CORRIDOR No.
LOBBY No
VERANDA No
SENATE CLUB
OR PLAN :

This is number one hundred and seventy-five in the
second numbered series of the
Miegunyah Volumes
made possible by the
Miegunyah Fund
established by bequests
under the wills of
Sir Russell and Lady Grimwade.

'Miegunyah' was the home of
Mab and Russell Grimwade
from 1911 to 1955.

Paul Strangio is Associate Professor of Politics in the School of Social Sciences at Monash University. A political historian and biographer, he has written extensively about political leadership and political parties in Australia. Before recent studies of the Australian prime ministers, his last book was *Neither Power Nor Glory: 100 Years of Political Labor in Victoria, 1856–1956* (2012). Paul has also been a long-time commentator on Australian politics in the print and electronic media.

Paul 't Hart is Professor of Public Administration, Utrecht School of Governance, Utrecht University, the Netherlands. A former professor of political science at the Australian National University, since 2007 Paul has been a core faculty member of the Australia and New Zealand School of Government. He writes about political and public service leadership, crisis management, policy evaluation and public accountability. His latest book is *The Leadership Capital Index: A New Perspective on Political Leadership* (2017).

James Walter is Professor of Politics in the School of Social Sciences at Monash University and a Fellow of the Academy of Social Sciences in Australia. He has published widely on biography, political psychology, leadership, political thought and policy deliberation. His last book, before recent studies of the Australian prime ministers, was *What Were They Thinking? The Politics of Ideas in Australia* (2010).

Prior to the present volume, the authors jointly published *Understanding Prime-Ministerial Performance: Comparative Perspectives* (2013), and *Settling the Office: The Australian Prime Ministership from Federation to Reconstruction* (2016).

THE PIVOT *of* POWER

AUSTRALIAN PRIME MINISTERS and POLITICAL LEADERSHIP, 1949—2016

Paul Strangio, Paul 't Hart & James Walter

THE MIEGUNYAH PRESS

THE MIEGUNYAH PRESS
An imprint of Melbourne University Publishing Limited
Level 1, 715 Swanston Street, Carlton, Victoria 3053, Australia
mup-info@unimelb.edu.au
www.mup.com.au

First published 2017

Endpapers: Front, *Department of Works & Railways – Provisional Parliament House Canberra – Main Floor Plan* (1924); Back, Parliament House Construction Authority, 1990.

Cover design by Design by Committee
Typeset in 11/15pt Minion by Cannon Typesetting
Printed in China by 1010 Printing International Ltd

National Library of Australia Cataloguing-in-Publication entry

Pivot of power/by Paul Strangio, Paul 't Hart, James Walter.

9780522868746 (hardback)

9780522868753 (ebook)

Includes index.

Prime ministers—Australia—History.
Politicians—Australia—History.
Australia—Politics and government—History.

Other Creators/Contributors:
Hart, Paul 't, author.
Walter, James, 1949– author.

Contents

Prime Ministers of Australia: 1949 – 2016

Prime Minister	**Period of Office**
Robert Menzies	19 December 1949 – 26 January 1966
Harold Holt	26 January 1966 – 19 December 1967
John McEwen	19 December 1967 – 10 January 1968
John Gorton	10 January 1968 – 10 March 1971
William (Billy) McMahon	10 March 1971 – 5 December 1972
Gough Whitlam	5 December 1972 – 11 November 1975
Malcolm Fraser	11 November 1975 – 11 March 1983
Bob Hawke	11 March 1983 – 20 December 1991
Paul Keating	20 December 1991 – 11 March 1996
John Howard	11 March 1996 – 3 December 2007
Kevin Rudd	3 December 2007 – 24 June 2010 27 June 2013 – 18 September 2013
Julia Gillard	24 June 2010 – 27 June 2013
Tony Abbott	18 September 2013 – 15 September 2015
Malcolm Turnbull	15 September 2015 –

Introduction

FOLLOWING HER FALL from power in 2013, Australia's first female prime minister, Julia Gillard, was asked whether in retrospect she thought she had been ready for the position upon ascending to it three years earlier. Gillard retorted: 'I think I was as ready as you can be. You don't get a bloody manual for it'.[1] It is true that upon assuming the highest political office in the land, new occupants receive no instruction book to guide them on their journey. Nor are prime ministers the beneficiaries of an equivalent to the ritual in the United States where departing presidents leave handwritten notes in the Oval Office for their successors, offering them words of advice and encouragement.

What they do inherit is a repertoire of practices and expectations, gained by observing their immediate predecessors during their own ascent to power. There is in addition the infrastructure of office: hard-won resources developed by successive incumbents. Few attend closely to the history from which the repertoire they take for granted, or the resources at their command, has emerged. Yet what one English scholar has written about the British prime ministership similarly applies to its Australian counterpart: 'the job … is a product of history. History deals each new incumbent a certain hand, the bundle of customs, practices and expectations that go with the office'. In short, the role is 'organised by history',[2] and it is this on which our investigation is focused.

In the first volume of this study of the Australian prime ministership, we charted the office's development from its prehistory in the self-governing colonies of the second half of the nineteenth century and through the first fifty years of the Commonwealth to the defeat of Ben Chifley's Labor government in 1949. The architects of the Commonwealth constitution anticipated that the office would enjoy pre-eminent status in a federated Australia—one prophesised that it would be 'the blue ribbon of the highest possible ambition'.[3] Their own experience of parliamentary politics in the colonies, where executives were constrained by legislatures in conditions in which party systems had not yet consolidated and governments were frequently transient, had not filled them with anxiety about a powerful executive. As a necessary concession to achieving Federation, however, they designed a constitution that confined the authority of the Commonwealth to ensure that in the newly created nation the rights of the states—particularly the smaller ones—would not be subjugated.

By restraining the Commonwealth, its founders placed fetters on the authority of prime ministers, especially in key fields like finance and industrial relations. They were left to butt heads against frequently uncooperative state premiers and other rival power centres. Concluding that the office's limitations were unequal to the challenges of nation building, a majority of incumbents in the first half of last century sought to amend the constitution. Mostly, however, their attempts to augment the federal government's powers through referenda proved futile. Fulfilment of the potential of the prime ministership was also hindered by other factors. Party alignments were unstable in the infant Commonwealth and even when the system settled, the fractiousness of the major parties remained a thorn in prime-ministerial sides. In addition, incumbents had access to only rudimentary administrative support. Ministerial offices were a distant innovation and the bureaucracy remained modest in size and weak at policy generation for decades.

Consequently, the prime ministership was a frustrating occupation for much of the first half of the twentieth century. Nevertheless, the major incumbents of those decades—Alfred Deakin, Andrew Fisher, Billy Hughes, Stanley Bruce, Joseph Lyons, culminating in the creative wartime tandem of John Curtin and Ben Chifley—each left their mark on the office and variously contributed to the realisation of its potential. By the 1940s it had been established as a platform for national leadership—so much so that at the decade's end a senior government minister was moved to observe that 'the office of the prime minister is becoming more and more the pivot around which the whole government machine turns'. The exigencies of World War II had facilitated a decisive realignment of financial power from the states to the Commonwealth. The Labor leaders Curtin and Chifley, but also their Liberal Party opponent and successor Robert Menzies, had learned from bitter experience that maintaining a strong, disciplined party, which itself depended on a coherent philosophy, was the sine qua non of successful executive leadership. The creation of new agencies and the mobilising of experts to manage the war effort and advise on postwar reconstruction had also laid the foundation for the modern Australian Public Service. Moreover, learning from the communication initiatives and shortcomings of his prime-ministerial predecessors, and exploiting new technologies, Curtin had illustrated the indispensability of media management to fostering the public connection.[4]

While the collective endeavours of Curtin, Chifley and their fellow early prime ministers had 'settled' the prime ministership by mid last century and bequeathed to their successors a repertoire for national leadership, the evolution of office was far from complete. In this volume we turn to the story of that evolution from the Cold War to the information age: from the second prime-ministerial coming of Robert Menzies in 1949 to Tony Abbott's short-lived tenure of 2013–15 and his replacement by Malcolm Turnbull. As in the preceding volume, we focus on three elements. The first is the institutional framework of the office; the second is the political, economic and social contexts in which the prime ministers governed; and the third involves the character, leadership styles and beliefs of the individuals holding the office. Because we are interested in illuminating continuities in prime-ministerial experience, especially in relation to shared challenges particular to specific periods, we have again mostly followed the practice of clustering two or more leaders together in a chapter rather than treating office holders individually.

Themes from the first volume recur. For instance, there is a repeated pattern of oscillation between 'personalisers' whose idiosyncratic traits and style drive them to seek domination, and process-oriented leaders who are more inclined to abide by the existing 'rules of the game' in exercising power. In this volume we observe this reflected in the transitions from Gough Whitlam to Malcolm Fraser and Kevin Rudd to Julia Gillard. Yet in the later twentieth century, the potential for 'personalisation' is amplified by the significantly more powerful infrastructure of office and the loosening of other traditional constraints, a point we return to below. This allows some leaders more easily to exert their will. Thus there emerges the potential for 'prime-ministerial government'—at some times enhancing decisive executive action, at others causing a deterioration in responsible cabinet government.

In this volume too we observe that the fortunes of prime ministers are shaped by what one might call the wheels of political time. Does their term of office coincide with a period when the circumstances are ripe for the forging of a new policy direction? Or do they take office when existing policies and institutional arrangements are more or less in place and need to be consolidated? Or, the most difficult set of circumstances, does their office holding coincide with a gradual decay or even an acute crisis of the prevailing order? All prime ministers, in other words, are not created equal.

We are also reminded that productive prime-ministerial leadership is seldom an outcome of an individual acting alone, regardless of how supremely gifted or lucky is the incumbent. It is far more likely to arise when the office holder forges strong collaborative relationships at the centre of power. In particular, we again witness the efficacy of a leadership tandem: while a more tempestuous pairing, the combination of Bob Hawke and Paul Keating has echoes of the successful nation-building partnership of their Labor predecessors, Curtin and Chifley.

Notwithstanding such similarities, this volume deals with an era of profound change that has impacted the prime ministership. There are further accretions of Commonwealth power at the expense of the states.

The bureaucracy vastly burgeons. Ministerial staffers arrive on the scene and expand in number and influence. The international dimension of the role grows dramatically. The advent of the 'celebrity' medium of television recasts the relationship between leaders and the public. More recently, party bases have dwindled substantially from their mid-twentieth-century peak and electoral volatility has increased. Moreover, intensifying globalisation has altered the locus and freight of decision making, and the digital revolution has further disrupted long-existing patterns of political communication.

A number of these developments have contributed to a marked elevation of the 'metabolic rate' of the prime ministership.[5] Modern office holders have at their disposal an elaborate support apparatus, but beyond the experience of their predecessors of yesteryear they are subject to remorseless pressures and are relentlessly exposed to the public gaze. The transformations of recent decades have also fuelled a trend towards leader-centred politics. The augmentation of institutional resources within government executives has been concentrated around leaders who have also enjoyed increased autonomy from their parties, including greater licence to determine policy. Perhaps most defining of all, the heightened media focus upon leaders and their personalities means they now loom larger in how citizens think, and make decisions, about politics.

This phenomenon of leader-centred politics has been given various labels: prime ministerialisation, presidentialisation, personalisation and—as noted earlier—prime-ministerial government. Whether it necessarily translates into expanded power for prime ministers remains, however, a contested issue. While the potential for leader dominance has undoubtedly grown, the office has on the current evidence simultaneously become more precarious for incumbents. Their stories suggest that the authority granted contemporary prime ministers is accompanied by escalated expectations and increased accountability pressures. Where those expectations are disappointed, prime ministers risk abrupt termination. In turn, those expectations are more than ever before tied to media performance. Authority flows less automatically from holding the office itself. It has become performative: prime ministers are increasingly required to be compelling public storytellers—crafting narratives of themselves and their governments. Yet as political leaders become de facto celebrities, as is the case with celebrities in show business, they are vulnerable to a rollercoaster of public adulation, ridicule and condemnation.

To be sure, this volume has been written in the shadow of continuing prime-ministerial turbulence. Though instability in the office has been a periodic feature of Australian politics from the time of Federation, the volatility of the past decade has been striking. Since 2007 there have been five prime ministers, three of whom have been deposed as a result of coups within their party rooms. It is a rate of turnover unparalleled since the first decade of the Commonwealth when the party system was still in formation.

Against this backdrop of upheaval, this volume considers how the present leadership churn originated in the seismic changes of recent decades. We suggest that the late-twentieth-century developments that strengthened the authority and raised the prominence of the prime ministership, and were capitalised upon effectively by Hawke, Keating and John Howard, carried within them the seeds of the current fragilities. Other questions emerge: have the demands of the office become so onerous, and its performative and managerial functions so contradictory, as to be virtually irreconcilable? Is the scrutiny it receives so unforgiving that its effectiveness as a leadership platform is now threatened?

If the prime ministership is diminished from its heyday of late last century, we ought not to forget that its history demonstrates it is a resilient and adaptable institution. The role has recovered from earlier troughs. But at a point when the office has rarely appeared so confounding, revisiting that past is timely indeed.

1

THE POLITICS OF CONSOLIDATION: ROBERT MENZIES

On 4 April 1960, *Time Magazine* announced to its international readership that 'things are looking up down-under': Australia was emerging 'out of the dreaming'.[1] Its cover image was a modernist version of iconography, a portrait by William Dobell of Robert Menzies, who had then been prime minister for just over ten years. The backhanded misappropriation of an Indigenous concept in the article's title might now be read as indicative of the era, but its purpose was clear: Australia had shrugged off its colonial origins and was being applauded as an enterprising modern economy with a vibrant lifestyle. And its arrival on the world stage owed everything to the leadership of Robert Menzies. He had become the longest-serving Australian prime minister (and would continue for another six years). And he had travelled a long way since his ignominious resignation after his first term as prime minister nearly twenty years earlier. In doing so, he had already had a profound influence on public life.

Robert Menzies' long tenure as prime minister in the mid twentieth century (1949–66) has ensured that his performance has been revisited by both critics and champions ever since. He has become a foundational figure in the way the role has subsequently been understood. Even trenchant opponents acknowledged the iconic status he came to occupy: 'He looked like a PM, he behaved like a PM and he had the presence of a PM'.[2] The drama of his first brief, tumultuous term (1939–41) and the bitter intra-party conflict that precipitated his resignation have rightly been seen as forcing him to reconsider how power should be exercised. The steps he took to regain office reveal the lessons he had drawn from that searing experience. His behaviour would have to be modified: impatience curbed, arrogance reined in and openness to others practised. The Country Party—commonly a partner in non-Labor coalitions—had refused to serve under Menzies during most of his first term, and would have to be appeased. The failure of the United Australia Party (UAP) demanded significant organisational change and attention to the values for which the leading anti–Labor Party stood. This in turn required close attention to how the seemingly successful centralisation of Commonwealth powers under John Curtin and Ben Chifley could be challenged.

It would take Menzies eight years—from 1941 to 1949—to accomplish these goals and regain the prime ministership. His achievement provides one of the outstanding examples of opposition leadership in Australian politics. So successful was it that the great liberal pioneer Alfred Deakin has been overshadowed, and the most competent pre–World War II conservative prime minister, Stanley Bruce, is largely forgotten. Menzies has come to be seen as the authentic voice of Australian liberalism. He is rightly acknowledged as the founder of the Liberal Party. No-one recalls its first manifestation (1909–17), nor the circumstances that caused it to be rebadged as the Nationalist Party and then the UAP, for Menzies effectively remade the party in the 1940s. Successors such as John Howard (Liberal prime minister from 1996 to 2007) have asserted that their purpose was to prosecute Menzies' agenda in a new age.[3] Only John Curtin's rescue of the shattered Labor Party after James Scullin's 1931 defeat, and Gough Whitlam's fight (1967–72) to develop a policy program, reform his party and bring it back into contention after twenty-three years in the wilderness, can match Menzies' initiative.

And only Curtin and Menzies could be said to have managed the transition to office in a manner that saw their primary objectives substantially realised. In each case, what was developed in opposition formed the bedrock for what was done in office.

Reinventing Australia's Anti-Labor Politics

Menzies' loss of office in 1941 was devastating. As he left the crucial party meeting in which his decision to resign was announced, he is said to have remarked to his private secretary, with tears in his eyes, that 'I have been done … I'll lie down and bleed awhile'. His biographer concluded that his spirit was broken.[4] He retreated to the backbench, where he was to remain until 1943. Yet it was soon apparent that his ambition scarcely faltered. There were repeated efforts to find an alternative and influential public role, many of them involving attempts to return to England and the British War Cabinet (all blocked by Winston Churchill), and at least one proposal (a diversionary tactic initiated by Churchill) that he should succeed Richard Casey as ambassador to Washington. This was thwarted by John Curtin's cabinet.[5] Of more consequence was that within six months of relinquishing the prime ministership, Menzies commenced a series of radio broadcasts that would be the catalyst for, as he later reflected, 'the revival of liberalism in Australia'.[6] His intention was to establish unity of purpose within the fragmented remnant party that the UAP had become. Effective advocacy of a philosophy for the contemporary anti-Labor cause would restore public attention and see him become the voice of a new party.

'The forgotten people', one of Menzies' radio broadcasts, delivered on 22 May 1942, has become a touchstone for the analysis of his appeal to a substantial Australian constituency.[7] Regarded as 'one of the few classic statements of the Australian Liberal philosophy',[8] it has been perceptively analysed by political historian Judith Brett, who draws our attention to the way it represented the opposition between socialism and individualism in a context where liberal values—if the ascendance of Curtin and Chifley continued—could possibly be eclipsed.[9] Eschewing the 'false class war' that he associated with Labor's politics, Menzies spoke for 'the forgotten people', those situated between wealthy elites and the organised labour movement. This group comprised, in his view, the backbone of the nation. Menzies skilfully created a moral category

> whose members are defined by their political values, social attitudes and moral qualities as much as by their social and economic position … the logic of the speech is the members' possession of these virtues as *individuals* rather than members of a class. As a moral category, the middle class has no material economic boundaries; anyone can belong to it through identifying with the values associated with it.[10]

Within this group, individual purpose was represented as anchored within the domestic context of the family and obligations to it. For Menzies, the patriotic instinct was rooted in the defence of hearth and home; the genesis of responsibility was to give one's children 'a chance in life'; the imperative behind community engagement was to be 'lifters, not leaners'. Such ideas, grounded on 'independence of spirit', real life being lived away from the public sphere and a limited role for the state, were to be progressively elaborated throughout the 1940s.[11] While war continued and Curtin's appeal for collective effort held sway, with the promise of a new world to be delivered through managed postwar reconstruction still resonating, Menzies' ideals gained little traction. But he had planted a seed that would flourish once attention turned from the privations of war towards the prospects for peace.

The seed was nurtured not only by Menzies but also by progressive thinkers in business. They had been willing to work with Labor governments in the total war effort. Now they envisaged a postwar world in which the benefits achieved through business–government cooperation were to be sustained by transferring the initiative from the bureaucratic managers of the war economy to private sector leaders. Such views were disseminated in an influential pamphlet, *Looking Forward*, developed by an economist, CD Kemp, and published in 1944 by a pioneering think tank—the Victorian Branch of the Institute for Public Affairs (IPA)—of which he was then director. Individual rights were represented as sacrosanct. Keynesian economics and a role for the state were accepted, but 'public works … should be regarded as a balancing factor rather than a permanent field of government activity'. Indeed, planning of the economy in which government maintained the initiative would lead to totalitarianism. In contrast, 'efficiency ... promoted under a system founded in competitive free enterprise ... holds out to all participants ... incentives to give of their best'.[12] Menzies was already closely engaged with Kemp and the Victorian IPA; their ideas would be fundamental to the program of the party he was now engaged in establishing. Menzies was dominant in crafting the policy platform for the anti-Labor cause in the election of 1943, and even more crucially in 1946 and 1949.

The work of institutional reform was pursued in concert with this development of the program for contemporary liberalism. One of the first steps was to 'ginger up' the opposition. An indicative instance illustrates the tactics Menzies adopted to insist that the UAP should act on its beliefs. The UAP had advocated that Australian conscripts should be deployed in all areas where the Japanese were to be fought. Yet despite divisions in party opinion, the leadership (including Menzies) agreed not to move an amendment of Curtin's proposal to allow for only limited deployment of conscripted militia in the South-West Pacific. UAP leader Billy Hughes—expelled from the Labor Party for proposing conscription in 1916—gained satisfaction from seeing Curtin forced to adopt this measure. He thought in time compulsion would be extended to other theatres, but an amendment at this point would see the Bill abandoned or would provoke an unwanted election.[13] When the Bill was debated, however, Menzies, with two colleagues, recanted. He argued that 'this is a world war and ... no limit can be set in the duty of Australia in relation to it'.[14]

They failed to alter the Bill, but their action triggered furious denunciation by Hughes, and some thought Menzies and his allies were damaged by their stand. But his sometime critic, media proprietor Keith Murdoch, believed Menzies 'had gained in the hearts and minds of hundreds and thousands of people in the street'. The incident provoked Hughes to call the first party meeting since his assumption of party leadership (succeeding Menzies) over a year before. There was talk among Menzies' friends of a spill of positions, which Menzies resisted: instead, he drafted a statement 'of a very frank kind about the

Government and our problems' and persuaded sixteen UAP MPs to sign it. Calling themselves the 'National Service Group', these dissidents handed the statement to Hughes on 31 March 1943. Their intention vigorously to seek party reform was apparent.[15]

The 1943 election saw the UAP decisively defeated. In its wake, established support organisations disintegrated. The view that wholesale party reform was now imperative became widespread. When the parliamentary party met, despite Hughes' efforts to forestall any immediate decision on leadership, his incompetence in meeting procedure led to chaos that was only quelled when Menzies suggested, with parliament to meet the following day, a leader must be chosen forthwith. He argued that 'the continuation in office of our election leaders would lead to shouts of ridicule and that the public would never take us seriously again'.[16] The meeting was unanimous in its support. In the ensuing contest, four candidates (including Menzies) stood; after he won half the votes on the first ballot, the rest dropped out and Menzies was elected. Remarkably, the devious octogenarian Hughes was not done: when he nominated as deputy, other contenders withdrew. The 'Little Digger' would retain some of the limelight, despite all. Press reception was cool: there were still doubts about Menzies, but he held the reins.

In October 1944, Menzies convened a unity conference of disparate non-labour organisations from all states with a core group of UAP MPs. There, as he recalled, 'I faced a state of affairs in which I must dedicate myself to bringing fourteen organizations into one, under one banner, and with one body of ideas'.[17] It was agreed to unite, to form one party, to be known as the Liberal Party of Australia. A second conference in December met to devise organisational principles, including that the party 'would raise and control its own funds … free of any possibility of control from outside itself and would determine its own destiny'.[18] In the following year, six state divisions were launched, a federal constitution was implemented, a federal council met and a federal executive was elected, 761 branches were formed with 94 500 members, and a federal secretariat was established. The Liberal Party of Australia was formally launched on 31 August 1945.[19]

The Liberal Party was now committed to Menzies' leadership, largely rid of the ex-Labor element that had joined in the interwar years, and with a national organisation and a more coherent philosophy than the UAP had communicated. It was at last in a position to challenge the Labor government effectively, or so it was thought. Early frustrations and the loss of the 1946 election were to dash such optimistic assumptions. It proved hard to encourage a pan-Australian conception of the party and to overcome state-mindedness—rivalries and disputes with local organisations intent on protecting their turf continued to fester. There were also reverses in state elections.[20] Menzies travelled extensively and fought the hardest campaign of his life for the federal election, but Labor prime minister Ben Chifley was equally wide-ranging and active.

Menzies called for a contest not about details but over fundamental principles: free enterprise, and recognition that development was the result of initiative, risk-taking and ambition:

> These things are not produced by Government Departments … They will be produced in the future as in the past by letting the citizen understand that there are still rewards for the courageous and the intelligent and the vigorous, and that the enterprise of the individual citizen is the essential foundation of the development of the State.[21]

His subtext was the threat of 'socialist' planning taking over everyday life. Chifley's message, an appeal to allow his government, having successfully managed the war, now to manage the peace and to deliver on the postwar reconstruction that had been promised, still prevailed.

Menzies and his followers were devastated by the election outcome: 'we may expect undisputed Socialist rule', he said, 'a steady weakening of the authority of the law, especially the industrial law, and continuing depression of individual initiative'.[22] There was speculation about whether Menzies could retain the leadership, or even wanted to do so, and comment in a draft party executive report on the election about 'a section of the people' hostile to Menzies who would have nothing to do with the party because of this. Menzies excised that comment before the report was presented. Soon after, the parliamentary party unanimously re-elected him leader. Notwithstanding disappointment and internal criticism, he still appeared 'the indisputable chief'.[23]

Menzies would face further frustration within his party in 1947–48, but gradually the tide turned, partly because of the growing appeal of his message (augmented by a 20-month radio broadcasting campaign leading up to the 1949 election) and partly because of the difficulties the Chifley government encountered. The Labor government had not gained the powers it thought necessary fully to pursue its reconstruction and social justice agenda through referenda in 1944 or in 1946. Its efforts to achieve more limited ends through other means led to compromise and disappointment. Australia's membership of the Sterling Bloc left it hostage to Britain's desperate financial predicament, unable to address shortages and compelled to retain rationing: the public saw this simply as pig-headed imposition of continuing control. A series of strikes, especially on the coalfields, and attempts by the Communist Party to consolidate control of key unions, were put down by the Labor government as firmly as any anti-Labor administration might have done, but provoked division in the broader labour movement and brought the 'socialist menace' strongly to popular attention. Chifley's overreaction to challenges to his government's banking legislation—his failed attempt to nationalise the banks—was a disastrous misjudgement that amplified such concerns and played into Menzies' hands. Labor's persistence in asserting that progress depended on ongoing government oversight finally provoked 'the forgotten people' to mobilise: as the *Sydney Morning Herald* remarked during the 1949 election campaign, 'the "white collar" men are fighting'.[24]

Then there was Menzies' message. He had spoken consistently since 1943 in terms that resonated with the 'forgotten people' speech and the themes of *Looking Forward*, and invariably articulated Liberal Party policies in those terms. This was augmented from April 1948 by the Liberal Party's astute use of radio broadcasting, lavishly funded by Australian and British interests keen to rid themselves of a 'socialist' government. Menzies' sober claims were ingeniously elaborated through a quiz program (addressing everyday individual problems with answers that drew on Liberal philosophy), and a series of fifteen-minute spots on more than eighty radio stations produced as a quasi-serial in which 'John Henry Austral' spoke for common sense and individual initiative while ruthlessly lampooning the Labor government. It foreshadowed what was to be the most expensive election campaign in Australian history to that time.[25] When it came to the campaign proper, rather than simply listing promises, Menzies remarked, 'We believe that politics is a high and real conflict of principles'. 'Are we', he asked,

> for the Socialist State, with its subordination of the individual to the universal officialdom of government, or are we for the ancient British faith that governments are the servants of the people, a faith that has given fire and quality and direction to the whole of our history for 600 years? … In 1946 you could vote Labor, reasonably supposing that it was a party of reform and not of socialisation. In 1949 it is clear that a Labor vote is for the socialist objective and nothing else.[26]

For all the battle over policy detail that ensued, it was this message, invoking individual freedom and ambition in the face of the socialist menace, that was most influential (as pioneering pollster Roy Morgan and Chifley himself later remarked[27]). The Coalition, now led by the Liberal Party, won the 1949 election. The seed Menzies had planted in 1942 had flourished. Now the task was to ensure his authority in government.

Despite his remarkable achievement in effectively founding a new party, Menzies' authority initially was not as assured as it would later appear. Even with an influx of new Liberal MPs in 1949, there remained sceptics in the party, with reservations based on his earlier prime-ministerial performance. And the new Liberal MPs themselves, more zealous about free enterprise than was Menzies, were frustrated by his willingness to heed the advice of those public servants inherited from the Curtin–Chifley era. There were to be close-run elections in 1951, 1954 and 1961, as we will see. Paradoxically, his governments were most productive in roughly the first eight years, but his authority was only to become certain towards the end of that period. And it was in the 1960s, when his party and parliamentary supremacy was beyond question, that questions about what his governments had actually done began to bite.

Five elements undergirded the authority Menzies eventually wielded. First, the ameliorative liberalism he espoused in the 1940s—that is, a liberalism that put the individual first, but insisted that with every right came a responsibility and acknowledged a role for the state in mitigating the effects of misfortune, or the omissions of markets—now translated into a policy program for managed prosperity for which the electorate gave the Coalition credit. Second, the Cold War played into Menzies' hands: the communist threat confirmed dire predictions Menzies had made during the 1940s (and now he predicted a third world war); and internal divisions over communism split the Labor Party, with a proportion of the Catholic Labor vote syphoned off by the emergent Democratic Labor Party (DLP) and delivered to the Coalition via second preferences. Then Labor leader Herbert Vere 'Doc' Evatt's erratic performance in responding to these challenges gave Menzies the ammunition to destroy him, and the means of heightening ideological divisions. Third, Menzies proved much more adept at managing colleagues than in his earlier incarnation. In particular, his effective working relationship with the Country Party was in stark contrast with the antipathy exhibited earlier in his career and, despite some rocky passages, ensured the survival of the Coalition. Fourth, his trust in and reliance on his public service advisers established a pattern for executive–public service relations. And finally, Menzies' ability to absorb information, handle a brief, deliver speeches (whether prepared or extemporaneous), and perform with both wit and controlled aggression, and his sheer experience, made him a parliamentary performer without peer.

Managed Prosperity

The postwar decades are frequently characterised as a golden age of relative stability and economic growth and, by some, as evidence of the wisdom of Menzies' rule.[28] Economic historians offer a more sober account, in which Menzies and his governments scarcely figure; Ian McLean, for instance, concluded that 'Domestic economic management was such as to do no serious harm, no small achievement in itself, though it is doubtful it can be accorded a major role in securing the prosperity Australians enjoyed'.[29] Menzies was blessed in taking office when he did. The catalyst for much of the prosperity over which he presided lay in events that preceded his term of office. Wartime industrialisation and diversification; the augmentation in the scale, location and composition of manufacturing to satisfy war demands; and the increase in technical sophistication it required were preconditions for the growth that followed. Much closer economic relations (and a mutual aid agreement) with the United States in promoting the Pacific War saw Australia emerge in an enhanced financial position when hostilities ended. The migration program introduced by Chifley's government in 1946 would provide the labour needed for development. The liberalisation of trade in commodities following the postwar General Agreement on Tariffs and Trade (GATT) advantaged Australia. Pent-up domestic demand—a 'backlog' accumulating since the Depression and then held in check by wartime restrictions—in combination with population growth (migration plus a 'baby boom') would accelerate consumption, providing incentives for innovation and large-scale investment. This momentum was not unique to Australia: the international economy flourished, and Australia was integrated into the global trading system, so it shared in a general postwar boom.[30]

In four respects, however, Menzies framed and facilitated that Australian prosperity. First, Menzies' administration was as committed to national development as the Labor governments of John Curtin and Ben Chifley had been, but the aim now was not government dictation of how that was to be achieved, but rather to 'help the individual to help himself, to create a climate … favourable to his activity and growth'.[31] Second, Menzies agreed that there must be partnership between government and business, but not with the sort of 'directorate' once envisaged by Labor's reconstruction planners. Bureaucrats in government employ should work with, not dictate to, the entrepreneurs whose energy and initiative would drive the economy: enterprise should lead. Third, that did not, however, mean that planning, regulation and intervention were irrelevant: 'Where government action or control has seemed to us to be the best answer to a practical problem, we have adopted that answer', said Menzies. 'But our first impulse is always to seek the private enterprise answer.'[32] Fourth, the tolerance of government action was accompanied by an acceptance of the expanded bureaucracy (and indeed many of the personnel) recruited in the 1940s. This in turn meant that Keynesian econocrats would continue to flourish relatively unimpeded, save that programs and spending would be directed not towards the provision of welfare and benefits (as Labor had intended) but oriented instead to encouraging enterprise and the subsidisation of private choice.

Housing policy illustrates the Menzies government's approach to the social dimension of economic management, and its departure from the initial postwar reconstruction model. Australia had emerged from depression and war with a housing crisis. Labor in government had focused upon public provision, believing that private enterprise did not have the capacity to meet the shortfall. It negotiated a Commonwealth-State Housing Agreement (CSHA) in 1945, under which the Commonwealth offered low-interest loans to the states for housing construction, primarily for rental to low-income families. Targets were set, but rarely were Commonwealth aspirations met.

For Menzies, housing was not just a practical issue but a marker of liberal values. It had been a critical element in his 'Forgotten People' broadcast. There, he emphasised the home as the foundation of national life, the redoubt of the family and the product of (and reward for) individual enterprise.[33] It was an appeal resonant with long-term Australian values concerning home ownership.[34] It was congruent with current experience: where governments could not deliver, you must do it yourself—and many did. And this chimed with the pioneer legend, a reaching back by resourceful individuals to the energy and improvisation of the imagined past.[35]

It was not that Menzies' government vacated the field. Rather, it adopted policies that promoted private investment and consumption. The long postwar boom underwrote just such an approach. Under Menzies, CSHA funding was redirected. Instead of the focus on public provision for rental purposes, especially for those on lower incomes, there were new measures in 1956 allowing Commonwealth funding to be made available to building societies for home lending, the introduction of a home savings grant scheme a little later, and in 1965 the introduction of national housing insurance to encourage lenders to offer loans at a higher level against valuations.[36] Here was the public subsidisation of private choice in full flower. Menzies saw it as a reassertion of the 'proper' relations between federal and state governments[37]—provision for the disadvantaged would be left to independent state housing commissions, undermining Labor's attempt at an integrated plan for public housing. Suburbanisation was entrenched. Rates of owner occupation rose dramatically. Arguably there was a democratisation of home ownership and a recognition by the left of the advantages of suburban life for the ordinary Australian.[38] The housing story of the 1950s and 1960s was widely rated a success, and redounded to Menzies' credit. Until, that is, its unforeseen consequences started to bite.

The recognition and encouragement of private choice became the governing rhetoric of the 1950s, with Menzies its chief exponent. Yet, as noted earlier, there was a large measure of acceptance of public social and economic planning,[39] and a reliance on the public service. Menzies, in effect, set the terms of reference, then depended on his officials for policy content, delivery and implementation. It was a golden age not only for the economy, but also for 'the mandarins'.[40] However, popular understanding of 'expert' decisions was mediated by Menzies, and always in terms intended to engage with his promise to 'the forgotten people'.

The Menzies government combined industry protection—which, in the hands of his minister for commerce and agriculture and then trade, Country Party leader John McEwen, saw tariffs reach unprecedented heights—with at least some elements of demand management. Control of taxation gave government the means to resource major infrastructure projects (for instance, the Snowy Mountains Hydro-electric Scheme, initiated in 1949 by Chifley but brought to fruition under Menzies) and to step up public investment when private demand slackened. Population management and social engineering were endorsed; for instance, direction of migrant labour to areas of need (also introduced under Chifley). Initiatives thought central to economic development—the expansion of tertiary education (following the Menzies-initiated Murray Report, 1957), for instance—were funded by the Commonwealth. Menzies' faith in the public sector allowed the postwar public service to play a significant role in the achievements of the Menzies era. These included advances in relative equality, and hence social integration; mediation of the balance of advantage between different economic groups; regional equalisation through federal programs; and the near universalisation of educational access and standards.[41]

The incremental realisation of such aims reinforced Menzies' authority. Yet progress was not always smooth. On the one hand, the government took advantage of increasing revenues for its investment in infrastructure and to assist private investment. On the other, consumer demand driven by the 'backlog' of depression and war was allowed relatively free rein. That drove prices up and inflation was a recurrent threat. In one instance it was exacerbated by the Korean War (commencing in June 1950), when high demand for commodities, especially wool, drove a price boom. Income growth spread into the domestic economy and into increased expenditure on imports. Belief in countercyclical intervention in such cases then induced government economists to recommend 'disciplinary' measures to curb inflation and control the balance of payments. In 1951, reacting to the Korean War boom and galloping inflation, the government produced a 'horror' budget cutting public spending and increasing taxes. In a later instance, in 1960, it induced a fierce 'credit squeeze'.

The public reaction was adverse: anger and dismay were fiercely expressed in 1952, and Menzies came close to losing the 1961 election. The politically embarrassing alternation of 'hell-for-leather-expansionism, punctuated by sharp deflationary measures',[42] influenced contemporary perceptions of the Menzies era. More significantly, his promise that 'progress is not to be based upon the poverty or despair of those who cannot compete' was undercut: 'discipline' and deflation ensured periodic retreats from social policy.[43]

This 'stop-go' pattern signified the tension between Menzies' political objectives and his reliance upon the influential 'Treasury line'.[44] Privately, he was given to sardonic observations about 'Treasury witchcraft' and its failure to understand public relations.[45] But his public expression of responsible economic policy was usually dependent upon the Treasury brief. It would lead to internal conflict and policy inconsistency when, for instance, Menzies sided with Roland Wilson (secretary of Treasury) in Wilson's periodic conflict with John McEwen and Jack Crawford (secretary of the Department of Trade), and with influential economist HC 'Nugget' Coombs (successively governor of the Commonwealth Bank, 1949–60, and the Reserve Bank, 1960–68), over who should exercise authority in the provision of economic advice. It would reach its apogee when Menzies, on the advice of Wilson, impugned the 1965 report of a Committee of Economic Inquiry (chaired by Dr James Vernon) that his government had established in the wake of the 1960–61 credit squeeze. The Vernon Inquiry recommended the establishment of an Advisory Council on Economic Growth, but Wilson would not brook an alternative source that might challenge Treasury and Menzies killed it.[46]

In overall terms, however, notwithstanding episodes of disenchantment, the public was willing to accept that the Coalition government was author of their improving economic circumstances—real GDP increased at an annual average rate of 4.2 per cent in the 1950s and 5.1 per cent in the 1960s[47]—and Menzies could persuasively be represented as the architect of their good fortune. He was blessed indeed.

'The Great World Struggle'

There has been a long tradition of Australian anti-socialism—George Reid's Free Trade Party adopted the anti-socialist banner in 1906. Menzies was schooled in this tradition. But liberals continued to defend freedom of opinion and expression, even when they abhorred an opponent's philosophy, as did Menzies until the late 1940s. By then, however, influenced by the deteriorating relations between East and West, and by Australian and overseas strategic analyses of the emerging Cold War, Menzies had come to believe in the imminence of a third world war in which a communist fifth column would undermine Australia. His initial diffidence about banning the Communist Party when first urged by Percy Spender and other party stalwarts to do so was overcome. Communists now represented a threat so extreme that the liberal commitment to defending civil liberties had to be set aside. Menzies declared in his 1949 election campaign: 'The Communist Party will be declared unlawful, and dissolved'. He promised that illegality would be attached to any new association following communist tenets, and members of the

Communist Party would be disqualified from government employment and from office in any registered industrial organisation.[48] Once elected, he commenced implementing these proposals.

The Cold War was another gift for Menzies. The notion of a continuing crisis of national defence and of the state action (and decisive leadership) necessary to address it was not peculiar to Australia, but it was well suited to Menzies' purposes. The Korean War gave real point to the threat he had forecast before the 1949 election. The encouragement of a mentality favourable to a security state afforded him means of reinforcing his image as a strong leader. His access to secret intelligence gave him the whip hand in parliament and in the media. The huge investment in defence added to the inflation roller-coaster, but it also allowed for continued government intervention in the economy in ways that served his interests. As prosperity increased, the threat that all that had been gained would be swept away by the enemy remained a potent incentive to stay the course with the Coalition.

Above all, the anti-communist crusade led to the disintegration of effective opposition from Labor and provided the platform on which Menzies would destroy its leader, 'Doc' Evatt. The confluence of these strands further ensured Menzies' ascendancy. Critics have argued that Menzies' utilisation of what he called 'the great world struggle' was entirely opportunistic, a cynical, orchestrated strategy for defeating Labor.[49] His biographer, AW Martin, however, demonstrates persuasively that this is to oversimplify what was core to Menzies: his conviction that there would be another war.[50] Menzies could undoubtedly see the advantage Cold War politics delivered to him, and his astute political calculation played its part, but it was also a crusade driven by belief and principle.

The demand for 'semi-war' preparations and industrial capacity to provide for potential conflict was another incentive for commitments to increased productivity, technological development and industry protection that shaped postwar economic development. Menzies wanted defence and development, 'guns and butter', all at once. The Snowy Mountains scheme, for example, was not only represented as an investment in necessary infrastructure but also as meeting the power shortage necessary for defence. High spending exacerbated economic volatility, which constrained Menzies' ambition. He could not reproduce a United States style security state in Australia. Pursuit of these twin goals led not only to an overheated economy—inflation and currency instability—but also to constrictions on productivity related to the domestic consumer backlog. Yet Menzies could use the rhetoric of Cold War challenges to gain public support for sacrifice, and the desperate need for action as an excuse for failing to introduce stronger anti-inflationary measures. Cold War imperatives were thus married to developmental aspirations and to managed prosperity.[51]

In conjunction, there was the determination to outlaw the Communist Party of Australia (CPA). In 1950 the government introduced legislation with that objective, relying on the Commonwealth defence power. The CPA and some unions immediately initiated a constitutional challenge. In March 1951, the High Court declared in their favour, finding that the Act was invalid in that it was aimed at specific persons or bodies rather than regulating or proscribing specific conduct, the factual nature of which should be tested by courts.[52] The government then decided to take the issue to the people. A referendum to change the constitution would be conducted following an early election.

Menzies triggered a double dissolution election to take place on 28 April: Labor, he said, had 'used its Senate majority to slow down the machinery of government; and did violence to our legislative programme'.[53] The impending referendum was mentioned in his policy speech, and the government was returned on a strongly anti-socialist platform. A confidential internal report by state secretaries of the Liberal Party would later record their belief that anti-communism had been a significant factor in the Coalition victory.[54] The referendum, proposing the addition of a new section to the constitution to empower the Commonwealth Parliament to make laws in respect of communists and communism where this was necessary for the security of the Commonwealth, was to take place on 22 September 1951.

Evatt may well have been torn between his awareness that the referendum threatened the stability of the Labor Party, given the intense anti-communism of its Catholic supporters and MPs, and his international reputation as an advocate for human rights and civil liberties. He had, when attorney-general in the Chifley government, been a notable agitator for such causes and an assertive participant in the establishment of the United Nations. Should party welfare or high principle (and personal reputation) govern his action? In the event, he opted to lead the 'No' campaign, and with such success that it delivered an improbable victory. Just three months before the referendum, 80 per cent of respondents in a Gallup Poll had said they were 'likely' to vote 'Yes' to a proposal to ban the CPA. And during the campaign, the press was almost universally hostile to Evatt and his cause (though his speeches, like Menzies', were regularly reproduced).[55] Yet on the day the national vote registered a slim majority 'against' Menzies' proposal (2 370 009 vs. 2 317 927 'for'), albeit with a significant informal vote. Only two states, Queensland and Western Australia, supported the measure. The loss was a setback for Menzies, but it had the effect he may well have predicted: it would, in conjunction with Evatt's mismanagement of his colleagues, provide further momentum towards the disastrous split in Labor's ranks that was to follow.

There were remarkable parallels between Menzies and Evatt. They were born in the same year, 1894. Though neither was from a particularly disadvantaged family, each had gained educational benefit, and escape from their small town origins (Jeparit in Victoria and East Maitland in New South Wales, respectively) by winning scholarships to elite metropolitan schools: Wesley College, Melbourne, in Menzies' case, and the selective Fort Street Boys' High School, Sydney, in Evatt's. Both were outstanding students at university and went on to brilliant legal careers. By their early thirties, each had large and flourishing practices at the bar. Evatt was appointed the youngest justice of the High Court of Australia, aged only thirty-six. He was a significant scholar as well, having completed a law doctorate (LLD, 1924, published 1936) and published three further books of legal and political history before 1940. Each had served in state politics before entering the federal sphere. Both had served as Commonwealth attorney-general and travelled overseas, beginning to attain an international reputation in that capacity, before attaining party leadership. Each thought that they were the pre-eminent champion of liberalism (for Evatt had decided in 1915 that the Labor Party was the only party committed to 'true liberalism'[56]). They were, equally, inordinately ambitious and incapable of concealing it. Perhaps these very similarities provoked what became an intense rivalry: they loathed each other. Their antipathy boiled over in 1954, in the third act of 'the great world struggle': the Petrov affair.[57] And it was here that Menzies' distinctive advantage over Evatt became apparent.

Despite his achievements and brilliance, Evatt's fatal flaw was a persistent suspicion of, and inability to read, others. He was unreasonably demanding of inferiors, always impatient, occasionally devious, insensitive about the effects of his imperious incursions into the lives of those around him, mistrustful of anyone who might have pretensions as an equal, and passionately competitive when confronted. It was a paranoid style.[58] Norman Makin, a ministerial colleague in Labor's wartime governments and later ambassador to Washington under Evatt (then minister of external affairs), remarked that

> it was inevitable he would come into head-on collision with any contemporary of his time … There was undoubtedly a great inward upsurge of feeling that impelled him to do and say things which sent 'sparks flying from the anvil'. He was fearless, but failed correctly to assess an adversary.[59]

Menzies, in contrast, was now an adept reader of others. He had governed the arrogance that had impaired his assessment of opponents from 1939 to 1941. The accounts of those who worked with him in the 1950s, and especially his private correspondence, show him to be a close observer of behaviour, a connoisseur of gossip and an astute judge of character and motives.[60] He would deride Evatt's 'fitting on his shaggy brow the halo of martyrdom', and was especially attentive to accounts of his misadventures, which he translated into comic stories.[61] The veneer of humour scarcely conceals the malicious glee Menzies took in capturing Evatt's faults. Much of Menzies' own account of 'the Petrov Spy Case' revolved 'around the personality and actions of Evatt … a strange and controversial figure'.[62]

Vladimir Petrov, third secretary at the Soviet Embassy, defected on 3 April 1954, bringing with him documents that purported to reveal Soviet espionage in Australia. Menzies had been forewarned of a possible defection by Charles Spry, director-general of the Australian Security Intelligence Agency (ASIO), in early February, but later claimed not to have remembered the name that had been mentioned. Menzies was immediately briefed when it occurred but said nothing of the defection for ten days, since 'the formalities of diplomatic communication had to be attended to'.[63] Then, on the night of 13 April, only a day before parliament was to rise prior to an election he had called for 29 May, Menzies announced Petrov's defection to the House of Representatives, and his proposal to establish a Royal Commission into Soviet Espionage. It was a revelation that appeared stunningly to confirm suggestions of communist subversion made as early as 1948 by party figures such as Richard Casey and Percy Spender, and much amplified in 1952 when the Liberal maverick WC Wentworth questioned Casey (then minister for external affairs) about a leak of confidential material to a communist paper, eliciting from Casey a reference to a 'nest of traitors' in the public service.[64] The opposition did not oppose the proposed royal commission but, significantly, Evatt—having an engagement in Sydney—was not in the House when Menzies made his announcement.

The following day, parliament's last sitting day, Evatt endorsed the royal commission, and the opposition subsequently approved its terms of reference. However, Evatt bitterly denounced the government for its discourtesy in failing to inform him of the impending announcement, proceeding in his absence and not consulting about the workings of the commission. Menzies always insisted that the slight was unintended: he had not known in time that Evatt was not to be in the House. Whether or not that can be believed, in fact, Evatt was rarely if ever briefed on security matters. Menzies and Spry (who had been appointed early in the Menzies regime) had decided that Evatt's unpredictable behaviour disqualified him from access to sensitive confidential material.[65]

Menzies, along with his colleagues, believed in the 'nest of traitors' hypothesis. He was well aware that ASIO kept a register of known communists and suspected sympathisers, some of whom were public servants; indeed, Spry had reported to cabinet on these matters in 1952.[66] Their beliefs would eventually be vindicated: not perhaps as definitively as might have been hoped when the royal commission's report was delivered, but years later when analyses of transcripts from the Soviet embassies in London, Washington and Canberra proved there was espionage in the West and that local communists were willing agents.[67] The Petrov affair was not simply contrived to frame Labor. Menzies' actions were not wholly opportunistic, but, again, a mixture of conviction and calculation. The circumstances and timing of the announcement, Menzies must have guessed, would provoke Evatt's innate suspicion: he was primed to overreact.

Menzies said no more about Petrov or espionage during the 1954 election, but colleagues did so. The royal commission commenced some twelve days before the election and though no witnesses were called initially, the 'communist threat' was again brought to public attention. The government squeaked home by a narrow margin. Evatt was devastated, sure that he had been destined for victory and that the Petrov defection had been engineered to his disadvantage. When documents before the commission then appeared to suggest that members of Evatt's staff had been sources of information for Soviet contacts, Evatt was convinced of a conspiracy and sought leave to represent two of them before the commission. There he embarked on a fishing expedition and became increasingly erratic and intemperate, and his leave to appear was withdrawn. The commissioners would later comment adversely on Evatt's 'constant reiteration of vague charges of infamy', all of which 'turned out to be fantastic and wholly unsupported by any credible evidence'.[68]

Evatt then turned on the 'conspiracy' in his own party. For years he had done his best to conciliate the right-wing, vehemently anti-communist Catholics in the Labor Caucus. Now Evatt lashed out at them, issuing a press statement on 5 October 1954 in which he accused 'a small group' of repeated disloyalty intended to assist the Menzies government, and proposed to report its members to the federal executive for 'appropriate action' at the forthcoming federal conference.[69] They were, he suggested later, backed by 'an outside, semi-fascist body' financed by big business and Liberal politicians.[70] His target was the

Catholic Social Studies Movement, inspired by BA Santamaria, whose publication *News Weekly* was referred to in his public statement as their 'organ'. The Movement (as it was commonly called) had infiltrated the Labor Party's own Industrial Groups, intended to combat communist influence in trade unions. Evatt's earlier conciliation of Movement activists and the 'Groupers' having failed, they now became the target of his rage and frustration.[71]

Anti-communists in the party, already unsettled by Evatt's role in the 1951 referendum campaign and dismayed by his performance at the espionage royal commission, were provoked beyond measure by his statement. Simmering tensions between more and less radical factions in the party now erupted into a self-destructive civil war. Over the next year, splits occurred in most state branches and at the federal level, leading to the creation of the Australian Labor Party Anti-Communist (ALP-AC), which later became the DLP. The ACL and later the DLP would thereafter direct second preferences to the Liberal Party: Labor was about to be driven into the wilderness.[72]

When the royal commission's final report was debated in October 1955, Evatt tried again to revive his case—this time with the advantage that the report, while finding evidence to sustain the case that espionage indeed took place, found nothing that could lead to charges against any Australian individual being laid. Here, surely, was the proof that it was all an attempt to discredit himself and the Labor Party. Yet again, he seriously misjudged the situation, producing a long, fevered and at times incoherent speech, traducing ASIO and the commissioners—and in the course of which he remarked that he had written to Russian foreign minister Vyacheslav Molotov asking if certain documents Petrov had produced were genuine, and that Molotov had replied that they were forgeries, fabricated on the instructions of 'persons interested in the deterioration of Soviet–Australian relations'.[73]

Opposition members, who had been given no warning, were stupefied; the government benches dissolved in laughter. The speech Menzies made in reply was brilliant, forensic in its demolition of Evatt's argument, and exceptionally cruel.[74] The reference to Molotov, he remarked, will 'satisfy all sane and sensible people that the right honourable gentleman, suffering from persecution delusions, is introducing us into a world of sheer fantasy'.[75] His closing riposte was that 'honourable public opinion' would acquit those whom Evatt had vilified in his speech.

> But the same honourable public opinion will not acquit the man who made these reckless and villainous charges ... I am therefore compelled to say that, in the name of all these good and honourable men, in the name of public decency, in the name of the safety of Australia, the man on trial in this debate is the right honourable gentleman himself.[76]

The next day in what, given the circumstances of previous weeks, amounted to a theatrical climax, Menzies announced that he had advised the governor-general to dissolve the parliament and to call an election for the House and for half the Senate, to take place on 10 December 1955. It had been just eighteen months since the 1954 election. The official rationale was that a Senate election was necessary by 30 June 1956; this would bring the elections for both Houses into alignment. Menzies also referred to needing a mandate to solve the present 'economic crisis'. It was evident to all that the government was seizing an advantage—Evatt denounced the reasons given as a deception—but even the Labor deputy leader, Arthur Calwell, conceded that the tension and excitement of previous weeks had made parliament unworkable and an election would 'clear the air'.[77] At the 1955 election, the government achieved a secure majority, assisted by the preferences of the ALP-AC. Menzies believed that Evatt's 'strange advocacy' had been 'most damaging to his own party' and that he 'had ruined himself as a real political force'.[78] No doubt, that had been exactly Menzies' intention. 'The great world struggle' had delivered an immense domestic dividend.

Commonwealth Statesman

Menzies' ambition was not limited to the domestic sphere. The drive that led him to travel to London in the early years of World War II, to be at the centre of affairs rather than at the periphery, with such cost to his party and eventually to his reputation, remained unabated. Now the energy with which he engaged in 'the great world struggle' was a signal to those he identified as 'great and powerful friends'[79] of his eagerness to be seen as one with them. This time, his effort was not solely to gain entry to the British power elite but to be seen as a leader in the British Commonwealth. From that vantage, he could influence not only other Commonwealth countries but also the important 'powerful friend', the United States. It was a rational calculation. Menzies would gain more traction and more attention as a leader in such a transnational collective than he would speaking for Australia alone.

Menzies succeeded in building an international reputation as a Commonwealth statesman. Arguably, it was an instance of strategic decision making—adopting one tactic for the international audience, and another for domestic consumption where there was growing concern about regional relationships. However, while Menzies could offer a tenable defence against the charge that his governments were not sufficiently alert to the geopolitical realities of Australia's region,[80] the focus on London and Washington that ensued profoundly shaped Australian foreign policy in the 1950s and 1960s. He never missed Commonwealth Prime Ministers' Conferences, and invariably extended these trips to visit Washington. He became friends with successive British conservative prime ministers, Anthony Eden and Harold Macmillan. He met with every American president and developed close relations with their advisers, such as Dwight Eisenhower's secretary of state, John Foster Dulles—Menzies' facility as a persuasive advocate of their interests made him a valued public speaker in both countries.

Australia's loyalty ensured some access to the intelligence resources of these Cold War allies. Certainly Menzies' engagement—sometimes as an intermediary—in the complex interrelations between these parties gained him international recognition and a stature that could be represented in Australia as serving strategic interests, especially by encouraging continued US engagement in the Asia-Pacific region. He was well aware of Australia's reliance on American power, but privately he still felt that moral leadership depended on Britain, as he assured Macmillan in 1959:

> deeply as I respect the Americans and realistically as I understand their immense power and significance, I have for a long time felt that they

> are not yet ripe for the intellectual and spiritual leadership which many people have assumed they can give. Great Britain still has the major resources in this field.[81]

Menzies impressed Australia's allies. The American ambassador to Australia, in advance of Menzies' first official state visit to the United States following the 1955 Prime Ministers' Conference, reported back to the president's counsel that he was 'easily the coming spokesman of the Commonwealth: one of the most effective advocates I have ever seen in action … We are fortunate in having such a friend'.[82] And in 1959, in a speech reported in Australia, Macmillan would describe him as 'perhaps the greatest figure in our Commonwealth today'.[83]

Such alliances led Menzies to commit Australian military support to the United States in the Korean War almost immediately it was announced in 1950; to Britain in its battle with communist insurgents during 'the Malayan emergency' between 1950 and 1960; and to the US intervention in Vietnam in 1962. He was easily persuaded to agree to a British request to conduct atomic tests in Australia between 1952 and 1963: Menzies took the decision unilaterally but met no resistance in cabinet. The hope was that this would lead to a sharing of nuclear technology: it was never realised. 'Blind loyalty'[84] was also said to be the catalyst for Menzies agreeing to lead a delegation to Egypt to negotiate a means for ending the Suez Crisis in 1956.

The Suez Crisis arose when the Egyptian president, Gamel Abdel Nasser, having been rebuffed in attempts to raise finance from Western powers to build new infrastructure, decided in July 1956 to nationalise the Suez Canal and use shipping tolls as an alternative source of funds. The canal, a major artery for international trade, had been managed by a French/British consortium since 1869 under a 99-year agreement with Egypt. After Nasser's announcement, the British and French were intent on restoring their control, but as an outcome of a hastily convened international conference, they agreed to a plan devised by Dulles to explore Nasser's willingness to entertain negotiations that could lead to a new convention governing the canal. It was agreed that Menzies should lead a small international committee to open discussions with

Nasser. Menzies, against the advice of his own ministers, Richard Casey (external affairs) and Philip McBride (defence), had given unconditional support to the British position and been an outspoken participant in the conference. He insisted that he had nothing to do with the decision that he should lead the delegation: he had been 'drafted' by British prime minister Anthony Eden and Dulles.[85] In the event, he was caught between his loyalty to Britain and US determination that armed force was to be avoided. Before discussions with Nasser concluded (during which Menzies had already informally warned him of the possibility of military intervention if amicable agreement could not be reached), president Eisenhower unconditionally rejected the use of force. Nasser rejected the delegation's proposals.

In early November, Britain and France, in collusion with Israel, invaded Egypt. The intervention was short-lived: immediate US censure and UN intervention along with isolation by the diplomatic community forced their withdrawal, and in March 1957 the canal reopened under Egyptian control. Britain's pretensions as a world power were shattered. It effectively ended Eden's career and forced his successor, Macmillan, to focus on the restoration of US relations. And, though he would never admit it, it was a debacle for Menzies. The pessimistic forecasts of his more pragmatic colleagues, Casey and McBride, were confirmed. Menzies, despite his efforts, was not forewarned of the British and French invasion. Nasser's insistence during negotiations that what was proposed to him by Menzies' committee amounted to colonialism struck a chord with developing nations, including those in the Commonwealth. This was a catalyst for battles to come. And at least some of the Liberal-oriented progeny of 'the forgotten people' were so outraged by Menzies' participation in the British reversion to 'the jungle of power politics, imperialism and nationalism' that it sparked a transition to a lifelong affiliation with the Labor Party.[86]

The Commonwealth architecture to which Menzies had been so committed began to crumble. In part it was simply the dawning reality that Britain had been seriously weakened as an economic power: it could no longer afford, for instance, to be strong in both Europe and Asia. It was also because former colonial dependencies were alert to anything they perceived as signifying a residual colonial mentality among the Commonwealth's senior statesmen. Having been anointed as such, Menzies took his role as an adviser to leaders of 'less mature' polities (precisely the category in which he had placed Nasser[87]) seriously. It was not always appreciated. And in 1960,when he took up the cudgels for his 'great and powerful friends' once more at the UN General Assembly—Menzies having now assumed the external affairs portfolio himself—he was again depicted as on the wrong side of history.

After a breakdown in US–Soviet summitry, Indian prime minister Jawaharlal Nehru had proposed a motion at a special meeting of the UN General Assembly on behalf of five 'neutralist' nations calling for renewed contact between Eisenhower and Nikita Khrushchev. Having taken no advice from his own officials, attorney-general Garfield Barwick (who Menzies had initially sent to lead a delegation to the meeting before belatedly deciding to attend himself) and James Plimsoll (Australia's representative at the General Assembly), Menzies moved an amending resolution. It would expand the summit to include Britain and France alongside the United States and Russia, but without regard for the non-aligned nations supporting Nehru's motion. It had been discussed with Eisenhower and drafted in consultation with Macmillan and the US State Department. It attracted only five votes and precipitated a furious denunciation from Nehru in the assembly. According to Australia's US ambassador, Howard Beale, Menzies never forgave Macmillan and Eisenhower for this 'great humiliation'.[88]

In 1961 Britain played an equivocal role in South Africa's departure from the Commonwealth, despite Menzies' efforts to retain its engagement. When Macmillan then handed the chair of the Prime Ministers' Conference to Nehru rather than to him, Menzies was deeply offended. His disillusion with Macmillan was complete and he now despaired about the Commonwealth's future. 'If I survive the next election', he told his staunch ally Eric Harrison, formerly the Liberal deputy leader and now high commissioner in London, 'I will not be in a hurry to attend another Prime Ministers' Conference in which the balance of power has changed so much and in which my own views have become so relatively unimportant'.[89]

As his international dealings made evident, Menzies maintained a hierarchy of values the assumed superiority of which relegated other positions to inferior status. His statement that the Americans were not yet ready for spiritual leadership was as nothing relative to the condescension visited on 'lesser' civilisations. Egyptians, he said well before the Suez fiasco, were 'a dangerous lot of backward adolescents mouthing the slogans of democracy, full of self-importance and basic ignorance'.[90] And his telling interpretation of Nehru's harsh criticism of his role at the UN was that it revealed how thin the civilised veneer was: 'He sneered, he distorted what I had said, he was grossly offensive. All the primitive came out in him'.[91] AW Martin makes the case that Menzies' attitudes were simply those of a man of his times,[92] and yet some colleagues, equally committed to great power connections, such as Paul Hasluck, Garfield Barwick and Richard Casey, not to mention their senior officials, were more attuned to how the times were changing. Their advice was ignored. At a time when the British themselves were attempting to deal with decolonisation through the Commonwealth, which was surely Macmillan's objective, Menzies' unreflective assertion of superior British values was bound to be wrong-footed in the end.

Yet Menzies, advantaged by the postwar situation in which Australia adopted an independent voice rather than allowing its international relations to be refracted through the British Foreign Office, undoubtedly spoke for what he conceived to be Australian interests. Empire loyalty and common cause with desired allies were factors, as was his ambition to be seen as a statesman, but he was motivated by national interests. He was sometimes humiliated when acting on what he took to be the shared concerns of great and powerful friends, yet it is an oversimplification to assume he was driven simply by deference. The Commonwealth was for him not just a valuable association but also a platform from which he gained a vantage not available to him simply as the Australian prime minister. It was not his only platform: he travelled tirelessly and worked hard to build the alliances and gain admission to the councils on which Australian foreign policy would rely in the postwar decades. He won considerable regard in doing so. From the earliest years of his administration, he set a benchmark in international engagement that later prime ministers would strive to emulate.

Menzies' Boys

One of the striking features of the way in which Menzies worked was his trust in and reliance on the public service. He profited from the institutional development that had taken place under John Curtin and Ben Chifley, but established a pattern of relationships between the bureaucracy and the executive of which Stanley Bruce—an earlier prime minister committed to the 'science' of administration—can only have dreamed, and that has scarcely been matched by any of Menzies' successors. It gave 'the seven dwarfs'—notable bureaucratic chiefs of great intellect but short stature—the scope to drive the professionalisation of the Commonwealth public service.[93] Douglas Copland, the economist who had advised every prime minister from Bruce to Menzies, remarked during Menzies' first prime-ministerial term that he spent more time with his 'experts' than with his ministers.[94] It was a pattern that would become amplified during his second term. John Bunting, later secretary of the Prime Minister's Department (PMD), but one of the bright young men who had been recruited to the Department of Post War Reconstruction in the 1940s, observed that during his period of opposition leadership, Menzies was in the habit of catching up with senior bureaucrats in King's Hall as they passed to and from their ministers' parliamentary offices. He took it as a sign of the neutrality that Menzies ascribed to senior public servants: their loyalty to the government of the day was taken for granted.[95]

Once in power again, Menzies resisted pressure from his party colleagues to dispense with senior officials who had been influential in the period of Labor's ascendancy, and was proud of it.[96] Nugget Coombs, architect of much of Labor's postwar reconstruction agenda, and Peter Lawler, a young public servant and member of the Labor Party, each had cause to testify to Menzies' assumption that they could serve his government just as efficiently as they had his predecessors, despite their political allegiance.[97] Tony Eggleton recalled his surprise at Menzies' remarks when he went to see him as a candidate to join Menzies' office as press secretary:

> He said, 'I don't know anything about your politics and nor do I want to know … I don't mind what your politics are: the only thing is, do

> you feel comfortable about working for me and my government? And, if you are, that's, that's all I need to know'. And then, as I got to work with him, he said … a number of times, 'Oh, I'd like you to ring so and so in the Department to get this piece of information …' And he'd say, 'Oh, it's interesting … he's a Chairman of one of the ALP branches in Canberra … If you hear he's a Labor fellow, don't worry: he's a very good chap'.[98]

'Stiffly formal in address until a newcomer was accepted', said one of his private secretaries, William Heseltine, 'the process of acceptance once made was complete. We were admitted to meals, to meditations, to family life and to the joys and discomforts of travel in a way both complete and immensely flattering'.[99] The trust and confidence Menzies extended to both his staff and his senior officials allowed some of them to join an inner circle to which few of his political colleagues had access. They became part of his special 'family'.[100] And like family, they were as concerned with Menzies' health and wellbeing as with policy objectives. Thus, Allen Brown, a Coombs recruit, appointed initially as secretary of PMD by Chifley, and ever a consummate professional, would implore Menzies not to attend the 1952 Commonwealth Economic Conference despite its 'intrinsic importance' for Australia: 'You know that you are run down physically and very tired; you are picking up every stray wog and finding it very difficult to get rid of them … Going to a northern winter and the fog of London cannot improve this'.[101] Implicit in Brown's message, and clearly expressed by Heseltine, was that 'one of the remarkable things about this rather shy, cold and detached man is that he was capable of evoking the warmest feelings of affection in all who worked for him'.[102]

John Bunting, who succeeded Brown as secretary of PMD in 1959, gives the fullest account of how this affection tempered working relations: 'the boys' (as Bunting called them) were not only his advisers but his companions.[103] 'He enjoyed their company as much as he appreciated their official ministrations.' But there were limits: it was 'a personal, though not undue official friendship'.[104] A suitable distance between ministers and senior officials was to be observed. Nonetheless,

Bunting observes, for Menzies 'talking was relaxation' and, especially on his frequent and gruelling international trips, at the end of the day 'Menzies looked for "the boys"—and companionship'.[105] 'The boys' knew their place, their duty to the boss and what was expected. The ambitions of politicians on the other hand, except for those few whose allegiance to Menzies' cause was always clear, had to be managed: they might turn on him as they had once before; he might be forced to disappoint their aspirations; and the best of them might eventually be his rivals.

Ben Chifley, that 'expert in human relations', had achieved full rapport with the senior public service.[106] Menzies, with little of Chifley's gift, might have been expected to falter. Instead, by manifesting trust, respecting professionalism and expecting integrity, he too achieved just such a rapport. It was this approach that, as Alan Davies noted, saw a 'relatively free hand given to bureaucrats in running their enterprises; the reliance on experts ... a high level of bureaucratic innovation'.[107] In Paul Hasluck's view,

> it was Menzies who was mainly responsible for seeing that the Commonwealth Public Service was re-established after the war as an efficient, non-partisan and self-respecting institution. This was among his major achievements. Through him, too, some of the greatest public servants in Australian history found the opportunity throughout the 1950s and 1960s to make their own independent contribution to Australian government and maintain the traditional place of the public service in the government structure.[108]

Bunting, endorsing another senior official, Jack Crawford, makes the case that it was

> an integrated enterprise ... between the Prime Minister (and ministers) and public servants. From this integrated effort came, without fuss or advertisement by the officials, a great deal of the material that was translated into policy by the Government, and led to much of the achievement of the whole Menzies period.[109]

A consequence of the reliance on senior officials was that Menzies' prime ministerial office (PMO)[110] remained small, though equally bound to him by affection and loyalty. Heseltine, in the mid-1950s, served as Menzies' private secretary (seconded from PMD) and noted that there was a personal secretary, Hazel Craig (who had worked for both Curtin and Chifley); a press secretary, Hugh Dash (who was also assisted by a secretary); three typists (one of whom managed the office switchboard); and two cabinet room attendants—a complement of nine. Dash was something of a court jester, but he also served as Menzies' 'eyes and ears in the … press gallery—and indispensable late night drinking companion and competitive raconteur'.[111] There was no place in his office (or those of any other minister) for a 'political appointee'.[112] Years later, towards the end of Menzies' final term, when Eggleton joined the PMO, little had changed. The office remained small, and all policy advice came from the PMD.[113]

The 'integrated enterprise' between the executive and senior officials did not mean that all things ran smoothly. Menzies did not invariably accept advice from his cabinet colleagues, or 'the boys', especially when their pragmatism was at odds with his values and ambitions in relation to the Commonwealth, his relations with 'great and powerful friends' or the utility of the UN. At times, Menzies may have wished that his occasional expression of private misgivings (the sarcastic comments about Treasury witchcraft peppering his letters[114]) had translated into public action, for instance in relation to accepting the advice not only of Treasury but also 'the boys' that led to the 1961 credit squeeze, substantial public dissatisfaction and near defeat at that year's election. The relatively free hand given to bureaucrats may well have allowed 'the seven dwarfs' to make substantial independent contributions to policy; it also led to clashes between some big egos. Roland Wilson's fiercely combative promotion of the 'Treasury line' led not only to intermittent warfare with Jack Crawford (and John McEwen) over trade policy, but to the dismissal of the government-commissioned Vernon Report. Allen Brown's aspirations to give the PMD powers more effectively to coordinate others and to serve as an independent source of advice to the prime minister had Menzies' support. Yet the staffing changes this entailed were thwarted by the chairman of the Public Service Board, Fred Wheeler. 'Independence' when it came to economic analysis was continually obstructed by Wilson. Nonetheless, Brown had succeeded in persuading Menzies of the importance of a more activist department with a broad policy role. Menzies issued a memorandum in 1955 that expanded the services PMD was to provide to the prime minister, fundamentally altering the functions of the department. It would take decades for Brown's vision to be realised, but the groundwork had been laid.[115]

On the matters that were closest to Menzies' heart—a robust public service, promotion of higher education, and the development of the national capital—and for which he would later claim credit, the influence of 'the boys' is indisputable. His pride in his contribution to the development of what he persisted in calling the 'civil service' was manifest, and his periodic and astute reorganisation of cabinet and administration were significant, but the drivers of improved administrative practice were figures like Allen Brown and his successors.[116] The 'heroic' representation, to which Menzies' own account contributed, that he had saved Australian universities in the late 1950s through initiating an expert inquiry and instituting Commonwealth funding measures, was not entirely accurate.[117] He was initially tardy in responding to the urgings of 'the boys'; he was not the originator of Commonwealth support (it had commenced in a small way in 1943, under Curtin); he did not invent the idea of what became the Murray inquiry—for a time he opposed it. But as AW Martin points out, 'that idea developed, partly as a result of discussions among officials in his own Department and partly through the pressure of committed academic agitators ... the way was prepared for him to act when attention to the mounting university crisis became unavoidable.' And once converted, 'he used all his power in Cabinet and party to have a good committee appointed and to see that its recommendations were implemented'.[118] Grant Harman, having assessed the story of higher education reform, remarks that credit for the developments between 1949 and 1966 should go as much to the influential advisers of the period as to Menzies but concludes that none of it would have occurred without Menzies' strong commitment.[119]

The same inference could be drawn about Menzies' role in the active development of Canberra, generated not only by expert advice but also by his own frustrations with the quotidian details of dysfunction in the experience of living there, and in managing government in the 'bush capital'.[120] It would lead to the introduction of the National Capital Development Commission (NCDC).[121] Finally, even trade and industry development, in which Menzies had less of a claim to centrality than in the other three domains, was drawn into his story of achievement. He would brandish the landmark Japanese trade treaty of 1957, which economic historians now regard as 'arguably the most significant economic policy innovation during the Menzies era',[122] as a counter to the criticism that he had been too focused on London and Washington.[123] In fact, while the Japanese treaty could not have gone ahead without Menzies' endorsement and support, credit properly belongs to John McEwen, minister for trade (1956–63), and then secretary of the Department of Trade, Jack Crawford.

Indicative of the Menzies era, in all of these cases, there is a strong impress of the British connection. Brown and Bunting's refinement of PMD took advantage of visits (and staff postings) to the British Cabinet Office. When vice-chancellors suggested Sir Keith Murray, chairman of the British University Grants Committee, should be invited to lead the inquiry into Australian universities, Menzies immediately opened negotiations directly with Murray in England. Menzies himself was the prime mover in the appointment of Sir William Holford, a famous British urban planner, to advise on the development of Canberra and of the NCDC. All were later justifiably recounted as signal achievements. Only in the area of trade, where Menzies acknowledged McEwen but accentuated his own role,[124] was his story easily faulted. McEwen's own memoir persuasively demonstrated that he had primary carriage of the Japanese trade treaty initiative. Crawford later revealed that McEwen would have gained even better terms for Australia in renegotiating the Ottawa Agreement that had regulated trade with Britain since 1932 had Menzies not intervened to increase the level of preference afforded British manufacturers. Australian business conglomerates of the time were scathing about Menzies' perceived deference to the British Treasury, much preferring McEwen's forthright economic nationalism.[125]

The Art of Politics

Menzies published two essays on 'the art and science of politics', one in 1948 before he regained the prime ministership, and a second in 1970 after his retirement.[126] Further experience had not changed his views. These essays capture the skill sets that he emphasised in his exercise of leadership, and can frame our discussion of how he managed cabinet, his party (and the Coalition), parliament and the public stage. He stressed that a leader must understand 'political science'—facts, evidence, values and their institutional contexts—but then he must communicate, which requires 'art'. He articulated 'liberal' values and was prepared to leave the 'scientific' input to 'the boys'. His skill was in assimilating the brief they provided once the principles he advocated had been understood. For Menzies' own preoccupation, which he universalised as the leadership role, was with the 'art' of politics: 'to provide exposition, persuasion and inspiration'.[127]

> The art of politics is to convey ideas to others ... to persuade a majority to agree, to create or encourage a public opinion so soundly based that it endures ... This means that, political science having been applied and a thoughtful and competent judgment arrived at, the art of speech or of written language becomes supreme. For good or even great ideas can be quite infertile unless they are clearly conveyed to others.[128]

For Menzies, then, leadership was a discursive practice, intimately tied to public performance. Talking was not only 'his relaxation', as Bunting observed, but also the essence of politics. It was how he managed men and created impressions. It was at its peak in parliament, which was Menzies' natural forum. It was there that his capacity for 'exposition, persuasion and inspiration' flourished. He relished the public theatre it allowed. Previous Labor leaders had checked him—Curtin with his own (very different) rhetorical flair, and Chifley with laconic plain speaking that sometimes made Menzies' judiciously contrived performance seem precious. Menzies had learned the lesson. He still prepared carefully but called more on his undeniable talent for the extemporary and for humour, often with deadly effect. Against Evatt he dispensed with the chivalry that had largely prevailed between himself, Curtin and Chifley.

His bent for ruthless demolition was unleashed. Once he had bested 'poor old Bert' (as he referred to Evatt privately), there were few who could take him on convincingly in the chamber.

Menzies' showmanship extended not only to parliament and the public stage but also to informal settings: Sundays at The Lodge, usually involving dinner parties with 'the boys' and select luminaries; drinks with his ministers in the anteroom after cabinet meetings; chats with backbenchers in King's Hall; discussions in lobbies at meetings of Commonwealth prime ministers.[129] His performance would demonstrate a command of detail, but almost always leavened with humour. He played off colleagues: Coombs described Country Party leader Artie Fadden as the ideal straight man for Menzies' amusing performance.[130] Joviality was intended to offset aloofness; wit was meant to disarm. In informal contexts it usually involved comic stories but could also become a weapon: his one-liners were used against interjectors; his capacity for lethal put-downs in political debate evinced flashes of cruelty he seemed unable to resist. For those regularly associated with Menzies, his anecdotes could become all too familiar;[131] but many continued to find them a delightful aspect of their interactions with him. Those encountering him for the first time were often captivated.

Menzies created a leadership persona, a public face that not only served to disarm, impress and manage others, but also to mask the 'shy, cold and detached man' that some of 'the boys', such as Heseltine, perceived. It also concealed the shrewd character assessments taking place. Woe betide the minion, however, who misinterpreted the jovial performance as genuine fellow-feeling. Gavin Souter notes that after Menzies the 'superb raconteur' had provoked peals of laughter from a group of backbenchers with the punchline of one of his anecdotes, one of them went

> so far as to slap the Prime Minister on the back and say: 'You old bastard!' The laughter ceased. Menzies said, 'Good evening gentlemen', and left the room. As [Labor MP] Leslie Haylen wrote about a similar incident between the leader and some of his followers, 'the Godhead had withdrawn beyond the veil'.[132]

Menzies' marked sense of amour-propre was not to be breached, and his capacity to freeze out those who trespassed was yet another means of control.

In cabinet, the 'science' side of the equation was manifest in the periodic reorganisation of administration, committees and portfolios through which Menzies incrementally increased efficiency. 'Science' was also part of Menzies' preparation: 'he read his Cabinet papers and the notes prepared by his department. He always studied his brief'.[133] There was experimentation with high-level advisory bodies to coordinate policy. A cabinet secretariat was established and innovations in note taking and process were introduced by Allen Brown. Brown was also instrumental in Menzies' 1955 decision to split the executive, with twelve ministers of cabinet rank and ten ministers outside cabinet. Cabinet discussion was also unusually open to the incorporation of experts—departmental officials who could present material and participate in debates. That said, cabinet was intensely partisan: the likely impact of decisions in disadvantaging the opposition was manifest in discussion.[134]

As for 'art', the discursive mode was apparent in the frequent resort to informal, bilateral discussion outside cabinet through which Menzies, with select ministers and officials, collectively determined the policy imperatives of the day. Outside the room, in discussion, Menzies managed tensions with those who sometimes disagreed, or who felt their advice had been ignored. There was art, too, in the way Menzies constrained strong personalities and potential challengers in his ministry, frustrating their wishes (Richard Casey), arguing that regional balance in cabinet required them to remain in lesser portfolios than their talents deserved (Paul Hasluck), holding out until their patience was exhausted then offering an attractive exit option (Percy Spender, Garfield Barwick), until, having dispensed with rivals, he could exercise patronage in selecting his successor (Harold Holt). We will return to these instances.

Inside cabinet, Menzies' capacity to persuade was a combination of his skill in elucidating the principles of a position, and his ability then to 'patiently let each minister have his say and then disentangle the argument, presenting in his summing up the points that mattered and those that were secondary and the major questions which Cabinet must first decide'.[135] He succeeded, argued Hasluck, not because he was authoritarian or domineering but because he was the best man there.[136]

Menzies' 'art' could not be exercised so easily in managing the Coalition, especially after Artie Fadden relinquished the Country Party leadership to the tough, wily John McEwen in 1958. McEwen's ruthlessness and commitment to his own departmental objectives and party interests equalled Menzies' own. And when McEwen failed to get his way, he would launch public campaigns for his policies, albeit not always successfully.[137] Menzies' suspicion of McEwen—whom he dubbed 'Le Noir', signifying his Machiavellian capacity[138]—would increase. But he could not afford again to allow the Coalition to divide in acrimony, as it had during his first prime-ministerial term. Careful negotiation and compromise rather than persuasive art were necessary.

Menzies could command the party room. His mastery of parliament and his 'creation' of the party itself overawed most Liberal MPs: the standing he had achieved carried great weight. His ability to put an argument could not be gainsaid. There was a succession of individuals with whom he engaged because of their conspicuous loyalty, or perceived talent, or they amused him.[139] But he did not stroll down to the parliamentary dining room to dine with his backbenchers, as John Howard later would, nor establish routines for regular availability. He would chat amiably with groups in the corridors—ad hoc contact seemed the preferred mode—but would withdraw abruptly if the interaction displeased him. And so there were recurrent stories of the backbench's dismay—significantly, in 1952 with reference to its feeling that 'Government [should] take more notice of party and public feeling, and less of the "expert" guides who have led it astray'.[140] In 1957, Peter Carrington, British high commissioner (and later a close friend of Menzies), reported to his superiors that 'His relations are unsatisfactory with his own backbenchers who resent what they regard as his cavalier treatment of them. He has seldom met them during the last year, and there is a growing feeling … that they are not consulted as they should be'.[141] These patterns would surge and abate, but never entirely dissipate. Evidently, there was a hierarchy of those to whom Menzies would attend in forming his views, and once 'thoughtful' conclusions had been reached, neither backbench nor public opinion would much sway him from what he knew to be 'right'.

In consequence, in the public realm too, Menzies' 'magic' was not as far-reaching as is sometimes suggested. His talent as a speaker might have been thought a signal advantage on the public stage.[142] It had won him great acclaim abroad. Yet there were countervailing factors at home. There was the loyalty of Labor voters, and their abiding fury at the man who had contributed so much to the division of the party. There was an undercurrent of feeling that

> over small things the Government has not always had a happy touch … a general feeling … and Mr Menzies does not take sufficient pains to counteract it—that he is not as closely in touch as he should be with the bread and butter issues … which affect … the interests and concerns of the average Australian.[143]

Above all, there was the tutelary air of a man who, having gained the knowledge needed for the 'right' decision, was so intent on advocacy that he failed to listen to those whom he was trying to persuade.

Skill in exposition, quickness on his feet, humour and facility in dealing with interjectors could not always override these obstinate facts. Neither could his undeniable courage, manifest in a willingness to perform in circumstances where he could be assured of a hostile audience, always win over objectors. Therefore, eloquence did not always give him control of an audience, and artfulness did not invariably allow him to deal well with dissent, or to control his temper. Repeatedly, in successive campaigns, a few meetings descended into bedlam.[144] Yet all this notwithstanding, Menzies' 'art' meant he consistently commanded public attention. He was always the lead story.

The occasional difficulty of public meetings could be offset by Menzies' command of other means of communication. Radio delivery, at which he had proved so adept in 'the revival of liberalism', remained his favoured medium. Like Joseph Lyons, he had a talent for broadcasting. He was less comfortable with television when it arrived, but he predicted that it would be the next important medium. And there too, once he found the formula he wanted, which was 'to appear that he was in your living room, reasoning with you',[145] he got the best of the opposition. Respondents, whatever their political preferences, agreed on his eloquence in his first televised policy speech.[146] Menzies might also have used the press to communicate, like Curtin, but here a distinct ambivalence cut in.

The direct communication integral to Menzies' conception of the political art could be served by radio and to some extent by television, but he believed that the selectivity and editorial intrusions of print journalists distorted and trivialised his message. He longed for someone 'first class' to intervene, like Curtin's legendary press secretary, Don Rodgers,[147] but overlooked the effort Curtin made to relate directly with the gallery. In fact, press secretaries such as Charles Meeking and Hugh Dash proved to be loyal intermediaries. In the early 1950s Menzies held regular press conferences, but over time they became ever fewer and more perfunctory. Only a few journalists were willing to confront him: most were afraid to trade punches with a man so able with an acerbic comeback.[148] He was immune to requests for comments in passing, telling importunate journalists they could learn what he had to say by listening to him in parliament. He once warned Dulles that a propensity for thinking aloud in public about alternative options rather than deciding exactly what was to be said and sticking to it allowed journalists to cherry pick what they wanted, contributing to Dulles' reputation for inconsistency.[149]

Menzies' relations with journalists in general had never recovered from his perception of their hostility towards him during his first prime ministership and in the long campaign to win power again. His suspicion concerning them fostered mood swings: he could veer from genial and friendly one day to cold, distant and contemptuous the next. His gibes against them could be cruel. He made little effort to charm the men who presented him to the public.[150] His variable relations with the great press proprietors were factors. He was friendly with Frank Packer (Consolidated Press) and John Williams (Herald and Weekly Times), both of whom he knighted—their papers remained effusive in their support. He had long been close to Keith Murdoch (*Adelaide Advertiser*, Melbourne *Herald*, Brisbane *Courier-Mail* and others), who had played an influential role in the formation of the UAP and whom he had controversially appointed director-general of information at the beginning of World War II. In contrast, despite early sociable links with Warwick Fairfax, Menzies came to regard the influential Fairfax press, especially the *Sydney Morning Herald*, as consistently unfair and poisonous in its reporting on his administration.[151] In the end, through patronage on the one hand and a war of attrition on the other, Clem Lloyd concluded,

> Menzies established an ascendancy over the Gallery as absolute and assured as his dominance of parliament, ministry, party and electorate … It was a gradual process, but the overwhelming effect of the long Menzies hegemony on political journalism was one of pervasive enervation.[152]

There could be limited critique of the Menzian art of politics thereafter.

Authority Assured

By the late 1950s, Menzies' authority was assured. Decisive victory at the 1958 election, said AW Martin, 'put the Coalition Government in a seemingly impregnable position, marked definitive confirmation of Menzies' ascendancy over his followers and, equally, conveyed a widespread air of inevitability about his leadership of the nation'.[153] The nation-building initiatives he had inherited from the Labor governments of the 1940s had been consolidated, but now with an emphasis on private enterprise rather than social planning and individual choice rather than collective direction. The institutional changes he had championed, especially in relation to public service efficiency, had also been consolidated. The mandarins he had encouraged were at the top of their game: they were, as Bunting noted, contributing much of what would be understood as the Menzies legacy. For all the glitches in stop-go developmentalism and in managing economic policy and the (expensive) imperatives of a Cold War security state, the increase in prosperity was demonstrable. Even if luck had played a large part, the government reaped the reward.

The Labor Party had been split and driven into the wilderness, and DLP preferences now cushioned the Coalition. Notwithstanding the debacle of Suez, Menzies' role in the Commonwealth, staunch support of Anglo-American Cold War politics, and courting of 'great and powerful friends' had made him a player on the world stage, and recognised as such not only there but also at home. Many of the objectives closest to Menzies' heart had been achieved or were in train. It was all of this that *Time Magazine* praised in the cover story with which we commenced this chapter. Attention to how Menzies approached his political work has been necessary to explain how he reached this point of assured authority by 1960. It is also the basis on which we can assess his ongoing influence on the role of prime minister.

Pre-war anti-Labor parties had always looked to leaders for salvation, sometimes parachuting Labor defectors into the role, but theirs was a patchwork enterprise, constantly wrestling with philosophical coherence. Menzies' strong direction of the postwar Liberal Party certainly cemented leadership predominance, but now with organisational stability and vigorous branches whose support surmounted earlier perceptions that the cause was the creation of shadowy business conglomerates, and would change tack according to their needs. Most importantly, there was now a clearly articulated philosophy associated with a constituency Menzies persuasively represented as bound together not merely by interests but by moral imperatives. He demonstrated the congruence of leadership and philosophy that not only ensured the ongoing viability of the Liberal Party as one of the great Australian parties, but also became an aspiration for Labor too as it fought to recover from the split of the 1950s. Strong leadership and an associated narrative (ideally with a moral core) was now the expectation on both sides.

Others had pursued a role on the international stage—Hughes during World War 1 and its aftermath; Bruce as high commissioner in London, after losing office; Menzies himself in attempts to influence the British War Cabinet; and Evatt as Labor attorney-general and participant in the formative debates at the UN. Yet no prime minister had achieved a reputation as an international statesman such as that Menzies attained in the 1950s. This too would become an abiding expectation of Australian leaders thereafter.

The development of a stable partnership between executive government and the public service 'as an efficient, non-partisan and self-respecting institution' was, as Hasluck observed, 'among his major achievements'.[154] It was not without a downside, and was not fully endorsed by all of his successors (not least on his own side). But the necessity of ensuring administrative competence and the institutional availability of expert professional advice in pursuing political objectives, foreshadowed by Bruce, and demonstrated by Curtin and Chifley, was now firmly established by Menzies as a constant in the Australian polity. We will see that there is a good story to be told about the contribution of the Australian Public Service (APS) to Australian life: its genesis can largely be attributed to Menzies.

Criticism of Menzies would never abate, even in the years of his greatest success, but nevertheless, enduring memories of his 'ideal of party cohesion, electoral success, parliamentary domination, tight cabinet control and stable government'[155] would become the touchstone not only for later Liberal leaders but for all prime ministers. That much of it was achieved through the 'art of politics'—careful preparation allied with eloquence, wit, quick apprehension, extemporisation, controlled aggression, ruthless deposition of opposing leaders, and above all public theatre—was an aspiration coveted by many but achieved by only a few (perhaps most notably Gough Whitlam and Paul Keating). Yet leadership communication and capturing the public stage as had Menzies would become increasingly important later in the twentieth century.

The way Menzies worked, the manner of his performance, established a leadership repertoire that had enduring effects both on public expectations and on leader candidates themselves. It was a benchmark that was as liable to show up incapacities—as it would in his most immediate successors, Harold Holt, John Gorton and William McMahon—as to encourage achievement, but it was rarely forgotten. And almost coinciding with the moment at which it was most fully realised, when Menzies had held the prime ministership for a little over ten years, his standing began to ebb.

2

THE BURDEN OF SUCCESSION: HAROLD HOLT, JOHN GORTON AND WILLIAM McMAHON

Robert Menzies was never spared criticism, but by the late 1950s his dominance of parliament, party and public forums was unquestioned. In the 1960s, attitudes changed. In some quarters Menzies was represented as a source of pervasive dissatisfaction with politics. Yet he would depart, in 1966, at a time of his own choosing, managing an orderly transfer of power. That his successors—Harold Holt, John Gorton and William (Billy) McMahon—retained office for nearly seven more years, extending the Coalition hegemony to twenty-three years, was itself remarkable. But they too would be disparaged.

Such a transition was evident in many Western polities. The leaders whose administrations were synonymous with relative stability and postwar recovery—Dwight Eisenhower in America, Konrad Adenauer in Germany, Harold Macmillan in Britain, Charles de Gaulle in France, Louis St Laurent in Canada—left the scene. In their wake there was frequently instability or dissatisfaction. They were turbulent times, and the strong leaders who seemed apt to the inwardly focused national rebuilding required after war, and enjoyed relative security of tenure while engaged in those endeavours, now appeared as paragons in relation to their successors, or their reputations were subject to revaluation. Menzies was no exception.

Challenging Menzies' Reputation

In 1965, Allen Brown, the secretary of PMD until 1959 and one of Menzies' 'boys', wrote to him from Oxford about a book he had been reading, Donald Horne's *The Lucky Country*: 'He doesn't approve of you. In fact, on all matters [of] which I can claim to know anything at all, he is wrong-headed and ill-informed'.[1] Horne's influential book famously declared that 'Australia is a lucky country run mainly by second rate people who share its luck'.[2] Of Menzies he remarked, 'It is a feature of … [his] long rule that little of what he does seems to matter much. His great talent is to preside over events and look as if he knows what they are all about'.[3] Horne's argument, as he acknowledged, reprised that mounted by former Fairfax editor John Pringle in 1958 (the year of one of Menzies' greatest electoral triumphs): that the idealism with which the Liberal revival started had

> dwindled throughout its long period of office. Corrupted by the easy prosperity of the boom years, with little to fear from a divided and degraded Opposition, the Liberal–Country Party Coalition has found it easier to cope with the dangers of inflation by the very controls which it had previously denounced, and to maintain its political position by beating the anti-Communist drum … Today it has the appearance of a complacent, lazy government which owes its success more to good luck than to good management.[4]

Horne revisited the argument, cataloguing the events of the early 1960s to represent Menzies as the man who always took the easy shot, a great actor ruthless in political battle but uninterested in policy, lazily dependent upon his officials, inattentive to the shift in Australian values and society, and with a preference 'to frustrate talent, to surround himself with a firebreak of mediocrity'. He concluded that Menzies' bitter humiliation by his own party in 1941 'seemed to make him decide that it was better to survive than to govern well'.[5]

Menzies lugubriously remarked after retiring in 1966 that 'I am learning what it is to be attacked in a snide sort of way without being able to make any retort ... I have long been given to understand that in my own period of office nothing happened except, of course, that I did win elections'. And so he decided to write 'something' in response to 'Mr Horne's book and such other miserable scribblings'.[6] It was *The Measure of the Years*, a second volume of memoirs (preceded three years earlier by *Afternoon Light*), in which he paid particular attention to his chief policy achievements. Although methodical and logical, many cavilled at what he left out and found Menzies' writing curiously stilted in comparison with the magic of his public performance. His books earned comfortable royalties but did not achieve the sales of Pringle or Horne. Books other than Horne's—such as Don Whitington's *The Rulers*—offered a more accurate insider view of parliament in the Menzies years but did not capture the public imagination. Arguably Horne had a lasting influence on how 'The Menzies Era' would be understood.

Neither Pringle nor Horne conceded that Menzies' 'idealism' drew on the heritage of Victorian liberalism in which individual choice and free enterprise are first principles, but where state action will be applied if it is the best remedy.[7] Certainly, he disappointed the more earnest advocacy of free markets by some of those elected with him in 1949, but it was not a case of betraying the promise Menzies had made to 'the forgotten people' in the 1940s: he had remained consistent. Menzies maintained reliance on and trust in the public service. Rather than signifying a lazy shuffling off of responsibility, we agree with Hasluck that the development and promotion of the public service was one of his grand achievements. There is ample evidence from contemporaries in the 1960s and from later analysts that there was no slackening in Menzies' working habits, interaction with officials, travel, parliamentary performance, application to policy detail, command of cabinet, or engagement with political challenges. It is difficult to sustain the charge of laziness and complacency.[8] Yet Pringle and Horne would not have gained such attention and influence had their arguments not struck a chord. Understanding why helps to set the scene for what was to follow when Menzies retired, for as Horne also remarked, 'With Menzies gone all the main characters will be different; they will no longer be defining themselves in relation to *him*; we just don't know what they will be like. There is a state of concealed crisis in Australian politics, unpredictable in effect'.[9]

Menzies' Shadow

Peter Carrington, conservative politician, high commissioner to Australia (1956–59) and a notable British peer, was impressed and charmed by Menzies.[10] He became a friend and supporter, willingly engaged in the response to Menzies' critics. He referred to the metaphor 'under the beech tree nothing grows' not to endorse the assertion that Menzies was so dominant that any other initiative was stifled, but to refute it.[11] Tellingly, he overlooked the point made in one of his first reports to London in 1957, that the Menzies' government 'is far too much a one man show'.[12] Later, Carrington argued that while Menzies was powerful and authoritative, to suggest that others were not given opportunity to express their views is to underestimate the quality of cabinet discussion, underrate personalities such as Artie Fadden, Richard Casey and John McEwen, and ignore Menzies' devotion to the parliamentary system.[13] It is hard, however, to avoid the conclusion that the eventual cost of running 'a one man show' was that some of the most notable and able of his ministers—such as Casey, Percy Spender, Garfield Barwick and Paul Hasluck—departed or reined in their ambitions, not because Menzies compelled them to do so (something he vehemently denied[14]) but because his dominance and longevity impacted on their work or blocked their aspirations.

Casey had been appointed by Menzies ambassador to Washington during Menzies' first government, some thought as a means of getting him out of the way. Later, as external affairs minister in the 1950s, he would make a substantial contribution to Australia's relations with Asia. Yet his biographer records that Casey found Menzies impossible to work with, and in 1956 was humiliated when his advice on Suez was ignored and caused Menzies to lobby against him (in favour of Harold Holt) in a ballot for deputy leader of the party. He would retire from parliament in 1960 when appointed to a British peerage.[15] Five years later, Menzies, at last willing to nominate an Australian to the post, recommended that Lord Casey become governor-general (though Casey was his second choice—he had first offered the post to British admiral and war hero Sir John Collins, who declined[16]).

Spender was first encouraged to enter politics by Menzies. An impressive parliamentary performer in the 1940s whose leadership potential was recognised (and who manoeuvred to ensure he was in striking distance should Menzies go), he was an activist minister for external affairs (and a Cold War warrior) after 1949. His command of foreign policy challenged the convention of prime-ministerial dominance in international relations. His leadership aspirations were clear. Once he concluded that the prime minister was immovable, and that Menzies' supremacy in Cold War relations with 'great and powerful friends' undermined his own authority, Spender opted to exercise his influence in other ways, initially as ambassador to Washington.[17]

Barwick was a prominent lawyer, brought into politics as a celebrity candidate at a by-election in 1958, then appointed attorney-general. In December 1961 he became minister of external affairs. Menzies regarded external affairs as a key portfolio: he took it on himself in 1960–61. Barwick was another whose achievement and capacities seemed fitted for leadership. Despite early success in the attorney-general's role, manifest diplomatic ability and a growing passion for foreign affairs, Barwick was eventually to fall out with the old guard of the party and with Menzies over trade practices (he wanted to restrict the powers of manufacturing cartels) and concurrence with British policy in the confrontation between Malaya and Indonesia (he would treat Indonesia more circumspectly and shared US scepticism about British policy). Attempts to balance these tensions led to political difficulties in parliament.[18] Frustrated, out of favour and aware that he had not built the party following to succeed Menzies, in 1964 Barwick expressed an interest in the High Court. When the chief justice, Sir Owen Dixon, unexpectedly announced his intention to retire shortly afterwards, Menzies insisted that Barwick should make up his mind immediately. Barwick, feeling under duress, agreed to put his name forward and was appointed. 'The old man kicked me out', he said. 'I don't know what else I could have done about it.'[19]

Menzies indicated that it was a choice Barwick had made of his own volition and denied that pressure had been applied.[20]

Hasluck had as much cause as any to resent the constraint under which he had laboured in Menzies' cabinets but nevertheless persevered. He wrote generously about his old leader later. Yet he was buried in the territories portfolio for years and denied the opportunity he craved—external affairs—when Barwick was parachuted in. Even after succeeding Barwick, and despite his anti-communism and support for forward defence, his inclination was for circumspection in committing to Vietnam solely on American terms, but he capitulated to Holt and McEwen in the interests of cabinet solidarity (and with deference to Menzies' wishes).[21] Only years later would Menzies concede that Hasluck was 'the ablest Minister for External Affairs Australia has ever had'.[22]

McEwen was an aggressive leader of the Country Party and a disputatious deputy prime minister. His contribution to landmark achievements such as the Japanese Trade Treaty, and to industry protection, is well understood. And he was, according to Horne, the sole minister who called Menzies' bluff.[23] It was McEwen's challenges that pushed Menzies closer to Treasury than might otherwise have been the case. When the Country Party leader, deputy prime minister and treasurer Arthur Fadden resigned, Menzies exercised his prerogative to pass the Treasury portfolio to a Liberal Party ally, his deputy leader, Harold Holt. McEwen still made political capital out of his industry connections and record in trade negotiations. By 1962, Menzies was privately speculating that McEwen might be plotting to seize the succession for himself by discrediting Holt, refusing to serve under him and persuading Liberal MPs to vote for a Country Party prime minister. Indeed, Menzies intimated that it was for this reason that he must remain 'chained to the political chariot wheels' for yet another election while time ran out for McEwen and Holt's stocks could be salvaged.[24]

His private determination to ensure McEwen did not gain the upper hand over Holt aside, given the circumstances, Menzies and his supporters could sustain the view that he did nothing to precipitate the decisions of able men in seeking other opportunities. Yet the outcome by the 1960s was that, McEwen notwithstanding, those best placed to ensure robust debate in cabinet and the party room had departed or, like Hasluck, allowed loyalty to override their doubts. On Menzies' part, it is not surprising that long tenure, with an incremental accretion of power and experience, should encourage the expectation that his judgement should prevail.[25] On one occasion, having carpeted a senior foreign affairs officer who had unwittingly expressed a view at odds with his own, only to learn that the official had been following the instructions of the then external affairs minister, Barwick, he expostulated, 'What! Barwick! That new boy!'[26] Cabinet historian Patrick Weller notes that in the 1950s, fundamental differences could be expressed and debate in cabinet was willing, but

> Whether that vigorous debate continued into the last years of Menzies' reign is questioned by observers: the ministers of his own generation were replaced by a younger cohort that was more in awe of the long-serving prime minister. He was reputedly less patient with views he did not accept.[27]

These then were the grounds on which Horne could argue that Menzies had surrounded himself with 'a firebreak of mediocrity', and that led Weller, in looking across Menzies and his immediate successors, to conclude that there had been 'an emperor and three pale shadows'.[28]

Unforeseen Consequences

In the early 1960s, economic and social transitions that were a consequence of the decisions taken by Menzies' administrations over the previous decade began to produce effects that would impact on the government and on Menzies himself. An early signal was the economic turmoil of 1960 and 1961, arising from 'managed prosperity', but culminating in the near defeat of the Coalition government at the 1961 general election.

In early 1960, influenced by a buoyant economy, cabinet decided to remove import restrictions that had been 'temporarily' imposed in 1952 to protect foreign reserves. This fuelled a new boom and, fearing a trade deficit, the treasurer, Harold Holt, introduced a mildly deflationary budget in August. It was not enough. Labor leader Arthur Calwell (who had succeeded Evatt in 1960) described it as a 'stay put' budget brought down by a 'stand still' government.[29] In November, Holt introduced much more rigorous 'supplementary' measures to restrain excessive growth—the 'credit squeeze' that was to result in recession, some highly publicised company failures, an increase in overdraft rates, and a significant rise in unemployment (to a then unprecedented postwar level of 3 per cent in mid-1961). It was a strategy devised by economists in the increasingly influential PMD.[30]

As community outrage, business anger and media criticism mounted, Menzies and Holt were advised by their officials to stay the course. During 1961, they were assured by their advisers that these measures were having the intended effect, and Menzies took heart in noting that Britain was taking similar deflationary action.[31] The economist CB Schedvin saw these events as indicative of Holt's intellectual dependence on Wilson.[32] The *Australian Financial Review* opined that the bitter reaction of business to the government's actions was 'aggravated by the suspicion that the treasurer had only the vaguest idea of what they were supposed to achieve'.[33] Holt would claim during the 1961 election campaign that the damage had been contained and despite discomfort 'the economy has now passed through the phase of readjustment and is beginning a steady advance'.[34] While Calwell made a forceful attack on the government's economic management in his 1961 policy speech, Menzies remained aloof from the core economic arguments in his, effectively asking to be judged on his record.[35] Calwell denounced this as arrogance and complacency.

The *Sydney Morning Herald*, long critical of Menzies but never heretofore a Labor supporter, agreed. It gave Calwell much informal support behind the scenes while publicly noting Menzies' 'lofty paternalism, his unshaken complacency, his bland dismissal of a major social and economic problem as "some temporary unemployment"'.[36] It concluded some weeks later that 'since, after 12 years of office, the Government can offer no further suggestions except to stand on its record, we would prefer to take the alternative and to give Labor its opportunity'.[37] The electorate almost concurred. The Coalition was returned with a single-seat majority, suffering its worst electoral result since 1946. Holt bore the brunt of public anger. It was this setback and the resulting disquiet within Coalition ranks that fed Menzies' suspicion that if he was to retire, McEwen might challenge the wounded Holt. However, the charge of standing haughtily above the fray and of complacency was directed at Menzies himself.

An additional feature of the 1961 campaign, little noted by commentators at the time, was the extent to which people with 'conventional' views were disengaged from politics,[38] while in parallel there was agitation by new social movements around the margins. Student activists, inspired by the Immigration Reform Group that had emerged in the late 1950s, campaigned against the White Australia policy. Demonstrations explicitly aimed at Menzies' tolerance of apartheid (he had opposed moves to force South Africa out of the Commonwealth over its racially discriminatory policies) would morph into protests against Australia's own immigration policies and eventually into activism supporting Indigenous rights.[39] The Australian peace movement organised petitions for peace and 'universal disarmament',[40] and seeded opposition to Australia's military commitment to its great and powerful friends: the grounds on which the anti–Vietnam War movement would later build.

These incipient social movements, usually seen as flowering in the late 1960s, were evident much earlier than is commonly assumed. And their emergence served to highlight Menzies' rigidity: he would not adapt as conditions changed. The 'moral middle class' to which Menzies originally appealed[41] might have retreated into convention and relative disengagement,[42] but some of their children, advantaged by prosperity and educational opportunities unknown to their parents, were engaging with new moral issues. The conditions that Curtin, Chifley and Menzies had worked so hard to achieve had proved favourable to the development of views inimical to the values to which Menzies still clung.[43] While responsible ministers saw the emerging shift in social mores—Hubert Opperman in relation to immigration, Casey and McEwen in relation to Asian engagement, Hasluck in relation to Aboriginal policy, and even Holt on White Australia—Menzies stalled. Older voters would still find merit in his stance, but the erosion of his standing with the rising generation was beginning.

Some of these issues—such as liberalisation of immigration policy and removal of the marriage bar against women in the public service—were put on hold pending his departure.[44] Others were more difficult to ignore. The increasingly important defence relationship with the United States (especially the promotion of regional security through the ANZUS Treaty), the growth in trade with Asia, and the success of the Spender-inspired Colombo Plan for cooperative development in South and South-East Asia were all to the credit of the Coalition government. In contrast, Menzies' continued insistence on the importance of the British connection in the face of Britain's efforts to facilitate decolonisation through Commonwealth agencies and to enter the European Economic Community was seen in an increasingly critical light.

The young Queen Elizabeth's Australian tour in 1954, the first by a reigning monarch, had been immensely popular, accentuating Menzies' profile and playing to the Coalition government's advantage (it concluded scarcely a fortnight before the announcement of Petrov's defection). Response to a return visit in 1963 was more restrained, and Menzies' efforts to celebrate her return provoked satire. His quotation from a little-known Elizabethan poet, 'I did but see her passing by, and yet I love her til I die',[45] in a speech intended to compliment the Queen, appeared to embarrass her. It was ridiculed by some as sentimental sycophancy. During the same visit, the Queen conferred on Menzies one of the highest-ranking British knighthoods—the Most Ancient and Most Noble Order of the Thistle—the highest honour bestowed upon an Australian to that time. In fairness to Menzies, it appears he knew nothing about this in advance. It was a genuine measure of the regard in which he was held in Britain. Not since Edmund Barton had an incumbent Australian prime minister been knighted. Yet it further accentuated that he was the 'Queen's man' in a context where multilateral relationships and a more independent foreign policy, encouraged by his own ministers, were in vogue.

Public perceptions of Menzies' penchant for the cosy environs of empire obscured the extent to which foreign policy in the 1950s had successfully fostered a better alliance with both Britain and America, and indeed masked the emphasis on Asia and the Pacific that had been initiated by Spender and carried forward by his successors. In most cases they managed to sustain productive relations with Menzies in these endeavours. For example, Spender had clear objectives in his approach to the ANZUS Treaty negotiations and good relations with supportive officials in External Affairs. Despite clear differences between Menzies and Spender, Spender's conceptual clarity enabled them to work together to achieve more than Menzies had thought possible.[46] Casey was less successful in persuading Menzies to be more cautious in committing to the British during the Suez Crisis, but he too managed to maintain the focus on Asia and the Pacific.[47]

In the 1960s, the previous emphasis on quadrilateral talks between Australia, the United States, the United Kingdom and New Zealand was abandoned as Australia eagerly sought involvement in Vietnam. The twin imperatives of containing communism and demonstrating loyalty to the United States overrode good alliance management: there was no exit strategy. Menzies and Hasluck got the advice they wanted from their officials, partly through ensuring some diplomats were kept out of the loop.[48] While they were initially able to persuade the public that this was an essential defensive commitment (its popularity would help ensure a Coalition victory in 1966), it would prove a costly exposure. Liberal Party president John Elliott claimed in 1988 that it lost the party the support of a generation.[49]

There were no exit strategies either when adverse aspects of domestic policies that had been integral to Menzies' appeal emerged. For example, the importance of the home to a satisfactory life had been central to his 'forgotten people' speech. His governments had incrementally adapted Labor's Commonwealth-State Housing Agreement—initially intended to boost public housing for rental to low-income families—to instead promote private investment and consumption. During the 1950s and early 1960s this appeared to be a policy success. By the mid-1960s, problems were becoming apparent. Suburban expansion, left to developers, market forces and individual decisions, was ad hoc and often poorly planned. Chronic shortages of land and housing persisted, leading to a highly inflationary real estate market. The result for many was unfavourable, with some aspirant owners financially overstretched and those too poor to buy paying prohibitive rents. The biggest losers were precisely those on whom Labor's 1944 initiatives had focused: by 1975, fewer than one-third of Australia's poor could be accommodated in public housing.[50] Not until the late 1960s would a Coalition government attempt to address these problems, but by then the new Labor leader, Gough Whitlam, had captured the debate over housing and urban development.

Much of the blowback would come after Menzies had departed the scene. It would be the task of his successors to respond to change and to the unforeseen consequences of Menzies' long rule. Meanwhile, despite the narrow escape of 1961, Menzies' ascendance was undented. Critics and satirists underestimated his command of parliament and the public domain. And Labor kept on giving.

In 1963, in the midst of a contentious debate about a proposed US naval communications base in Western Australia over which the Labor Party was divided, the party's parliamentary leader and deputy leader—Calwell and Whitlam—were photographed waiting outside a meeting of the party's national conference for a policy decision. Journalist Alan Reid had cleverly captured the moment, tagging Labor's real decision-makers the '36 faceless men'. It was a boon to the Coalition, still intent on the Cold War and the US defence relationship. In October, Menzies, without consulting his party, called a snap election for late November, a year earlier than was expected. He would fight it principally on foreign policy grounds, and on Labor's unwillingness to face up to what was needed in a dangerous world. Coincidentally, US president John Kennedy was assassinated during the course of the campaign.

There were stormy campaign meetings, including 'ban the bomb' demonstrations, but the government was returned with a 22-seat majority. High-profile Labor MP Dr Jim Cairns insisted that Labor must move to the left: the 1963 election had been decided 'by fear, and superstitious and impractical people who fell easy victims to "the big lie"'.[51] Coalition supporters in contrast again celebrated the miracle achieved by Menzies' timing and flair. Even the *Sydney Morning Herald* conceded

> Such results are not achieved by little men: they are the public rewards of men of outstanding achievements and ability. The Prime Minister's

> mastery of politics, his long service … in the highest seat of government, and his formidable reputation in international councils have generated a political momentum of their own which the Labour Opposition has been quite unable to offset.[52]

With the government's position once more secure, speculation about Menzies' retirement ensued. Still, concerned about national security, he persevered for two more years, working with Hasluck in External Affairs, and with defence minister Shane Paltridge, to entrench the Vietnam commitment and the US alliance. Defence, and concerns that the confrontation between Malaya and Indonesia would lead Australia into conflict with Indonesia, were primary themes in a half Senate election in 1964. Compulsory military service, with young men conscripted on the basis of a birthdate chosen by ballot, was introduced in 1964. In April 1965 it was announced that a regular Australian battalion would be sent to join US forces in Vietnam. In September Holt brought down a 'guns before fun' budget, and Menzies announced that another 350 men would be sent to Vietnam and that the intake of national service conscripts would be increased in 1966 (the first national service conscripts were sent to join regular forces in Vietnam in April that year). There were some protests: the first anti-war 'teach-ins' in universities began. Yet opposition at this stage was desultory. Economic steadiness now seemed assured and so Holt's position was reinforced. Menzies turned seventy-one in December 1965 and decided his work was done. On 20 January 1966 he announced to the assembled Coalition parties that he was retiring forthwith.[53]

'A Nicer Man than the Prime Minister Sometimes Needed to Be'

Harold Holt, or 'Young Harold' as Menzies invariably called him, would later be referred to ruefully by Menzies in the words above.[54] He was fifty-seven when he succeeded Menzies as leader of the parliamentary Liberal Party and hence prime minister. He had waited thirty years for the opportunity—aside from Menzies, he was the only member of the former UAP still in parliament. Holt had trained as a lawyer. Associated with Menzies even before entering politics, he challenged former Labor prime minister James Scullin in the 1934 federal election, contested another safe Labor seat in a subsequent state election, and in 1935 won a safe UAP federal seat in a by-election. In 1939 he served briefly in Menzies' first ministry. Aged thirty, he was then the youngest man to have held federal ministerial office. He was displaced, however, when the Country Party rejoined the Coalition and its ministers had to be accommodated. Holt then enlisted in the army.

Holt was recalled to Canberra by Menzies only months later after three senior Coalition ministers died in an air accident. Following the September 1940 election, he was given a full cabinet position as minister for labour and national service. His energy and zeal were soon evident. He proved an able administrator, drawing people of different abilities and dispositions together. An early mentor was the ubiquitous Roland Wilson, secretary of Holt's department in 1940. Holt regretfully supported those whose opposition led to Menzies' resignation in 1941, and was not a prominent contributor to Menzies' efforts to create the Liberal Party. Yet Menzies, typically not a forgiving man, forgave Holt,[55] perhaps recalling the administrative talent displayed in 1940–41. After the 1949 election, Holt was reappointed minister for labour and national service, to which the portfolio of immigration was added.[56]

Holt's easy public demeanour, with something of a playboy air, was deceptive: he was hardworking, persistent and ambitious. His ascent, first to deputy leader of the party in 1956, then to the key Treasury portfolio in 1958, was indicative of the favour he won in Menzies' eyes. By then, many of the strong personalities prominent in the first Menzies governments had departed. As treasurer, Holt again came under the influence of Wilson. 'Treasury generally approved of the appointment: Holt had the requisite seniority and skill in cabinet to win a brief, and he did not have a dangerously independent mind or a personal agenda.'[57] With strong support from the mandarins, he oversaw the establishment of the Reserve Bank and lengthy planning for the smooth introduction of decimal currency, adding to his reputation for diligent administration.[58] He was also the bearer of Treasury's criticisms of the Vernon Report in cabinet, though it was Menzies who delivered the statement repudiating the report in parliament. Holt's reliance on the mandarins left him exposed: he followed their advice and hence bore the flack for the 1960 'credit squeeze' and the near loss of the 1961 election. Menzies' concern that Holt must be given the time to recover from this setback was a factor in his own decision to stay on through the 1963 election and beyond. Holt was clearly by then the chosen successor, and on Menzies' retirement it smoothly came to pass. Holt could boast that it was a bloodless succession: in January 1966, he became prime minister 'without stepping over anyone's body'.[59]

Despite the thirty-year wait and his silver hair, Holt's winning smile, athleticism and retention of a boyish air contrasted with 'the old man' who had dominated national life for so long. Subsequent image-making would rely on this relative youth and vitality to convey a sense of glamour. It was an intentional contrast with Menzies, who could amuse, charm, persuade and entertain when he chose, but who remained formidable, detached and formal in most contexts. Holt was sociable and seemed open to all—approachable by backbenchers and journalists, and on the way to his office willing to chat even to tourists visiting Parliament House. He recognised that he could not be a Menzies and defined his style of 'team' leadership accordingly:

> There is the type of leadership that is so far out in front of the team that there is danger of lack of cooperation, lack of warmth and some loss of effectiveness. There is the leadership that can lead but, at the same time, be close enough to the team to be part of it and be on the basis of friendly cooperation. I will make that my technique of leadership.[60]

It was an attempt to explain his preferred mode as a conscious differentiation from Menzies: a return to 'first among equals' rather than the 'Godhead' who might withdraw behind the veil. The danger was, in opting to be chairman rather than emperor, he was departing from the template to which his colleagues had become accustomed and might find his authority diminished. A decisive chairman can be an enormously effective leader, as was the later Labor prime minister Bob Hawke, but one focused on keeping all parties happy can face incremental attrition, as was the case with UAP prime minister Joe Lyons throughout the 1930s.

Some of the party elders saw Holt's amiability and relative lack of intellectual rigour as political weaknesses, and felt he should be schooled in the skills now needed. Hasluck, who had contested the deputy leadership following Holt's elevation by the party room but been defeated by the high-pressure voting tactics adopted by Billy McMahon, was one who thought Holt's impetuosity should be curbed.[61] That Hasluck, believing that merit alone should guarantee advancement, never worked to garner colleagues' votes and consistently failed to gain the prizes that Holt won indicates a misunderstanding of Holt's shrewdness. Holt may have lacked intellectual rigour, but he was intelligent, widely experienced and conscious of the need for sound advice close at hand. He appointed Keith Sinclair, former editor of the *Age*, as a speechwriter: the first prime minister to introduce such a position. He wanted to bring a trusted officer from Treasury into the PMO: Bunting warned that it might be seen as a Treasury takeover. Instead, Peter Bailey from PMD was appointed to head the office—an 'on-the-spot' departmental adviser.[62] Criticised later as an attempt to institute a presidential style of leadership,[63] it was the smallest of moves towards the enhancement of the PMO that would be undertaken in the 1970s.

Alert to public expectations, Holt turned to his press secretary, Tony Eggleton. Though Eggleton had previously worked for Menzies, Hasluck disapproved of him and of this turn to the 'strange and glamorous but quite fanciful world of "public relations"'.[64] Holt, however, was conscious that his reputation would be influenced by the way he was represented in the media.[65] Eggleton shaped Holt's media relationships and modes of communicating policy decisions. There were three innovations: Holt's office in association with the gallery devised rules to regulate attendance and procedure at press briefings; meetings were recorded and transcribed by his staff and a memorandum circulated to indicate statements that were for attribution, those for publication without attribution, and those that were 'off the record'; and Holt would allow radio and television reporters then to attend his office to record attributable statements for broadcast.[66] It was the beginning of the PMO intentionally fashioning the leader's image. That said, Holt was more open with the press than Menzies had been, generating the interviews and picture opportunities that Menzies spurned, and more accommodating when asked to adapt his presentation for television. He would give the first extended interview any prime minister had granted to the ABC's *This Day Tonight*, the catalyst for broadcasting 'rules of behaviour' that would shape such engagements thereafter.[67] Menzies had predicted late in his term that television would become the important medium for engaging with the electorate, but it was Holt and his advisers who began to grapple with the demands of the medium.

Things went well at first. The government moved to address the issue of immigration reform. Holt saw this as 'of fundamental importance in the development of Australian foreign policy and the search for friendly relations with non-European countries'.[68] Holt and his immigration minister, Hubert Opperman, reintroduced measures that had first been mooted in 1964 but rejected by Menzies: the *Migration Act 1966*. Conditions for naturalisation and entry for non-Europeans were liberalised. Although reforms were cautious (there was still opposition not only within the Coalition but also in the Labor Party), critics from Asia and the UN were mollified. These were the necessary first steps in dismantling the White Australia policy.[69]

Every Coalition minister for external affairs from Spender on had worked to foster good relations with Asian neighbours and trading partners, but Menzies' direct engagement was sporadic. Holt was the first prime minister to travel extensively and invest personally in building such bilateral relationships. An engaging personality, he showed some flair in diplomacy, but occasionally Hasluck's prediction of impetuosity was confirmed, as in Holt's decision that Australia would open an embassy in Taiwan—described by a former Australian diplomat as a 'foolish and naive off-the-cuff decision' made by 'an amiable man … who knew almost nothing about foreign affairs'[70]—and later his controversial invitation to Nguyen Cao Ky, prime minister of South Vietnam, to visit Australia.

Naturally, Holt also initiated his own relationships with the allies so assiduously cultivated by Menzies, hosting visits to Australia by British defence minister Denis Healey and US vice-president Hubert Humphrey. In 1966 he travelled to the United Kingdom to meet prime minister

Harold Wilson, and to the United States to meet president Johnson. The engagement with Johnson was intended to foster trade concessions and greater access to US intelligence, the latter to be advanced by stressing Australia's dedication to the alliance in prosecuting the Vietnam War, but these objectives were never achieved.[71] This manifestation of American indifference to Australian interests was not publicised: forward defence was the public rationale for Australia's commitment.

Holt had first encountered Lyndon Johnson in Melbourne in 1942, but it was Holt's visit to Washington in July 1966 that sparked what his wife, Zara, described as his 'most spectacular friendship' with Johnson.[72] They hit it off. But, carried away by the occasion, again Holt misjudged, adding to a formal speech an extemporary remark drawing on what had been the Democrats' 1964 presidential campaign slogan: 'I hope there will be a corner of your mind and heart which takes cheer from the fact that you have an admiring friend, a staunch ally that will be "All the way with LBJ"'.[73] It was seriously to misread the Australian reaction. What had been intended as a friendly and lighthearted remark was interpreted as another manifestation of sycophancy.[74]

In October 1966, Johnson visited Australia, the first incumbent American president to do so. It was testament not only to the burgeoning relationship between these leaders but also to the increasing investment by Holt in supporting America in the Vietnam War. He shared Menzies' view of the seriousness of the communist threat and the necessity of securing US commitment to the security of South-East Asia. In March 1966, soon after assuming office, Holt had announced a trebling of the Australian troop commitment (from 1500 to 4500) and the first inclusion of national servicemen in the task force. Such decisions, the 'All the way with LBJ' remark, and Johnson's visit were all conducive to the growth of the anti-war movement, still relatively small but now with enough momentum to generate effective demonstrations (and media coverage) during Johnson's visit. Given the proximity of the 1966 election (Holt had announced as early as August that it was to take place on 26 November), it evidently did Holt no short-term harm: 'the most powerful man in the world … had come to visit the prime minister of Australia as a personal friend, a month before the federal election'.[75]

Holt went into the election campaign convinced that Vietnam was the key issue, and he spoke accordingly. The war had already provoked violent protest and civil unrest. In June 1966, Labor leader Calwell was shot, though not seriously wounded, following an anti-conscription rally. Calwell thought the war in Vietnam was 'a cruel, unwinnable civil war' and asked 'the Australian people not to cast a blood vote for the Holt Government and conscription'. At times he spoke intemperately, as if the campaign was for a plebiscite on conscription. It sat uneasily with his promise to deliver social service benefits.[76] The outcome was a landslide win for the Coalition and Labor's most severe loss since 1931. Holt had achieved a greater victory than any achieved by Menzies, with a then record majority of seats, and a still unsurpassed two-party-preferred vote of nearly 57 per cent. It was the end for the septuagenarian Labor leader Arthur Calwell, who was replaced by Gough Whitlam in early 1967. It was widely thought a vindication of Holt's commitment to the US alliance. But the Vietnam story was not over.

Holt had been given a mandate that should have assured his authority, but nothing would be so bright again for him, or for the Coalition government. On the one hand, such a win induced complacency, especially among new members who knew nothing of the struggles of managing 'the Keynesian war economy' while maintaining electoral support. On the other, as the largely unchanged cabinet settled down for the long haul, Holt's defects as a 'team' leader came more persistently to the fore. In cabinet, Menzies had shown how to allow ministers their voice and when to intervene decisively, but Holt's style in both cabinet and party room was closer to that of the earlier Coalition prime minister Joe Lyons—striving for consensus and reluctant to force issues when it could not be achieved. One of his ministers, Don Chipp, would later remark that Holt

> was a gentle man who rarely showed signs of temper or of adopting the firm authority of a strong leader … Holt did not have the personality to control the dissidents … During 1967 … Party Room debates featured growing aggression and new-found bravado, which would never have been contemplated in Menzies' time.[77]

With Holt's weaker grip on cabinet, there was a greater need for PMD to advise on policy coordination across departments, but then Holt began to read PMD briefs—intended to assist the prime minister's deliberations rather than to be broadcast to colleagues—in cabinet. Bunting had to ask that Holt take responsibility rather than appear to be adopting a PMD line.[78] In parliament, Holt proved no match for Whitlam, the new opposition leader.

In the course of 1967, a series of damaging incidents occurred, all of which demonstrated not only Holt's misjudgement, but also his indecisiveness in taking control of events, and of colleagues. There was the VIP flights scandal, in which questions were raised about the alleged misuse of the RAAF's Special Transport Squadron (responsible for carriage of the prime minister and other 'very important' persons). Holt was wrongly advised when miscommunication between the Department of Air, PMD and Holt's office led to his claim in parliament that there was no record of passenger manifests from which such questions could be answered. But when the error was discovered, out of loyalty to his friend, Peter Howson, minister for air, he indulged a period of messy evasion and dissembling before the government leader in the Senate, John Gorton, lanced the boil by tabling the records there.[79] Holt's reputation for decency and integrity suffered a serious blow.

There was a backbench revolt over Holt's resistance to reopening an inquiry (following an earlier royal commission initiated by Menzies) into the loss of HMAS *Voyager* after a collision with HMAS *Melbourne* in 1964. Having for months fended off those disappointed with the initial royal commission's report, and persistent claims that there was new evidence to be considered, Holt buckled and allowed for the matter to be debated in the House. Then, following a fiery maiden speech in that debate by Liberal MP Edward St John, during which an infuriated Holt breached protocol by interjecting, he back-peddled again, allowing the matter to return to the party room, and subsequently announcing that there would be another royal commission. It was interpreted as a failure to control his backbench, and an inability to withstand negative media and public pressure. The suspicion that Holt could not lead in a crisis began to be voiced.

Then there was the running sore of the Vietnam engagement. Holt had increased the Australian troop commitment in March 1966, again in December (after his election win) and again in October 1967, to a peak of over 8000 men. He was as committed to security as Menzies, driven by his overall interest in Asia, piqued by the British withdrawal from 'East of Suez' (over which he felt he had been misled by Harold Wilson), and fortified by his friendship with president Johnson—who also subjected him to intense pressure. Hasluck, equally committed to anti-communism and national security, but never an uncritical friend of America, advised caution in appearing too decidedly responsive to US demands. He was ignored. To his credit, Holt consistently sought to explain foreign policy decisions, especially in relation to Vietnam, in parliament, a practice that Hasluck began to follow. But when Holt tried to explain the rationale for perseverance in his Deakin Lecture in July 1967, a Liberal supporter observed, 'it had become evident that the Prime Minister could not explain Government foreign policy—and in particular, Australia's military commitment to Vietnam'.[80]

Holt became the Australian leader most clearly associated with the war. He was thus the target of the anti-war movement, which was now being energised by the activities of student radicals. There had been serious casualties (eighteen Australian soldiers killed and another twenty-one wounded) in the battle of Long Tan in August 1966, and by late 1967, Holt, worried about increasing casualties (now over 200), and with polls showing more than half the electorate opposed to any increased participation, decided the ceiling of Australia's commitment had been reached.[81] The fulsome support of only a year earlier was eroding: there had been worrying by-election losses during the year and in the half Senate election on 25 November, the government's vote fell from the historic high of 56.9 per cent in 1966 to 42.8 per cent.

Holt took some comfort from one battle that he had won: he had faced down John McEwen. Relations between McEwen and treasurer Billy McMahon had become increasingly poisonous over the course of 1966 and 1967: McEwen (and Trade) remained resolutely protectionist, while McMahon was the first treasurer actually qualified in economics, free-trade inclined, and backed by a strong department. McEwen had also adopted a more assertive role in cabinet and party debates: some thought as a counter to Holt's weakness. Matters came to a head when, just prior to the Senate poll, Australia announced it would not follow Britain in a currency devaluation. Cabinet had accepted Treasury advice despite a conflicting argument from the Department of Trade. McEwen, overseas when the decision was taken, disagreed and publicly criticised the decision. Holt privately took him to task, threatening that the Liberal Party would govern alone if he persisted in defying the cabinet decision, and then publicly repudiating the deputy prime minister's statement. McEwen backed down.[82] 'In a year of drift and decline', said ALP speechwriter Graham Freudenberg, 'it was Holt's best day'.[83]

There had been other achievements in 1967 that would have longer-term cultural significance: the establishment of the Australian Council for the Arts (ACA), on the advice, and initially under the direction, of Nugget Coombs; and, more importantly, the passage of a referendum changing the constitution to enable Aboriginal people to be counted in the census and giving the Commonwealth the capacity to legislate for them (which had formerly been prohibited). Both of these were foundational to initiatives later governments would undertake. Nonetheless, the concerns of his backbenchers were not allayed, and Menzies himself concluded the cause had been Holt's 'besetting sin … he wanted everyone to love him … the result was he made a muck of everything in his second year. He would have lost the next election. It was a dreadful performance. Dreadful'.[84]

There would be no opportunity for recovery. On 17 December 1967, during a weekend break at his retreat at Portsea, on Victoria's Mornington Peninsula, Holt disappeared while swimming in heavy seas off Cheviot Beach. His body was never recovered. He would be remembered as a decent, amiable man who had misjudged his strength in taking to the surf that day and, perhaps, in taking on the highest office in the land.

Breaking the Mould

The Menzies succession was disrupted. Holt had not only been favoured in 1966 but was also seen by media opinion leaders as the 'obvious' choice. This time there was no such contender. Yet the favourite son's wholehearted adoption of the Vietnam commitment had already sown unease about the US alliance; his cautious reforms of the White Australia policy, in Indigenous relations and in promotion of the arts were laudable but remained indicative rather than fully implemented; and, above all, his apparent failings in team leadership had been a disappointment. It would emerge that some Liberal MPs (including party whip Dudley Erwin and a future prime minister, Malcolm Fraser) had been planning to confront him about such concerns in the period immediately before his death. Their initial thoughts about an alternative had settled on John Gorton, only recently appointed government leader in the Senate.[85]

Holt's death brought other factors and other aspirants into play. Billy McMahon, an ambitious schemer, immediately contacted colleagues trying to organise an early meeting of the party and began to canvass support, but John McEwen acted first. Deputy prime minister by virtue of his position as Country Party leader, McEwen had routinely been named acting prime minister by Holt when the latter was travelling. McEwen's antipathy to McMahon was intense: he moved quickly to inform the governor-general, Lord Casey, that the Country Party would refuse to serve in the Coalition if McMahon was prime minister. Casey was concerned to ensure the Coalition government's stability until the Liberal leadership was resolved. He appointed McEwen as prime minister. McEwen then announced publicly that he would stand aside once the Liberal Party had resolved on a new leader, but the Country Party would refuse to remain in the Coalition if that leader was to be McMahon—he had effectively been blackballed.[86]

In the event, there were four candidates: John Gorton (minister for education and science), Paul Hasluck (minister for external affairs), Leslie Bury (minister for labour and national service) and Billy Snedden (minister for immigration). Essentially the contest was between Hasluck and Gorton—the other two would be dispensed with on the first ballot. Gorton, relatively unknown to the public, worked actively to secure support in the party and to raise his profile, proving particularly effective on radio and television in the run-up to the party room meeting. It was the precursor to what became one of Gorton's most notable capacities:

his informality of approach served him well on television and won electoral support. Menzies had acknowledged the growing significance of television in engaging with the electorate; Holt had pioneered 'rules of engagement' with the medium; now Gorton demonstrated that modes of presentation adapted to television could win not only the electorate but also the party room.

Hasluck, true to form, did not campaign at all other than to distribute a letter to Liberal MPs and senators announcing his candidature. Menzies privately lobbied on his behalf. It is thought that most of the ministry supported Hasluck, but Gorton had strong support in the Senate and the backbench was eager for a new style of leadership. In the final ballot, Gorton prevailed. He was sworn in as prime minister on 10 January 1968. He contested Holt's Victorian seat of Higgins in the ensuing by-election on 24 February, and moved to the House of Representatives before parliament reconvened in March.[87]

John Gorton had a materially secure but unsettling childhood. He was unaware that his mother was not married to his father until after she died: he was aged seven. Then he was sent to live with his father's estranged wife where he first met his older sister, and had only intermittent contact with his father until, in 1927, the wife decided to return to her native England, taking his sister with her. Returning to his father, he was dispatched to boarding school. This experience encouraged early self-reliance and a toughly competitive streak. Gorton was slow to trust others, easily offended, always ready for a fight, but eager to please and searching for acknowledgment. He was privately educated and sent abroad to Oxford University to take a degree, but afterwards was called to work on his family's rural smallholding in northern Victoria. He served in the air force as a fighter pilot during World War II, surviving two air crashes that led to facial reconstruction, then returned to run the family orchard.

Gorton was one of the Liberal phalanxes elected in 1949. Independent and irreverent, he did not initially appeal to Menzies, and waited until December 1958 to be appointed to the ministry. After having held a number of junior ministries, he was appointed as minister assisting the prime minister in education and science towards the end of Menzies' reign and played a significant role in the implementation of reforms flowing from the Murray Report, the extension of state aid to private schools and, following a recommendation from the Australian Universities Commission (AUC), the establishment of colleges of advanced education.[88] His ability was evident, but not until Holt's accession was he brought into cabinet and appointed full minister for education and science. It was his toughness, intelligence and independent-mindedness that attracted colleagues as Holt's difficulties became apparent. And once Gorton gained the public eye, it was his breezy air, directness and disregard of convention that appealed in contrast to Menzies' patrician dominance and Holt's effort to appear all things to all people. Tall, lean, with war injuries having given him a ruggedly distinctive appearance, he seemed an attractive option.[89]

If it was strong leadership that was sought from the new prime minister, Gorton promised to deliver. At once he marked his difference from Holt:

> The prime minister ... is not to be chairman of the committee so that a majority vote in the committee says what's going to be done. He should put to the cabinet or the committee what he believes ought to be done, and if believes strongly enough that it ought to be done, *then it must be done.*[90]

Something similar might have been said about Menzies, but Menzies had learned in 1941 that merely to insist on his own way was fruitless. Following his reincarnation as prime minister, Menzies may well have been 'the best man there', but he knew when to allow his colleagues to talk, when to listen, when to speak, and when to intervene with authority.[91] Gorton, when it came to the point, would simply insist. Malcolm Fraser, initially a political friend and supporter, eventually concluded that Gorton thought it was a sign of weakness to change his mind.[92]

Gorton was in a hurry: he had told friends during the frustrating years of waiting for preferment that he was in politics to do things. He had an agenda, and it was not that of Menzies. He was a resolute nationalist and wanted a foreign policy that was not subject to the wishes of great and powerful friends; he championed cultural enterprises, and would not only bring Holt's ACA into being, with a board he chose, but also go further to inaugurate a national film development corporation;[93] and he was a believer in the use of Commonwealth power to achieve national objectives—a centralist in a party committed, as Menzies carefully explained, to appropriate devolution of power in a federation.[94] Those who supported Gorton's election as party leader underestimated the extent to which his agenda and his determination would impact upon the way government operated. He proved more forceful and innovative than Holt, and impatient with the processes and institutions Menzies had established. Menzies' 'boys' were rudely interrupted.

Distrustful of John Bunting, and wanting his own man, Lenox Hewitt, by his side, Gorton split his department in two, shunting Bunting and some of his senior officers into a new Cabinet Office and installing Hewitt as secretary of PMD. Hewitt, chairman of the AUC, had impressed Gorton when they worked together on education reform. Aggressive, demanding and controlling, Hewitt was said to spend more time in Parliament House than in the department. He personally governed the flow of paperwork to and from the prime minister.[95] Hewitt became Gorton's 'go to' man, 'the substitute for everything Gorton needed and could not immediately get'.[96]

Simultaneously, Peter Bailey was sent back to PMD and Gorton appointed a 22-year-old, Ainsley Gotto, formerly secretary to the party whip, as his principal private secretary. It was a controversial appointment not only because of its departure from convention—she was not a bureaucratic insider—but also because Gotto's youth, attractiveness and gender provoked innuendo about the nature of her relationship with Gorton. Rumours of an affair were later dismissed by Gorton's biographer, who also questioned the degree of her influence.[97] Yet it was a relationship that prefigured the later notorious dalliance between Labor deputy prime minister Jim Cairns and his private secretary, Junie Morosi, and the pronounced co-dependency between Tony Abbott and his senior staffer Peta Credlin. At the very least, Gotto controlled access to the prime minister.

Gorton's interventions were unusual and foreshadowed the sorts of changes later prime ministers would make to ensure loyalty and responsiveness in the PMO and within the agencies with which they were most closely associated. They also foreshadowed some of the problems that would later become acute. Gotto and the PMO served to make Gorton increasingly detached from his backbench. And Hewitt

> … in one sense … served his master very well. He guided him, supported him, and helped him cut through the time honoured practices. But for Gorton to be more successful he had to have the full cooperation of the public service and Hewitt … made things difficult for him by alienating too many senior public servants.[98]

Nevertheless, Hewitt left a lasting structural legacy: 'He recruited sharp and aggressive policy specialists … Hewitt and his recruits established a more assertive place for PMD in policy generation and advice that came to be accepted in the following decade'.[99]

It followed that Gorton's approach to cabinet was not only more assertive than that of Holt, but also less tactically adroit than that of Menzies. He was brusque and gave no credence to bruised egos. On the one hand, he closed down or confronted competitors. For instance, he removed his closest leadership rival, Paul Hasluck, by securing his appointment as governor-general (succeeding Lord Casey in 1969) and joined with McEwen to wage a relentless battle against McMahon. On the other, he was heedless of reaction when exercising patronage in favour of his supporters, forming a so-called 'cocktail cabinet' with a select inner circle. Hiving off the Cabinet Office left his closest bureaucratic ally, Hewitt, out of the room, and hence PMD was dependent on what Gorton communicated on how decisions were to be interpreted. There were instances where Bunting, now cabinet secretary, sought clarification on how decisions had been recorded, when qualifications were removed and decisions rendered as more definitive than initially drafted, or more attuned to Gorton's objectives.[100]

Gorton was deemed lazy (or, as Tony Eggleton put it, a 'Monday to Friday' prime minister) because he did not work the long hours of his predecessors, insisting that a prime minister should be able to live a normal life. But there was no diminution in the regularity of cabinet meetings. There, at first, Gorton was at his best: attentive to detail, incisive and, unlike Holt, quick to make decisions. He could win through well-prepared, decisive argument rather than simple assertion. Yet there were occasions when he joined battle, such as in collaborating with McEwen to gain support for McEwen's initiative, the Industry Development Corporation, against the opposition of McMahon and Treasury, and simply announced cabinet's acceptance, though most opposed it. And over time, as he refused to curb his gregarious party-going and relatively heavy-drinking lifestyle while the pressures of the job increased, there was a deterioration in performance and in judgement. It would provoke opposition, discontent and eventually a revolt that brought him down.[101]

Gorton's style was most evident in cases that engaged his core principles. His pugnacious assertion of Australian independence, for example, would not only change the course of foreign policy but also transform the man who had once said, 'do not make me look at any more culture than I want to look at', into an adherent of cultural nationalism. Political scientist Ian Ward argues that 'Gorton sought to distance himself from the British sensibilities of the Menzies era and find new ways of thinking and talking about Australia.'[102] It was this that drove his commitment to implementing Holt's ACA and to the establishment of the Australian Film Development Corporation: matters seen as marginal by most of his cabinet, which thus enabled him to own these projects. The ACA was established not (as had been expected) as a statutory authority but as an element within PMD. And the chair of the committee appointed to advise on support for the film industry, Peter Coleman, later said that its conclusions 'were predetermined by the wishes of an impatient Prime Minister'.[103]

Far less marginal to Gorton's colleagues, however, was Gorton's predilection for asserting Commonwealth power against the states. Although a supporter of the assimilation policies adopted by the Menzies government in the 1950s (and largely developed by Hasluck as minister for territories), Gorton was concerned about Aboriginal welfare and appointed his friend, the maverick MP WC Wentworth, to prepare a policy for Aboriginal advancement. It met with opposition in cabinet and underwent a number of changes before being taken to a ministerial meeting with the states. Gorton made it clear that the Commonwealth, following the 1967 referendum, took its new constitutional responsibilities seriously and would take a lead in Aboriginal affairs. Predictably, the states and some of his ministers were disturbed by what they saw as centralist interference in their responsibilities.[104]

More significant was Gorton's unequivocal assertion of Commonwealth supremacy in the financial relationship with the states at the 1968 Premiers' Conference. It followed a period of increasing agitation by the premiers. They argued that the formula for disbursing Commonwealth funding under the uniform taxation regime now failed to meet their needs, and contravened the Liberal Party's 1948 commitment to 'the maintenance, unimpaired, of the federal system'. Gorton did not give an inch. He told them that they could not enter the income and payroll tax fields; the Commonwealth could veto forms and levels of state taxation; those who had not complied (Victoria and Western Australia, with a receipts tax) would be given two years to abandon such measures; and if they failed to do so or other states entered the field, it would be taken into account in the distribution of Commonwealth taxation revenue. In fact, Gorton was relaying a decision proposed by McMahon as treasurer and wholly supported by cabinet, but it was seen by the press and the states to be another unforgivable Gorton incursion.[105]

A further provocation was Gorton's unilateral decision to claim Commonwealth control over the territorial sea and continental shelf resources, and the assertion in cabinet that the Commonwealth was under no obligation to inform the states of the course it proposed to take. It was too much for David Fairbairn, minister for national development, who queried Gorton's centralist tendencies, and when told the prime minister would not be changing, announced he could no longer serve in a cabinet led by Gorton. And it impelled some of the premiers to join with those who would undermine Gorton.[106]

Foreign policy and defence were fields that immediately engaged Gorton's agenda. Though as strongly anti-communist as his predecessors, he was sceptical of alliance relationships in serving Australia's interests. It was a disposition reinforced by Britain's notification that it would withdraw all its forces from South-East Asia by 1971, and by the US decision to review its military commitment to Vietnam following heavy losses in the Tet offensive by North Vietnamese forces of January 1968 and the intensification of protest in America. US president Johnson subsequently announced a limit on troop commitments, cessation of bombing in most of North Vietnam, and that he would not be seeking a further term as US president.[107] The core tenet of foreign policy under Menzies—to keep both Britain and America engaged in the region—was failing. Gorton was convinced that multi-party defence agreements were no longer enough: he favoured the development of an independent defence capacity—fortress Australia rather than forward defence. This had three consequences: a renewed commitment to an Australian nuclear capacity; a vacillating search for the Vietnam exit strategy; and the public emergence of divisions in a field where the executive had formerly advanced one view. Gorton's tendency to act unilaterally provoked such divisions—indeed, conflict with his defence minister, Malcolm Fraser, would finally precipitate his downfall.

Australia had long sought engagement in nuclear research, and potential nuclear capacity. Chifley had sanctioned British missile testing at Woomera in 1946, hoping to access new weapons and promote industrial research. And Menzies endorsed British nuclear testing on the Monte Bello islands in 1951 and at Maralinga in 1954, entertaining similar hopes (it has been argued that his commitment to the British and French position during the Suez Crisis was in part intended to win support for access to their nuclear technology).[108] Gorton, meanwhile, had long been a member of the so-called 'bomb squad': it fitted his insistence that Australia should stand up for itself, and now regional change appeared to support his view.

Hewitt, at PMD, supported Gorton's nationalism. Proponents of the established foreign policy favouring forward defence were sidelined. Hasluck, minister for external affairs since 1964 and now the leading voice of foreign policy orthodoxy, was sent to Yarralumla. Influenced by the Australian Atomic Energy Commission, Gorton forced through cabinet a proposal that a nuclear power station be established at Jervis Bay on the east coast (it would never be implemented). There ensued a battle between Gorton (with PMD and the Department of National

Development) and External Affairs (which favoured the established policy position) over whether Australia should sign the Nuclear Non-Proliferation Treaty (NPT) then being negotiated. To sign would curtail Australia's nuclear options. External Affairs eventually prevailed and Gorton signed. Yet his obduracy had extracted concessions no-one expected from the US: it allowed for more transparency in the way the NPT would be operationalised. Gorton's threat to 'go it alone' gave him an edge in such circumstances, but it was also the catalyst for conflict with colleagues attempting to negotiate a five-power regional defence agreement, especially Malcolm Fraser.[109]

Australia had been heedless in its commitment to the Vietnam War. President Richard Nixon (elected in November 1968) had announced US troop withdrawals, 'Vietnamisation' of the war was now US policy, and on none of these matters was Australia consulted or forewarned. There was no strategic vison of what Australia should do in these circumstances. The historian Peter Edwards argues that it missed an opportunity to reduce its exposure at that moment while Gorton vacillated between hawkish and dovish positions and the ministry was divided between those committed to the dominant paradigm of the preceding twenty years, and those (like Gorton) seeking new ideas.[110] Fraser would later concede, 'We had no impact at all on American strategy or policy. We had no information. The students who were demonstrating on the campuses of American universities had more influence over the conduct of the war than did the Australian Government'.[111]

In Australia, too, anti-conscription and anti-war sentiment could no longer be ignored. Between October 1968 and October 1969, polls showed opinion moving to support withdrawal: by August 1969, a majority favoured bringing troops home.[112] It proved not to be a highly salient issue in the election of October 1969, though there was widespread consciousness of it,[113] and its confluence with a range of factors indicative of dissension within government, conflict in the federation and Gorton's erratic performance led to a 7 per cent swing against the Coalition. The government survived, but all the gains won by Holt in 1966 were wiped out. It was the greatest electoral swing since 1931, and the worst against the principal non-Labor party since the UAP rout of 1943.[114]

In the aftermath, there was a challenge to Gorton's leadership: McMahon and Fairbairn stood against him at the 7 November party room meeting. Gorton survived and his rival McMahon was demoted from Treasury to External Affairs, but significantly, in the lead-up to the challenge, McEwen had announced that his veto on McMahon was withdrawn, linking it with a reference to the need for all policy decisions to be discussed in cabinet: it was a direct strike against Gorton's personalised mode.[115] As the Vietnam problem dragged on—the great Vietnam Moratorium campaign commenced with a mass national demonstration on 8 May 1970—McMahon covertly sought to undermine Gorton, and the McMahon-aligned Packer press conglomerate mounted a stridently anti-Gorton campaign,[116] but the telling conflict came to be with the newly appointed defence minister, Malcolm Fraser.

A series of events persuaded Fraser that supporting Gorton, his former political friend, had been a mistake. Fraser, with his departmental secretary, Sir Arthur Tange, strove for a five-power defence arrangement between the United Kingdom, Australia, Malaysia, Singapore and New Zealand. Convinced that Gorton, now sceptical of forward defence, did not understand it and would wreck a crucial conference if it was to be held in Canberra, he arranged with his British counterpart, Peter Carrington, for it to be conducted in Singapore. Fraser was forced to resort to brinkmanship against US counterparts in renegotiating a contract for the Australian purchase of F111 fighters. He succeeded, but in the process he learned that president Nixon had told Gorton a year earlier that the United States would never change its terms: Gorton had neglected to tell him. He also took issue with Gorton over the latter's enthusiasm for providing that Australian troops could be called out to quell a domestic civil disturbance in Papua New Guinea despite Fraser's opposition and that of the Defence Committee.[117]

The final straw, for Fraser, was a dispute about civic action—troops giving aid to the civilian population—in Vietnam during Australia's projected withdrawal. The dispute initially did not concern Gorton: it was sparked by Fraser's belief that the army's leaders in Vietnam had unilaterally decided to terminate civic action without reference to himself, the department or cabinet, and contrary to government policy.

As media interest in this conflict between the minister for defence and the army grew, *Australian* journalist Alan Ramsey reported that the army chief, Sir Thomas Daly, had met with Gorton and had accused Fraser of disloyalty to the army and of trying to discredit it and its junior minister, Andrew Peacock. Daly immediately denied that he had said this, with Gorton's concurrence, but Ramsey revealed that Gorton had been given an opportunity to refute the allegation before publication and had not done so.

Fraser concluded that he had no option but to resign. Gorton had met with Daly without reference to his minister. That he had not been informed was, in Fraser's view, a contravention of due process, and Gorton and his office may have allowed misinformation to spread. In any case, he did not have Gorton's confidence.[118] On 8 March 1971, he tendered his resignation to the governor-general, with copies going to the prime minister and the leader of the Country Party. The next day, he made a statement in the House, concluding:

> The Prime Minister, because of his unreasoned drive to get his own way, his obstinacy, impetuous and emotional reactions, has imposed strains on the Liberal Party, the government and the public service. I do not believe he is fit to hold the great office of Prime Minister, and I cannot serve in his government.[119]

The following day, at a Liberal Party meeting, there was a motion of confidence in Gorton's leadership. When the vote was tied, 33–33, Gorton symbolically (since it was not allowed for in the rules) cast a chairman's vote against himself: in effect, he resigned. Billy McMahon was elected leader. In a surprise move, Gorton stood as deputy and won, then opted to take the Defence portfolio.

'Tiberius with a Telephone'

Billy McMahon was sixty-three years old when he assumed the prime ministership—older on first assuming the office than any other incumbent (bar John McEwen, who held office for only twenty-three days between Holt and Gorton). But he was fit and energetic and might have been the best prepared—certainly the most experienced—of any, since he had already held ministerial office for twenty years. Indeed, his initial rise had been rapid: elected in 1949, he was promoted to the ministry in 1951 (as minister for the navy and for air) and elevated to cabinet as minister for primary industry in 1956. Menzies did not like him but recognised his drive, intelligence and shrewdness, and McEwen, later a bitter enemy, had been similarly impressed and lobbied for him. It was an uncharacteristic mistake: the intensely ambitious McMahon soon mastered his brief, brought matters to cabinet without McEwen's knowledge, and argued against his senior minister.[120]

Nevertheless, his rise was unchecked. He moved from primary industry to the portfolio of labour and national service (1958–66), in which role he was identified with fighting unions where communists dominated and was responsible for the contentious legislation that authorised conscription for national service (1964). Then, after Holt had replaced Menzies, and having defeated Hasluck in the contest for deputy leader of the Liberal Party, he took the plum role of treasurer. It was the position, he said, he had always wanted. He was the first treasurer with a degree in economics and was regarded as remarkably effective and a doughty combatant in cabinet, albeit with the backing of a strong department.[121] In 1969 he would, after challenging Gorton, be moved against his wishes to External Affairs (where he introduced specialist policy research branches, dealt with the unpopular Vietnam War, and changed the department's name to Foreign Affairs). Yet, notwithstanding his evident ability, long participation in executive government and wealth of experience, he is generally considered a failed leader, the least effective of all Australian prime ministers.[122]

The causes of McMahon's misfortune were manifold. He took the top job at a time when the Coalition was more rancorous and divided than it had been since the collapse of the UAP in the early 1940s. The tied party-room vote had persuaded Gorton, finally, that he could not prevail. Yet it also revealed on one side a level of sympathy for Gorton's nationalist independence and on the other a rupture in the sort of liberalism that Menzies had championed. McMahon, always more free-trade inclined than the meliorist Victorians (Menzies, Holt and

Gorton) who had dominated the party, began as treasurer the reversion to the principles of Alfred Marshall—the Cambridge economist who had first championed neoclassical economics—at a time when Treasury itself was abandoning Keynes.[123] Gorton and McEwen had conspired to thwart this enterprise, and then demoted him to External Affairs. Yet intimations of the economic change that would undermine the postwar orthodoxy were already appearing: wage costs and consumer prices were rising, there were exchange rate difficulties, unions were becoming more strident, unemployment was increasing and inflation threatened.[124] It was a time that demanded a leader who could unify the party and build a team that could address the challenges of transition and convey the message of reform. McMahon proved manifestly unsuited to this task.

The reasons lie in a complex of personal circumstances, political experiences and working practices that inhibited the very capacities now demanded. First, like Gorton, a materially secure—indeed, in McMahon's case, wealthy—background had not insulated him against early tribulation; McMahon lost his mother at four and his father in his teens and was raised by relatives. Second (also akin to Gorton), it seems he emerged with a suspicion of others, but he had none of Gorton's imagination or talents for charm and directness: rather, he was chronically distrustful and devious. Patrick Weller, a political scientist rarely given to psychological speculation, described him as paranoid.[125] This fed into a third difficulty in that it ensured that relations with others were either entirely transactional—a tactical exchange of information or a favour that served his interests—or else precarious and combative. He was a demanding, ungrateful and unreasonable boss.[126]

McMahon appealed to some, like the media mogul Frank Packer, by showing off or trading inside information.[127] Repeated breaches of cabinet confidentiality, partly to demonstrate his access to inside dope, but especially in the cause of undermining rivals, led to him being derided as 'Billy the Leak'. Always on guard against those who might thwart his ambition, his deviousness inevitably provoked distrust in others. The doubt started at the top: Menzies described him as 'that untrustworthy little scamp'; the formidable Roland Wilson retired from Treasury because he could not abide McMahon. Among a long list of

Liberal colleagues who shared Liberal MP Leslie Bury's disquiet—'I have an intense antipathy … I don't like anything about him'[128]—the most acute and scarifying evaluation, written three years before McMahon became prime minister, was by Paul Hasluck:

> The longer one is associated with him, the deeper the contempt grows and I find it hard to allow him any merit. Disloyal, devious, dishonest, untrustworthy, petty, cowardly—all these adjectives have been weighed by me and I could not in truth modify or reduce any one of them in its application to McMahon. I find him a contemptible creature … [129]

Gough Whitlam, with incisive wit, would later capture McMahon in a phrase: 'Tiberius with a telephone'. (Tiberius, a famously tyrannical, reclusive and vengeful Roman emperor, had used his networks to gather intelligence with which to conduct a reign of terror against the Roman elite, an allusion not lost on readers of a then popular novel, Robert Graves' *I, Claudius*.)

Yet McMahon had won early preferment, constant inclusion in successive ministries and finally the prime ministership for one reason: he gave his life to the job. He knew his brief and studied the submissions of his colleagues—he was, some report, the best-informed man in cabinet once Menzies departed. He was one of the few who dared to take on John McEwen. It gained him grudging admiration and toleration, but it encouraged a working style inimical to what was now needed. The strength that had made him a successful minister was focus on and application to a particular brief; he was unable to adapt to the multi-tasking, team building and collective management demanded of a prime minister.

On assuming office, McMahon immediately removed Hewitt, brought PMD and the Cabinet Office back together, with the department henceforth to be called Prime Minister and Cabinet (PM&C), and reinstated Bunting in the top job. Normality, he implied, had been restored, and he would focus on consultation with individual ministers, coordination and ensuring the 'cabinet machinery' functioned effectively to guarantee accountability, and attention to and speedy resolution of the 'ever changing problems of Government'.[130] Admirable objectives, but his predilections ensured they would not be achieved.

John McEwen, who had in 1969 withdrawn his notorious veto on McMahon as a strike against Gorton, retired just a month before McMahon became prime minister. The loss of McEwen's experience, political wiles and capacity to demand cabinet discipline was destabilising. There was no counter to McMahon's caprice. It was never a harmonious ministry—ministers were moved precipitately; cabinet leaked against him, and Gorton was an open critic until McMahon demanded his resignation in August 1971 for having published newspaper articles critical of cabinet.[131] Gorton then became the de facto leader of other disgruntled ex-ministers on the backbench.[132]

McMahon argued towards the end:

> I have learnt … that I now must make more decisions than I had the intention of making when I first became the prime minister. I wanted to be head of a team. I wanted to delegate the authority to the relevant Ministers … I couldn't get the work done quickly enough and I found frequently that the political approaches to it were not as good as I thought they should be … I gradually started to change, and I have been changing a little more quickly as the days have gone by.[133]

A one-man band was back. No longer dealing with a defined task in a discrete portfolio but rather many demands, McMahon veered to and fro, indecisive and inconsistent: the complaint was that he failed to give leadership in any direction.[134] Legislative business was mismanaged, leading in May 1971 to a mammoth sitting of the House where multiple Bills were forced through. Liberal MP Jim Killen protested that the executive was overriding parliament. When McMahon proposed an additional minister and introduced legislation to appoint assistant ministers to deal with the complexities of government, he faced furious criticism. Liberal senator Magnus Cormack argued that it was executive overreach at the expense of parliament.[135]

Notwithstanding division and disorder, and McMahon's own cynical dismissal of Gorton as having failed because 'he tried to do things',[136]

McMahon's government cautiously attempted, like those of his predecessors, to address Menzies' unfinished business. There was attention to budget rigour: the 1970–71 budget was a balanced one, and a deflationary budget followed for 1971–72, but by mid-1972, as its stocks fell, the government reverted to handouts and tax cuts. The Australian Institute of Marine Science and the Australian Wool Corporation were created. The issue of offshore minerals was kept off the agenda and McMahon made efforts to placate the premiers. The Gorton government, while vowing not to 'cut and run', had incrementally reduced the Australian military presence in Vietnam after 1969 by not replacing troops whose tour was completed, but McMahon is credited with the decision to withdraw all Australian troops, announced in August 1971. McMahon attempted to diminish Labor's appeal on social issues and deficient planning by establishing the National Urban and Regional Development Authority and the Department of Environment, Aborigines and the Arts (to which Hewitt was appointed). There was Commonwealth funding for childcare centres, the pensioner means test was abolished and the Henderson commission of inquiry into poverty was instigated. McMahon eased his party towards sufficient accommodation with China to facilitate trade, though he was badly wrong-footed by criticising Whitlam's temerity in actually visiting China to meet its communist leaders just as Richard Nixon announced his own impending visit. In the circumstances, McMahon's tenacity was remarkable.[137]

Yet even what was achieved was not adequately communicated. McMahon was comprehensively outperformed in parliament, as both Holt and Gorton had been, by the opposition leader, Gough Whitlam. His assumption that the demonstration of knowledge entailed the endless iteration of statistics made him a boring speaker. Holt and Gorton had shown the importance of adapting communication to the now dominant medium: television. McMahon did not perform well on television or on the hustings. He was not helped by a thin voice that seemed querulous rather than authoritative. Approval of McMahon fell from 55 per cent to 25 per cent in the first twelve months and never recovered. By February 1972, support for Labor was at 49 per cent, the Coalition 40 per cent and the DLP 7 per cent: Labor had exceeded the rest of its political adversaries combined.[138] Arguably, the government rallied thereafter, helped by its reactive attention to social issues and the promised handouts of its final budget: the swing against the government in the election on 2 December 1972 was only 2.5 per cent, significantly less than that against Gorton in 1969.[139] But it was enough to unseat the government. The Menzies era was at an end.

Afternoon Light

Robert Menzies titled the first volume of his memoirs *Afternoon Light*, signifying his reflections as old age approached and the light faded. Afternoon light casts long shadows, and in one respect Menzies' lengthy dominance overshadowed the later years of his administration. Many of the strong personalities had gone. His ways had become settled, and resistance to social change, some of it induced by his own policies, set in. In another respect, he cast a long shadow over his successors. His capacities—rhetorical fluency, command of parliament, facility in broadcast media, selective ruthlessness in dealing with opponents, cabinet control, party management, professional bureaucratic relations and stable government—set a benchmark for how a prime minister should look, sound and act. Each of them recognised the challenge and tried to define the leadership task differently, in ways that suited their own preferences.

Holt, the favoured son, tried to carry on the Menzies project but aspired to be the equable chair rather than the big man. He was too nice to be tough when needed, so debate in the cabinet and party room became unruly and unfocused; too slow to act decisively when mistakes were recognised; and too beholden to friends in crises to protect the perception of integrity so central to his appeal. His authority leached away.

Gorton would make no such mistake. He would simply break the mould and practise a different sort of strong leadership: when the arguments were over, what the prime minister decided *must* be done. Arguably he was the most talented, innovative and imaginative of the three who followed Menzies. He would take over the unfinished business of the Menzies years and push it in new directions, stressing Australia's independence and cultural identity and talking up its place in the world. But he was also impulsive, idiosyncratic, too careless of the egos he had to manage, incapable of picking his battles and recognising when to withdraw, and inattentive to the tide of internal opposition that would overwhelm him.

McMahon was the manipulative schemer who did whatever it took to get to the top, and once there, did not know what to do with the prize. He too professed himself the chair, but one who would set directions and delegate. Yet he lacked direction. Furthermore, delegation demands trust and confidence, and this in a party that was now deeply divided. The gamble was that for all his faults, he had been a good minister and maybe could succeed as prime minister. But there were critics on every side. Everything he did undermined the confidence of his colleagues in their leader, and his chronic distrust of others left him unable to let them get on with their jobs. In consequence, he 'found' that he had to do more and more himself. It was a failing strategy.

Thus it was that the 'state of concealed crisis in Australian politics' Horne had forecast in 1964 played out. None of the successors fully addressed the challenge presented by the unfinished business of the Menzies years. And none lived up to the leadership expectations he had set. Only one man seemed to have the knowledge, wit, capacity for public theatre, considered ruthlessness, philosophical consistency and command of parliament that might match Menzies. It was Gough Whitlam, leader of the opposition.

This is not to suggest that what Holt, Gorton and McMahon achieved was inconsequential. Each of them saw the new demands generated by social change and the deficiencies that remained to be addressed, and they responded. Active regional relations and Asian diplomacy were accelerated, especially by Holt. They took important steps to change migration policy, with legislation that was foundational to what the Whitlam and Fraser governments would do, ending the White Australia policy and paving the way for multiculturalism. There was fresh attention to Indigenous policy, with new agencies to support it and an insistence (by Gorton), following the landmark 1967 referendum, that national government take the lead. Holt and Gorton introduced the infrastructure to support the burgeoning cultural aspirations of a country breaking out of the cosy environs of empire. The new sense of independence was encouraged not only by the political response to Britain's withdrawal from South-East Asia, with active steps to loosen British ties, but also by the pugnacious nationalism of Gorton: this created a context propitious for what Whitlam would later accomplish. McMahon saw the traction Labor was gaining with its focus on the unforeseen consequences of leaving cities, housing and development prey to ad-hoc consumer choice and developer preferences. His launch of an authority in this sphere would be the platform for Whitlam's more ambitious initiatives for urban and regional regeneration. Though Holt was the leader most identified with the Vietnam War, it was Gorton who began the wind-down and the McMahon government that took the decision to bring the troops home. There was belated recognition that the good times might be ending and of the need for new models and budget rigour under McMahon, even if at the end political desperation induced a reversion to budget handouts.

Donald Horne, a Menzies critic, acknowledged that the change wrought between 1966 and 1972, even if fashioned by imperfect leaders clutching at straws, was the catalyst for a 'time of hope'.[140] The governments of Gough Whitlam (ALP, 1972–75) and Malcolm Fraser (LCP, 1975–83) would build on these initiatives and gain much of the credit for those that succeeded, but they would have been much harder to achieve had not Holt, Gorton and McMahon broken the ground.

Finally, as Menzies' successors wrestled with how to manage their job, facing what they conceived as new challenges, and lacking the supreme self-confidence of their predecessor, they demanded more personal support. Interwar prime ministers had all struggled to acquire the resources and to identify the levers with which to exercise national leadership. A kind of settlement had been achieved by the late 1940s, with the Commonwealth acquisition of financial power and the emergence of an effective federal public service. These gains had been consolidated by Menzies. It was no longer enough.

Holt, Gorton and McMahon began tentatively to augment the infrastructure surrounding the prime minister. Initially, modifications were small. Holt, dissatisfied with the minimal PMO that had sufficed for Menzies, appointed additional staff (a speechwriter) and sought to bring a trusted lieutenant with him from Treasury; Bunting intervened and Peter Bailey was brought in from PMD instead. This small innovation was represented as an attempt to institute 'a presidential style of leadership'. Gorton was more radical: he dispensed with Bailey and appointed Ainsley Gotto, a political staffer, within the PMO, a profound break from Menzies' practice. More notable still, he dispensed with Bunting, split the PM's department and appointed Hewitt, his own man, as secretary. While Menzies had enjoyed close relations with Bunting, there was also an explicit observance of appropriate roles, which none of 'the boys' would breach.

Hewitt and Gorton seemed oblivious of such role boundaries: Hewitt was there to provide whatever the prime minister needed and in the heat of policy conflict did not hesitate to offer his own views. Hewitt also expanded the capacity of PMD, appointing policy specialists: it was the harbinger of a more assertive role for the department. McMahon may have appeared to restore normality with the reamalgamation of PM&C and the return of Bunting, but the message was not forgotten. McMahon then tried to address what he felt to be an untenable workload for the executive by experimenting with assistant ministers and adding to the ministry proper. He was savaged by his colleagues for attempting this unseemly arrogation of power by the executive. As Magnus Cormack angrily asserted,

> Now I can see with great sorrow and an enormous amount of apprehension that we are moving into an area where there is a new component of power, namely, the convenient marriage of Ministers and the bureaucracy, by which Parliament will be overruled.[141]

What he was observing was as nothing in comparison with what was soon to come.

3

HARNESSED BY HISTORY: GOUGH WHITLAM AND MALCOLM FRASER

It is, perhaps, the most familiar televised event in Australian political history. Replayed countless times in subsequent decades, with tens of thousand of viewings on YouTube, it has been the focal point of numerous books and articles, and an elegiac television miniseries. What happened is on record: its meaning is contested to this day. In the scene it records, a small dark man reads a proclamation, hedged in by banks of people—evidently part of a much larger, roiling crowd. Police are visible in the background. His announcement is barely discernible, given the noise. Behind him stands a tall, imposing, silver-haired man with a bitter smile. The crowd is chanting 'We want Gough!' The smaller man—it is David Smith, secretary to the governor-general—concludes his announcement, saying 'God save the Queen'. The taller man—it is Gough Whitlam—now serious, takes the microphone. 'Ladies and gentlemen [laughter and applause] … Well may we say "God save the Queen"', he begins, 'because nothing will save the governor-general'. His brief, extemporaneous speech—with its measured cadence but invective targeting the governor general, Sir John Kerr, and Malcolm Fraser, 'who will undoubtedly go down in history … as Kerr's cur'—is now famous, his opening words the subtitle of a book that aims to present 'the speeches that made Australia'.[1]

It was the scene on the steps of Parliament House at 4.45 p.m. on the afternoon of 11 November 1975. Smith, referring to section 57 of the constitution (on the circumstances under which the governor-general may terminate parliament), had announced Kerr's decision to dissolve parliament on that day. An election would be held on 13 December. Kerr's proclamation was countersigned Malcolm Fraser, prime minister. Whitlam, who had governed as Labor prime minister since December 1972, had been dismissed by Kerr shortly after 1 p.m. Fraser, leader of the Liberal Party, was commissioned (without Whitlam's knowledge) immediately thereafter. His brief was to secure the passage of supply Bills, which had been blocked in the Senate by the Coalition parties. That done, on Fraser's 'advice', parliament was dissolved. Fraser had been prime minister for less than four hours, but he would fight the election as the incumbent. The political deadlock of October–November 1975, created by the Coalition's refusal to vote on annual appropriation Bills in the Senate, was thus resolved. Whitlam's impassioned speech was the denouement of what had been represented as a constitutional crisis. Indicative of an intense political and psychological battle between Fraser, Kerr and himself, it is remembered as one of the great, dramatic instances of antagonistic leadership in Australian politics. The play of emotions and enmity it generated would shadow the 1975 election, which Fraser went on to win in a landslide. Fraser then held office until 1983.

Now consider this: in 1991, Whitlam and Fraser astounded their erstwhile supporters by standing together, upraised hands clasped, on the back of a truck in Fitzroy Gardens, Melbourne, campaigning against the sale of Fairfax media to foreign interests. In 1999, they appeared together in a television advertisement, advocating a vote for an Australian republic during the referendum campaign in that year.[2] There were other issues on which they made common cause and campaigned together in their later years. Indeed, each testified to a special friendship, and Fraser would remark on Whitlam's death in October 2014:

> He always had an independent mind. He had his way of looking at things and he was a very important person in Australia's life ... He didn't carry animosity forward. He didn't carry personal bitterness. He was a much bigger man than that ... He took issues as they were: on issues of race, on issues of discrimination ... on the idea of Australia's place in the wider world, we had a pretty common view ... [H]e changed the way Australia started to look at itself.[3]

The great rivals, whose mutual antipathy had once equalled that between Menzies and Evatt, were reconciled. The received view was that Fraser had changed; he had moved to the left. He rejected that interpretation: 'I see the [Liberal] party as having moved leagues to the right and I see the Labor Party having moved leagues to the right of Gough Whitlam's period ... We both bemoaned a bit of this when we met. The whole political spectrum is entirely different'.[4] There is substance to this. It can be demonstrated that they shared views such as those Fraser identified above by comparing continuities in their policies on such issues.[5] Each had a broad commitment to national independence and to the postwar nation-building agenda. Certainly, philosophy and personality ensured that their approaches to achieving those objectives were different—their methods and modes of working were poles apart. Still, they faced a common problem: a complex of economic challenges that undercut Whitlam's reform ambitions, and that even Fraser—more attuned than his predecessor to the shifting ground—proved unable to address. They would be coupled in historical memory by the drama of the Dismissal and paradoxically united by their common nation-building objectives. Yet each was defeated by a global economic transition that undermined what they took for granted. Nevertheless, in Whitlam's effort to achieve substantial reform, and in Fraser's attempt to manage the volatility that threatened the economic orthodoxy of their day, they jointly transformed the prime ministerial office itself.

Whitlam: Rallying the Opposition

Before being in a position to transform the prime ministership, Gough Whitlam had first to transform his party and its platform. Elected in

1952, he had served throughout the disastrous Labor split and watched Menzies destroy Evatt and disable Calwell. The lessons of party unification, a leader with a philosophy, a dominating parliamentary performance and ruthless despatch of rivals were not lost on him. His passage to party leadership and effective opposition was as remarkable in its way as Curtin's rescue of the demoralised and divided Labor Party after 1935 and Menzies' creation of the Liberal Party after the collapse of the UAP in 1943. In each case, they seized a failing cause, developed a new agenda for action and dragged their party back into contention and finally into government. It was this combination of party rejuvenation and a vision for government that set them apart. Quite apart from their performance in office, they were the three great opposition leaders of the twentieth century.

Whitlam, born in Melbourne in 1916, was nurtured in a family with liberal humanist values, a concentration on education and literacy, devout Christianity and a strong service ethic.[6] He grew up among the children of public servants and politicians, and from the age of twelve, in Canberra. His father worked in the Attorney-General's Department and was appointed Commonwealth Crown solicitor in 1936. Whitlam later remarked, 'Some are born centralists, some achieve centralism, some have centralism thrust upon them … the years I spent growing up in this city did something to strengthen my convictions about the role of the national Government in the nation's affairs'.[7]

Whitlam studied arts and law at the University of Sydney. Following the outbreak of World War II, and before completing his law degree, he enlisted in the RAAF and was called to active service in 1942. In 1945 he joined the Labor Party: the catalyst was the defeat of the Curtin government's '14 powers' referendum in 1944. Following his discharge from the RAAF, Whitlam completed his law degree and joined the NSW Bar. After winning Labor preselection as a candidate for the Sydney City Council, then running unsuccessfully for Sutherland Shire Council and later the state seat of Sutherland, Whitlam won preselection for the federal seat of Werriwa in 1952. When the sitting member died, Whitlam mounted an energetic campaign and won the seat at the ensuing by-election with a 12 per cent swing to Labor, trebling his predecessor's majority.

While an anti-government swing occasioned by the 1951 'horror budget' played a large part in his success, Whitlam's assiduous canvassing helped. Campaigning proved to be one of his strengths.

Even before his election, Whitlam had impressed party elders: 'Chifley had a high regard for Whitlam. He said we had to get men of that calibre into parliament, and he strongly supported him in the machine out there at that time'.[8] After taking his seat in early 1953, his talents did not equally impress his parliamentary peers. Educated, articulate and too clever, 'Whitlam would tell you himself that he had more brains than anybody and you might as well know it ... People knew that, but they didn't want to be told'.[9] Whitlam conceded that initially he won few friends: 'That vintage was notably cold for the whole time we were in caucus together, with a few exceptions ... most of the others didn't like anyone coming into the closed circle'.[10] Those 'few exceptions' were crucial. They were the men who saw Whitlam's promise and contributed the political nous, insider knowledge of the machine and capacities that Whitlam lacked. They appreciated the fluency, detail, wit and boldness—evident even in his maiden speech[11]—that promised superior parliamentary performance. His command of information and quick thinking allowed him to deploy his knowledge to maximum effect. He seemed ready to address the grievous state of the party. He appeared capable of reviving the social democratic mission of Curtin and Chifley, but now applied to contemporary problems.

It took time, however, for those relationships to jell. Initially, Whitlam worked alone. He used parliamentary resources to explore current problems and their solutions. He became adept at relating what he found to the contemporary adaptation of party philosophy. His abiding belief was that the community should provide for individuals those necessities that an individual could not obtain alone. This was the proper project of government. As he put it,

> The approach is based on this concept: increasingly the citizen's real standard of living ... [and] his scope to participate in the decisions and actions of the community, are determined ... by the availability and accessibility of services which the community alone

> can provide and ensure. The quality of life depends less and less on the things which individuals obtain for themselves … from their personal incomes and depends more and more on the things which the community provides for all its members from the combined resources of the community.[12]

The broad parameters of those things 'the community' should provide gave Whitlam wide scope for what became a personal research project. It was driven by the problems he saw around him. They were the shortcomings and difficulties of suburban life—housing, transport, schools, health services, civic amenities, welfare provision—manifest in his own struggling electorate, elaborated to national scale and related to what government 'should' do. He sought information from all quarters, generating comprehensive files and notes. He used questions on notice to access Commonwealth resources, gaining data from the departments serving the government he intended to displace. The parliament, Whitlam said, 'is the best forum for the documentation and dissemination of information. For an Opposition developing and promoting new policies, it is indispensable'. The inspiration for what became the Whitlam program was 'mundane', distilling 'a decade of documentation'.[13]

The success of Whitlam's research project was manifest. To his already apparent rhetorical gifts was added an extensive array of policy-relevant knowledge. It gave him the capacity not only to demolish the government's arguments in the House but also to outshine his colleagues, including the fading Evatt and then Evatt's successor, Calwell. He began to gain internal allies. Some, like Chifley, had seen his calibre from the first: 'Norman Makin, George Lawson—those Chifley and Curtin Ministers couldn't have been more helpful or gracious'.[14] Others soon appreciated his potential for developing a new party agenda and addressing the institutional roadblocks to its success. Lance Barnard, later to be deputy prime minister, was an early convert. He persuaded Whitlam to stand as deputy leader in 1960 against long-serving and hardened party men and, with Pat Kennelly, engineered his success.[15] It was indicative of what became a pattern: party insiders with particular skills or capacities would pair up with Whitlam to achieve specific objectives: together they would overcome the disabling effects of the 1950s split and make the party a credible alternative government.

Whitlam, with backing from such allies, began to climb the party ladder. In 1959, he was elected to the Caucus executive. 'People thought that he'd be performing the kind of job the work he'd been doing suited him for', said Labor MP Jim Cairns. 'He'd be thought of, maybe, in government, as a modern, up-to-date, law changing Attorney General.'[16] In 1960, when Calwell finally took over from Evatt—who had been appointed NSW chief justice by an accommodating state Labor government—Whitlam contested the deputy leadership against more senior rivals Eddie Ward, Les Haylen and EJ Harrison: 'I just approached it as one of those occasions in which one had to participate in the normal progression. If one won, that was satisfactory; if one lost there was no disgrace in being beaten by men who'd all been there longer'.[17] Despite Calwell's antipathy (he expected Ward to win) and what some in Caucus thought was a precocious bid, Whitlam succeeded, thanks to the support rallied by 'numbers men' Barnard and Kennelly.[18] Aged forty-three, Whitlam was the youngest Labor deputy leader in forty years.

Whitlam wanted to reorganise party structures. Menzies' skilful exploitation of the '36 faceless men' jibe in 1963 made him determined that the domination of extra-parliamentary officials, at the expense of Caucus and the elected party leaders, must alter. The 1963 election defeat reinforced Whitlam's conviction that reform must address the party's image of being a state- and union-dominated body. According to John Menadue, who was to be head of PM&C under both Whitlam and Fraser,

> From about '64 on Gough set out on a campaign to destabilise the controls of the Labor Party. Looking back … this was Gough's 'crash through or crash' approach, which was exhilarating, worrying, sort of hang-on-to-your-hat, here we go, confronting people in the party.[19]

It meant taking on the factions, encroaching on the party executive's ways of doing things, introducing open and transparent decision-making. Whitlam saw a parallel between his situation and that facing Menzies after the crushing defeat of the UAP in 1943: the task was to rebuild the party.[20] Getting there, however, was not plain sailing. Whitlam mixed persuasion with confrontation. His capacity in attracting loyal allies, especially Barnard, party secretary Cyril Wyndham, and Wyndham's successor, Mick Young, was crucial. But he also took on the old guard and the party shibboleths with impatience and a combative manner that intensified resistance.[21]

Whitlam decided Calwell was not up to these challenges. Whitlam had fallen out with him as early as 1955, during the impassioned internal debates over the party split, and in 1964 he began openly to question Calwell's leadership. In 1965, in a battle over banning unity tickets (where disparate groups combine forces to run their candidates on a joint ticket for elections—a tactic that had seen Labor collaborate with communists in Victorian union elections), Whitlam forced a backdown by putting his personal position on the line, threatening to resign and precipitate a spill that would undermine Calwell. In 1966, in a contentious debate over the party's opposition to the policy that Menzies had used so effectively against it, state aid to private schools, Whitlam publicly castigated the federal executive, calling its members 'the twelve witless men', and only narrowly avoided expulsion. The following year, party policy was changed.

With Holt's stunning election victory in November 1966, it was all over for Calwell. When Caucus met on 8 February 1967, Whitlam was elected Labor Party leader. Whitlam, with Wyndham, embarked on reform that would incorporate the four federal leaders in both the federal conference and the federal executive—a decisive shift in the balance of power away from paid officials and towards the parliamentary leadership.[22] He allocated defined responsibilities for shadow cabinet portfolios in Caucus. Their previous absence had generated multiple views and self-appointed spokesmen, rather than concentrating energy and encouraging expertise.[23] Finally, in the cause of achieving national coordination and policy consistency, he initiated intervention into recalcitrant state branches.

In the heat of another confrontation in 1968, over a Victorian left–inspired attempt to refuse a right-wing Tasmanian delegate a seat on the federal executive, Whitlam resigned the leadership to trigger a vote, challenging the party to endorse his position or replace him. He prevailed, but only narrowly. His challenger, Jim Cairns, had memorably asked, 'Whose Party is it—ours or his?'[24] Whitlam was chastened: he had been slow to learn the compromise that was needed to change the constitution of the party executive (allowing elected parliamentary leaders to be installed). He would now rely on what others could do to assist in clearing the hurdles to reform. In 1970, for instance, it was Clyde Cameron, Wyndham and later Young who defeated the Victorian radicals. Cameron was a left-wing 'fixer' initially (and thereafter intermittently) hostile to Whitlam. He nonetheless worked with him to contrive the successful intervention into the obstructionist Victorian branch of the party. It was an essential element of party reform.[25] Whitlam could not simply 'crash through'. Successful reform demanded allies with knowledge, experience of political tactics and command of party processes.

Whitlam's second imperative was 'the program'. Another set of extra-parliamentary allies—advisers and outside experts inspired by the agenda Whitlam was promoting—was attracted once he became party leader. It seemed a way of attaching their ambitions to a larger cause. Peter Wilenski, a public servant and sometime academic, spoke for many in explaining the appeal: 'I thought he was the sort of fellow who would lead a great reform government, and I was quite happy to be associated with [that]'.[26] John Menadue and Race Mathews, working in Whitlam's office, developed links with community activists, academics and professionals, creating policy networks that fleshed out the grand plan. Others, like Pat Troy, architect of the blueprint for urban renewal, volunteered their services. Wilenski was recruited to rethink ministerial offices, the PMO and relations with the APS.[27] The support networks developed to mobilise ideas were carried into government and institutionalised within ministerial offices.

Whitlam identified problems, gained all he could from Commonwealth sources, but then sought alternatives from these experts who supplied the detail for his grand plans.

> I ... try and work out means of achieving what I think are my Party's objectives—how to marshal the examples in other countries, how to

> marshal the advisers in this country—and then try to work how to explain it to people. I think that's probably what I've done best ...[28]

Whitlam initiated a policy explosion. He could claim later that 'the party platform is studded with things I was the first to suggest',[29] but his office created the policy networks on which program elaboration relied. In these networks, relationships were developed with professional and semi-professional associations, opening up new constituencies for Labor. Thus was developed a program based on the pressing domestic issues with which the Coalition had struggled—development, housing, education, health, for example—and on a newly independent stance in the world.

Increasingly, Whitlam was seen as the man with the answers, especially in parliamentary debate. The government was seen as reactive, when, for instance, it responded belatedly to Whitlam's growing momentum in addressing problems of the cities by establishing the National Urban and Regional Development Authority. And prime minister Billy McMahon would appear ludicrous when he attacked Whitlam for visiting China in July 1971 to meet with premier Zhou Enlai, only to learn within days of US president Richard Nixon's overtures to the Chinese leader via Henry Kissinger. Whitlam had argued for recognition of China since 1954: his visit was the antecedent for a new relationship and a significant change in Australian relations with Asia.[30]

A corollary of this mode of program development, with lasting effects on the capacities of subsequent prime ministers, was that the informal infrastructure developed to support Whitlam in opposition was intended for translation into government. Planning began for a wholesale reorganisation of ministerial staff and the PMO.[31] One objective was to retain the broad advisory networks developed in opposition by the Whitlam team. Another was to supplement the options provided by the APS, and to shake up the APS itself. Whitlam held the public service in high regard: he had known some of its leaders through his father, and was conscious that the careers of many of those in senior positions originated in the initiatives of Curtin and Chifley. Many in the party, and on his own staff, however, suspected that those who had become

Menzies' 'boys' were now habituated to the Coalition's world view, and would not readily adapt to Whitlam's ambitious reform agenda.

Peter Wilenski, then a public servant on temporary leave at the Australian National University (ANU) in Canberra, was approached by one of Whitlam's advisers, Dick Hall, for ideas. Hall then instigated a meeting six months before the 1972 election, in which Whitlam asked Wilenski for papers on three things: a reorganisation of the public service, a draft administrative arrangements order for the new Labor ministry, and the organisation of the prime minister's personal staff. Wilenski undertook to prepare these on the condition that they would be delivered only if Whitlam won government. When he did, Wilenski became his initial principal private secretary, and started the rollout of these plans.[32] The intention was that the APS would remain a key source for policy advice, but that advice would now be contestable. It would not work out entirely as planned, but in the longer term it would be the catalyst for a fundamental amplification of executive power.

Anticipating Government

By 1969 it appeared that the wind was in Whitlam's sails. The Federal Party Conference adopted much for which he had argued. Whitlam's command of the policy agenda—'the program' that had become the party's platform—was comprehensive and potentially transformative. Whitlam's performance at that conference, which was open to the media for the first time, allowed the public to see the qualities that had ensured his domination of parliament. Parliamentary insiders—unsettled Coalition MPs, former Labor sceptics, the press gallery—had already begun to think that Labor might unseat Gorton's increasingly fractious administration, despite the substantial Coalition majority bequeathed by Holt's victory in 1966. The influence of such opinions was later captured in David Williamson's *Don's Party* (1971), a play satirising the hopes and disappointments of Whitlam's suburban supporters on the night of the 1969 election as it became clear that the dream was not then to be realised. Nonetheless, the election was a worrying portent for the Coalition: Holt's gains were nullified, Labor won eighteen additional seats (with a 7.1 per cent swing), and Gorton's leadership was rendered even more precarious.

Still, there were paradoxes that might have signalled difficulties ahead. Perhaps Whitlam was conscious of some of these. He had, for instance, himself identified the problem of personalised leadership, castigating the imperious, confrontational Billy Hughes as having 'undermined the Labor Party's trust in the very concept of leadership'.[33] Yet his own approach—commandeering the platform, preferring to 'crash through' rather than to negotiate agreement—was another such exercise. In 1971, he commented on the hurdles at which Australia's most talented leaders had fallen and the frustration and tragic trajectory that seemed to bedevil their efforts:

> ... our chief men and our chief efforts have been singularly associated with failure and frustration ... There is a deep poignancy in the fate of a remarkably long list of our chief figures ... Deakin outliving his superb faculties in a long twilight of senility; Fisher forgotten; Bruce living in self-chosen exile; Scullin heartbroken; Lyons dying in the midst of relentless intrigue against him; Curtin driven to desperation and to the point of resignation by some of his own colleagues at the worst period in the war.[34]

In hindsight, it might be read as a prescient foreshadowing of what he was facing, a spur to the urgency of all that he attempted and a suspicion of the fate awaiting someone with his ambition to change the world.

A further dilemma was that Whitlam's plans, and his promise to demolish any impediment to their realisation, appealed strongly to some but made others apprehensive. He could certainly inspire. His persona was what first drew the party's elder statesmen, then the staffers and advisers who developed the networks and generated the detail to deliver his program, then the professionals attracted to specific elements of what was offered, and finally the enthusiasts who flocked to his campaign rallies in 1969 and especially in 1972. But such leaders struggle to unify an electorate. For all the enthusiasm they generate, they also deter those so wedded to things as they are that they are unwilling to listen to detailed argument or are made anxious by the changes proposed. There is a dualism then—some will share a sense of common problems and respond to a leader seeming to address them; others will be cautious, or downright suspicious, of anyone claiming to have the answer to what has challenged the rest of us. Such leaders also provoke unusual hostility among those affronted by the very principles on which they act. They are divisive figures. Yet there is always the danger that those susceptible to the inspiring message, and surrounded by like-minded others, will interpret their own enthusiasm as indicative of a broader public mood. It would be a recurrent problem for Whitlam and his circle.

Despite the significant Labor gains in 1969, and increasingly adverse polling on McMahon's leadership, the public did not warm to Whitlam. In the October 1970 Senate election, Labor's vote fell to 42.2 per cent from the 47 per cent achieved at the House of Representatives election in 1969. Not a single Gallup Poll in 1971 pointed to a Labor victory. Indeed, in August the Gallup Poll and the first of the Australian Nationwide Opinion Polls pointed to the Coalition being returned with an increased majority.[35] Focus group research commissioned by the Labor Party that year showed it to be ahead of the Coalition as the party with the best approach to most policy areas and to outscore the Coalition on party image, but feedback on Whitlam was 'at best neutral and at worst extremely negative'. He was evasive, lacked warmth, and argued at such length that people began to doubt him and judged him 'not a Labor man'.[36] Surprisingly, while there was consensus that McMahon was pompous, boring and not a good prime minister, the sort of man who 'would kiss you on the cheek and stab you in the back', he was also seen as 'forceful, shrewd and direct'. His advantages over Whitlam were reinforced by a sense that Labor lacked 'credibility … as an alternative because of overwhelming negatives'; there was a 'widespread acceptance of the government as "probably knowing more about things" and therefore [sic] general willingness not to question their actions'.[37] Early in 1972, an analysis of the support in public opinion polls for the parties and party leaders suggested that it 'was going to be very hard for Whitlam to win the next election; but quite easy for McMahon to lose it'.[38]

It was decided to address the 'very hard' element in this equation by mounting what has since been regarded as a decisive breakthrough in political marketing: the 'It's Time' campaign.[39] Directed by Mick Young, who had in 1968, as Labor's South Australian secretary, devised the country's 'first recognisably modern, marketing driven campaign', this campaign, political academic Stephen Mills argues, introduced three innovations.[40] First, it directly confronted the Labor tendency to value the purity of principles as more important than electoral expediency. Whitlam had denounced this in 1967 'as a philosophy of failure', and the 1972 campaign focused on electoral success as the primary purpose of campaigning. Second, it capitalised on the revolution in market research and in television advertising. This was a substantial leap from the efforts Menzies, Holt and Gorton had made to adapt to the demands of the dominant medium. Rather than rely on what had by the 1970s become television conventions of political representation—studio discussions, interviews and prerecorded talking heads—'It's Time' was framed as a marketing exercise. It was designed to address precisely those factors that party-commissioned focus group research had indicated as negatives in public attitudes to Whitlam. Images of Whitlam's childhood, school days, career and wedding were intended to humanise him, to tackle the impression of a cold, distant, political automaton. It explicitly promoted 'the leader'. Furthermore, it spoke to the heart, not the head: it was a message of hope and trust, not policy costings or policy detail. In the famous television advertisements, with then-popular celebrities singing the 'It's Time' anthem,

> not a single policy is hinted at … not a single solid clue is given about the future of Australia … It's Time for what? No specific answer is given: indeed the slogan's ambiguity was intentional according to Paul Jones who invented it: 'You say "It's Time" and they'll fill in what it's time for … whatever is important to the individual. There's nothing to disagree with. It's the perfect statement'.[41]

Third, with Mick Young not only party secretary but also national campaign director, it was the first time either party had campaigned on a genuinely national scale, with coordination and discipline imposed from the centre, and state branches singing to its hymn sheet.

The Labor Party won the federal election on 2 December 1972. A survey on the day of the poll found that 53 per cent of respondents said they had voted ALP, and of those, the highest proportion, 38 per cent, gave as their unprompted reason 'It's time for a change'. Sixty-one per cent of those who had previously voted for other parties made this response, and 40 per cent of first-time voters followed suit.[42] It was not a sweeping victory: with a swing of 2.5 per cent, Labor won a nine-seat majority in a House of 125 (the outgoing Coalition's majority had been seven seats). For all the criticism of McMahon and his administration, it did not represent a decisive rebuff of the Coalition. But Labor's campaign had been effective in countering popular reservations about the party and its leader evident in polls and focus group research prior to the election. Mick Young argued that the 'It's Time' campaign was just the final push needed. The hard graft of party reorganisation and policy dissemination had been done well before the 1972 campaign, and the credit was Whitlam's.[43]

A Transformational Agenda

Whitlam and his followers, euphoric in victory after twenty-three years in the wilderness, believed that Labor 'had been given a specific mandate to implement each part of the program set out in the 1972 policy speech'.[44] Whitlam's own sense of the mandate never wavered: 'we raised expectations about what the national Parliament could achieve in Australia and convinced a sufficient majority that those expectations could be met'.[45] Others close to the campaign were more dubious: the soon to be minister for labour, Clyde Cameron, for instance, believed Whitlam had won the election largely because McMahon had lost it.[46] Political scientist Murray Goot concluded that on the evidence of the party's own research, 'Whitlam's program was not widely understood. If that's the case, one can hardly say that the slogan encapsulated the program or that the electorate endorsed it'.[47]

It is clear, however, that Whitlam had been central to four endeavours. He had generated a comprehensive plan for policy action. He had developed around himself an advisory system that facilitated policy development. He had made the party more professional and pragmatic, more amenable to national direction and more attuned to the parliamentary executive. And he had waged a campaign in which, arguably for the first time, the leader stood in for the party itself. Each of these would have ramifications for his performance in office. Together they reinforced the implication of ownership in his persistent reference thereafter to 'My Government'.[48]

Nothing more clearly indicated the conviction of a personal mandate, the urgency of action, and Whitlam's characteristic leader-centric mode than what he did first. Famously, he established an interim ministry of two, himself and Lance Barnard, with the cooperation of the governor-general, Paul Hasluck, who chaired the Executive Council (the body that gives formal legality to cabinet decisions, technically including all ministers but typically comprising a minimum of two): 'Lance Barnard held fourteen portfolios. I contented myself with a more modest thirteen'.[49] The duumvirate would operate for fourteen days (5–19 December 1972), until counting in close contests concluded and the Labor Caucus could meet to elect the full ministry. That occurred on 18 December, with the full ministry sworn in the following day. The duumvirate held no cabinet meetings, but decisions seen as imperative were taken—essentially through deliberation and announcement or as actions of the Executive Council—with a record subsequently kept by PM&C.

Whitlam has meticulously documented both the preparation for the interim ministry and its decisions.[50] There were some forty, including: the release of conscientious objectors who had refused national service in Vietnam; commencement of discussions to recognise the People's Republic of China; announcement of an inquiry into Aboriginal land rights; convening an interim committee of the Australian Schools Commission; reopening an equal pay case in which the McMahon government had intervened; abolition of the sales tax on contraceptive pills; support for sanctions against Rhodesia and for the self-determination and independence of colonial nations; and significant reorganisation of government departments, entailing abolitions, mergers and new entities.[51] It was a startling revelation of what could be done when propositions had been long considered in opposition and were capable of implementation. It signalled the new government's direction.

Moreover, it was also government by executive fiat and indicative of its future. Graham Freudenberg, Whitlam's speechwriter and the first historian of his government, conceded that the outcome would include:

> the clash between the old ways and the new spirit; small episodes with large consequences; decisions inadequately explained or thought through; the gap between decision and successful execution; the tensions between the permanent public service and political staffs; opposing concepts of the national interest ...[52]

Its defiance of convention also resonated with a presumption common among the government's opponents, 'pervading everything to the very end, in so many powerful circles, the unspoken denial of the legitimacy of the Whitlam Labor Government'.[53]

The Whitlam government survived barely three years, from 5 December 1972 to 11 November 1975. It was interrupted by a double-dissolution election and an attendant campaign in May 1974. In the circumstances, it was remarkable how much was achieved. The long years of preparation led to a plethora of policies and an institutional revolution. Much would be thwarted, compromised or incomplete when Whitlam lost office, and yet the political landscape was changed in lasting ways. Whitlam's program focused on five broad policy priorities: education, health, social reform/social welfare, cities, and foreign policy. In each of these, there were to be substantial achievements.

In education, the landmark initiatives were the creation of a schools commission and the ongoing influence of its report on needs-based school funding, and the abolition of fees for tertiary education. Each would later be modified by the Hawke/Keating Labor government. In both instances, however, the participation of the Commonwealth in education provision was amplified in ways that would last. In health, it was the introduction of a universal insurance scheme, Medibank. This was so hard-fought that its enabling legislation had to await the joint sitting following the 1974 double dissolution. Then it was ramped up quickly and effectively, but looked doomed when the successor Coalition government incrementally dismantled it. Yet it would be revived (as Medicare) by the next Labor government and would remain an impregnable feature of the Australian system thereafter. In social welfare, the remit of the Henderson poverty inquiry (initiated under McMahon) was expanded; the inauguration of no-fault divorce was accompanied by the introduction of the Supporting Mothers benefit and improved access to long-term child care; and the Australian Assistance Plan introduced provisions for regionally based social administration and citizen participation. The *Racial Discrimination Act* (1975) and provision for the Commonwealth to purchase land to be held on behalf of (and transferred to) Aboriginal communities were significant advances in both human rights and Indigenous policy. Multicultural reform signified the end of assimilation.

The government's grand urban objectives were thwarted, but Commonwealth leverage ensured that at last comprehensive sewerage systems were rolled out in the capital cities. In foreign affairs, there was an emphasis on decolonisation and human rights, a notable increase in the proportion of gross national product devoted to international aid, a determination to bring Papua New Guinea to self-government and independence, an emphasis on establishing relations with countries in the region, and a new assertion of 'equal' relations with great and powerful friends (for example, within ANZUS) to establish decisively Australia's independent voice in world affairs. There were, in addition, measures to promote cultural development. The Holt/Gorton ACA was enhanced with the introduction of the Australia Council in 1973. Gorton's support for film production was reinforced by the establishment of the Australian Film and Television School in 1975. Gender equality was also advanced, not only through equal pay and employment practices but also with the pioneering appointment of a special adviser to the prime minister on women's affairs. The appointee, Elizabeth Reid, was empowered to monitor ministerial and departmental decisions to ensure that their impact on women was taken into account.

Institutional Reform

The broad overview above simply indicates the government's range and its dominant policy ideas. To understand how the prime minister engaged with these objectives—and what contemporary and enduring effects that had on performance of the role—we must consider Whitlam's working style and how institutional resources were utilised and transformed. In policy terms, Whitlam was the best prepared of any of the Australian prime ministers. With so much predetermined, a great deal that could be achieved by administrative action rather than legislation could be implemented rapidly. For instance, in one of the fields closest to Whitlam's heart, foreign and defence policy, which he details comprehensively in his personal account,[54] 'implementing policy ... is ... largely stroke-of-the-pen-stuff ... there is not usually a need for the often lengthy and potentially frustrating processes of parliamentary approval through legislation'.[55]

In areas demanding development, a responsive public service, major and often contentious domestic change, complex legislation and careful implementation, extensive forethought can only be the beginning. There must be concerted work within the policy community, followed by consolidation of cabinet and Caucus support, and attention to parliamentary tactics. A preparatory move, then, was to attend to the policy community itself. As indicated earlier, this entailed implementation of the plans Wilenski had outlined for augmenting ministerial staff and the PMO itself, and for public service reform. The aim was to bring opposition advisory networks into government. Multiple sources of advice would ensure robust debate.

The initial plan was that the PMO would manage government priorities, coordination across portfolios and differentiation of political demands from policy objectives. Within a year, however, it was evident that the PMO was too small to handle such a complex brief.[56] It was decided instead to strengthen the policy and coordination capacities of the PM&C. Arguably, PMO influence declined thereafter. Wilenski himself rated it only a 'modest' success relative to initial aspirations. A study in 1976 concluded: 'The work done by ministerial advisers varies considerably, but their part in the policy process has been essentially limited and confined'.[57]

There are four reasons, however, to qualify that conclusion. First, from that point on, prime ministers had better information than their colleagues. So they had a greater capacity, if they chose, to control their cabinet and the government. Second, the institutionalisation of ministerial advisers allowed for a politically engaged group with strong network ties to be drawn into the parliamentary political process. As one commentator remarked,

> when I walked into Parliament House earlier this year [1973], I would have known half the personal staffs who had already arrived through nothing more conspiratorial than a left-liberal history in the local Labor Party, the Sydney and NSW Fabian Societies, the anti-Vietnam movement … It was as though part of a whole generation had marched through King's Hall and filtered through to the various ministers' offices.[58]

These networks allowed advisers to reach out into the party, academia, the media and the community in a way never open to the APS. This outreach activity remained an important potential of the private office under future prime ministers.

Third, these network activists were immediately to hand in a way that traditional public servants could not match. Soon the effect was noticed. On one hand, the public service was gingered up, forced to argue for and justify its case in an unprecedented way, its inner working opened up to scrutiny and challenge. On the other, however, the lack of clear role definition for ministerial staff and of systematic accountability (since they were assumed to act in the minister's name) would eventually have a pernicious effect. As early as 1974 it was evident that Treasury sensed the erosion of its influence over economic decision-making:

> Treasury's up to the minute submissions have had to meet the view of ministerial advisers who … have been overwhelmingly hostile witnesses. There is a feeling within the Treasury that the balance has been rather lop-sided: that ministerial advisers get to make comments to ministers entering cabinet, but that the Treasury does not get anything like a fair chance to reply.[59]

Being the agent at the principal's side was no small advantage. As Clyde Cameron commented:

> at the prime ministerial level … staffers regard themselves as being more powerful than ministers or private members of parliament. Indeed, they

> almost invariably do have more influence with their prime minister than do the ministers … in all cases, the staff can, and do, influence a minister's relations with his peers and senior public servants. This is crucial in the case of the prime minister.[60]

Fourth, even if initial degrees of PMO influence were debatable at the time, it would become clear over the next forty years that the reforms under Whitlam were the catalyst for a remarkable elevation of the role of the PMO within the core executive.

The appointment of private office advisers was, and was intended to be, a challenge to the APS. It was accompanied by revision of portfolios, complemented by departmental mergers, some rationalisation and one entirely new entity: the Department of Urban and Regional Development (DURD).[61] While there had been prior preparation by the Public Service Board (PSB) to respond to Labor's machinery of government proposals, the advice of Wilenski and a small ginger group of young public servants was influential, though he had only two meetings with Whitlam before the election.[62] Immediately the election result was clear, Wilenski contacted the secretary of the PSB and commissioned an administrative arrangements order, to implement the proposed departmental changes. The real importance of the Wilenski report, according to Freudenberg, 'was that it allowed the politicians, inexperienced as they were in administration, to establish an immediate ascendancy over the public servants'.[63]

Despite the scepticism expressed by Whitlam's advisers, one of the most successful of his ministers, Bill Hayden, believed there was 'widespread goodwill towards the incoming government and, generally, an evident keenness on the part of the public service to faithfully serve it'.[64] The far-reaching nature of administrative reform and the pace of change, however, did unsettle the mandarins. Experimentation with new bodies—such as a group to advise on government programs, the Priorities Review Staff (PRS), which would also prove only a modest success—appeared threatening to central agencies. PM&C at first, far from being a key actor in coordination, was left trying to catch up with what was happening and to reconcile other players to change.

The Treasury, having presented a bleak report on economic prospects to a government whose program depended on continued growth and a prime minister whose policy focus was not on the economy, was not included in Whitlam's initial meeting with the secretaries of PM&C, PSB and Foreign Affairs.[65] Neither PM&C nor Treasury would be comfortably reconciled with the Whitlam government.

In late 1974, when Whitlam's inner circle determined that the PMO was not itself equipped for the complex task of driving policy, Whitlam controversially appointed his former private secretary, John Menadue, as secretary of PM&C to succeed John Bunting, occasioning an outcry of 'jobs for the boys'.[66] It was indicative of a determination that PM&C should have an activist policy role rather than serving only to facilitate and coordinate. Menadue set about this task, bringing the PRS (formerly under the special minister of state) into PM&C, establishing a Policy Coordination Unit, transferring the women's adviser from the PMO into PM&C, and attracting talented policy analysts from across the APS to the department.[67] These initiatives built on, but significantly enhanced, the structure introduced by Lenox Hewitt, with similar intentions, under Gorton. No subsequent government has reversed this enterprise. It formalised the duopoly of policy resources—PMO and PM&C—available to the prime minister alone, an advantage no successor prime minister would sacrifice.[68] Menadue's was not to be the only departmental appointment from within the inner circle: Wilenski was appointed secretary of the Department of Labor and Immigration soon after, and Wilenski's successor as Whitlam's principal private secretary, Jim Spigelman, was appointed secretary of the Department of the Media in 1975.

These were substantial interventions in the way the APS operated. They were accompanied by an unprecedented resort to special inquiries, ad-hoc committees and consultants, and eight royal commissions, including the Royal Commission on Australian Government Administration (RCAGA). The RCAGA, chaired by the indefatigable Nugget Coombs, was appointed after the 1974 election. Its terms of reference were so broad as to leave it 'wandering through relatively uncharted territory with little guidance'.[69] It invited departmental submissions and initiated wide-ranging research, often conducted by specialist task forces, but it had to work fast, and the fall of the Whitlam government meant its report was not delivered until 1976, to the new Coalition government. It was a signal of intent. Circumstances prevented its realisation as a catalyst for change. Yet the issues it identified—concern for a 'responsive' public sector; greater attention to personnel, structures and the efficient allocation of resources—were those that later administrations would pursue with gusto.

Whitlam's New Order: the Case of DURD

The short history of the one new department introduced by Whitlam, the Department of Urban and Regional Development, illustrates how innovative intentions, policy implementation, fiscal constraint and administrative process played out in the policy community. Whitlam's concern with urban problems had long been evident. Pat Troy, a planning engineer and ANU academic, had provided advice (and speechwriting) to Whitlam, and to then urban affairs spokesman Tom Uren, since 1968. Troy was seconded to DURD a week after the 1972 election and given a fortnight by Uren—minister for urban and regional development—to produce the blueprint for the new department. DURD's ambitious and expensive program entailed whole-of-government objectives, involving urban regeneration and rehabilitation, regional growth centres and new cities, land acquisition and public housing, and specific improvements (such as the extension of urban sewerage). DURD had no financial or legislative control over other departments, but its task was to coordinate reform on a national scale.

A program of such range and complexity needed time to develop and to be bedded down: it was not to be granted that time. But its fate illuminates four generic problems in the way the Whitlam government interacted with states, stakeholders and the bureaucracy. The first was the attempt to impose a particular vision of Commonwealth–state relations, with national reform driven from Canberra, that did not make for easy negotiations with state counterparts. The second was the disparity between enthusiastic program specialists and professional bureaucrats within Whitlam's administration. Whitlam defended the program specialists and the integrity of his program, in which urban reform was a signature element, at all costs.

Third, it was intended, as Whitlam himself stated,

> that DURD was to be a major department of state, virtually co-equal with Treasury, dealing with the urban budget and coordinating departments with urban responsibilities ... [but] the Public Service Board refused to classify the senior positions in the Department at levels equivalent to Treasury so that it could attract people of higher calibre from other parts of the bureaucracy.[70]

This resistance provoked the ire of a government intent on creating a more responsive public sector, but it ensured that DURD remained subsidiary to the central agencies. Fourth, Treasury was increasingly concerned with reining in expenditure, yet DURD's commitment to expensive urban reforms, and Uren's success in prosecuting the case in cabinet, ran counter to the Treasury line. This provoked antagonism—which persisted throughout the life of DURD—and anticipated on a small scale the broader conflict over economic policy that cruelled the government after 1974.

Relations between the Whitlam ministry and Treasury reached their nadir in preparations for the 1974 budget. In this, coincidentally, a DURD officer played a catalytic role. Treasury had failed to persuade the government to accept a sharply deflationary package soon after the May election, and again in August, despite Whitlam's support (he lost the battle in cabinet and Caucus). It then approached its objective in another way by presenting figures to cabinet in the budget round that—at least in the eyes of the ministry—were intentionally misleading. Mike Keating, a former Treasury official then working as a divisional head in DURD (and later to become secretary of PM&C), pointed out to Tom Uren that the documents on which Treasury based its argument for cuts in spending and an increase in taxes could not be correct. Uren swiftly conveyed the message to his colleagues. As Bill Hayden has stated, Keating

> illustrated that the figures in fact implied a substantial surplus, that is, a fierce reinforcement of the contraction already underway. There was

> near enough to pandemonium in the Cabinet as ministers revolted at what they believed was deliberate deception by the Treasury.[71]

With Treasury discredited, the expansionary budget that followed owed more to views espoused by the new deputy prime minister, Jim Cairns, than to the arguments put by treasurer Frank Crean. Cairns would soon after replace Crean as treasurer. Some believe that Labor's disastrous detour into unorthodox funding channels in late 1974 that culminated in 'the loans affair' was a direct result of the government having slipped the Treasury rein. Treasury had forfeited its opportunities to influence the course of events.[72] As an incidental by-product of the conflict, DURD was again a winner in the 1974 budget. But time was running out: DURD was abolished by the Fraser government in 1976.

Whitlam's Executive Leadership

Despite the preparation for reform and institutional innovation, consolidation of Whitlam's program depended on political efficacy in government. The skills that made him a great opposition leader continued to serve in inspiring followers, in campaigning and in domination of parliament. But now there were the very different demands of team building, Caucus management, cabinet discipline, ministerial oversight, policy implementation and day-to-day administration.

Whitlam's rise within the party, the transformation of the party executive with the incorporation of the parliamentary leadership, the professionalisation of media relations and national campaigning, and not least his attention to the Menzies model all signified a shift away from Labor's collective tradition and towards a more leader-centric mode. Yet Caucus customs would die hard, and Whitlam lacked Fisher's skill as a conciliatory chair, Curtin's deft resort to party machinery and capacity for inspiring respect, and Chifley's instinctive gift for human relations. Whitlam was first and foremost an advocate. Impatient to be heard, he could not sit back to listen and moderate from the chair. In consequence, in 1972 Caucus rules were changed to allow him to be the first Labor leader *not* to act as Caucus chair. Enabled to speak, he was forthright and largely respected for being so. He was supported by loyal allies, such as Barnard and Fred Daly (leader of the House), who organised the numbers for him. He could rely on the power of patronage (such as the allocation of portfolios) and the reluctance of colleagues to check a leader who had brought them into office. Whitlam would thus count on a personal vote rather than patiently canvassing support.

Yet when argument or deference failed, Whitlam was all too willing to resort to confrontation. A journalist assessing Whitlam's first year in office noted, 'Instead of winning them by persuasion, [Whitlam] tries to intimidate the weekly meetings of his … fellow Labor MPs. Sometimes he gets away with it. On several occasions … he has been rebuffed'.[73] Every Labor leader faces such problems, but given party expectations, a Labor PM must 'keep reviewing the ways by which [Caucus] can be given a voice in decision making. It is the failure to consider this factor which may lead to continued disputes with backbenchers'.[74] Whitlam sometimes provoked Caucus by announcing an initiative cabinet had discussed on Monday at his regular Tuesday press conference before it had been considered by Caucus, which met on Wednesday. Caucus' occasional reaction to Whitlam's failure to acknowledge its prerogatives was perhaps as much an assertion of its rights as an expression of dissent, but the succession of disputes—over an incomes referendum, over tariff policy, over tax concessions, and most significantly over the nature of the 1974 budget—fuelled accusations of 'government by crisis'.[75]

The performance of the Whitlam ministry was patchy. Caucus had decided that there were to be twenty-seven ministers, all of whom were to be in cabinet. It was unwieldy and entailed last-minute alterations to Whitlam's transition plans simply in order to create portfolios. None of Whitlam's ministry had cabinet or administrative experience. Barnard as deputy prime minister was initially a calming and stabilising influence, but he was replaced by Cairns in 1974. Crean, in the Treasury portfolio, tried to rein in excess but could not carry the fight in cabinet. He was replaced by Cairns (albeit briefly), whose influence had outweighed Crean's in framing the 1974 budget. Bill Hayden, who delivered the government's more settled and decidedly less expansionist final budget, was belatedly appointed treasurer in 1975. There were some standout performers, such as Hayden in the delivery of Medibank and Uren in urban reform. Others combined major misjudgement with episodic brilliance. For example, attorney-general Lionel Murphy's leadership of a raid by Commonwealth police on ASIO in 1973 when it failed to produce material he had requested was one of the early calamities of the government. But he also engineered significant family and environmental law reform and established the Australian Legal Aid Office.

Efforts to rationalise work and impose order and direction—through, for instance, the establishment of standing committees of cabinet envisaged in the transition plans—only began to bear fruit towards the end of Whitlam's reign. Standing committees withered after the 1974 election, with ad-hoc committees becoming more important. The most effective of these—such as the Expenditure Review Committee (ERC)—demonstrated the potential of the committee system.[76] The ERC would be a continuing feature of successor governments. The supposition that all ministers were 'equal' was belied by the fact that Whitlam controlled what could be considered, determining the flow of business to committees and to cabinet itself.[77] Frequently in cabinet, ministers would be so cowed by the mass of paper and Whitlam's insistence that decisions move at a rapid clip that he gained compliance. Yet if opposition to a proposal he favoured seemed likely, he would suggest there be full debate, which would unroll endlessly until opponents began to drop out, 'hammered into surrender by exhaustion and frustration'.[78]

Sometimes there would be pushback. Ministers, having lost in cabinet and believing their appointment to be the gift of Caucus rather than of the prime minister, occasionally resurrected issues or reopened battles there, eroding cabinet discipline and adding to public impressions of disorder. Above all, there was simply the speed of the line: Whitlam pushed too much through cabinet too fast. 'There was no let up from the pressure for action from the very first', said one minister, while another remarked publicly, 'the Government may be going a little too far too quickly'.[79] By July 1975, parliamentary counsel CK Comans noted that his office was faced with an excessive amount of legislation to draft: 'We do our best to maintain a standard, but there is far too much'.[80] The abiding impression of the Whitlam cabinet, concluded Patrick Weller, 'was its lack of coherence … At no stage was there an attempt, or even apparently an expressed desire, for cabinet to take a clear view of where the government was going. The pace was always too hectic … policy seemed to lurch from crisis to crisis'.[81]

The way Whitlam dealt with such crises confirmed the underlying problem: he was a poor manager, seemingly uninterested in supervision of his ministers, focusing on areas that interested him (such as foreign affairs) and leaving others to get on with their jobs. He was the only one in a position to know all that was happening but was inattentive to coordination. His ministers, heavily overburdened, concentrated on their own portfolios and took little notice of what was going on elsewhere. It was a situation ripe for strong-minded individuals to act of their own volition, as did Murphy, or for small coteries to act independently without wider consultation or thought of the collective rationale, as did all those entangled with minerals and energy minister Rex Connor in the fatal 'loans affair'.

Connor had a grand scheme to keep control of the processing of Australian resources in Australian hands, and when conventional methods of funding could not be gained, sought to raise huge international 'petro-dollar' loans through unorthodox channels via a shady Pakistani intermediary, Tirath Khemlani. Connor was authorised by an Executive Council minute describing the loan as for temporary purposes, so it did not have to be approved by the Loans Council. When, after escalating difficulties, his authority was withdrawn, Connor continued to deal covertly with Khemlani, despite having assured Whitlam (and via Whitlam, parliament) that he had ceased to do so.[82] When it came to light, Connor was dismissed. In parallel, on a smaller scale, treasurer Jim Cairns enlisted another doubtful intermediary, George Harris, who assured him that considerable funds could be accessed for government purposes through sources in the United States. Cairns provided a letter referring to a brokerage fee should Harris succeed. He would later deny in parliament having provided such a letter, apparently believing he had never signed it.[83] The opposition had the evidence, and Whitlam sacked Cairns from the ministry and as deputy prime minister.

When problems like these came to light, Whitlam, astonished that someone had let him down, would lose his temper and, as one minister put it, 'begin to chuck us out like chess-men'.[84] Thus, one-time allies Crean, Connor and Cameron, and even his loyal confidant and party mediator Barnard, would lose his support—in very public circumstances. Some were dismissed for not prevailing in the battles they had been expected to carry (Crean and Barnard), or for disagreement (Cameron). Others were sacked for more evident transgressions (Connor for duplicity and for having caused Whitlam to mislead parliament; Cairns also for having inadvertently misled parliament over the existence of the Harris letter). While Whitlam had sufficient cause to act in cases like that of Connor and Cairns, collaboration, oversight and management might well have prevented the escalation of fiascos that led Malcolm Fraser, by 1975 leader of the opposition, to decide that in the loans affair, he had found a circumstance so 'extraordinary and reprehensible' as to justify the denial of supply by the Senate.

Whitlam Defeated, Fraser Ascendant

Whitlam was finally brought down by a confluence of critical factors. The first was the public perception of policy overreach, incoherence and—courtesy of the loans affair—incompetence and possibly corruption. Such perceptions were amplified by other issues. A program based on the assumption that 'we do not have to ration scarcity but plan abundance'[85] was incompatible with the economic deterioration that was increasingly evident. Whitlam had overrated parliament as the forum where solutions must properly be resolved. His judgement was confounded when dealing with an opposition always determined to challenge the legitimacy of his government, and a leader, Malcom Fraser, who was as obdurate and fearless as Whitlam himself.

Whitlam's program had been conceived during the 'long boom' and assumed that prosperity and growth would continue. His commitment to public provision of services and investment in education, health and urban reform while simultaneously fostering wage growth and lowering unemployment depended on steadily increasing revenue—'the great assumption' that, as John Howard (Fraser's treasurer and later himself prime minister) argued, was shared by both sides of politics.[86] In the early 1970s, transitions in the international order undermined that assumption, and the feasibility of such a program. The economy Whitlam inherited was already underperforming, with rising unemployment, significant inflation and decreasing economic activity. Treasury, convinced that Keynesian orthodoxy was failing, had argued for more rigour during the McMahon administration but with limited success. Indeed, Whitlam targeted the Coalition's failed economic management in his 1972 policy speech. But he had no crystal ball to indicate that the boom was over or to help him address conditions that affected all the Western economies.

The growth driven by reconstruction was over. A rough consensus between labour, business and government about managed prosperity had sustained growth while containing wage hikes and inflation, but it eventually fostered a belief that relative prosperity was the norm. As conditions deteriorated, that consensus broke down. The international financial system came under strain as the emphasis on liberalisation undermined the Bretton Woods fixed-exchange rate regime. International inflation was exacerbated by US policies to finance the Vietnam War and Lyndon Johnson's welfarist 'Great Society' program. The oil price shock initiated in late 1973 by the Organization of the Petroleum Exporting Countries, or OPEC, spread cost increases through all economies, provoking widespread dislocation, recession and unemployment. The expectation that inflation could be contained by allowing unemployment to rise was confounded. Increasing inflation, slowing activity and higher unemployment were experienced simultaneously. Stagflation had arrived.[87]

None of the advanced economies handled this complex of economic problems well. Indeed, Whitlam was later to show that Australia's growth rate prior to 1972 had been below the Organisation for Economic Co-operation and Development (OECD) average, while between 1972 and 1975 the rate was similar to the OECD average.[88] His government first attempted to manage worsening economic conditions by revaluing the exchange rate, by a startling 25 per cent tariff reduction, and by raising interest rates. Later it would resort to wage indexation and a Prices Justification Tribunal. But the goals of lower inflation were incompatible with increased public expenditure, support for wage rises and lower unemployment. Crean, as treasurer, was destroyed in the attempt to manage that incompatibility. The 1973 budget, driven by the government's ambitious reform program, saw a substantial commitment to an expanded public sector, and significant increases in government outlays. It was accompanied by a wages explosion. Treasury's case for a deflationary shock in 1974, supported by both Crean and Whitlam, was defeated in Caucus and in cabinet. Treasury dealt itself out of the debate by a manoeuvre that broke cabinet's trust, allowing Cairns' influence as chair of the Caucus Economic Committee to prevail and subsequently seeing him elevated to the Treasury portfolio. Not until 1975, after Cairns had been removed from Treasury to Environment and then sacked from the ministry, would his successor, Hayden, deliver a budget that argued for 'consolidation and constraint'.[89]

It came too late. Pre-existing commitments (and costs associated with an unexpected contingency, the cyclone that hit Darwin in December 1974) saw spending growth even higher, exacerbating the budget deficit. Over the three years of the Whitlam government, economic growth halved, unemployment doubled and inflation tripled.[90] The public experience was of diminishing prosperity and security. Few equated this with what the government had inherited, or the international circumstances leading to the parallel decline in other advanced economies. Accompanied by economic policy disputes within government, dubious loan initiatives and the sacking of key ministers, the perception that instability was due to incompetence was inevitable.

Whitlam's failing as a judge of character was key not only to his mishandling of key players in Caucus and cabinet but to what happened next. He thought the Coalition's attempt to confirm the illegitimacy of Labor governance had been seen off by its defeat in the double-dissolution election of 1974. That had been precipitated by the discovery of Whitlam's attempt to gain control of the Senate by offering DLP senator Vincent Gair appointment to an ambassadorship, creating a potential vacancy (and a Labor opportunity) in the projected May Senate election. It was thwarted by Queensland Country Party premier Joh Bjelke-Petersen, but it was represented by the opposition as such a challenge to orthodoxy that the Coalition threatened to block supply.

Enraged, and already having had Bills rejected in the Senate, Whitlam called a double-dissolution election. His government was returned, though with an even slimmer majority in the House and without control of the Senate.

The threat had not disappeared, especially after then Liberal leader Bill Snedden was ousted in March 1975 by Malcolm Fraser, who promised tougher leadership. Fraser took the fight over economic management to Labor in the House, and his comprehensive response to Hayden's budget in August proved him to be a doughty foe. Whitlam, still the master of the chamber, too readily assumed he could dominate Fraser in the way he had Holt, Gorton, McMahon and Snedden. He had not counted on an opponent as tenacious as Fraser. Thus, when the details of the loans affair were progressively revealed, and the Coalition seized on these as 'extraordinary' and 'reprehensible', and justification for deferring a vote on appropriation Bills in the Senate, Whitlam made contingency plans to hold out even if supply was denied, calculating that Fraser would crack before he did. He also assumed that it would be a battle fought out in parliament itself, not counting on the potential of a third party, the governor-general, to intervene.

John Kerr, appointed on Whitlam's recommendation in February 1974 to succeed Paul Hasluck as governor-general, had his own ambitions and other ideas. Fraser did not crack, but held his troops together in the face of mounting pressure. Kerr did not act simply on the advice of his prime minister, but instead sought covert advice on another way to break the deadlock. The impasse dragged on through October and into November. The lengths to which Kerr and those whose cooperation he enlisted went to conceal their intentions and mislead the prime minister only became clear later.[91] Yet colleagues at the time, such as Hayden and Crean, had seen enough warning signs to convey their concerns to Whitlam. Whitlam's attitude was, 'What can he do—he's got to take his advice from me'.[92] When Hayden said 'my … instincts tell me [Kerr's] going to sack us', Whitlam pronounced, 'No, Comrade, he wouldn't have the guts to do it'.[93] He was completely blindsided when the unthinkable happened: Kerr dismissed him, commissioned Fraser with an injunction to secure supply, then dissolved parliament until an election could be held. The formal grounds for dissolution were twenty-one Whitlam government Bills that had been rejected by the Senate. A context had been created in which Fraser could not lose, despite the rage of Labor supporters, the evidence that Kerr had deceived the prime minister, and the conviction of some that the Dismissal lacked constitutional validity.

The Herald of Crisis

Malcolm Fraser was one of those who interpreted life as an arena of struggle for competitive advantage in which the task is always that of achieving balance between individual self-interest and the restraint essential to civilised society. Individual aspiration must be encouraged, but robust institutions and strong leadership are necessary if the battle of each against all is not to lead to destruction.[94] Institutions, and the 'due process' painstakingly developed to ensure their functions, should be defended. It is a balance always in danger of disruption, so one must be constantly on guard. Crisis is always the potential. 'Life was not meant to be easy', as Fraser famously said.[95] It was not Whitlam's values and vision to which Fraser objected, but his inattention to institutional limits, disregard for due process, and the chaos and diminution of authority to which this gave rise.[96] These were the harbingers of social crisis. Fraser's message was that he would end the crisis, restore due process and provide the strong leadership needed to fend off the danger to Australian society.

By 1975, his willingness to risk all in responding to events he represented as crises was apparent. He had brought down John Gorton in 1971 in a battle over proper process. In March 1975 he had overthrown Bill Snedden, whose compromised 'middle road' leadership of the Liberal Party was no answer to the threat Whitlam posed. Finally, by December that same year, his brinkmanship and strategic instinct had terminated the 'illegitimate' Labor government. Some regarded each of these high-profile confrontations as driven by ambition, hypocrisy and brutal opportunism.[97] Even colleagues intimated that he invented breach of process as a rationale for aggressive action when it suited his purpose. But, in every instance, Fraser was convinced of the virtue of his cause.[98]

Once engaged, his courage in battle could not be doubted. Each of these coups were gambles that threatened his career, prospects, alliances, friendships and even his cause. Yet unremitting work, public profile and undeniable ability ensured he remained a senior figure in the party. He had no friends in his party after Gorton's defeat, few when he challenged Snedden, and was immensely unpopular with self-identified progressives in the electorate after the constitutional crisis. He did not seek popularity or friendship, but rather authority and respect. It was a message that cut through. He regained roles in McMahon's ministry and Snedden's shadow ministry despite undermining Gorton. He came eventually to be seen as the only foil to Whitlam. And he won some of the largest majorities in Australian history at the elections of 1975 and 1977.

Crisis and confrontation were his métier because their occurrence confirmed his implicit world view. Battle-ready, he was attuned to struggles in which his capacities could be exercised. Even when returning to his farm—'Nareen', in his western Victorian electorate of Wannon—far from relaxing he preferred finding problems to fix: he 'thrives on crises and emergencies', said his farm manager, adding 'when it's quiet in Canberra he will come down here and pick out little things to complain about. When the whole world is against him, he is happiest'.[99] More engaging still was the arena of adversarial politics and the issues he would tackle as prime minister: unstable government; contravention of institutional process; societal decline; the Cold War and economic crisis. He would not act alone, but this was the context in which authoritative leadership was essential. Crisis, then, was both a challenge and an opportunity—to prove himself. He would find, as we will see, that the opportunity was limited, and he would be judged by his inability to master what he had framed as the chief domestic 'crisis' of the time: the threat to managed prosperity.[100]

Fraser's background had steeled him for such a role. His childhood 'had given him extraordinary self-sufficiency, extraordinary shyness and, paradoxically, a strong desire to be heard'.[101] Raised on large family farms, where wealth and privilege were apparently belied by anxiety about money, relationships were distant, age peers were few and children were expected to be seen and not heard, Fraser emerged as a frugal, incommunicative loner.[102] He made few friends at the private boarding schools he attended. By then, he says, it was 'too late. The die was cast.

I had been solitary for too long so I was still in part self-contained or reserved or whatever. I don't think anything really was going to alter that'.[103] A competent but not outstanding student, he was nicknamed 'Freezer'. Nor did he make a mark at Oxford University, although there, his inherent curiosity about politics and society became apparent, and he discovered in reading the economic and historical analysts of that period the intellectual resources to refine his views of social fragility and the urgency of watchful defence. Frustrated by his early exclusion from adult conversation, resentful of the authority of his extroverted but often absent father and the regimentation of boarding school, and overlooked at Oxford, Fraser would strike back, entering politics in early adulthood and demanding a voice.[104] At last, in 1975, the political climate was conducive to what he had to say.

Defining Challenges

The challenges on which Fraser had based his narrative of a manifold crisis were threefold: international, economic and institutional. Internationally, his role as former minister for defence, principal defender of the Vietnam engagement in its dying days, advocate of forward defence and ardent exponent of the threat of Soviet expansionism had generated a reputation as a Cold War warrior. A protégé of Richard Casey, though also careful to develop and maintain relations with Menzies, he was the logical carrier of the 'great world struggle' into the new context. The rhetoric of struggle, sacrifice and obligation—and the importance of the American alliance—on which Whitlam's government had cast doubt was revived. It was for Fraser, as it had been for Menzies, a means of managing popular expectations and a warning of demands that might override domestic concerns.

Yet Fraser differed from Menzies. He was far more concerned, following Holt and Whitlam, with regional relations. The communist threat was reason enough for continued partnership with America, but the Soviet Union was his target and he never saw China as an expansionist power. He endorsed Whitlam's pioneering restoration of relations with China and had a pragmatic interest in encouraging trading relations. Unlike Menzies, he recognised the necessity of decolonisation and was concerned to promote enabling relations with, and democratic government in, third-world countries. Only by working with them could the seduction of communism be averted. The provision of aid and promotion of human rights were keys to success. Like Menzies, he regarded the Commonwealth as an important avenue for pursuing these ends, but it was apparent to all that there was no hint of racism in his make-up.

Participation in Commonwealth Heads of Government meetings augmented Fraser's international profile, gave him networks with third-world leaders and led to his productive interventions in debates on Zimbabwe's independence and on the ending of apartheid in South Africa. He was relatively successful as an international statesman, especially in Commonwealth circles, though some of his dearest aspirations were thwarted. His attempts to engage Western polities with North–South issues were thwarted, and he learned the hard way that the self-interest of powerful states and trading conglomerates would always trump free trade.[105] Nonetheless, his inclinations, as well as the regard he had won, led to continuing engagement in international affairs long after his prime-ministerial role ended.

There was continuity here with some of the concerns Fraser pursued in domestic politics, and these, he acknowledged, linked him back to Whitlam. Fraser identified as core issues their bipartisan engagement with human rights, immigration, promotion of multiculturalism, opposition to racism, and commitment to reinforcing Australia's independent identity.[106] On some of these issues—multiculturalism, immigration reform, admission of refugees—Fraser was more progressive than Whitlam had been. Admirers argued that he had 'cemented' Whitlam's humanitarian reforms.[107] Certainly, his constructive opposition to racial discrimination, and his acceptance of refugees and institutional elaboration of multiculturalism were celebrated, and were ranked by him among his proudest achievements. For him, these were all equally means of ensuring social cohesion and countering the divisions that would undermine it. But critics identified these issues as a distraction from the main task—economic reform—and a capitulation to progressive decadence.[108]

Yet Fraser was the prime minister who first placed the economic narrative at the centre of government, where it has remained ever since.

He was conscious that progressive initiatives were less salient for the domestic audience in a context of general anxiety about an unpredictable economic transition. Fraser had capitalised on economic challenge as the means of winning office. It was this that had brought him to power and on which his reputation would rely. In understanding the way he worked, its effects on the institutions of government, and his lasting influence on the prime-ministerial role, it is economic management that is most significant for our purposes.

Fraser's Economic Narrative

Fraser was hardly unique in thinking that sound economic management was imperative, and the task that Whitlam had conspicuously failed. His government adopted the 'fight inflation first' policy that had finally been accepted by Bill Hayden and was an article of faith in Treasury. The assumption was that excessive government spending fuels inflation and also requires higher taxation to avoid deficits. Government spending had to be cut and wage demands contained so that inflation could be managed: only then could unemployment come down. The postwar full-employment mantra was abandoned. An element of protection was maintained by continuing with Labor's wage indexation, though it too ceased in 1981. But the rhetoric of government cutbacks being imperative was consistent. Those engaged in budget review—similar to the ERC process introduced late in Whitlam's term—became known as 'the razor gang'.

Fraser was intent on being in control, not being controlled, and he consistently sought alternative sources of advice. Treasury presented only its preferred option and he would not be captive to the Treasury line. Fraser relished argument: it clarified his own position and sometimes reinforced his resistance when a specific option was asserted against his inclinations. In Treasury he found formidable antagonists, especially in John Stone—deputy secretary at the time Fraser took office but appointed secretary in 1979. Treasury, said Fraser, 'thought knowledge was power. They didn't want to give away any of their power and they didn't want to share any of their knowledge'.[109] Hence, he brought influential economic advisers into the PMO, and as Menadue and then Alan

Carmody transformed PM&C into a 'can-do' department, he would rely more and more on these resources to shape his thinking. His staff were instructed to work smoothly with Treasury, but John Rose in the PMO, along with Ian Castles and Ed Visbord in PM&C, would constitute an invaluable troika in enabling him to explore other possibilities. '[With] Stone and Wheeler [Stone's predecessor in Treasury] there was only one way of getting to an end-point', Fraser remarked, 'and that was the way they chose. They would never accept that there's always more than one way of getting to an end-point'.[110]

Despite prioritising inflation control, Fraser periodically engaged in battles with Treasury. The disputes began early. Fraser insisted on the introduction of tax indexation, which Treasury argued would destroy the government's credibility: Fraser won. There was constant argument over the size of the deficit. Treasury was so recalcitrant in supplying the data on which its recommendations were based that Fraser divided it into two, establishing a separate department of finance to concentrate on expenditure. Increasingly he turned to PM&C for alternative ideas and to check on Treasury figures. In late 1976, worried about Australian competitiveness, Fraser decided to devalue the Australian dollar and to introduce a managed exchange rate, against the advice of Treasury. It became apparent that he was not only to be informed but also would be closely involved in every economic decision. Control would be exercised by the prime minister and cabinet, and not dictated by bureaucratic preferences.[111]

The highly regulated environment of industrial relations was always problematic for Fraser. His initial response to the wages explosion initiated by Labor—and the high levels of industrial disputation left by its belated attempts to back away from 'pace setter' policies—was to promote communication and negotiation between employers, unions and government. He established an ombudsman: the Industrial Relations Bureau. Neither employers nor unions took it seriously. The Arbitration Commission frequently reached determinations that worked against government intentions. Fraser's subsequent attempts to introduce tougher measures were inevitably deemed union bashing, a charge he never overcame. A 'wages pause' negotiated with the states in the dying days of his government was one success, but Fraser felt finally that he had been constrained by the Arbitration Commission, embattled by unions and undermined by employer pusillanimity. His government had struggled to achieve balance without having control.[112]

In broad terms, however, Fraser succeeded in what had been his principal objectives: reining in government outlays, controlling the deficit, managing inflation and restoring orderly processes of deliberation. The results, said some, were meagre—on none of the measures were the effects as great as hoped—but they were seen early in his term as significant. The press represented the 1976 budget as having delivered what was promised. Most advisers (including Treasury) believed the extent of cuts was about right. Some business advisers thought that to have been harsher risked stopping the economy in its tracks.[113] Fraser himself would later regret that he had not cut more deeply in the first instance, but claimed that even Treasury secretary Fred Wheeler cautioned against more radical excisions.[114]

The effect for much of his term was to confirm the public perception of Fraser as a strong leader, prepared to take tough decisions. The argument of potential crisis demanding stringent measures remained consistent: as economic conditions marginally improved, the strategy seemed to be working. Arguably this ensured his dominance in the elections of 1977 and 1980. By 1980–81, 'the budget was in surplus. Industry profitability was recovering. Unemployment dropped to below 6 per cent'.[115] But when a short-term mining boom in 1979 was rapidly succeeded by a recession in 1982, the government was in trouble. The causes of both were outside Australia's control. The brief boom followed another oil-price shock, which drove up demand and prices for Australian commodities. It was short-lived: an international recession soon dragged commodity prices back down. The effects were exacerbated by a severe drought in Australia. Looking to an early election, Fraser reverted to a Keynesian, pump-priming budget, the effects of which were to be exacerbated when Treasury forecasts proved to be wrong: it had dramatically underestimated the downturn and the deficit would climb.[116] Fraser was immediately accused of having abandoned the gospel of restraint.

Those desperate attempts to rescue the situation—the expansionary budget and an early election before conditions deteriorated further—set Fraser's downfall in train. The planned election was delayed for a variety of reasons, including opposition within the party organisation and Fraser's ill health, during which time the budget assumptions unravelled. By the time he was ready to proceed, economic indicators had become increasingly unfavourable. On 3 February 1983, the day Fraser approached the governor-general to ask for a double dissolution, Labor terminated its own internal leadership debates by appointing Bob Hawke in place of Bill Hayden. With both unemployment and inflation again heading above 10 per cent and a deficit looming, Fraser reverted frenetically to the crisis scenario, now arguing how much worse the situation would be should there be any resumption of Labor's notoriously irresponsible economic management.

This time, Fraser's habitual narrative collapsed. Hawke, widely known and popular, countered talk of crisis with a message of hope and consensus, ending division and bringing people together to deliberate on sensible solutions. He neatly punctured Fraser's default themes—economic collapse and communist expansion—with ridicule. When Fraser suggested that people's savings would not be safe in the banks because Labor would plunder the banks to fund their 'mad and extravagant promises', Hawke jested: 'They can't put them under the bed, because that's where the Commies are!'[117] Fraser was floundering. Hawke ran a strong campaign. The electorate, said Liberal Party director Tony Eggleton, had become 'disillusioned and impatient with the government'.[118] On 5 March 1983, the Fraser government was defeated.

Essentially, Fraser's was a project of restoration, implicitly founded on the belief that proper processes and rigorous management would ensure the return of 'normal' conditions. Few of the measures he favoured would have been unfamiliar to Menzies. Fraser, as much as Whitlam, remained captive to what Howard called 'the great assumption'—as did Howard himself—of managed prosperity.[119] But that normality was being shattered by transitions in the world economy that not many understood. In Fraser's defence, few contemporary leaders were faring better. The apostles of neoliberalism—state withdrawal, and surrender of control of economic factors to the private sector—Margaret Thatcher and Ronald Reagan, were four and five years from election respectively at the time Fraser took power. Still, by the late 1970s, the advocates of a more radical market-oriented approach to structural reform were mustering, not least within his own party.

John Hyde, Jim Carlton, Peter Shack and others challenged the protectionist ethic of the National Country Party (NCP—the new name given to the Country Party in 1977) and of conservative Liberals. Most were new voices—Coalition MPs who had been elected in 1977 and 1980 after Fraser came to power, with a commitment to radical free market liberalism. They imported an economic zealotry[120] into the Coalition party room that ensured ministers were kept on their toes and forced to defend their brief,[121] but that can hardly have been better calculated to provoke Fraser's resistance. While his public authority remained, he was increasingly challenged by these colleagues. John Howard, appointed treasurer in 1977 and a belated convert to the free market cause, concluded that Fraser and his ministry saw the Liberal Party's 'return to office as a resumption of government prior to 1972': they did not understand the irreversible transition in the world economy taking place in the 1970s.[122]

Over time, such criticism became more trenchant. The domineering titan, happiest 'when the whole world is against him', would be accused of timidity, of being a leader too slow to adapt, reluctant to make the big decisions and leaving the heavy lifting to his successors: Bob Hawke, Paul Keating and ultimately John Howard.[123] Yet political journalist Paul Kelly, one of the critics who concluded that 'Fraser's dominance of his own time is not matched by his imprint on history', conceded that it was Fraser who refined the art of prime-ministerial government.[124] It was an achievement of consequence in understanding the role Fraser bequeathed to those who followed.

Refining Prime-ministerial Government

A trend towards 'leader-centric' government has been relatively uniform in majoritarian democracies since the 1970s.[125] In parliaments following the Westminster model, this is deemed the emergence of 'prime-ministerial government', in contrast to conventional cabinet government.[126] That is, it is government in which the prime minister is not just 'first among equals' in a cabinet exercising collective responsibility but also has a capacity to dominate that colleagues can override only in extremis. This is not the product of a dominant personality (such as that of Hughes or Menzies) or of unusual charisma (such as possessed by Deakin) but of institutional evolution. Advisory structures, the public service, political parties, parliament, executive practice and even media and communication technologies have transformed both the expectations of, and the resources available to, our leaders.[127]

In Australia, it was Malcolm Fraser's fine-tuning of the leader centrality forged by Menzies and of administrative reform initiated by Gorton and Whitlam that brought the possibility of prime-ministerial government to fruition. Fraser consolidated leader centrality by the way he worked in cabinet, in the party and in the use of media to communicate his purposes. He upgraded leadership resources by enhancing the advisory capacities of both the PMO and PM&C to ensure a range of options from which he could choose. While this encouraged competition in policy debate, the leader alone had a monopoly of the information flow, which increased his ability to dominate the cabinet and the party room. In some circumstances, it allowed him to circumvent both bureaucratic direction and ministerial preferences.

As a Liberal minister, Fraser had developed the administrative style that characterised his prime ministership—intense application, immense demands on his staff, advice from personal networks, canvassing a range of opinion as the precedent for every decision. Such predilections imposed heavy workloads on his ministers. Fraser was committed to cabinet and collective responsibility, but he dominated there through his idiosyncratic mode of consultation. He wanted consensus but would not act unilaterally. If decisions were not reached, items would be deferred and returned to, sometimes with new submissions sought and brought back. Everything—even matters that had previously been handled informally by PM&C—was now routed through cabinet. Fraser wanted formality because he understood the political value of collective decisions, but it meant that meetings were incessant.

Wanting the information on which recommendations had been based, and assurance that every aspect of an issue had been considered, he would interrogate his colleagues in a manner some found intimidating. It was not necessarily because he had a settled view, though he was prepared to reject ministerial recommendations when he had. For instance, he rejected the advice of his treasurer twice, on tax indexation and devaluation of the dollar, in the first year of his government. In general, however, he wanted to be persuaded. He relished argument and acted in a manner that invited it. Strong and self-confident interlocutors won his respect, but it foreclosed options that might have been presented by the less confident. 'He wouldn't override a cabinet majority against him', said one minister, 'he would just wear it down because he wanted people with him'. It was government by exhaustion: 'he knew what he wanted', said a cabinet official, 'but if he didn't have his colleagues on side, he kept them locked up until they caved in'.[128] He did not always prevail, but his sources of independent advice and reach across all areas of government gave him the advantage more often than not. It was an exercise of discipline: Fraser could represent decisions to his party room as collective, and to the electorate as decisions of 'the government', never his alone.

One problem marred this meticulous attention to cabinet management. Fraser abhorred Whitlam's failure to control his ministers. He would not make the same mistake. By rigorously controlling cabinet, drawing ministers in through exhaustive consultation and maintaining surveillance over policy areas, collective responsibility and proper process was to be restored. Yet this would not save him from the embarrassment of ministers resigning or being forced to stand aside for a variety of offences against proper behaviour or standards. There were eight—including his treasurer and his finance minister—during the course of his government.[129] It indicated a systemic problem. These untimely departures suggest that Fraser, too, lacked judgement. In his case, however, it was not due to impatience about getting on with the program or sheer inattention. He looked for skills, abilities and capacities that suited his purposes. But he was oriented to the task rather than the person, failing to take account of broader facets of character that might undermine performance or foreshadow questionable behaviour.

Fraser reinforced his authority by carefully tending to the Coalition relationship and by working particularly closely with the Liberal Party organisation. Himself a farmer, and from an electorate that could not be taken for granted, he was accustomed to working with the Country Party to shore up his base. His affinity with Country Party interests was apparent and in Canberra, senior Country Party figures—Doug Anthony, Peter Nixon, Ian Sinclair—became not only powerful allies in cabinet but also close friends. While their influence antagonised some Liberals, they reinforced Fraser's command. There was little of the tension or division that had periodically surfaced in previous Coalition administrations.

With respect to his own party, Fraser had a close engagement with the federal secretariat by dint of his intimacy with its director, Tony Eggleton. Eggleton travelled with Fraser during the 1975 campaign, and thereafter worked with him as closely as his most senior advisers. He was involved with informally vetting proposed staff members; put forward the idea that every cabinet submission must include a communication section; introduced question time briefing notes; and persuaded Fraser to establish a Government Information Unit (GIU).[130] Each morning, Eggleton sent Fraser notes on the party organisation's activities. He sat in on Fraser's strategy meetings and question time briefings, listened to question time in his office, and discussed how it had gone on his return. The relationship was so close it became contentious, with Eggleton thought to be devoting more time to parliamentary business than to that of the secretariat. Fraser, however, wanted the party organisation unequivocally behind him, and Eggleton argued that his ability to gain access and swift approval for what the organisation needed was an asset. Fraser had a direct line to Eggleton. 'It was because we could do things quickly together', said Eggleton. 'And we did.'[131]

Advancing Institutional Support

The manner in which Fraser's working style ensured his centrality and authority in cabinet and in the party was complemented by his adoption and development of the initiatives of his predecessors—Gorton and Whitlam. Fraser, like Whitlam, developed an advisory group while in opposition, the nucleus of which he carried into government. While initially he accepted the advice of PM&C that ministerial staff should be cut back, the PMO itself was not reduced from the level it had reached under Whitlam. As the only minister to retain an extensive staff, he enjoyed an even greater measure of policy dominance over his colleagues than had Whitlam. It was a resource that suited Fraser's intensely task-oriented, controlling administrative style.[132] Nonetheless, the office was initially set up in a conventional manner: at first there was no attempt to make the office a policy dynamo as had been attempted under Whitlam. Fraser worked closely with PM&C on policy and coordination. Indeed, in 1979, following a less than successful attempt (urged by the Liberal Party secretariat) to make the PMO more politically attuned, a career public servant was appointed to the position of chief executive: bureaucratic dominance was briefly restored.

It was not to last. Dissatisfied with the lack of political support provided by his office during the 1980 election campaign, Fraser turned again to the staff who had helped him win power. David Kemp, an academic who had served Fraser as a senior adviser in 1975–76, was brought back to head the office. Key staff were paid on a consultancy basis, with the intention that bringing their salary to near equivalence with permanent heads would signal their importance and status. The director of the PMO was now the apex of the whole ministerial staff structure, the point of direction and coordination. The PMO was the strategic hub where the flow of information from both party and public service came together, and Fraser ensured that it had the personnel and facilities to take advantage of this. By 1981, Fraser's PMO exceeded that of Whitlam numerically (twenty-three compared with twenty-one in 1974) and its senior officers were paid substantially more.[133] The PMO was a body of senior status and impressive credentials. The intention was not to compete with the APS in developing policy but to widen debate and to bring political sensitivity to bear on what was being proposed. It was a refinement of what Whitlam and Wilenski had aimed at, and now with the resources to make a difference. It was a decided extension to the prime minister's directive and controlling capacities.

Enhancement of the PMO was not intended to be at the cost of the APS. Fraser 'was himself an exponent of the Westminster system and worked by it', said Ed Visbord.[134] 'He believed in that system', affirmed John Rose, 'but he also believed in having these external, independent voices ... but he didn't want to have a political combat about it'.[135] Staff were accordingly instructed to work smoothly with their APS counterparts. For the most part they did: 'generally, the department and the office were as one and very strongly influenced each other ... we'd show each other papers ... What Rose advised to Fraser we knew and what we advised of course he knew', says Mike Keating (then in PM&C).[136] When tension arose, it was not primarily because of conflict between private office advisers and APS officials but usually for other reasons. One was Fraser's willingness to argue with and interrogate APS advisers as forcefully as he would his ministers. Another was his propensity directly to contact APS officials he deemed most appropriate for particular queries (at any time of day or night) without reference to their seniors. Above all, it was his use of PM&C to challenge or finesse departmental proposals about which he had questions. This last was the most significant, and it was a capacity former prime ministers had lacked.

The transition from Gorton's use of Hewitt to assure prime-ministerial direction of PM&C to the Whitlam, Wilenski and Menadue enterprise of giving it a policy capacity provided the foundation for Fraser's next step. When Fraser took office, Menadue was retained as secretary of PM&C. Fraser, according to Menadue, was not interested in the party affiliation of his APS advisers: 'People were more likely to be judged on their ability and honesty than on what side of the political tracks they came from'. Thus, 'Under Fraser, I continued to build up further the activist role of the department that I had started with Whitlam. It was necessary to be able to respond to Fraser's wide-ranging interests and energy'.[137]

After nearly a year, Menadue was offered an ambassadorial posting and Alan Carmody succeeded him as secretary of PM&C. Carmody, a 'can-do' man whose proclivities had been honed in McEwen's Department of Trade, was an activist attuned to the interests of the prime minister. He began a recalibration even more extensive than Menadue had envisaged. He was, said one of his senior officers,

> almost like a chairman of directors on a board but he wanted the board to be ... a full complement of people who knew what they were on about

> and who could do things … We ended up, after his re-organisation, having … more senior level people. We had, for example, division heads and special advisors at division head level as well.[138]

In 1977, there were eight divisions whose general descriptions covered nearly every facet of government operations and policy.[139] There would be some refinement and changes of name later in Fraser's term and thereafter,[140] but it was a pattern that has largely persisted since. It was intended that these divisions should give the prime minister reach across the whole of government. Fraser remarked that 'Carmody wanted to make sure that the department serviced the PM even better than the PM wanted'.[141] Patrick Weller observed that Carmody inculcated a much more active approach, with a decisive impact on the culture of PM&C.[142] One of his officers thought that 'Carmody basically saw himself … as the prime minister's alter ego. "I run this side of the House, he runs the Parliament"'.[143]

Carmody died suddenly in 1978, and deputy secretary Geoff Yeend was appointed secretary. Yeend (like Whitlam) had grown up in Canberra. He joined the public service in the 1940s and served in the hothouse for postwar mandarins, the Department of Post War Reconstruction, and then the PMD (as assistant to Allen Brown) in 1949. He had worked as private secretary to Menzies in 1954, and later as deputy secretary under Bunting. Few were better versed in the department's history or the ways of prime ministers. Calm under pressure, he was known as Mr Cool, and according to Menadue had 'a good political and policy touch' and was 'very professional and trustworthy'.[144] It was Yeend who had the capacity to recruit and encourage an effective team, bringing the final refinements to the sort of infrastructure Gorton, Whitlam and Fraser had wanted. Fraser at last had the support he sought and the means to monitor, question and intercede, if he chose, in every area of government. From being a department concerned with process, PM&C had become a policy powerhouse to which bright and ambitious public servants were attracted. It was also an incubator for future departmental secretaries, 'a place to learn the political demands of cabinet and ministers as a collectivity'.[145] The structure developed sequentially by Menadue, Carmody and Yeend remained intact for the next thirty years.

Getting the dynamics of cabinet, Coalition, party and infrastructural support right was essential to refining prime-ministerial government, but one further factor was a source of anxiety for Fraser. Fearless in battle with individuals, or the opposition, or an identifiable interest, when it came to the electorate he was much more cautious. Getting his message out, being understood, was of signal importance. Fraser was acutely conscious of electorate impressions and aware of the significance of media management. While Labor's 1972 'It's Time' campaign was 'a promotional vehicle for Whitlam',[146] the decisions had been made by Mick Young on the advice of the party's advertising agency. In 1973, contemplating his prospects, Fraser took the initiative himself, approaching John Royce Public Relations with a brief to boost his image. The agent assigned to his case, Alister Drysdale, invited journalists down to the prime minister's farm, encouraged stories about family life and hobbies, persuaded Fraser to generate stories by going out into the community and workplaces, and incrementally softened and humanised impressions. Drysdale showed the value of marketing experience when he defused a Labor attack advertisement. He began to advise on the drafting of speeches and media releases. Drysdale would go on to work as Fraser's press secretary in the PMO.[147]

From 1975, Tony Eggleton, party director and national campaign manager, dealt with the advertising agencies that produced the memorable 'Turn on the Lights' and 'Memories' campaigns in 1975 and 1977 (as well as the less compelling 'Wealth Tax' and 'Labor's Hit List' ads in 1980 and 1983). Since Eggleton interacted with him on a daily basis and, at his insistence, travelled with him during campaigns, Fraser was involved with every aspect of communication strategy.[148] In office, Fraser adopted news release practices characteristic of US election campaigning—arguably the forerunner of what is today virtually a 'permanent campaign'. He commented directly to television and released transcripts, encouraging the practice of monitoring and transcription that is now the fodder for the general media. He maintained press conferences but extended the use of doorstop opportunities (where he could say what he wanted without being questioned). The incorporation of press secretaries or of media-savvy advisers was a feature of the expanded ministerial offices introduced by the Whitlam government. Its drawback had been to allow the dispersed dissemination of information, sometimes from capricious ministers. Fraser ended this: the GIU suggested by Eggleton ensured control over information, since it was both the conduit for what the government wanted to say and an impediment to direct ministerial access.[149] Fraser's capacity to dominate the flow of policy information, deliberation, decision-making and communication of intentions and outcomes was now unrivalled by any predecessor, the structures now established a gift to those who would follow.

Whitlam and Fraser: Changing the Game

Whitlam and Fraser—strong personalities with big ambitions, neither of whom reached the heights at which they aimed—were undermined by historical contingencies. Whitlam's unusually detailed development of a program for government was limited by international economic disruption (later deemed the beginning of globalisation) that constrained *any* government's ability to achieve what he planned. Fraser's efforts to restore proper processes and economic responsibility in the face of that same transition were neither decisive enough nor fully attuned to the irreversible change and new currents of thinking sweeping the world.

Both were in some respect looking back rather than to the world as it now was. In Whitlam's case it was to how the social democratic agenda of Curtin and Chifley might be extended and renovated to address contemporary problems, in Fraser's to the restoration of managed prosperity that had prevailed prior to the rude interruption of Coalition rule in 1972. There was a disjunction between their aspirations and the times in which they had to operate.[150] The policy regime to which they were accustomed and 'the great assumption' that they took for granted was exhausted. For Labor, Whitlam became the model of how not to govern. For the Liberals, Fraser was the epitome of lost opportunity. He was said to be 'the last prime minister before the age of globalisation forced Australia to break from its introspective economic past'.[151]

Such arguments are persuasive to a degree, but they fail to capture the nuance needed to account for the enduring influence of these two prime ministers, both on the social world and—more specifically—on the office of prime minister. To flip the argument, only by trying to see them *through* context can we grasp the nature of their achievement, to understand where contingencies disrupted their plans, and where outcomes of lasting significance were realised.

They were indeed caught in difficulties that were none of their making, and committed to projects that seem in retrospect ill-suited to their circumstances. It may already have been thought by some that the Keynesian model was failing (some in Treasury were arguing for a return to Alfred Marshall and neoclassical economics in 1971). But no-one quite agreed about why. Fraser was introduced to the works of Friedrich Hayek and Milton Friedman and met both, but the free market push in his party room kicked off only in 1981.[152] A more radical market orientation might have been filtering through, but Whitlam and Fraser were not alone in being wary of its prescriptions. In 1980, US president Ronald Reagan, one of the presumptive apostles of the revolution, was running enormous deficits in America. In the United Kingdom, Margaret Thatcher gained prime-ministerial office in 1979, but it would be 1981 before her budget indicated the nature of her intentions and several more years before the full extent of her reform agenda became apparent.[153] Even the word 'globalisation' was not in common use until the mid-1980s.[154]

Thus, what *we* take for granted, the conceptual characterisation of what was happening, was not articulated until after Fraser left the scene. The new regime does not arrive fully formed, nor do orthodoxies collapse in a moment: it is a more fragmentary and incremental process than that. Whitlam and Fraser must be seen, as it were, as in the midst of this turmoil.

They were not about to sacrifice core convictions: Whitlam's belief in the transformative capacity of government; Fraser's persuasion that 'the people who are at the extreme on free markets don't really believe in social policy'.[155] But nor were they oblivious to the need to revise the orthodoxies of their time. Whitlam's dramatic reduction of tariff protection in 1973 (opposed by Treasury), his attempt to compel a more rigorous budget in 1974 (defeated at that time by cabinet and Caucus), and the final Hayden budget of 1975 were all indicative of reforms to come. Fraser's introduction of a managed exchange rate (bitterly opposed by Treasury) was the precursor for one of the celebrated reforms of the Hawke–Keating era: the floating of the dollar. And he alone reframed the narrative of government as being centrally about economic management.

Their legacies were as much about personality and style as about the contingencies that hobbled them. Whitlam's case is unusual: profoundly optimistic, inspirational and an enormously comprehensive programmatic thinker, he set out to 'plan for the ages, not just for this life',[156] but he lacked the patience for cabinet discipline or Caucus management and the administrative and people skills for routine governance. Much could have been handled better, and perhaps have gone further, given a disciplined cabinet and an effective team, even in the context of an ambitious program running up against a deteriorating economy. It is fitting, however, to have looked closely at his long preparation for government because, despite all, 'the program' was the genesis of an enduring legacy.

The principles Whitlam's government established through reforms relating to human rights, health insurance, independent foreign policy, environment, heritage, electoral reform, multiculturalism, school and university funding, equal pay, land rights and family law, for example, in some cases have become the bipartisan consensus, and in others may have been developed and modified, but never abandoned or forgotten. Even the great experiments that were shut down (like DURD) had significant outcomes (the cities were sewered). Many books have been produced by scholars, activists and politicians revisiting the Whitlam years:[157] when it comes to debate about foundational issues of social reform and active government Whitlam's administration remains the test-bed of possibilities.

Fraser was quite the obverse. His plan was not about a new world—he was, according to Menadue, underprepared for government[158]—but about proper process and rigorous administration. He would address the chaos left by Whitlam, defend against a threatening world and restore the economy. By no means an optimist, dogged rather than inspirational, preoccupied with establishing authority to govern from strength, committed to a philosophy rather than a social vision, and task-oriented to a fault, he would ensure order was maintained through micro management. Drawing cabinet in through extensive consultation, imposing discipline on the party room through presenting the 'collective' decision, and keeping the organisation close and communication controlled enabled him to govern for nearly eight years in uncertain times. They were all the capacities Whitlam had neglected.

Between 1975 and 1981, Fraser might credibly have claimed to have delivered on his promise of responsible economic management. The collapse of 1982–83 challenged the legitimacy of that narrative. It would be the catalyst for trenchant criticism from his own party. Fraser's greatest achievements were, as even critics acknowledged, in social domains.[159] Many were aligned to the unfinished business of the Whitlam years. Whitlam introduced human rights legislation; Fraser established the Human Rights Commission. Whitlam and his immigration minister, Al Grassby, were credited with the advent of multiculturalism. Fraser and adviser Petro Georgiou created the Special Broadcasting Service and established the Australian Institute of Multicultural Affairs (later transferred to a branch of PM&C). Where the Whitlam government had a niggardly migration program, Fraser's immigration reforms provided for non-discriminatory services and the largely successful settlement of large numbers of Indochinese refugees (on a per capita basis, the most generous of any Western country). Fraser regarded these as 'my proudest achievements'.[160]

While Menzies, Holt and Gorton had recognised, and begun to adapt to, the emergence of television as the dominant communication medium for political purposes, under Whitlam and Fraser there was a transformation in its use, and in the relationship of the prime minister with the electorate. While party loyalty was then still significant in voter support, leader images began incrementally to gain ground in 'selling' the party message. The 'It's Time' campaign, a national, coordinated marketing campaign promoting Whitlam himself, was the breakthrough. It was the most striking instance, to that time, of what would become commonplace in later years: the prime minister standing in for the party. Fraser had personally resorted to PR advisers in his bid for power. He accepted the attention that must now be devoted to a leadership image. Moreover, he would be integrally engaged with communication strategy during campaigns, with central control of everyday communication through the GIU and with pioneering American media strategy in Australia.

One of the most profound legacies of the Whitlam and Fraser years was their extension of prime-ministerial capacity and elevation of the prime minister's role. It was a result of their interpretation of pragmatic imperatives rather than empire building. Yet the outcome was a pronounced refinement of prime-ministerial government. In renovating the advisory and departmental infrastructure for their purposes, the great antagonists of the 1970s succeeded in changing the game for every prime minister that followed.

Whitlam, having built up advisory networks in developing his program, wanted to carry them into government with him. Those who worked with him at first intended the PMO to supply the drive and coordination for program implementation. This proving insufficient, attention turned to strengthening PM&C itself. Thus began a significant transformation of the resources available to the government, especially the prime minister. Fraser seized on these elements, building up an influential PMO and working to turn PM&C into a policy powerhouse. His distinctive emphases on control and process brought administrative order to the initiatives commenced by Whitlam. It enabled a reach across government available to no previous prime minister, command of information available to no-one else, the generation of alternative sources of advice, and a means of dominating cabinet and contending with recalcitrant departments—as Fraser's orchestration of interaction between his advisers, PM&C and other departments (especially Treasury) demonstrated.

The new duopoly of advice particular to the prime minister was always intended to work cooperatively, and for the most part did so. It would not always be the case in the future, but in the 1980s—under the Hawke and Keating governments—the cooperative interaction between the PMO and PM&C, deploying and strengthening the resources created by Whitlam and Fraser, would impel policy innovation. There was limited resort to prime-ministerial government. Bob Hawke's capacity to orchestrate dispersed leadership though the most talented cabinet since World War II, and above all his partnership with Paul Keating, were the foundations for transformational reform.

4

AGENTS OF CHANGE: BOB HAWKE AND PAUL KEATING

> Hawke and Keating individually were outstanding, but they were best as a team. While it is not easy to make comparisons, there are—at least in my mind—only two great partnerships in Labor history. One is Chifley and Curtin and the other is Hawke and Keating. Together and individually they shaped and sculpted the policy mix … and in doing so helped forge a different and better nation.[1]

As SECRETARY OF the Australian Council of Trade Unions (ACTU) throughout the prime ministerships of Bob Hawke and Paul Keating, and an intimate collaborator in their governing project, Bill Kelty's assessment of their place in the Labor leadership pantheon is not an impartial one. Nevertheless, the historical parallel he draws between their partnership and that of John Curtin and Ben Chifley has a compelling force. Following the eventful, traumatic Whitlam intermezzo, the governments led by Hawke (March 1983 – December 1991) and Keating (December 1991 – March 1996) finally managed to restore Labor's credentials as a party fit to govern.[2] Together they won and retained office at five consecutive elections, in doing so surpassing the Curtin–Chifley record to deliver an unprecedented run of success for Labor. Moreover, like their mid-twentieth-century predecessors, Hawke and Keating's partnership was not merely momentous for Labor but shaped the long-term policy direction of the nation. In office they pursued a plethora of economic, institutional, social and foreign policy reforms in what amounted to a thirteen-year experiment in event-making leadership.[3]

If Hawke and Keating constituted the second great leadership tandem of the Australian Commonwealth, theirs was a more tempestuous relationship than that of Curtin and Chifley. The latter were men of modest sensibility and enjoyed a mutual respect and affection that all but precluded rivalry or jealousy between them. There was no scrambling over one another for the crown—Chifley was devastated by Curtin's death in office that paved the way for him to inherit the prime ministership. That both men died early also ensured that there would be no retrospective tussle between them over how they ought to be remembered by posterity. Instead, their kinship is the stuff of folklore as embodied in their immortalisation as political brothers in arms in a striking statue in the nation's capital. By way of contrast, the Hawke and Keating partnership entailed an accommodation of titanic egos. Though blessed with complementary talents, theirs was a partnership of creative tension and competitive in spirit. And while still in government, their relationship soured into open conflict, with Keating eventually tearing down Hawke to claim his opportunity as prime minister. Out of office, their record of collaboration has been sullied as well by sporadic bickering over ownership of their reform legacy. Keating, in particular, has seemed to feel a burning injustice at not being accorded sufficient recognition for Labor's achievements in office.[4]

Yet, as Kelty insists, there is little doubt that Hawke and Keating were 'best as a team' and were, for the most part, remarkably like-minded in their governing project. The reform legacy of their administrations was grounded in an ability to craft the necessary proposals, build political coalitions and obtain public support for a succession of sweeping changes. In deregulating the Australian economy, they committed a 'heretical act' for a Labor government.[5] Hawke and Keating drove a dramatic departure from the Keynesian economics embraced by the Curtin, Chifley and Whitlam Labor governments and the ameliorative liberalism Fraser was never quite prepared to abandon.[6] Such policy audacity required Hawke and Keating to persuade, seduce and sometimes stare down not just the opposing side of politics but their own party's traditionalists, of whom there were many. Continuing long after they both had lost office, Hawke and Keating were criticised for selling out to 'economic rationalists' in the bureaucracy, getting too cosy with 'big business' and 'hijacking' their party on a path that led away from its core values.[7] One critical observer judged that Hawke and Keating forged 'a political culture utterly divorced from Labor's traditional beliefs in class politics, government intervention, solidarity and egalitarianism'—a claim disputed by both men and many former members of the government.[8]

There were numerous tense confrontations along the road to reform during the Hawke and Keating years—not just in the form of political battles to effect proposed changes, but also because some of their policy changes produced unintended consequences. Throughout the Hawke–Keating era, proactive reform and reactive economic troubleshooting went hand in hand.[9] Time and again, Hawke and Keating were forced to make deep spending cuts, juggle electoral promises and disappoint Labor's core constituencies. The economy overheated in the second half of the 1980s. Its cooling could not be managed by a 'soft landing' through monetary policy adjustment but came in the form of a nasty recession in the early 1990s that drove up unemployment, undermined the government's fiscal position and devoured much of Keating's political capital by exposing the limit to his self-professed mastery of the national economy's levers.

Debates about the impact of this thirteen-year period of Labor governments will continue to be waged, but the subsequent fate of the Australian economy has lent considerable credence to Hawke and Keating's claims that their reforms 'set up' the country for the long period of growth and middle-class prosperity that was to follow.[10] Not all that was set in motion between 1983 and 1996 endured. The Howard Coalition government retained the neoliberal compass of economic policy and, eventually, continued on the path of more intense engagement with Asia that Hawke and Keating as prime ministers had both paved. But it showed less appetite for environmental conservation than Hawke had done, and it put the brakes on Keating's push for Indigenous reconciliation and an Australian republic.

The Hawke and Keating governments arguably represent a peak in the authority and efficacy of the Australian prime minister. By 1983, the office of prime minister was well institutionalised. Fraser had further strengthened the coordinating role of PM&C, a key lever of the office. Hawke and Keating strengthened the other key lever, the PMO. They staffed it with high-calibre public servants with a strong public policy orientation and experienced political operators alike. Particularly under Hawke, these two sources of prime-ministerial initiative and oversight worked well together. Neither dominated the other; the inevitable competition and tensions between them were, by and large, managed effectively.

A pivotal source of strength was the close partnership between prime minister and treasurer. A marriage of convenience at first, the Hawke–Keating compact was rooted in a shared appetite for economic modernisation, a willingness to take political risks in bringing it about and—for the most part—a keen understanding of their interdependency. Hawke brought personal popularity, deft chairmanship of cabinet and political cunning; Keating brought policy bravado, dominance in the party room and parliament, and a captive press gallery. Both understood and appreciated the complexity of institutional reform and were willing to listen to expert advice on how to go about it. They were at their most effective when working alongside one another, just as Curtin and Chifley had been.

Overall, the Hawke and Keating governments were led with vigour, astuteness and considerable courage. In fact, during the post-Howard discomfiture of the prime ministership and the growing laments about the 'end of the reform era', both Hawke and Keating—whose records in office had been regarded with ambivalence even by their own party for much of the preceding decade and a half—enjoyed rising esteem. Amid a yearning for a time when governments were less beholden to short-term, poll-driven politics and possessed clarity of purpose, and for leaders more willing and better able to persuade the community to embrace deep change, the Hawke–Keating years were held up as the benchmark that the contemporary political class was failing to reach.[11]

Bob Hawke: the Consensus Messiah

Before he became prime minister, Bob Hawke had been a magnetic presence on the public stage for a decade and a half. He was a quintessentially Australian trade unionist turned politician. The Hawke public persona was that of a sports-loving, hard-drinking, blokey and self-consciously vain alpha male. Yet he was also the exceptionally gifted child of an idealistic Congregationalist minister and a doting mother utterly convinced of her surviving son's greater purpose in life—his elder brother Neil died of meningitis at seventeen—who became a highly educated yet practical thinker and political operator par excellence. Combining a powerful need for achievement with a powerful need for affiliation, Hawke was a remarkably effective trader in hope who enjoyed as easy a rapport with rugged local punters at a country pub as he did with well-heeled corporate executives on the northern beaches of Sydney and a broad array of foreign leaders.

Hawke opened up his family life to an intrigued public to an unprecedented extent (echoing Joseph Lyons' pioneering but pre-television era effort).[12] On the wings of it, he became elected Victorian 'Father of the Year' (in 1971), notwithstanding his frequent and long absences from the family in service of his union work, his political career, his passion for sports and various extramarital pursuits. Cast into the public spotlight along with her husband, his wife Hazel turned into the most visible and admired wife of a prime minister since Enid Lyons (who unlike Hazel would later build an independent political career on that foundation).

Yet Hawke was also a consummate professional. Joining the ACTU as a research officer in 1957 and rapidly rising to the position of advocate, he assumed responsibility for presenting the unions' annual wage case before the national wages tribunal, the Conciliation and Arbitration Commission. He was a talented negotiator who was not only respected by the trade union side but also by the employers. Securing victories in some of the high-profile disputes of the era catapulted Hawke to the national stage. It provided him with a stepping stone for a political career. He first ran successfully for the presidency of the ACTU (in 1969), then for the presidency of the Australian Labor Party (in 1973). He managed to combine the two roles for seven turbulent years. Mobilising, advocating and mediating his way through, Hawke sought to forge common positions between the industrial and political wings of the Australian labour movement. He involved himself in all the major issues of the era, both within Australia and overseas: Vietnam War protests, the Whitlam government and its dismissal, the Middle East conflict, the economic impact of the oil shock and the labour movement's fight against Fraser's 'fight inflation first' policies.

By the late 1970s, Hawke was one of the best-known and most popular figures in public life. Once he finally made the move to parliament—it had been mooted, and thwarted, several times before—landing in the safe Victorian Labor seat of Wills in 1980, the messianic quality to his rhetoric about 'consensus' and 'reconciliation' contrasted sharply with the grave and divisive tones emanating from the Fraser government. Though his temperament and style proved not optimally suited to the tribal partisanship of the parliamentary arena, his public brand had become so strong that there was an element of inevitability to his rise to the Labor Party's leadership after only the briefest of apprenticeships. The party room, however, was ambivalent, with many Caucus members respecting the current opposition leader, Bill Hayden, who had replaced Whitlam in 1977 and had performed credibly in the 1980 election. They also resented Hawke's undisguised conviction that the leadership was his manifest destiny. Though Caucus knocked him back when he first challenged Hayden for the leadership in July 1982, as the Fraser government tied itself in knots over stagflation and became locked into paralysing battles with the unions, Hawke's bridge-building narrative of national consensus grew increasingly compelling. Most decisive, however, was his colleagues' growing acceptance, however reluctant, that his unique public popularity would provide the decisive ingredient for the party to return to government. A besieged Hayden finally bowed to the mounting pressure for him to step down in favour of Hawke just hours before Fraser called a snap election for March 1983 in an attempt to exploit the leadership struggle in the Labor Party.

The bloodless coup outfoxed Fraser, transfixed the public and saw an array of press gallery journalists scramble to get the authoritative account of Hawke's rise to power into the bookshops.[13] Not all captured the full significance of the occasion. For the first time in its history, the Labor Party elected a federal leader whose personality and public persona were the key sources of his authority rather than his standing with and loyalty to the party itself. The decision to install Hawke was to all intents and purposes an admission that he had an appeal that transcended the party and would ensure a desperately desired election victory. Indeed, at the 1983 election, Labor campaigned under the slogan 'Bob Hawke Bringing Australia Together'—note 'Bob Hawke', not 'Labor'.

The man in whom Labor set its store practised a politics of intimacy.[14] An overtly emotional man, Hawke shed public tears when faced with infuriating or tragic situations. His own emotional complexity 'always made him forgive and embrace every enemy in an attempt to assuage his own guilt [and] meant that he had access to the sacrament of confession without having to adopt the discipline of religion', observed long-time Hawke cabinet minister (and eventual co-architect of his downfall) Graham Richardson.[15] Hawke's temperament proved 'an enduring asset and an occasional cause of defective policy', according to finance minister Peter Walsh.[16]

There was a more complex character lurking underneath the self-assured crowd-pleaser who had tamed his demons and who 'continued throughout his prime ministership to believe in an almost mystical union between himself and the people'.[17] Strong empathy with the plight of constituents who were doing it tough coexisted with displays of 'profound egotism'.[18] Craving love, Hawke was also given to contemptuous disregard of criticism.[19] Steeped in the class war environment of 1960s trade unionism yet evangelically pursuing social consensus as the essence of his bid for government, Hawke, 'the patient negotiator, the accommodating chairman, the champion of consensus, the reconciler of conflict, could also be impetuous, headstrong … and pugnacious'.[20]

He was a master public communicator and yet an indifferent performer in parliament, regarding it 'with the kind of disdain that the self-made businessman has for an MBA course at a university'.[21] Rising to fame as a champion of the Australian workers' cause, he nevertheless was a staunch advocate of the alliance with the bulwark of capitalism—the United States—and as prime minister would spend considerable energy pursuing a role as peacemaker on distant shores.[22] Hawke had a sense of destiny about exercising leadership, and yet he struck his chief collaborator Keating—well before their relations soured—as one 'who doesn't know what he wants to do with the country, what he wants to do with his life, or where he wants to lead the Government'.[23]

Perhaps because of his conspicuous contradictions and fallibilities, Hawke not only captured the Australian public's attention, but a large portion of them also gave him their affection. His early biographer (and lover and, much later, second wife) Blanche d'Alpuget detailed his protracted struggles with alcohol, the ugly excess to which he was given when inebriated, and the family tensions, told side by side with gripping accounts of heroic (if not always successful) feats of political passion, courage, commitment and resourcefulness, acted out on stages ranging from Melbourne to Jerusalem. Hawke's larger-than-life public persona and his self-proclaimed—and much vaunted—'love affair with the Australian people' struck a powerful chord, making him appear refreshingly different from the aloof Fraser. It elicited reservoirs of public goodwill, forgiveness when he erred, and empathy when he suffered. The latter was most notable when in August 1984 as prime minister he broke down publicly (and was effectively deflated as leader for a significant period of time) upon learning that one of his daughters, herself a young mother of an infant, was in the throes of a punishing heroin addiction.

The last typical 'Aussie bloke' to become prime minister—fondly nicknamed 'Hawkie', likened to 'Hoges in a pinstripe' in Canberra (referring to the ocker persona of comedian Paul Hogan)[24]—Hawke in many ways was an improved version of Gorton, an earlier 'larrikin PM'.[25] Where Gorton proved fundamentally unprepared for the job that had landed in his lap by accident, Hawke had the prime ministership in his sights from a very early age and had pursued it with singular determination. When his great objective came closer to attainment, self-will enabled him to transform himself from an articulate, yet heavy-drinking working man's advocate into a disciplined and teetotal leader of the nation. Where Gorton proved erratic in his administrative practices, Hawke was methodical. Where Gorton turned out to be a solo flyer, Hawke proved a highly adept team builder. Where Gorton antagonised colleagues, Hawke mostly charmed them, and only confronted and pressured them when needed. Loving the cameras and appreciating their power in making and breaking political leadership aspirants, Hawke trumped Gorton—who had demonstrated an early affinity for communicating through the medium of television—to become the first fully accomplished Australian politician of the modern media era.[26]

Personal popularity thus formed a key source of Hawke's leadership capital. Viewed with the hindsight of Labor's unprecedented electoral success, it is easy to forget that in the course of the second half of the 1980s, that asset was put at risk amid the increasingly heated debates about the 'neoliberal' economic reform agenda Hawke was seen to be unleashing on an unsuspecting party and country. Many in middle Australia struggled to keep up with the depth and pace of the changes crafted by Hawke and Keating, in particular the greater level of uncertainty about their incomes, mortgages and indeed their jobs that was associated with these reforms.[27] Hawke's ostentatious socialising with the rich and famous and his friendship with big-end-of-town business figures normally associated with the anti-Labor side of politics, such as transport magnate Sir Peter Abeles, bred resentment among Labor supporters who were struggling to adjust to the market-driven realities. Many felt Hawke had become aloof from the party and the real-life experience of the working class it represented: it was being transformed into a vehicle for his self-aggrandisement. As one Victorian branch secretary complained to national secretary Bob McMullan:

> The A.L.P. is our party [and] no one member is above it, we are not happy with Bob Hawkes [sic] domination of it, if elected members are not strong enough then rank and file will have to look more closely at preselection. Bob Hawke never mentions the A.L.P. but my party, my government.[28]

These concerns intensified as the years wore on. In the last election Hawke fought as prime minister in early 1990, against a background of interest rates at dizzying heights and portents of an impending recession, Labor scraped back into office on second preferences. The collapse of its primary vote below 40 per cent was a harbinger of a sustained decline in the party's base constituency. Thus it was not until the memories of the traumas of economic transition, the shocks and the resentments (particularly among Labor heartland voters) of the 1980s and early 1990s had dissipated and the long-term dividends of their reform program became clearer that the more recent narrative of Hawke and Keating as heroic change agents could fully flower. And by 2010, respect for Hawke's performance as prime minister had rebounded to such an extent that in a comparative rating exercise conducted among historians, political scientists and journalists, he came second only to his lifelong hero John Curtin at the top rank of Australia's national leaders.[29]

An Era of Reform

When the Hawke government took office, Australia was falling behind in the global economy. It suffered from a large and deepening current account deficit; steady decline in the terms of trade; rising foreign debt; double-digit unemployment as well as double-digit inflation; and a falling exchange rate relative to other nations.[30] Speculators and competitors were seeking to exploit these weaknesses. If Australia was not to slide any further, the policy stalemate that had paralysed Fraser's attempt to tackle these issues had to be overcome. Hawke accordingly staked the early years of his government on forging a breakthrough in the way Australia was managing its stagflation-ridden economy. The first manifestation of that effort was the National Economic Summit, conducted at Parliament House in televised proceedings, where his gospel of consensus was enacted in a tripartite setting of business, union and government elites. It was Hawke's first appearance in parliament as prime minister: speaking not to the elected representatives of the people but presiding over a gathering of hand-picked economic and social elites.[31] There was much scepticism, not least among the invitees, about the idea. But Hawke's ability to enthuse the participants about making a fresh start, burying old hatchets and transcending the trench politics of class, proved infectious. The summit yielded a sense of optimism and possibility, a psychological mood shift that soon began to filter into the 'real' economy.

The summit vindicated Hawke's belief in the power of corporatist-style forms of consultation that had been pioneered but not always sustained by Curtin, Chifley and Whitlam.[32] As Keating adviser Don Russell recalls:

> When Hawke and Keating were elected in 1983, Australia had lived through two quite awful wage shocks ... where because of the centralised wage fixing system and the arbitration process it meant that once the economy starts growing and you got a wage increase somewhere as a result of growing demand for labour, the system was so tightly regulated that it just pumped that wage rise through. And so ... there is almost consensus that Australia is deeply flawed, trapped in low growth. But they come to office with the [Prices and Incomes] Accord, which was very much a Hawke device. Keating very quickly sees it as a plus, mainly because of the relationship he developed with Bill Kelty and the rest of the ACTU.[33]

In the years to come, there would be more summits, more councils, more broad-based consultation mechanisms across a range of sectors and issues—with predominantly positive effects in breaking policy deadlocks and the relational climate between labour and capital away from the mutual vilification of the Fraser era.[34] The Accord process between the government and the ACTU tied the unions to policies of wage moderation, fiscal restraint, tariff reduction and market-based reforms that were to follow in the next thirteen years, providing them with job growth, tax breaks, a social wage, improved education and training, and a robust social safety net in return.[35] The business sector, though not an active partner in the Accord, was a prime beneficiary of the arrangement.

The summit was not the only significant event early in the life of the Hawke government. The momentous decision to abandon the fixed exchange rate of the Australian dollar (and to remove most exchange controls) was endorsed at a meeting of the cabinet economic policy committee on the afternoon of 9 December 1983.[36] It rubberstamped the resolution of a hastily convened meeting earlier that morning chaired by Hawke and attended by Keating, key advisers from both their offices, and senior officials from the Reserve Bank, Treasury and PM&C, which itself had been preceded by a flurry of meetings and urgent conversations over the previous twenty-four hours. In turn, a float of the dollar had been the subject of fitful discussion within the government, Reserve Bank and Treasury for several months. The final scramble to take the decision had been triggered by a large inflow of foreign currency in the preceding week and alarming reports of another impending massive inflow (in total, some $3 billion). Market sentiment was that the dollar was undervalued and currency traders were anticipating an appreciation. These episodes of speculators directing their money to Australia, betting on exchange rate decisions of the Reserve Bank to reap windfall profits, were becoming endemic. They caused major difficulties for authorities in managing the money supply and setting the exchange rate. Moreover, with appreciations of the currency having to be made in response to the capital inflows, the dollar was consistently overvalued, making Australian exports uncompetitive and putting upward pressure on inflation. It all contributed to a sense that a drastic policy change was necessary.

Earlier, during the first days of the Hawke government, a spectacular 10 per cent devaluation had been put into effect to stop massive capital outflows that had been triggered at least in part by Fraser's campaign rhetoric evoking the imagery (and memory) of Labor mismanagement of the economy. The spectre of the Whitlam government's economic malaise haunted Hawke, treasurer Keating and other key government ministers. They were resolved to be conscientious stewards of the national economy, no matter what. As Hawke later wrote:

> The Whitlam Government did many good things but its strengths were not economic. I was determined that the Hawke Labor Government would distinguish itself as a better economic manager in that respect over our Opposition. I intended to turn the Government's performance as an economic manager into an asset rather than a liability.[37]

Convinced that opening up the economy was inevitable, Hawke's PMO advisers as well as those within PM&C were advocating the idea of structural currency reform from the start. Hawke accepted their advice and became a supporter of a float. Keating, still finding his way in the portfolio, faced strenuous opposition to a float within his department, in particular from its powerful secretary, John Stone. The leadership of the Reserve Bank, on the other hand, strongly favoured the idea. By way of compromise in late October 1983, the decision was made to float the forward rate (the exchange rate today for settlement later) but to keep the spot rate (the exchange rate at the present time) under government control. The December crisis provided the last push for a full float.

In the years after the decision, the float would emerge as a key battleground in the legacy wars waged between Hawke and Keating as they feuded over which of them should be regarded as the reform's principal architect. Keating's biographer Troy Bramston argues, however, that 'both deserve the credit … Hawke and Keating could not have taken this momentous step without each supporting it'.[38] Yet historian Frank Bongiorno has made the more salient point about the nature of the decision-making behind the float: '[it was] the ultimate top-down kind of reform that became synonymous with the Hawke government … it is both striking and symbolically powerful that most of cabinet and all of caucus were excluded from considering an issue that would matter so much for the nation's future'.[39]

One consequence of the float was that Stone saw the writing on the wall and left the public service. His departure paved the way for new cadres in Treasury who were to work closely with Keating throughout much of the thirteen years of the Labor government. This was no coincidence. In a break with tradition, Keating had quickly decided that he wanted a close partnership with Treasury, but he was also confident he could prove the intellectual equal of its officers, and said, 'I did understand one thing—power': he would make it work for him.[40]

In the meantime, with the floating of the dollar, Australia was now firmly locked into the international financial system. The ramifications were enormous. It was a '"make or break" decision, taken without reference to the party. Once the currency was floating the bulwark against full financial deregulation sustained an irreparable breach'.[41] The float set the stage for a raft of market-oriented economic reforms that generated intense controversy and whose impact was as much psychological as it was economic. First, backed by the outcome of a review of the proposals of the 1981 Campbell inquiry into the financial system—the recommendations of which had proved so vexing for the Fraser government—Keating announced in early 1984 that sixteen foreign banks would be licensed to operate in Australia. The announcement was anathema to the Labor faithful who had been nursed on resentment of the private banks (the so-called 'money power'): a resentment going back to the fiasco of Chifley's attempt to nationalise the trading banks and long before. It set the stage for a showdown at the party's July national conference. If the approval of entry of foreign banks was settled on factional lines, Keating nonetheless put in a virtuoso performance in selling the policy to delegates. 'He was charming, he was humorous, he was absolutely devastating and derisory of anyone that argued against him', recalled a member of the government.[42] The conference delegates also endorsed the floating of the dollar and interest rate deregulation. The NSW Labor premier and national president of the party, Neville Wran, marvelled at Hawke and Keating's audacious achievement, comparing it to 'stealing the holy water from the church'.[43]

In July 1985, another economic summit took place, paving the way for significant reform of the tax system. Keating's proposals included a broad-based consumption tax—a form of taxation the ALP had always regarded as 'regressive' and therefore undesirable. It was only put to the summit after lengthy and heated cabinet discussions, and it proved a step too far. Facing strenuous opposition from business as well as the unions, Hawke the realpolitiker cut his zealous treasurer loose and did a backroom deal with the unions. He dropped the consumption tax and settled for a politically less ambitious reform package.[44]

Still, the Hawke–Keating tandem kept the reforms coming. Most of the time, they could count on the support of ACTU leader Bill Kelty. The close partnership and personal friendship that developed between Kelty and Keating in particular were pivotal in turning the Accord into a powerful and longstanding pact between the government and the Labor Party's most important constituency. The Hawke/Keating governments implemented sharp tariff reductions to expose Australian business to global competitive pressures. They also moved into so-called 'micro-economic' reforms—changing competition laws, privatising public enterprises and breaking down their monopolies. The government mostly got its way with assets sales (in airlines, banking and telecommunications), but not without causing convulsions at party national conferences in 1988 and 1990. Finally, Keating as prime minister even managed to convince the ACTU and Labor to let go of the centralised wage-setting and arbitration system; it was superseded by enterprise bargaining.[45]

Hawke and Keating's appetite for economic reform was in no small measure driven by fear that Australia was falling behind internationally, a sentiment shared by other ministers with access to information about the economic realities.[46] They accepted that in a rapidly globalising economy, Australia's prosperity would come to depend on its competitiveness, its agility and capacity for innovation. By harnessing market forces, Hawke and Keating hoped to generate the kind of tax revenue that would be required to fund Labor's traditional commitments to social justice. The fundamental challenge to their governments, however, was not the underwriting of trade protection, centralised economic management and comprehensive welfare provision, but to lead the country's adaptation to a globalising, deregulated economy. In effect, they 'not only engineered a political and economic transformation, but also a reformation of Australians' perceptions of vulnerability'.[47]

In its later years, the Hawke government made another significant policy departure: it began to value preservation of the environment. In a number of instances, it was prepared to sacrifice blue-collar jobs to preserve forests and habitats. The 'greening' of the Labor government was most notable in Hawke's third term. The NSW right's factional powerbroker, Graham Richardson, 'Hawke's political troubleshooter',[48] acted as an unlikely but energetic ministerial advocate for the environment, partly out of conviction but also driven by strategic electoral considerations (it gained Labor increasingly important preferences from urban post-materialist voters). Preserving trees at the cost of jobs was distinctly unpopular among the ALP's traditional constituencies. There was significant conflict and acrimony within cabinet, Caucus and the party about it, but on most occasions Richardson obtained Hawke's and Keating's support and prevailed.[49]

The Astute Chairman

Hawke's key lever for wielding his power as prime minister—apart from his election-winning popularity—was first and foremost managerial. He was a highly effective chair, a smart organiser, and a confident delegator who was clever enough not to allow his supreme sense of self-regard to stand in the way of harnessing the drive and capabilities of his cabinet colleagues. Hawke's role model as prime minister was John Curtin, whose emotionality he could relate to and whose self-control, practical wisdom and political astuteness he admired.[50] He operated as the spider in a carefully constructed web of core executive arrangements; his 'imprimatur, or at least his acquiescence, was necessary for every major act of government'.[51]

Hawke combined a presidential style of structuring processes and chairing meetings with a genuine belief in fair and due process. He rarely exerted his will or dominated debate, instead creating the space for the highly talented frontbench, advisers and senior bureaucrats to argue their case.[52] He encouraged robust debate when it really mattered, in cabinet but certainly also among his inner circle.[53] He had a methodical approach to paperwork, consulted widely, was generally easily available to ministers, and respected cabinet government.[54]

In performing the managerial component of the prime-ministerial role, Hawke possessed considerable reserves of what today is called emotional intelligence. This helped to smooth feathers that otherwise would be ruffled and genuinely won over people:

> [He] gave every person he dealt with a sense of having acquired a special relationship with him or having obtained a special insight into him. This was as true for Cabinet ministers and foreign leaders as it was for those who drove his car, typed his letters, protected his security … Like a Chinese puzzle, Hawke's inner sanctums contained smaller and more

> select compartments; but he had the skill and the inexhaustible energy and natural charm to make most people feel they had at least glimpsed the doors and, sometimes, to have entered one of the compartments.[55]

Hawke came into office committed to continue along Fraser's path of strengthening the prime minister's institutional resources. He demanded public service responsiveness to the views of the government. At the same time, he knew better than to become captive to an inner circle filled with partisan loyalists. Upon coming to office, a Ministerial Staff Advisory Panel was established to centralise and regularise the formerly ad-hoc process of selecting ministerial staff—all appointments were subject to the prime minister's approval.[56] The government subsequently passed legislation in 1984 that formalised these arrangements and afforded greater clarity to the employment status of staffers (including for public servants seconded to ministerial offices). The legislation has been described as a 'crucial step in legitimising partisan advisers within the political system and provided a mandate for ministerial staff to take an explicit role in policy-making and political control'.[57] In other words, it was an important development in further embedding ministerial private offices in the machinery of government and in the institutionalising of competition in the provision of advice.

Hawke had an overweening ego but intuitively understood that it had to be checked. His PMO was anything but an echo chamber of its boss' views. Hawke's office was relatively small by contemporary standards. It comprised no more than seventeen staff—around one-third of the size of Julia Gillard's PMO.[58] It was a successful hybrid of imported public service and academic brainpower, and no-nonsense political operators drawn from unions and the Labor Party, such as Bob Hogg and Peter Barron. Hawke insisted it should always be led by a public servant, not a political appointee. Hawke's chief of staff (1988–90), Sandy Hollway, who had come from PM&C, recalls Hawke was emphatic on this:

> His view was 'I want somebody who understands how the broader government out there works. I mean broader, the whole sort of technocratic managerial bloody arm of government. If I want politics, I'll go

> somewhere else but I want somebody who understands that and can link me into that as well as help me manage government effectively'.[59]

The Hawke office thus had the prime minister's ear but was never a solely political outfit. It was a triangular arrangement in which people with policy nous and understanding of government machinery worked alongside political advisers and media experts. It was not overbearing in how it engaged with the other parts of the government, yet it was uncompromising in keeping its boss sane. Graham Freudenberg, Whitlam's and Neville Wran's speechwriter, accepted a part-time appointment in Hawke's PMO. Coming on board, he recalled he

> often winced at the brutal frankness with which Peter Barron, Geoff Walsh, Bob Sorby or Bob Hogg [all political advisers] could bring Hawke down to earth … Hawke's principal private secretaries, Graham Evans, Chris Conybeare, Sandy Hollway and Denis Richardson, were more circumspect, in the older public service tradition, but not less firm in curbing his ebullience and sometimes his excesses. In an office never short of prima donnas, there was remarkable cohesion, concentration and direction.[60]

There was moreover a degree of stability of personnel. Except for influential economic adviser Ross Garnaut (who left in 1985 to become ambassador to China), the key staffers in the original PMO did not start leaving until three-and-a-half years in. By that time, their departures did little to diminish Hawke's capacity to manage the policymaking process—his growing experience in the job enabled him to master its responsibilities and workload comfortably.[61]

When taking office, Hawke had resolved to reduce the dominance in the policymaking process that PM&C had acquired under Fraser. Nevertheless, he remained keen to hear its views. Hawke used PM&C as a coordinating body facilitating the cabinet process, and as a resource to undertake specialist initiatives.[62] Notwithstanding the occasional tensions, Hawke's PMO generally worked well with the department and the wider public service. In fact, Hawke's office moved over time from being staffed mainly by political appointees to a point where most advisers were recruited from the career bureaucracy.[63] His first principal private secretary (chief of staff), Graham Evans, recalled that:

> [H]e expected me to make certain that all of the people, whether advisers, ministers or public servants, who needed to be able to put a point of view to him, got that opportunity... Hawke was perhaps unusual, too, in that he knew from the outset how he proposed to operate, and his approach was not unlike that of a company chairman.[64]

The sense of discipline, stability, consultation and fairness also pervaded Hawke's management of cabinet. In 1983, Hawke had to allocate portfolios across the unusually large talent pool—'the most formidable group that Labor had ever assembled for government'.[65] They were elected from a Caucus some of whom were still brooding over Hawke's coup against Hayden. Hawke, however, resisted the temptation to punish Hayden loyalists and allowed Hayden to take his own pick of portfolios (he chose foreign affairs). Breaking with Labor's tradition of having large and potentially unwieldy and fractious cabinets, he opted in 1983 for an inner cabinet of thirteen and outer ministry of fourteen. The Caucus elected the twenty-seven members, but the prerogative for choosing the cabinet members was given to the four parliamentary leaders and was exercised 'in practice principally by Hawke'.[66] The decision to create an inner cabinet was ratified by Caucus despite reservations from within the party's left. Hawke informed the media that the rationale for its creation was 'efficiency ... which is going to be the hallmark of the Government'.[67] Proving too compact—for example, initially, the finance minister was excluded—cabinet was incrementally increased to seventeen by Hawke's second term. At the same time, the personnel of both the cabinet and ministry as a whole remained largely unchanged during Labor's early years in office, providing another source of cohesion.[68]

In another departure from Labor's past practices, Hawke insisted on cabinet solidarity. There would be no tolerance of a minister backtracking when it came to defending collectively reached cabinet decisions in Caucus. Again, the experience of the Whitlam government provided Hawke with a cautionary lesson in what not to do:

> Whitlam presided over a Cabinet which was in a permanent shambles. It included the full ministry of twenty-seven and was far too big and unwieldy. Beyond that, the government was continuously rent by a lack of Cabinet solidarity. Unhappy with what the Cabinet decided, ministers raced off to the Caucus and unravelled Cabinet decisions. The making and unmaking of policy was conducted in the media with maximum bloodshed for the Government and the party.[69]

The two institutional changes that Hawke wrought were interconnected: 'by endorsing his proposal for a Cabinet of 13, caucus had given the Prime Minister a powerful weapon to enforce solidarity: exclusion from the Cabinet of any minister unwilling to accept solidarity on an issue'.[70] The sole left-aligned member of Hawke's first cabinet, Stewart West, tested Hawke's resolve on the matter when in November 1983 he refused to be bound by the decision to support uranium mining at Roxby Downs in South Australia. He was briskly demoted, and only reinstated five months later after committing unequivocally to cabinet solidarity. It was to be the only such breach for many years; they would only recur and become debilitating towards the latter stages of the government.[71]

Hawke effectively used key cabinet committees, which were smaller, less fragmented and more easily managed, to steer the main reform agenda and impose fiscal discipline on the ministry. The most notable among them was the ERC. Hawke and other ERC members, especially Keating, spent inordinate amounts of time working line by line through budget items and asking ministers to come in and argue their case. Cabinet discussions on the most controversial issues—tax and other economic reforms, environmental conflicts—could be protracted and heated, although Hawke and Keating nearly always prevailed. In addition, judicious use was made of carefully composed ad-hoc committees to deal with particularly thorny issues. Cabinet meetings then would serve more to formally endorse committee recommendations than to have full-fledged discussions about the underlying issues.[72] With the effectiveness of the committee structures becoming apparent to Hawke, the full ministry began to meet less frequently. This left some junior ministers, who felt they were on the outer, 'cranky and unsettled'.[73]

At the same time, Hawke did encourage ministers to take the initiative. At the first meeting of the ministry, Hawke stated: 'there are only two circumstances in which I will become involved in your portfolios. First, if you ask me, and second, if an issue arises that has whole-of-government implications'.[74] By and large, he stuck to this principle throughout his term. He did not dominate cabinet discussions as had Whitlam and Fraser.[75] Instead, he preferred to confer individually with each minister about the general priorities and direction of the portfolio and then allowed them wide latitude in designing and pursuing initiatives, backing them up in cabinet, Caucus and country when needed. In this vein, he worked closely with industry minister John Button on industrial restructuring, finance minister Peter Walsh on asset sales, and environment minister Graham Richardson in staring down vehement opposition—including from within the ministry—to pro-conservation decisions about Tasmanian rainforests and Kakadu National Park.[76]

Though cabinet deliberations could become strained when the stakes were high and consensus elusive, Hawke worked to preserve an atmosphere of collegiality. He was a relaxed chair, tolerating long disquisitions from passionate ministers, but ever astute in summing up the thrust of the debate in ways that suited his needs yet left no-one so unhappy as to object. He was not afraid of granting dissenting ministers the opportunity to state their views in cabinet, and could do so because he was effective in establishing and maintaining a good sense of morale and discipline.[77] If he had to let a minister down, he would strive to do so as gently as possible.[78] Notwithstanding his generally relaxed and chairman-like posture, when discussions became robust, Hawke could be an energetic contributor to the debate himself. Then attorney-general Gareth Evans recalls one instance in his diary entry for a January 1985 cabinet meeting:

> For example, re a Barry Jones [minister for science] proposal to appoint Peter Garrett [then an activist rock star] to the increasingly surreal Commission for the Future, Bob Hawke says, 'This must be the stupidest recommendation ever to come before this Government: it is a grotesque

> abuse of the intelligence of this Cabinet', to which Bill Hayden interjects: 'Don't be obscure Bob, tell us your real views'.[79]

During the 1983 election campaign, Hawke had been adamant that the government would be making public policy decisions, not the public service. Yet there was no shake-up of departmental heads on Labor assuming office. Even fairly vociferous conservatives within the bureaucracy, such as Treasury secretary John Stone, kept their jobs.[80] Hawke sought to ensure responsiveness through structural reforms instead. He encouraged finance minister John Dawkins to advance proposals that eventually ended up in the 1984 *Public Service Reform Act*, which according to contemporary observers entailed 'some of the most significant changes in the Australian Public Service since 1922'.[81] The legislation created the Senior Executive Service as a means to break down bureaucratic silo mentalities and increase the responsiveness of the upper echelon of bureaucrats to the government's strategic priorities. Secretaries were put on five-year contracts and could thus be rotated across departments and removed more easily. Ministers were empowered to bring in consultants to work in their departments for periods of less than three years. The role of the (independent) Public Service Board was decreased and some of its responsibilities transferred to the (government-controlled) Department of Finance. Moreover, after the 1987 election, Hawke restructured the cabinet: the number of departments was reduced from twenty-eight to eighteen, largely mirroring the number of 'portfolio' ministers in cabinet (sixteen; in addition, there were thirteen non-portfolio ministers).[82] The aim of these changes was to strengthen the capacity of cabinet to act as a coordinating body.[83] There was also a strong and much discussed push towards more 'managerialism' in the running of government: the use of monetary incentives to direct and discipline public agencies, and of performance-assessment procedures to keep managers and staff on track.

Despite being the longest-serving and arguably most successful Labor Party prime minister, Hawke was never really a creature of the party. Valued for his election-winning abilities but viewed with suspicion by party loyalists and driving a program of economic reform that broke with nearly a century of Labor orthodoxy, Hawke maintained a fundamentally pragmatic relationship with the party—and the factions—that put him in office. He kept the party in power in Canberra; it accepted, however resentfully on occasions, that he along with Keating would run the government largely as they saw fit. Once in charge, Hawke's lack of emotional investment in Caucus allowed him to 'display little discomfort or remorse in culling Labor's herd of sacred cows', making him 'the perennial newcomer, an outsider, an interloper' who had to work hard to get the reforms he championed accepted.[84] As a result, the loyalty that he commanded depended to a large degree on continued electoral success. It was transactional, not tribal, and therefore finite.

A stabilising influence within the Hawke government was the formalising at the federal level of the hitherto predominantly state-based Labor faction system. The establishment in 1984 of the centre left (it emerged around key ministers, including Hayden, Dawkins and Neal Blewett) confirmed the institutionalisation of factionalism. Thereafter, very few members of Caucus were not aligned to one of the three factional camps (socialist left, centre left, right).[85] Factional arrangements centralised authority within the government and 'further reduced the role of Caucus, which tended to act more as a final court of appeal for members who could not be accommodated by debate within their own factions and negotiations between faction leaders'.[86]

Hawke was affiliated with the right—unusually for a prime minister, in the early years of the government he attended some of the faction's meetings—and cultivated close relationships with its chief powerbrokers in NSW and Victoria, Graham Richardson and Robert Ray respectively.[87] In exchange for influence on appointments, they delivered the numbers in Caucus. Hawke also maintained civil relations with the centre left, which Hayden described as a 'lonely hearts club squeezed between two super powers'.[88] On the other hand, he had a long history of enmity towards the socialist left, especially in Victoria, viewing it as a destructive and in many ways intractable force. Over the years, however, his icy personal relations with stalwarts of the left, such as Tom Uren, improved, and his invitation in 1987 to its senior minister (later deputy prime minister under both Hawke and Keating), Brian Howe, to join the ERC heralded something of a coming in from the cold for the left. Towards the end of Hawke's prime ministership, the factional basis of his authority fractured. Arguably, he signed his political death warrant in the wake of the 1990 election when he refused Richardson—who had done much to bring about this victory by courting the emerging urban green vote—the ministerial portfolio he preferred. Furious, Richardson switched his allegiance to Keating. The ensuing leadership struggle saw a breakdown of factional discipline: for example, the Victorian right remained loyal to Hawke whereas the NSW right threw its might behind Keating.

During the Hawke government, the communicative skills of its principals were complemented by further professionalisation of government media strategy. Hawke relied on television and broad coverage of 'big tent' events—the summits—to command public attention. Keating, in contrast, dazzled the press gallery and ensured its 'God journalists' (as journalist and academic Margaret Simons dubbed them) carried his message to the public. In addition, the government adapted the small-scale media units introduced by Whitlam and Fraser to create Labor's National Media Liaison Service (NMLS), with dedicated staff in Canberra and state capitals. It was ostensibly an information agency but was soon nicknamed 'aNiMaLS' by the gallery—testimony to its aggressive promotion of the government and its monitoring and dissemination of statements and action that would embarrass the Coalition. It was a lesson in news management not lost on successor prime ministers.[89]

The 'Double Act'

Hawke's governments resembled those of Curtin in that their internal dynamics were shaped to a considerable extent by tandem leadership exercised by a duo of prime minister and treasurer. Once rivalry had clouded the collaboration, both Hawke and Keating repeatedly scrambled to claim credit for the government's economic reform successes, but the record shows that this credit must be shared. Perhaps in recognition of this joint leadership, it has become common parlance to speak of the 'Hawke–Keating' governments when describing the 1983–91 segment of Labor's period in power.[90]

Finding themselves joined at the hip more by accident than by design after winning government in March 1983, both men soon learned that they fundamentally agreed on what needed to be done. Long-term Hawke and Keating cabinet minister Neal Blewett recalls:

> From the outset they shared a common perception of the economic challenges that faced government and country: in the immediate context of 1983 the need for fiscal restraint, and by 1986 contraction, and the need in the longer term to restructure the Australian economy to make it competitive in a globalising world. And they shared a similar approach to dealing with the deficit in a most untypical Labor way: not by increasing taxes, which they sought to reduce, but by expenditure cuts.[91]

Each also quickly realised that the other was indispensable to the achievement of shared goals: 'The foundations of the Hawke–Keating relationship were ambition and pragmatism, but there was also … "a natural fit" on policy goals. Both were committed to the pursuit of traditional Labor values in a changing world'.[92] Keating remembers the strength of the bond he and Hawke forged during their early years in government:

> At that stage, to use the corporate analogy, Bob was chairman of the board and managing director and I was chief financial officer … in that first year he and I were thick as thieves. He'd press the button on his intercom and say, 'What are you doing mate?' I'd come up and have coffee or tea, and he'd offer me a cigar … We were on such a roll in that first year and the economic changes we wanted were coming through. Bob luxuriated in all that and so did I. It was a genuine friendship, not just one born out of pragmatism.[93]

Keating biographer and former staffer John Edwards concurs about this meeting of minds: 'Hawke and Keating ultimately fought for the leadership of the party, but they almost never disagreed about policy'.[94] They both understood the need to work in partnership and within a year 'became one of the most successful teams since federation. They had a policy affinity, an efficient rapport and complementary political skills … Where Hawke was popular, Keating was dangerous. Hawke preached consensus and Keating wielded the economic knife'.[95]

Each developed effective policy networks with their officials and personal advisers. Hawke delegated to his ministers, instituting a practice of distributed leadership. So long as their partnership was effective, Hawke and Keating spoke with a single voice, which ensured that their authority was unquestioned. For eight years at least, they were invincible. As Don Russell observed,

> people tend to forget that Hawke and Keating were like that [gestures two fingers together] all the way through. They agreed on everything except one thing [leadership] until the end … I can remember only one time when Keating disagreed with Hawke … and Hawke always supported his treasurer except on [the proposal for a goods and services tax] … They dominated Caucus. They dominated the factions. The party machine: they dominated that … the two of them turned the country upside down and that was because … you couldn't go around them.[96]

Hawke delivered authority and good government. His career as the leader of the trade union movement had taught him the value of negotiation to reach solutions with which competing interests could agree. Hawke's specialty was the achievement of compromises, where each interest gained some but not all of its demands. Differentiating himself sharply from the combative rhetoric of Fraser, Hawke came to the prime ministership preaching consensus and reconciliation.[97] It was a stance oriented to process rather than to ideology that his critics would condemn as a fig leaf for Hawke's alleged lack of substantive ideas.[98] But they missed the point: Hawke was creating the forum in which ideas-driven political entrepreneurs like Keating could flourish.

While it was Hawke's team guidance and authority in cabinet and Caucus that kept the show on the road, it was Keating's passion for ideas that was essential to capturing the Labor Party, the unions and the business community. Keating 'could sell an idea better than anybody else in the government … He could cut through to the meaning and …

restate it in a useful form faster than any politician of his generation'.[99] Keating was well served both by his advisers and by a series of Treasury and Reserve Bank officials with whom he worked closely and in whom he inspired great loyalty and affection (which he reciprocated). But his ability to translate and adapt their advice into terms that persuaded not only Caucus and cabinet but also the media and opinion makers of reform objectives was unique. Cabinet colleagues who would not or could not 'get it' soon enough met with extended and energetically delivered lectures. And if nothing else worked, Keating was never shy of hurling some creatively worded abuse, for instance likening his more reluctant fellow ministers to 'a bunch of fucking economic Bourbons'.[100]

Neoliberal ideology prevailed neither self-evidently nor consistently, however. For one, there was often robust debate within and between Hawke's and Keating's offices and among the key agencies over issues of degree, framing, timing, tactics and perseverance. Those offices were occupied not just by Treasury-educated policy wonks like Don Russell and John Edwards, but also by experienced political operators steeped in the ALP's machine politics like Bob Hogg and Peter Barron. They were always on hand to provide politically attuned reality checks to any overbearing economistic doctrine that might buzz around. In interviews and memoirs, all participants in the ERC and the big cabinet discussions on deregulation, tax reform and annual budget preparations describe the process as rigorous and gruelling—hardly the kind of 'groupthink' that would have prevailed had there been a single shared policy paradigm.

The Hawke-initiated national policy summits were, partly, an educative process—peak bodies came together to talk, and the media reported their exchanges as part of the story of necessary change. Such tactics achieved gains in health, housing, community services, immigration and multiculturalism, education—even while the main game remained the economy. Each of these depended on the initiative of individual ministers, but the partnership with Keating was core. Driven by his curiosity about ideas and determination to make them work for him, Keating came to display an astonishing command of the economic realm. Starting in the second most complex ministerial portfolio with hardly any prior experience and no tertiary education, Keating began his term relatively unsure of his ability to master his brief. Hawke acted as a kind of mentor to him in the first months. Keating was also respectful of John Stone's expertise and ability to create political problems for a government that went against the Treasury view. The currency float decision was a critical turning point for Keating. It proved he could win out over Stone, it gained him the respect of senior Treasury and Reserve Bank officials, and major political credit through favourable mass media coverage and vocal business support. One of Keating's key Treasury advisers, Ted Evans, observed: 'Paul Keating is innately intelligent ... but more than being intelligent, he knew how to learn ... He showed quite an extraordinary ability: I have never seen a politician become so effective and acquire such extraordinary learning'.[101]

Like Curtin and Chifley, during the early years of their collaboration each testified to feelings of affection for and appreciation of the other during their working relationship. And like their distant predecessors, their success depended upon the remarkable complementarity of the attributes each brought to the partnership. Hawke's popularity generated political capital; Keating had the bravado to spend that political capital in the service of bold reform. Hawke made the public connections and ensured good government; Keating delivered the ideas that defined the agenda, with the political courage to act on them. It was the marriage of Hawke's organisational effectiveness and Keating's willingness to entertain big risks that worked so well.

Eventually, the ambitions that had fuelled the achievements of both became irreconcilable, with the Labor Caucus confronted with the choice, according to the colourful description of a former minister, between 'an egomaniac and a megalomaniac'.[102] Hawke's oceanic sense of wellbeing depended on public adulation; Keating's aspiration instead was to demonstrate his singularity by changing the world. Both men needed power to achieve their ends.[103] Hawke was willing to foster the ambitious treasurer as long as everything done in his name redounded to his credit. Keating, who possessed 'self-confidence to the point of infinity', was convinced of his entitlement.[104] He grew annoyed when his contributions were insufficiently recognised, believing emphatically that he was the powerhouse of the government and Hawke effectively its titular head; enraged when his initiatives were commandeered; and increasingly frustrated by Hawke's reluctance to relinquish the reins.[105]

It was Hawke's action at the beginning of 1991 in reneging on the so-called 'Kirribilli agreement'—the 1988 backroom deal struck between the prime minister and his treasurer for a handover of office following the next election, due in 1990—that ultimately transformed nearly three years of simmering leadership tensions into open conflict. By then their common project to remake the economy was under serious strain as Australia entered a recession in late 1990. Though undermining the reputations of both men, the economic downturn was more immediately damaging to Hawke, who struggled to cope in the adverse circumstances and found his key source of authority depleted by declining public popularity. Keating, who had warned Hawke in 1988, 'When I come at you, mate, I'll take your head right off!',[106] launched his first strike against Hawke's leadership in May 1991, saying he had a better chance than Hawke of leading Labor to victory. Unsuccessful, he resigned as treasurer and retired to the backbench. For Hawke, though, it was a brief reprieve. Bereft of Keating his powers to lead came into question, not least because of his unconvincing response to new Liberal leader John Hewson's *Fightback!* program—a 650-page economic policy manifesto, which proposed to revive the economy by taking neoliberal reforms to the next level and, among others, to introduce a goods and services tax (GST). In December, Caucus set a precedent by removing Hawke: the most successful prime minister in Labor history had also become its first to be voted out by the party room.

Paul Keating: the Brawler Statesman

The man who replaced Hawke as prime minister was born and bred in an Irish Catholic medium-sized business owner's family in the working-class and solidly Labor suburb of Bankstown in western Sydney.[107] Imbued by his family's deep-seated antipathy towards Menzies (his father, Matt, thought the Liberal leader 'a well-dressed conman'[108]), Paul Keating stepped into politics at a young age. His doting, ambitious mother egged him on, expecting him to aim high and succeed. He enjoyed a rapid, though hard-fought, rise in the NSW Labor Party, aligning himself with the right faction and soon emerging as its leading figure on the national stage. Made a cabinet minister by Whitlam in the dying days of his government, it was Keating who warmed up the crowd before Gough made his historic Dismissal speech on the steps of Parliament House on 11 November 1975.

A self-taught but avid student of Labor history, Keating shared Hawke's critical view of the Whitlam government. He had obtained his early mentoring in politics as the art of struggle from Curtin and Chifley's political nemesis, former NSW premier and Labor 'wrecker' Jack Lang. Lang, 'an indefatigable warrior', instilled in him the sense that battle was inevitable in politics, and that leaders must be prepared to take no prisoners when the situation so required.[109] Of all Australian prime ministers to date, Keating entertained the most explicit, romantic and aspirational view of political leadership, surpassing even that of Whitlam. Not one to be perturbed by suggestions that cooperative rather than dominant leaders meet with considerably more political as well as legacy success,[110] Keating always aspired to lead from the front, harnessing the power of conviction, the force of optimism, the beauty of vision and the courage to take risks. All this was backed up by a brisk determination to stare down, ridicule or walk over anyone standing in his way.[111] Ripened by years of waging reform battles as treasurer under Hawke, Keating articulated the credo that he would continue to live by as prime minister:

> it has to be real change and real reform, not some caprice off the top of the head, a good idea at the time; it's got to be something that has got structure to it, value. And to get it, you have to push the process beyond the consensus—but not long later drag the consensus up behind you … you've got to take the risks. But it's got to be a calculated risk, on the basis that you can educate the consensus back to you. If you can't, you and your change get chopped off.[112]

Keating's forte was really to run with an idea, a plan, a hunch even, examining it carefully, making it his own and then pursuing it relentlessly. Described by a close adviser as 'exceptionally bright',[113] Keating sold ideas through his comprehensive command of facts and policy arguments, delivered with zest, gusto, humour, irony, and spleen. Not a demagogue but a persuader, discussions and debates were his natural habitat. Whether in face-to-face encounters with journalists, fellow ministers or backbenchers, or in the combat zones of parliament, Keating thrived on collegial and competitive encounters with peers. He was less at ease in set speeches, mass gatherings, schmoozing with the punters on the campaign trail or on talkback radio. He liked governing for the people, not so much with the people. Where Hawke sought them out keenly in their social clubs, at their sports events or in their shopping malls, Keating had to be pushed by his minders to do so.

Eschewing many of the macho attitudes and mannerisms expected of western Sydney boys and NSW right-wing Labor 'hard men', Keating defied stereotype in the way he dressed (impeccably, Italian), how he drank (very little, preferring wine over beer) and the interests he pursued outside professional politics (niche antiques, classical music). A notable exception to the pattern was his rhetorical style. In his assessing it himself, he observed:

> My effectiveness in parliament is in the forensic analysis of an issue, the articulation of the key points and the sting in the tail. I wrap it in a political wrapper … It takes a lot of years to make hammers out of words, but they're not profane words. They're just plain words, arranged properly.[114]

This self-assessment characteristically erred on the side of generosity: Keating's penchant for raucous, colourful and bruising invective became the stuff of legend. Affectionately nicknamed 'the Jack Dempsey of Australian politics' (by fellow Hawke minister and left faction critic of Keating's reform program Tom Uren[115]), Keating did not hold back when it came to administering verbal punishment to political opponents. They were routinely characterised as 'gargoyles', 'perfumed gigolos', 'mangy maggots', 'fish that jump on the hook for you', 'bunyip aristocrats', 'gutless spivs', 'scumbags', 'pissants', 'intellectual hoboes', 'resident nutters', 'little desiccated coconuts' and 'pansies', who are 'going troppo', are 'all tip and no iceberg', 'need a Valium', and who will be 'squashed like rats' or 'done slowly'.[116] This was language used as a weapon, befitting a man who, as a student of Lang, saw himself as being 'in the grenade-throwing business'.[117]

Keating's bold leadership vision and his 'leading from the front' style harboured risks. It demanded enormous amounts of energy to convince so many people of so many things they did not necessarily want to hear, and for such sustained periods of time—energy that Keating did not always have. Even when Keating was still a relatively young treasurer, his first principal private secretary, Tony Cole, noted that he was 'playing brinkmanship with his health all the time'.[118] When he finally had achieved his goal of becoming prime minister, the energy balance and the allocation of his attention had become more erratic—puzzling, infuriating and at times worrying his closest advisers.[119] The other major risk of Keating's conviction leadership was that he would become too clever by half, too intoxicated by the grandiosity of his reform mission, incapable of self-regulation or even tactical retreat:

> His capacity to convince himself makes easier both convincing others and self-delusion ... His intensity, his obsessions, his attention to detail are part of that unremitting drive; they also make him prone to fantasies and self-inflicted wounds. The Keating motor, always running at full speed, sometimes badly overheats, causing the Keating political judgment to lapse.[120]

With so much of the emphasis being commonly placed on Keating's self-descriptions as a conviction-driven, self-reliant, even lonely political artist and weather-maker for Australian transformations—'out there on the stage doing the Plácido Domingo' as he himself famously remarked[121]—it is easy to overlook that throughout his career he was a prodigious collaborator. Keating in fact derived part of his clout as treasurer and prime minister from working together with people he could learn from, whose expertise and judgement he respected, whose values and instincts he trusted. Keating had an excellent nose for leveraging the expertise of others who could assist him in his quest to—in Keating lingo—'transform the place', ridding Australia of the 'Menzian torpor' in which he had grown up and that the Whitlam government had begun to shake.

The partnership with Hawke was only one of a number of key relationships that defined Keating's leadership. There was the longstanding entente cordiale with Kelty through several iterations of the Accord—though the relationship broke down in late 1995 over moves by both parties during a waterfront dispute, which escalated to the point of the unions hiring Bob Hawke to be their advocate—by then a patent affront to Keating's sensibilities.[122] Keating was also close to Treasury secretary (and subsequent handpicked Reserve Bank governor) Bernie Fraser and his eventual successor at Treasury, Ted Evans. Both were working-class boys who had made good. They shared Keating's world view and proved utterly dependable troops during the protracted 'economic trench warfare' required to achieve the 1980s reform program. They remained pivotal partners in the much more frustrating policy environment of the early 1990s.[123] Likewise, Keating grew very fond of another Treasury secretary, Chris Higgins, whose premature death caused Keating great distress. And then there was his chief of staff, Don Russell, with whom he developed an almost symbiotic relationship in the confines of the PMO.

Respected by his peers, inspiring to his close collaborators, Keating's relationship with the Australian public remained perennially complex. When still an increasingly impatient prime minister in waiting, he explicitly rejected the consensus-style politics that Hawke epitomised. After many years of delivering hard sells to the Australian public, and in the face of a nasty recession that he had first been unable to stop and then tried to normalise, he would never achieve the public support Hawke had enjoyed during his early years as prime minister. As treasurer he had successfully wooed the Canberra press gallery in a manner redolent of Curtin's deft cultivation of intimacy with key journalists.[124] Through them, he managed both to intrigue and educate the Australian people. Following the recession, which he had at first denied would come and then claimed to have been necessary ('the recession we had to have'), he began to lose the gallery's ear and a large section of the public stopped listening to him.

His relationship with the Labor Party organisation deteriorated rapidly when he became prime minister. There were serious altercations with party secretaries Bob Hogg and Gary Gray—who he detested and whose appointment as Hogg's successor Keating had unsuccessfully sought to block—over the management of Labor's 1993 and 1996 federal election campaigns. Keating wanted to run campaigns out of his office, and to be integrated with the story he had been telling the nation in the past decade; the secretariat insisted on the campaign being a party matter to be masterminded by the party organisation.[125] Long-time Labor minister and Keating's successor as party leader, Kim Beazley, echoed a view about Keating's prime ministership that became an ever more dominant narrative following the 1993 election, when he observed that

> basically Paul always wanted things on his terms … and with the Australian people you can't have things on your terms, you have it on theirs and part of the prime ministerial job is politics. Bob [Hawke] loved the politics, Bob really enjoyed meeting people and being popular and the rest of it, while Keating despised it.[126]

Keating speechwriter Don Watson observed that 'Keating and the Australian people were in gridlock. The people wanted Keating to recognize them. Keating wanted them to recognize him. They wanted to tell their story. He wanted to tell his'.[127] According to Watson, Keating 'seemed not to understand that he would make himself more popular and trusted if he played sometimes to the hollow centre of the job—to the ceremonial, sentimental, clichéd dimension of it. It was as if he would not let himself think such thoughts'.[128] Unlike Hawke, he was uncomfortable with the public's interest in his personal life. He tried to keep his wife Annita and their four young children away from the limelight as much as possible. His chief passions outside politics were antique clocks and classical music. They were important stress-relief mechanisms for Keating, who in Canberra liked to sneak off to Abels music store at the Manuka shops for hours. These were hardly pursuits that endeared him to the average Australian.

Keating did not want to conform to the demands of prime-ministerial performance in the late-twentieth-century's media democracy: courting and consolidating public popularity, and, when more energetic persuasion efforts simply don't work, settling for what the public will wear at a particular point in time. His unwillingness to do so should not have surprised anyone. His views on the role were well known and if anything hardened on the job once he had become prime minister. In Keating's conception, to accept that he could not afford to get ahead of public opinion would be tantamount to abandoning the very essence of what political leadership was about.

Keating would thus never be a popular prime minister, 'neither loved by the party nor liked by the people'.[129] Victory in the so-called unwinnable election of 1993 only tilted his way because he managed to cast his Liberal opponent, John Hewson, as even more unreliable, uncaring and arrogant than the Australian public saw Keating himself as being. That he then misread the election result as a mandate to pursue his even more 'out of the box' policies on national identity remained an uncomfortable truth that was best not discussed in the presence of the man who had done the impossible by winning Labor a fifth consecutive term in government.

There was simmering public resentment about the former treasurer's apparent lack of interest in the livelihoods of the many who were still deeply affected by long-term unemployment and financial setbacks caused by the recession of the early 1990s. In their eyes he had brought it about and the country was only slowly recovering. This anger and disaffection explain the depth of Keating's March 1996 election defeat and the relative ease with which his nemesis, John Howard, could expunge his prime-ministerial legacy and cloud his reputation. In the end, as Paul Kelly observed, 'it was his conception of leadership that made and then broke Paul Keating'—particularly his 'romantic conception of the strong leader' and its 'exaggerated emphasis on willpower'.[130]

The Erratic Animator

Keating was a far less methodical prime minister than Hawke had been. His ability to animate others and his authority in the cabinet room were instead rooted in the power of his self-belief, the contagious enthusiasm and intellectual brilliance he brought to bear in advocating his positions, his remorseless prosecution of the government's case against its critics, and his intense loyalty to colleagues even when this was politically very costly.[131] Keating dominated both cabinet and Caucus, yet proved ultimately more erratic in governing than he had when working in partnership with an equal. When Keating's ideas-driven reformist zeal was no longer checked by Hawke's appreciation of what was psychologically acceptable to the Australian public, there was always a risk of overreach.

Upon assuming the prime ministership, Keating had clear ideas about how he wanted to lead. It would be the antithesis of the Hawke style: 'I don't believe in aimless meetings where I sit mum trying to let a consensus develop for fear of showing my hand. That I reject as a style of leadership'.[132] Keating adopted a more centralist style than Hawke, preferring to make key decisions with, and on the advice of, a small number of confidants, which he then drove through the government's and the party's processes.[133] He relied heavily on a close circle of advisers housed primarily in his PMO and a second ring from the key central agencies, PM&C and the Treasury. The Keating system was not put in place overnight. In December 1991, after emerging victorious from the leadership struggle against Hawke, Keating had left the composition of cabinet and the outer ministry largely unchanged. It was a deliberate attempt to restore some sense of unity. Cabinet and party morale had sunk, and Keating understood he needed to rebuild not by purging but by mending.

Though he would closely collaborate with individual ministers on specific issues, cabinet as a whole began to play second fiddle in Keating's executive arrangements. Like Hawke, Keating wanted to be involved only in circumstances that were truly important or where the minister could not resolve it himself, but unlike Hawke he did not have an 'open door policy' that encouraged ministers to come in and just brainstorm, share their concerns, or try to read his mind. Thinking this a complete waste of his time, he instructed his staff to screen out those he regarded as aimless visitors.[134]

In the cabinet room, Keating was an accommodating chairman but never a consultative leader in the context of the broader cabinet system. Keating's style of chairing was remarkably low-key and tolerant of opposing views: he enjoyed the contest of ideas. Neal Blewett thought that initially Keating's cabinet operated in a 'more collegial' fashion than had Hawke's in the last years of his prime ministership.[135] Over time, however, Keating's commitment to formal cabinet meetings began to wane, as deputy prime minister Brian Howe later observed:

> Keating was less concerned to build the collective cabinet, particularly after 1993, by then he was pretty much running his own race. Prior to 93 I think he put a lot of effort into trying to build camaraderie and trying to take the cabinet very seriously, involve people much more … [After 1993] he's become much more withdrawn, much more focussed on his own agenda and much less interested in canvassing the views of the ministry.[136]

Howe refers to the 1993 federal election. Keating hailed the victory as one 'for the true believers' and now regarded the government as his own, seizing the opportunity to sidestep Labor's tradition of Caucus-led composition of the frontbench.[137] He proposed a list of thirty names for endorsement for the ministry and the factions and party room acquiesced.[138] This enabled him to rejuvenate the ministry—less than a third of the appointees had occupied frontbench positions in 1987—and populate cabinet with people who owed their positions only to him. What had seemed a one-off instance subsequently became the norm under Keating amid a gradual exodus of tired and jaded veteran ministers (among them Neal Blewett, John Button and John Dawkins), and replacements and reshuffles were required. By mid-1995 he had established dominance over the process of ministerial appointment. But at the same time, as Troy Bramston notes, 'Keating did not enjoy the same stability in the ministry, or indeed the quality of ministers, that Hawke had'.[139]

After the 1993 election, Keating restructured the cabinet process,[140] with most of the business re-routed to cabinet committees. The size of these committees was greatly reduced by excluding all the junior ministers. Cabinet committees became essentially decision-making bodies led by Keating and a small clique of very senior colleagues. The effect of all of this was to 'centralise power in the hands of the Prime Minister and marginalize the full cabinet'.[141] Those ministers who had had years of Hawke's steadying, process-driven, consultative leadership noted, and lamented, the change. They saw that Keating did not take the scheduling of meetings seriously and was often late. John Button felt Keating 'lacked Hawke's discipline'.[142] Others thought him 'disorganised and unpunctual'.[143]

Even some of his key aides in the PMO, like senior political advisor Mark Ryan, felt he 'didn't give his ministers enough attention'.[144] On tactical and personnel issues, he consulted ministers who were factional leaders, such as Brian Howe, Nick Bolkus and John Faulkner from the left, Peter Cook and John Dawkins from the centre left, and Robert Ray, Laurie Brereton and Graham Richardson from the right. Richardson's, Dawkins' and Brereton's closeness to Keating was based on portfolio interest and passion for policy (Dawkins), and factional and personal allegiance (Richardson and Brereton). Above all, the extent to which ministers (but also advisers and bureaucrats) got a hearing was determined by the extent to which the prime minister trusted the advice provided. Keating's resorting to hiding in his private bathroom from ministers—Gareth Evans among them—when he did not want to engage with them has become notorious.[145] As Jim Chalmers puts it in his detailed study of Keating's leadership style:

> Keating dominated colleagues; in the context of cabinet's operation he did so as a result of personal force and a compliant, handpicked ministry who tolerated his propensity to occasionally bypass the cabinet process and announce initiatives unilaterally. Cabinet consultation occurred during the Keating Prime Ministership at the behest of the leader, it was not forced upon an authoritative leader by a powerful ministry. Cabinet government was not an approach encouraged under his tenure; it was a *Keating* Government firmly in the evolving tradition of prime ministerial power.[146]

Keating's dominance reached the point where he announced major policy initiatives such as the privatisation of Qantas and the making of a security treaty with Indonesia before they reached cabinet. When Keating wanted or felt he needed to go solo, he could.[147]

As Kelly noted, the heart of Keating's administration lay in his office instead of in cabinet. For Keating, his office was a 'family affair', an inner sanctum where he was respected and commanded fierce loyalty, and provided him not just with advice but acted as a refuge where he could momentarily forget the requirements of day-to-day politics (which he came to dread).[148] In the confines of his PMO, he 'was among friends who were chosen ... It was a protective arrangement'.[149] Keating's faith in Don Russell was complete. He was variously described as Keating's 'right-hand-man' and 'alter ego'. When Russell left to become ambassador to the United States in mid-1993, none of three successors over the next couple of years (Russell returned to the PMO in late 1995 at the prime minister's behest) were able to replace him in Keating's heart.[150]

It illustrates a larger point: unlike Fraser and Hawke's methodical approaches to running their governments, under Keating nearly everything depended on individual relationships. Within the PMO, Keating wanted intelligent, highly educated—the joke was one had to have a PhD to be a Keating staffer—sharp and politically astute policy minds. Their expertise was what he wanted; their loyalty to him he reciprocated in kind and rewarded with opportunities for unprecedented policy influence. Moreover, the dynamics of the office and the wider advisory system of which it formed the hub were driven by policy priorities and political pressures rather than by systematic planning and coordination. Rather than stable structures and predictable processes, Keating preferred to work with project groups and committees directed towards specific policy initiatives or responding to specific incidents. It was government by brainstorming. This was most pointedly so in the confines of the PMO, which, said Don Watson,

> always had a large if not defining element of chaos about it: 'organised chaos' or 'creative chaos', Don Russell used to call it, but often it was just chaos or even 'hopeless chaos'... Paul Keating's government was almost

> always under siege or on the verge of it; and for better or worse, Paul Keating defined how the government travelled.[151]

The day-to-day routine of the Keating office was hectic, closely resembling the subsequent imagined portrayal of the American president's inner circle in the television series *The West Wing*:

> The computers buzzed, the phones rang incessantly and a clutch of personal assistants answered them ... Day and night, amid myriad other essential tasks, they [the PAs] typed away and took phone calls from everyone in the country who had a whinge. It was a clearing house for the culture of complaint ... Time was punctuated by TV stings and reality defined by what the news said reality had been in the preceding hour, or day or week, and what, as a consequence of this, it was likely to be in the foreseeable future ... Daily life in the PMO was a truth contest. All day long, truth was asserted, denied, demolished, reasserted.[152]

Keating's PMO came to be widely perceived as an exclusive club impenetrable to outsiders. The media ran stories to the effect that the prime minister and his staff were bunkered away in the office, operating in a vacuum and seemingly oblivious to the views of colleagues. It conveyed the impression that no-one and nothing else outside the inner circle counted for quite as much. The reality was more complicated. Keating rarely took advice on an issue without running it past another advisory group. He believed in redundancy, overlap and competition, instinctively seeking advice from many sources, attracting it from wherever he felt he could get the most value.[153] This could mean relying on his key PMO advisers, as he often did, but equally he might be listening to subject matter experts from Treasury, PM&C, the Reserve Bank. To the dismay of Labor traditionalists, he would, however, also seek out opinions from 'mates' in the media and the business world such as Kerry Packer and property developer Warren Anderson.

The provision of advice thus became a competitive process. Watson observed that he and his PMO colleagues 'competed every day with advice he took on the telephone'.[154] PMO social policy adviser

Mary Ann O'Loughlin recalled: 'as senior advisers to the prime minister, we're competing for him, absolutely. Because that's our job. We're competing to get his time, to get his attention'.[155] Competition did not stop at the doors of the PMO, either. Its key internal struggle—in Watson's terms: the battle between the pro welfare-state 'bleeding hearts' and the econocratic 'pointy heads'—was never far below the surface. According to Watson, the economists often prevailed. Another influential subgroup in Keating's advisory system were the diplomats, a group including Geoff Walsh, John Bowan, Ashton Calvert and Allan Gyngell, whose importance increased as Keating moved more and more onto the international stage.

With so much ambiguity about what was happening where and when, and who Keating was listening to about what, life at the office was a roller-coaster that not many endured for the full ride. Turnover at the PMO was high, leaving the prime minister more firmly in control but having to absorb early departures of people he valued immensely and found hard to replace. Towards the end, exhaustion and stress drained hope and energy within the office.[156]

One person who lost his job when Keating became prime minister was the secretary of PM&C and de-facto head of the federal public service, Mike Codd, who had grown close to Hawke. Keating saw him as being too supportive of Hawke's vision of 'cooperative federalism', which the new Labor leader rejected as too soft on the states:

> I always held Mike Codd in high regard. But he and I had completely divergent views about what was later called new federalism. As Treasurer I had opposed the idea of giving back to the states the pre-war taxing powers, in other words, moving away from centralised taxation. I was strongly opposed to that, and since it was essentially a scheme promoted rather formally by Mike Codd, he volunteered to resign.[157]

Keating replaced him with Mike Keating, with whom he built a close working relationship.

Institutionally, PM&C lost some weight in the transition from Bob Hawke to Paul Keating, despite it being fondly referred to as 'the other

Robert Menzies speaking in the 1949 election campaign. It was the culmination of his long struggle to revive his political career and remake the non-Labor side of politics. (Harry Martin, Fairfax Media)

Robert Menzies imperious at the lectern, April 1965. He exercised unparalleled authority as a platform speaker before live audiences even as that era of public communication was now coming to an end. (RL Stewart, Fairfax Media)

Robert Menzies, right, with 'young Harold'—his heir apparent, Harold Holt, January 1966. (News Ltd, Newspix)

Harold Holt, the first prime minister to travel extensively and invest personally in building bilateral relationships in Asia, embarks for Singapore, April 1966. (Don McPhedran, Newspix)

John Gorton, January 1968, shortly after becoming prime minister following the disappearance of Harold Holt: 'tall, lean, with war injuries having given him a ruggedly distinctive appearance, he seemed an attractive option'. (Ted Golding, Fairfax Media)

John Gorton flanked by a quizzical-looking treasurer, Billy McMahon, January 1968. Regarded as an inveterate schemer by his colleagues, McMahon earned Gorton's open contempt. (John O'Gready, Fairfax Media)

Awkward on television and on the hustings, Billy McMahon vainly signals victory on election day, December 1972. (News Ltd, Newspix)

The titanic rivals of 1975, Gough Whitlam and Malcolm Fraser, pictured in July of that year, would later find unity in shared values and causes. (News Ltd, Newspix)

Gough Whitlam campaigning in Melbourne, December 1975. Insiders could easily mistake the fervour of the crowds that rallied to his cause as indicative of a broader public mood—a supposition that collapsed at this election. (Michael Rayner, Fairfax Media)

A relentless taskmaster of his own government, Malcolm Fraser fights to keep control in the face of impending defeat, March 1983. (Fairfax Media)

An irresistible force: Bob Hawke, accompanied by his wife, Hazel, basks in his 'love affair' with the Australian public during the 1983 election campaign. (Paul Mathews, Fairfax Media)

After John Curtin and Ben Chifley, the next great leadership tandem in the history of the Commonwealth, Bob Hawke and Paul Keating, in the first blush of their partnership, August 1983. (Graeme Thomson, Newspix)

Bob Hawke's ebullience faded as Paul Keating closed in on his leadership, July 1991. (Andrew Taylor, Fairfax Media)

The 'brawler statesman' Paul Keating in full flight in the House of Representatives, August 1992. He had learned how 'to make hammers out of words'. (Michael Jones, Newspix)

A master of talkback radio, John Howard uses the medium to speak directly to 'mainstream' Australians, October 2004. (Mark Graham, Newspix)

John Howard bids farewell to his long-time chief of staff, Arthur Sinodinos, December 2006, a partnership that was integral to Howard's consolidation of 'prime-ministerial government'. (Andrew Taylor, Fairfax Media)

Kevin Rudd promising 'new leadership' during his triumphal 2007 election campaign. Focus groups revealed, 'there was no love for Labor as a party, brand, movement … It was all KR'. (Fiona-Lee Quimby, Fairfax Media)

'The gang of four' in session, April 2009. From left to right: Wayne Swan (Treasurer), Lindsay Tanner (Minister for Finance), Kevin Rudd (Prime Minister) and Julia Gillard (Deputy Prime Minister). (Gary Ramage, Newspix)

Julia Gillard, flanked by Wayne Swan (Treasurer) and Greg Combet (Minister for Climate Change), unveils the Clean Energy Future package, July 2011. A major reform that epitomised Gillard's capacity to close on measures uncompleted by Kevin Rudd, the politics of the carbon tax were disastrous for her. (Gary Ramage, Newspix)

Julia Gillard, October 2012: 'I will not be lectured about sexism and misogyny by this man. I will not.' (Kym Smith, Newspix)

Peta Credlin, 'the smartest and fiercest political warrior I've ever worked with', leads the charge for Tony Abbott on his war-like crusade for office, January 2012. (Alex Ellinghausen, Fairfax Media)

Four decades of prime-ministerial experience. From left to right: Malcolm Fraser, Julia Gillard, Bob Hawke, Tony Abbott (incumbent), John Howard, Kevin Rudd and Paul Keating, gathered at the state memorial service for Gough Whitlam, November 2014. (Dan Himbrechts, AAP Images)

A wounded Tony Abbott in declamatory mode after being confronted with a party room leadership spill motion less than eighteen months into his prime ministership, February 2015. (Ray Strange, Newspix)

Malcolm Turnbull was rapidly caught between voters' buoyant expectations of him and appeasing influential party views that chafed against majority public opinion. Here he glumly addresses the media the day after the July 2016 federal election with his government's survival hanging in the balance. (Andrew Meares, Fairfax Media)

half of the family' by Keating's PMO staff.[158] Keating discouraged PM&C from dictating to other departments. He gave as much weight to his PMO advisers as to PM&C in deciding whether a policy proposal should proceed. Without their giving the go-ahead, little got through to the cabinet level. The upper echelons of Keating's office were dominated by trusted former Treasury advisers.[159] This influenced the balance of power between PM&C, Treasury and Finance: the 'Treasury view' now got a prime-ministerial hearing alongside PM&C in a way that had never happened under Hawke.

However, under Mike Keating, PM&C did drive key policy initiatives such as the *One Nation* and *Working Nation* packages as well as the native title legislation. On issues Paul Keating really cared about, such as native title, he would work as intensely with the department as he would with PMO staff. Sandy Hollway, now deputy secretary in PM&C, recalled:

> He was very committed—determined to slog our way through the hundreds and hundreds of policy and practical and legal issues that the decision gave rise to. Always, always available to talk about it ... and get decisions and then work on them, and come back ... So much to the point where ... I think it hurt his prime ministership a bit that he was obliged to and, to his credit, willing to spend so much time on that one issue.[160]

The most important feature of the advisory system that emerged under Keating was its hybrid, unregulated nature: there were occasions when ministerial advisers at the PMO undertook the bulk of policy development, but there were also many instances in which PM&C set the agenda and drove the process. With a prime minister who was much keener on policy substance—usable ideas—than on orderly process, seamless coordination between the different clusters of policy development and policy advice was greatly needed but often in short supply.[161]

The Unrelenting Reformer

When Keating became prime minister, Australia seemed in almost as bad shape as it had been when the Hawke ministry took office in 1983. The recession cut deep, business confidence was low, the hundreds of thousands of long-term unemployed were despondent, and the government looked depleted. It fell to a prime minister who had spent eight years as a reforming treasurer to deal with these grim realities. As Bramston writes, 'Keating thought Hawke had robbed him of the best years of his life to become prime minister. He had had to wait too long, and the optimal time had passed. He was tired'.[162] Summoning the energy and willpower required now to lead the government in his own right thus was a challenge. Some ministers thought that he initially looked 'clueless' and lacked a sense of direction.[163] Keating himself recalled later that it took him several months 'to return to the prior level of intellectual gymnastics—to intellectual speed' after having spent the second half of 1991 on the backbench, seriously contemplating a future outside politics.[164]

Keating knew his time in office would likely be brief. The chances of winning the next election were slim at best. In keeping with his conception of leadership, he decided to 'err on the side of audacity because he knew most leaders retrospectively regretted their erring on the side of caution'.[165] A great believer in the use of conferred authority and the spending of political capital, he would continue to push for economic reform while at the same time initiating a new series of innovations aimed at nothing less than redefining Australia's national identity and its place in the world.

On the economic front, the Keating government reconverted to fiscal stimulus after years of restraint, in an attempt to bring down the now alarming unemployment figures. At the same time, Keating sought to sell the current recession as a pivotal exercise in breaking the spine of inflation. The 1992 policy statement *One Nation* was designed to provide the government's overdue answer to Hewson's *Fightback*! It allowed Keating to operate as a 'de facto opposition leader' to Hewson, who had barnstormed the country with a radical reform program that controversially included the introduction of a GST. Keating painted it as cold-hearted market liberalism, which abandoned the unemployed, the vulnerable and the Australian fair go, and held up *One Nation* as the embodiment of the alternative: active, constructive and kind government.[166]

Keating's relentless attacks on Hewson lifted the government's spirits, and *One Natio*n provided him with the narrative that helped him defeat the Coalition in 1993. It was followed in 1994 by the *Working Nation* package that contained an active and assertive labour market policy.[167] Both packages attempted to soften the blows that the withdrawal of protection had dealt to the now endangered bottom end of the labour market—Labor's traditional constituency. At the same time, Keating extended the macro-economic reform agenda of the 1980s, which was aimed at closing the book on the protectionist, centrally managed postwar economy.[168] If the new economic order was about openness, competition and market forces, then government had to make sure that these were properly regulated in order that they served the public interest. In particular, Keating saw himself as an institution-builder for the Reserve Bank, which had suffered a major loss of public prestige for its alleged mishandling of the onset of the recession. Keating championed the bank's independence and had to swallow what he regarded as its tardiness in releasing the monetary brakes on the fledgling recovery. Strong personal bonds of trust between Keating, Reserve Bank governor Bernie Fraser and Treasury secretary Ted Evans helped prevent what otherwise could have become another major showdown between a Labor government and the financial establishment.[169]

In the parallel universe of micro-economic policy, reform continued unabated. Keating's governments embarked on a wave of often intensely controversial privatisations. Gold-plated government assets such as the Commonwealth Bank, Qantas and the Snowy Mountains Corporation were brought to market.[170] The most sensitive and strategic reform, however, was the superseding of the near century-old system of centralised wage-setting by the Industrial Relations Commission by an enterprise bargaining model, legislated in 1993. It was the final and perhaps the most difficult chapter in the history of the Accord. The Keating–Kelty tandem once again proved pivotal, as trade unions, still smarting from the recession, feared this initiative would undermine their security. Kelty, however, shared Keating's view that the centralised wage system was incompatible with an open economy and that enterprise bargaining was essential for improving workplace productivity to the long-term benefit of employees. Moreover, Labor's model had the advantage of an extensive safety net, including a 'no disadvantage' test, as opposed to the Coalition's much more hawkish reform aspirations in industrial relations. Even so, selling enterprise bargaining to trade unions and the party was a bruising undertaking for Keating's friend and industrial relations minister Laurie Brereton. On the other hand, the government's enshrining of compulsory superannuation in legislation in 1992 was unambiguously embraced by the labour movement.[171]

But it was outside the economic realm that Keating articulated a new set of reform ambitions that would define his prime ministership. Collectively they became known as the 'big picture'. It took shape in a series of speeches and ad-hoc responses to unfolding events, igniting public controversy and inaugurating extended struggles for policy change and institutional reform.

Consider the sheer depth and pacing of the challenges Keating held out to the nation. Barely installed as prime minister, he leveraged Queen Elizabeth's February 1992 visit to launch a push for Australian constitutional independence. This enraged the Liberal opposition and the conservative press, which only emboldened the prime minister. By 1993 he had established a Republic Advisory Committee—chaired by the investment banker, lawyer and future prime minister Malcolm Turnbull—to investigate options for the creation of an Australian republic that set in train the process leading to a referendum on the question.

The opening up of the debate about the republic (and flag) was only the beginning of what began to look like a 'radical nationalist project'.[172] Two months later, Keating used the annual Anzac Day speech to play down the national myth that the battle at Gallipoli was seminal to the forging of Australian nationhood. Speaking in the Papua New Guinean capital Port Moresby, Keating argued that Australians should instead look upon Kokoda as the true sacred ground of Australian remembrance, since it was at Kokoda that Australian soldiers were fighting to protect Australia and its way of life. At Gallipoli, he implied, they had merely been sacrificing their lives in a war 'devoid of any virtue' and driven by 'loyalty to imperial Britain'[173]:

> The Australians who served here in Papua New Guinea fought and died, not in the defence of the old world, but the new world. Their world. They died in defence of Australia and the civilisation and values which

> had grown up there. That is why it might be said that, for Australians, the battles in Papua New Guinea were the most important ever fought.[174]

It was the opposite of courting popularity; Keating was trying to foment nothing less than a renewed national self-examination. A further two months later, Australia was compelled to face another historical myth underpinning its sense of nationhood. On 3 June 1992, the High Court recognised the land rights of the Meriam people, traditional owners of Murray Island in Torres Strait. The ruling in what became widely known as the Mabo case—after Eddie Mabo, one of the Meriam people who had initiated the legal proceedings in 1982—overturned the doctrine of 'terra nullius' ('land belonging to no-one') and established the concept of native title rights. In doing so, the High Court ruling also challenged the assumption that British colonisation in 1788 had delivered complete sovereignty of all land to the Crown, extinguishing any existing native title rights. In a speech in October 1992, Keating embraced the Mabo ruling and pleaded for reconciliation as a necessary step towards a new national self-confidence. Indigenous groups around the country were energised; miners and pastoralists were up in arms demanding blanket extinguishment of native title rights. Western Australian premier Richard Court led the charge against Keating's position. In the next eighteen months, the prime minister spent inordinate amounts of time—'too much', feared Mike Keating, who believed this absorption 'came at the cost to other things'[175]—navigating the treacherous terrain of crafting native title legislation that struck a politically viable balance between the contending values and interests. The ultimate result was the hard-fought and historic 1993 *Native Title Act*.[176]

Two months after the Mabo speech, Keating returned to the subject of reconciliation. On 10 December 1992 in Redfern Park near Sydney's CBD, in a rather awkward, wooden delivery, he spoke words that only slowly got through to the initially restless, mostly Indigenous audience:

> The starting point might be to recognise that the problem starts with us non-Aboriginal Australians … Recognition that it was we who did the dispossessing. We took the traditional lands and smashed the traditional

> way of life. We brought the diseases. The alcohol. We committed the murders. We took the children from their mothers. We practised discrimination and exclusion. It was our ignorance and our prejudice. And our failure to imagine these things being done to us. With some noble exceptions, we failed to make the most basic human response and enter into their hearts and minds. We failed to ask—how would I feel if this were done to me? As a consequence, we failed to see that what we were doing degraded all of us.[177]

The Redfern speech reverberated around the nation, stimulating intense public debate about the nature and impact of the British colonisation of Australia. It brought into the open the dark side of settlement history and of white dispossession of the Indigenous population. The 'culture wars' that it helped spark raged throughout John Howard's prime ministership and provided a springboard for the official apology to the stolen generations eventually delivered by Kevin Rudd in 2008.

In another element of his project of challenging Australians to reimagine their nation, Keating also embarked on an ambitious cultural policy, dubbed *Creative Nation*. Its objective was to enrich the nation's cultural fabric by nurturing the arts. And in foreign policy, the prime minister who as a young politician had once disparaged Asia as the place you fly over on your way to Europe, became a zealous campaigner for an Australia that saw itself and behaved as being part of the Asia-Pacific region rather than an Anglo/European outpost. His intensive diplomacy to persuade regional counterparts, including American presidents George HW Bush and Bill Clinton, to agree to an upgrading of the Asia-Pacific Economic Forum (APEC)—itself an initiative of Hawke's prime ministership—through the holding of regular leaders' meetings was just one expression of that emphasis.[178]

The new reform agenda came from Keating's heart as much as from his head.[179] On one level, it was a repetition of his performance as Hawke's tandem partner: Keating once again cast himself in the role of national agenda-setter in chief. But the substance of the agenda had little resemblance to the narrative of the 1980s. It was about Australia's nationhood, its past, its identity and its place in the region. It presented an altogether different dimension of Keating to the Australian public: that of an Australian nationalist, a patriot.[180] The 'big picture' was never purposefully designed up-front but emerged inductively. Keating was looking for a means to give purpose to his prime ministership, and to persuade the Australian people to have another look at him in the run-up to the 1993 election.

In federal–state relations, Keating's reform zeal was much more limited. He rebutted what he saw as moves by the states to claw back the powers of taxation successive federal governments had spent decades to obtain.[181] He nevertheless established the Council of Australian Governments (COAG) in 1992, a twice-yearly gathering comprising the prime minister, premiers and chief ministers, and the president of the Australian Local Government Association. Superseding premiers' conferences, it became the key forum for managing the federation.

Crucial bones of contention with the states were the drive for a national competition policy and the design of a legislative response to the High Court's decision on native title in the Mabo case. The former was not in place until 1995. To do so, Keating persuaded the premiers to accept a national regulatory regime that limited their own freedom to manoeuvre for competitive advantage, and the creation of a powerful national competition authority, the Australian Competition and Consumer Commission, to enforce it.[182] Legislating native title proved much tougher. Queensland premier Wayne Goss (Labor) and Richard Court (Liberal) had significant mining interests and conservative constituencies that were strenuously opposed. Substance and symbolism were closely intertwined. With the Liberal–National opposition fanning the fire, passions ran high during a protracted, intensive and exhaustive consultation and negotiation process orchestrated by Keating. He eventually confronted the premiers and stared down businesses and lobby groups. He placed prime-ministerial authority on the line and drove himself to the point of exhaustion to reach an acceptable agreement that the federation could bear. It was a major triumph. The Labor Caucus, often weary and restless with Keating, made the rare gesture of passing a resolution of congratulations for its leader, who had 'given Labor a sense of unity, new energy and a firmer sense of its direction'.[183]

Keating's 'big picture' was, in Kelly's words, 'a blend of idealism, ambition and megalomania laced with a thread of plausibility'.[184] Conscious of the political clock ticking, Keating tried as hard to put as much of it into effect as he could. Hence the frantic effort to enshrine native title in law (of which Aboriginal leader Noel Pearson remarked, 'Whitlam did the vision thing, Hawke did the crying thing and Keating did the doing thing'[185]), the foreshadowing of a constitutional referendum on a republic by the decade's end, the showering of money on the arts sector, the massaging of his regional counterparts to upgrade the status of APEC, and the brisk negotiation of a security treaty with Indonesia in 1995.

It was a lot for an unprepared public to take in: a prime minister who, like Gough Whitlam, was able to imagine a different Australia.[186] Keating's uncompromising pursuit of a grand policy vision kept those who truly believed in him enthralled, but it failed to sway much of the press gallery that was, by now, longing for new political talent to offset Keating's dominance. Indeed, from 1993 his relationship with the media had deteriorated to a state of mutual disenchantment, Keating barely disguising his contempt for journalists.[187] Moreover, each commitment mystified, annoyed or upset parts of the electorate, perhaps because they were all not only framed as pursuits of a better future but wrapped in repudiations of a past the voters were not prepared to disavow quite so far and quite so fast. And thus, collectively they decided to stop him, at the election on 2 March 1996.

Leveraging Prime-ministerial Power

In recent times, the Labor era of 1983–96—sanctified by influential accounts of the period—has acquired the patina of 'a political golden age'. Equally, it has developed into something of a millstone for Hawke and Keating's prime-ministerial successors by encouraging an expectation of the transformative potential of the office that others have been unable to equal. As Frank Bongiorno suggests, there is a tendency to mythologise the period:

> Giants once strode the land: politicians who did not allow themselves to be diverted by last week's focus group, this week's opinion poll or

> today's 24-hour news cycle. Yet one of the leading participants in that government, Gareth Evans, recently commented that 'it did not always feel that way on the inside'.[188]

Indeed, the reality is that the reform process was frequently messy and event contingent, fiercely contested (both inside and outside the Labor Party), brought unforeseen consequences, and was painful for the nation.

Even so, there can be little dispute that the Hawke and Keating governments changed how Australia functioned and how Australians thought of themselves. To some extent, they had to: globally governments of the late 1970s regardless of political complexion had become mired in stagflation. In the early 1980s, nearly everywhere in the Western world, governments bowed to the inevitable and began not only curbing public expenditure but also opening up their economies and harnessing competition in the provision of public services. Distinctive features of the Australian experience were that much of this 'neoliberal' work was undertaken by a Labor government, and the speed and depth at which the government effected these changes (rivalled only by New Zealand's Labour government, led by another effective reforming leadership tandem: David Lange and Roger Douglas).

In the thirteen years that Hawke and Keating governed, they also changed the Australian prime ministership. Each found ways to exercise the role that reflected their own expansive interpretations of what prime-ministerial leadership was to be about and that, at the same time, responded to the challenges of national leadership in the television age and governing in a globalising world. Hawke and Keating's executive arrangements strengthened the hand of the prime minister in the policy process. First of all, while ostensibly retaining Fraser's insistence on the centrality of cabinet government, they both relied more on cabinet committees—whose composition and processes they could more readily influence—than on plenary cabinet meetings.

Second, they expanded the PMO—it nearly doubled in size from Hawke to Keating—and turned it into a powerhouse of policy initiative, political coordination and message control. Yet its elevation was held in check by both prime ministers' insistence that it should in large part be staffed by people with policy savvy and public service experience. They made sure that the PMO worked closely with other key institutions, particularly the central agencies (PM&C, Treasury and the now separate department of Finance). The PMO was under standing orders to respect the expertise of the public service and to strike an appropriate balance between the exigencies of sound public policy and political feasibility. Under Hawke this was achieved through methodical insistence on orderly process, under Keating through the galvanising appeal of his policy ideas and the by now longstanding webs of relationships between key players in the core executive.

However, the latter years of Keating's tenure also pointed to the shape of things to come in the early twenty-first century: a bigger, powerful and more impregnable PMO that was fiercely loyal to the leader but less so to the leader's party or to the integrity of cabinet processes; that felt besieged by the pressures of managing an increasingly fast-paced news cycle and frantically sought to control the government's message; and that did not think twice about leaning on ministers and backbenchers who would not or could not toe the prime minister's line.

The party politics of prime-ministerial leadership changed too during the Hawke–Keating era. Hawke's was a personal brand that Labor had not quite seen before, and whose public appeal overrode any misgivings the party may have had about his limited socialisation into federal politics, or indeed his limited commitment to its traditional policy platform. Hawke and Keating jettisoned much of that platform early on in their government. They subsequently developed a pattern where, along with key senior ministers, they would more or less autonomously devise new policy projects. These would then be shepherded through the cabinet and past Caucus and the party organisation through a mixture of persuasion, cajoling and gagging internal opposition.

Inevitably, Labor's election campaigns became more personalised and 'presidentialised', following the more leader-centric model of its main competitor, the Liberal Party. Under Hawke and Keating, leader persona and personal performance began to trump party narrative. Then, armed with a personalised mandate, Labor prime ministers could be more assertive in imposing their will on the party. It increased their ability to lead from the front but also increased the risks of isolation and indeed alienation from the party base. Moreover, as Bongiorno notes, 'having abandoned the most significant weapon in its armoury—the ethical critique of capitalism—Labor now had to resort to maintaining a fragile, shifting alliance of voters that seemed forever in danger of falling apart under the impact of the latest economic crisis or policy disappointment'.[189] The debacle of the Labor Party's final election campaign in the Hawke–Keating era—its slogan: 'Leadership'; its sole public face: Paul Keating—indicated the fickle nature of the new power balance between leader, party and electorate that had emerged.

5

SPEAKING FOR THE MAINSTREAM: JOHN HOWARD

In 2006, *The Howard Factor*, a book celebrating John Howard's first decade in power, was published.[1] Triumphal in tone, commending skills said to have ensured his success, it suggested an impregnable leader. In 2007, Howard's Coalition government was defeated at the federal election, and he became the first prime minister since Stanley Bruce to lose his own seat. This abrupt transition in fortunes was indicative of a pattern. Howard was, in terms of longevity (prime minister, 1996–2007) and in relation to the achievement of the objectives he set for his government, one of Australia's most successful prime ministers. Yet the sudden reversal in his eleventh year in office was another swing of the pendulum in what had been an unusually jagged progression.

Most successful prime ministers make their way to the top through incremental advance: clambering up 'the slippery pole'. Certainly, other leaders had suffered defeat and come back into contention and remarkable success, most notably Robert Menzies. No-one, however, had quite the oscillations Howard endured in what almost amounted to a civil war within the Liberal Party over leadership in the 1980s, nor in the series of hair's-breadth escapes in which he snatched victory from near defeat in every election between 1998 and 2004, before ultimately failing in 2007.

Howard became Liberal Party leader in 1985, when then leader Andrew Peacock tried to wrest the deputy leadership from him in a tactic that failed, and subsequently stood down. It was not a successful sojourn, and when Peacock's supporters regrouped, challenged and defeated him in 1989, it was a setback so profound that Howard said the likelihood of him returning to the post would be akin to 'Lazarus with a triple bypass'.[2] Yet after Peacock failed, his successor John Hewson lost the 'unlosable' 1993 election, and a subsequent disastrous attempt to engender generational change with a 'dream team' of Alexander Downer and Peter Costello foundered, Howard was the last man standing. Re-elected party leader in January 1995, Howard led the Coalition to victory in the 1996 election with a near record majority.

There ensued a period of government in which policy success and repeated electoral victory encouraged some to argue that Howard's leadership had become as secure as was that of Menzies at his height, and that this was a manifestation of his uncanny ability to read the electorate. If so, it was a project that repeatedly teetered on the brink of disaster. At the 1998 election, the Howard government suffered one of the largest swings recorded against a first-term federal government, with Labor winning a majority of the two-party-preferred vote but failing to gain the marginal seats lost to the Coalition in 1996. In early 2001, opinion polls and commentators wrote the government off, but Howard rallied with spending initiatives (and government advertising) and began to make headway with strong statements on immigration. Then 9/11 elevated terrorism as an issue, and Howard was back in the game. In 2004, opinion polls ran consistently against the government for most of the year, but the erratic performance of Labor Party leader Mark Latham, and Howard's ability to play off Latham's idiosyncrasies, saw him prevail again. By then, the pronounced fluctuations in his political fortunes were irrelevant to his supporters: in surviving he became the titan of conservative politics.

Howard's achievement was significant, but the story is more complicated than is acknowledged by his supporters. It is these complications that make it so illuminating in understanding the contemporary prime ministership. Howard's lengthy tenure, bested only by Menzies, looks the more astonishing in comparison with the revolving door that bedevilled his successors. Considerable political agility and skilful communication tactics—especially defensive spin[3]—are part of his story. But it is above all the disciplined elaboration of prime-ministerial government, pioneered by Fraser but brought to fruition by Howard, that allowed him to become so dominant. Paradoxically, it was also in its exercise that the problems of centralised leadership became more apparent. They had always been inherent in the institutions introduced by Whitlam and Fraser, but were held in abeyance by distributed leadership under Hawke and Keating. Howard's shrewdness and pragmatism held them in check for much of his administration, but eventually habituation to centralised decision-making eroded his judgement and standing.

The way in which Howard worked, and the way he adapted what predecessors had developed, is of primary interest here. So significant was his dominance of the party, acquisition of authority, command of communication and control of the public service that we have focused on these, to the neglect of other areas about which more might be said (such as Commonwealth–international relations, or his gradual engagement with Asia). His administration was the bridge between one of the most successful periods of reforming federal government—between 1983 and roughly 2001[4]—and the turbulence that began to emerge following his third election victory and that was to become pronounced among the leaders who succeeded him in office.

The Inception

The youngest of four sons, John Howard emerged from what he described as a conservative, lower-middle-class family. His father was a small businessman, running a garage. His mother was a 'homemaker' with strong Methodist ideals, who had considerable influence over her youngest son. It was a family that felt its enterprise and values were synonymous with those identified by Menzies as characteristic of 'the forgotten people'. The family's conversations about politics, which Howard recalled, were indicative of their enthusiastic response to Menzies' appeal. Another idol was Winston Churchill, whose Christian name was given as a middle name to young John. Howard remembered taking a close interest—at the age of ten—in discussions of the 1949 election and his parents' delight at Menzies' success. Such influences fostered his ambition to become a politician. He prepared early, making his first public speech at age twelve (to thank a retiring headmaster) and undertaking debating at high school. It 'laid the groundwork', he said, 'for such speaking skills as I was able to bring with me into public life years later ... It was marvellous training'.[5]

Howard took a law degree at the University of Sydney and began work as a solicitor in 1962, when he was also state representative for the NSW Young Liberals. Within ten years he had become vice-president of the NSW Liberal Party and in 1974 was elected to federal parliament as the member for Bennelong. His commitment was manifest in his unstinting work for the party, and continued application and enterprise facilitated a swift rise from the backbench. When Fraser took power in 1975, Howard was appointed minister for business and consumer affairs, and in 1977 he became treasurer. Economic policy was a topic of heated debate in the party room towards the end of the Fraser administration. It was also an arena of contest between the prime minister's advisers and Treasury, with Howard awkwardly caught between the abrasive Treasury secretary, John Stone, the sources of alternative advice in the PMO and PM&C, and Fraser himself.

Treasury, at this stage, opposed many of the deregulatory measures advocated by the Liberal Party's 'dry' cohort. Fraser's advisers were pushing for incremental reform. Fraser himself was given to confrontational questioning of Treasury while attempting not to exacerbate Howard's predicament. Some accounts of the period argue that Howard was won over to the dry faction but was constrained by Fraser's resistance to the reform project.[6] The cabinet record provides little to substantiate this.[7] Fraser and Margaret Simons, drawing on archival records, give a more nuanced delineation of significant reform during Fraser's tenure, contesting the suggestion that Howard had lobbied for more radical measures.[8]

Yet it was a lesson both in realpolitik and in philosophy for Howard. Subject to competing arguments and in deteriorating economic circumstances, he had to master a pragmatic politics simply to maintain a grasp of his portfolio. He concedes that he commenced his 'ministerial career with anything but a strong commitment to economic rationalism', but argues that, 'I had, by the time of the Fraser Government's defeat in 1983, gone through something of an epiphany … In opposition I was to develop my views even further'.[9] This epiphany was the catalyst for Howard substantially modifying the ameliorative liberalism inherited from his idol, Robert Menzies. While the revolution in which 'the Liberal Party began to torch the edifices of its past'[10] was broadly based, it was Howard as prime minister who translated it into an effective philosophy of government.

First, however, there were thirteen long years in opposition, during which Howard would alternately drive policy, win and lose leadership, and doubt that he would ever rise again. Suffering, as former treasurer, some of the obloquy following the deficit revealed after Fraser's government lost office, Howard was easily defeated by Andrew Peacock in a bid for the party leadership in 1983. He did however retain the deputy leadership and the shadow treasury portfolio, which gave him the capacity to remain a policy driver. 'The last thing Andrew Peacock wanted in early opposition days was an intense debate about the philosophical direction of the Liberal Party on economic policy, especially industrial relations', said Howard. 'Yet that is what he got, because of my determination that the Coalition should take a more consistent pro-market approach'.[11] Howard became the torch-bearer in the party's internal revolution. Peacock, an urbane and diplomatic Liberal moderate, was more interested in public relations (and in blocking Howard) than in ideology. It was civil war. As then federal director of the party Tony Eggleton recalled: 'In those years in the wilderness … we had two Liberal Parties: the Howard Party and the Peacock Party'.[12]

Hawke tried to capitalise on Liberal divisions and on his personal popularity by calling an early election in 1984, but Peacock made an unexpectedly strong showing, reducing the Labor majority and reinforcing his leadership. Still, concerned by Howard's increasing profile as the voice of economic reform, and determined to head him off, in 1985 Peacock demanded an assurance that Howard would not challenge him. Failing to secure that, he attempted to oust him by engineering a vote for the deputy leadership. His preferred candidate lost to Howard. Peacock concluded that the situation was untenable and resigned. Howard was elected, 'leader by accident', as he put it.[13]

His initial tenure as party leader (1985–89) was an unhappy experience. Peacock supporters worked against him. Leaks and division undermined his authority. After over a year of this, the capricious and authoritarian National Party premier of Queensland, Joh Bjelke-Petersen, decided to save the conservative cause by making a run for Canberra. It was fanciful and doomed, but it diverted media attention from Howard's objectives. It split the Coalition on the eve of, and ensured its defeat at, the 1987 federal election. Howard's subsequent attempts to recapture the policy agenda were thwarted. *Future Directions*, a party manifesto launched in 1988, combined economic liberalism with a social conservatism undoubtedly representative of Howard's values, but at odds with the progressive social attitudes favoured not only by the Labor government but also by Liberal Party moderates. Howard's public reservations about multiculturalism (a policy domain he believed was 'owned' by Labor) and the rate of Asian immigration sparked public controversy, provoking in him an even more inflexible stance. He handled the backlash from elements within his party badly. Peacock supporters saw their chance: secretly they began to organise a challenge, revealing their intentions to Howard only the night before a routine party meeting at which they would call a vote. Given no time to muster support, he was ambushed. Peacock won the vote forty-four to twenty-seven.

Peacock's return was short-lived. After the Coalition was again defeated by Labor in 1990, John Hewson succeeded to the leadership, with Peacock's support. Hewson's tactic was to develop *Fightback!*, an even more radical economic reform package than that being implemented by Labor. It led to yet another defeat in 1993 at what had been seen, for the Coalition, as an 'unlosable' election against Paul Keating. Howard challenged again but Hewson held on, his numbers organised by the Peacock faction. In May 1994, Hewson finally faced the inevitable, defeated in a party-room ballot when colleagues gambled on generational change, electing Alexander Downer and Peter Costello as leader and deputy leader. Later that year, Howard's persistent rival, Peacock, resigned from parliament. Within months, a series of public relations disasters related to inept policy presentation shattered Downer's confidence. In effect, Downer then ceded the leadership to Howard. Following preliminary discussions between the two of them, on 30 January 1995, Downer stood aside and Howard regained the leadership, unopposed.

His obstinacy and inflexibility tempered by setbacks, his understanding of relationship building and political tactics sharpened, and his appreciation of how to communicate objectives finely honed, Howard had learned the necessary capacities for leadership the hard way.[14] He was now cautious about the way the reform message should be framed, and much too wily to be trapped in the way Hewson had been by Keating in 1993. Instead of a manifesto that might be misrepresented as *Future Directions* was, or detailed policy that could be attacked and demolished in the way *Fightback!* had been, he opted over the next year for a series of 'headland' speeches in which 'core values' were lauded and the claims of his party as the true author of Australian nation building were advanced. His message was that 'the changes I wished to bring about would more directly echo the instincts of the Australian people, rather than impose on them something new, and about which they would feel uncomfortable'.[15] Indeed, his central message during the 1996 election campaign was that he would restore the conditions in which Australians could once more feel 'relaxed and comfortable'. On 2 March 1996, Howard led the Coalition to an emphatic victory, achieving a 5 per cent swing and winning a 45-seat majority. He had served an arduous apprenticeship, twelve years working for the party, then twenty-two years in parliament, before attaining the prime ministership.

Howard would prove, in office, to be as preoccupied with control as Fraser had been, and as committed to the centralisation of power. But he understood that it need not mean taking everything upon himself as Fraser had. The trick was discipline: the discipline of a message that governed action and expectations, and of using the resources of office to ensure that others worked within the parameters he had established.

Howard's Message

By the late twentieth century, the belief that a leader must be a party's communicator-in-chief was well established. Howard was good on his feet, a deft debater, but was not a performer with the capacity for oratory, inspiration or theatre in the tradition of Menzies, or Whitlam, or Keating. It was easy for those enthralled by such figures to overlook the significance of what he was about. For he had rethought and adapted liberalism for his purposes, identified the coalitions of interests to which he must appeal (and those he could ignore), and devised a communicative style that without theatre or drama was extraordinarily effective. He disarmed by appearing to be an 'ordinary bloke'. He was committed to certain values, remorseless and disciplined in parliament, and a man with an acute sense both of what would reassure his party base and of what would satisfy the 'pub test' in what he called 'the mainstream'. He had also identified the best channels though which to disseminate his message.

Howard was said to have pioneered a 'small target strategy' during the 1996 campaign, talking in generalities and about values rather than policy specifics. He claimed that 'I did not come into office resolved to turn the nation on its head ... I had a project for government, but I was not so arrogant as to presume that I should inflict on the Australian people a new vision for the nation'.[16] Yet he had long shown commitment to a policy debate that his rival, Peacock, never wanted, and those who had been watching knew that he had been the Liberal Party's policy driver during the opposition years.[17]

Howard displayed policy consistency.[18] He was committed to continuing economic reform. A principal objective was to overturn the prevailing tenets of industrial relations, reducing union power and deregulating the labour market. Arguably, it was the remaining item of unfinished business following the reforms of Hawke and Keating, but Howard had stamped it as his own during the years of opposition.[19] It became an abiding area of policy contest during his administration. Labour market flexibility would, he said, engender productivity, driving growth, prosperity, jobs and choice.

There was also an insistence on deficit reduction to be achieved by further privatisation (sale of public assets) and public sector efficiencies (reducing government expenditure). Public sector modernisation would be accompanied by a transfer of service provision to the private sector (given appropriate market incentives, private enterprise would perform more effectively). Indeed, Howard claimed that particular entrenched 'elites' (bureaucrats and non-government activists in advantaged positions in, for instance, the 'welfare industry') dominated most programs and much service provision. They must be challenged by opening them up to market competition.

He spoke of liberating individual 'choice' as the best driver of resource allocation. He claimed that he was in touch with the core values ('self reliance, a fair go, pulling together and having a go') of 'the mainstream'. They were, he argued, essentially Australian and derived from Australian (and Liberal Party) history. By explaining how every policy initiative was based on such principles and relating it to the 'Liberal' narrative, he conveyed a sense of purpose. It was an ongoing elaboration of his pre-election 'headland' speeches.[20] It gave the market liberalisation of his times an Australian slant.

From 2001, historical contingency added another element to Howard's agenda: the importance of national security, crystallising around border protection and the 'war on terror' following the 9/11 attacks. He would use both to heighten his command of prime-ministerial government.[21] A dogged commitment to his objectives was paired with a politically astute ability to draw back, regroup and seek alternative options when impediments loomed. Yet he showed courage in tackling big issues—gun control legislation following a horrific massacre by a lone gunman at Port Arthur, and the bold introduction of a GST, for example—that won him respect if not affection.

He came to dominate his party and his era as an inventive and aggressive proponent of a distinctive world view. Political historian Judith Brett has shown how Howard, scorning the intelligentsia, determinedly committed to plain speaking, fashioned a powerful message. His was a calculated appeal to the 'battler', promoting the interests of 'the mainstream' and a common heritage against vested interests ('elites'), internal division, international challenge and foreign hostility.[22] Brett argues persuasively that Howard has been the most creative conservative political leader since Menzies. He expressed what a disconsolate electorate was feeling: that Labor's reform was top-down, an imposition by those in privileged positions with which the people were to comply. Instead, Howard downplayed the imperatives of the market in favour of a story about how careful change would deliver more jobs and more choice. He demonised the 'unrepresentative' elites said to have captured the Labor Party—he would govern 'for all of us'. It served to refocus understandable anxiety about reform as an 'objective' fear of a select few, encouraging people to mobilise behind a strong leader who would fight these special interests.

By renouncing the 'tribalism' of old politics to attract a mixed audience, Howard aimed to create new coalitions. The skill was recognising how to pitch his message to manage the tension between seemingly divergent interests. Economic reform, for instance, appealed to the self-interest of cosmopolitans (with skills, flexibility, capital to invest). But it could also be framed to persuade aspirational voters that delivering choice would provide pathways out of their current less-advantaged positions. He finely calculated those he could not win and hence whom he could afford to ignore, including church leaders, welfare advocates, academics and small-'l' liberals, indeed many of those whom Brett dubbed the 'moral middle class'[23] that had once formed the Liberal Party's core.

Howard argued that there must be 'a practical balance between the limits of government and the limits of markets, between laissez-faire economics on the one side and *a suffocating centralism* by government and bureaucracy on the other'.[24] In effect he turned away from what Paul Hasluck, Menzies' minister for external affairs, described as Menzies' greatest achievement: the development of a skilled, professional public service. Bureaucracy, Howard argued, could not be empowering or enabling: 'people motivated by high ideals, stirred by a sense of vocation, guided by local knowledge of their communities, and unashamedly desiring a reward if successful at their task, can help … better than a bureaucracy forced to work to rigid regulation'.[25] Because of its failure to recognise these truths, Labor was condemned:

> This is a path down which Labor, constrained by old loyalties, burdened by old ideology, simply cannot travel. The new concept of working

> through others, of being ally not superior, is simply impossible for a party historically committed to bureaucratic intervention … They simply cannot accept that others can be trusted with resources and with responsibility …[26]

Howard disrupted the positions established by Labor governments on immigration, asylum seekers and even Australian history.[27] He was suspicious of what had been a bipartisan commitment to multiculturalism. It was not a preoccupation with race but a concern for cultural compatibility that led him to encourage assimilationist rather than multicultural approaches. His argument was about containment of any disruption to core values. Indeed, having provoked controversy in 1988 by suggesting some reduction in Asian immigration, he would later support it since he felt that Asians' small business enterprise, family ideals and work ethic demonstrated values consonant with the Australian mainstream.

The hard edge emerged in his attitudes to asylum seekers and border control, and particularly the rhetoric adopted in relation to unexpected arrivals by boat, which appealed to those whose anxiety about change could be attached to issues of security. Furthermore, it boxed in Labor, which was represented as being 'soft' on 'illegal' arrivals, people smuggling and security. The paradoxical result was that the attention of both immigration progressives and anti-immigration cohorts was so focused upon the contentious refugee debate, that the liberal aspect of Howard's immigration regime was overlooked. Initially he slashed immigration, but after 1998, to promote economic growth, immigration rates were higher and more diverse than those under virtually any previous administration.[28]

Howard mirrored Keating in proposing that Australia comprised a people formed by shared circumstances, but he adroitly turned the narrative into an attack on Keating's 'history'. He saw that Labor had abandoned popular nationalism in its pursuit of economic reform, and its insistence on what 'we' must do to prosper in a global market. In response, Howard skilfully took over the 'Australian Legend',[29] once the preserve of radicals and the ALP, insisting that there was an 'essential'

Australian heritage to be defended, and turned its values—such as mateship—into a story of conservative individualism.[30] He also argued that Keating's history 'failed because it aimed to establish a form of historical correctness as a particular offshoot of political correctness'.[31]

This fed a more generalised attack upon selective historians and navel-gazing elites that, he said, endorsed a 'black arm-band' view of history. This was a term borrowed from a contentious speech by Geoffrey Blainey in 1984, to characterise historians who gave excessive emphasis to past wrongs.[32] Howard dismissed such alleged preoccupations with imperialism, exploitation, racism and discrimination: 'I believe that the balance sheet of our history is one of heroic achievement and that we have achieved much more as a nation of which we can be proud than of which we should be ashamed'. He was given to extensive commentary on 'national character [as] an important factor in achieving prosperity', the 'outstanding qualities which set us apart' and 'an Australian way—different and so often better than that of comparable societies'. Typically, he linked this with what he claimed were foundation values: 'self-reliance, a fair go, pulling together and having a go'.[33]

While Howard spoke of achieving conditions where people might be comfortable and relaxed and shared values could flower, the underside was an orchestration of fear—fear of elites who would block the realisation of dreams and (after 2001) those who would directly threaten Australian security, sovereignty and even survival.[34] The times suited him—just as opinion polls turned against him in 2001, the 'war on terror' erupted. Circumstances swung in favour of 'the garrison state' and Howard was handed a script that coincided precisely with his world view.[35] His fighting instincts were now in accord with the political climate he faced.

Communicating the Message

Howard observed in 1996 that 'for many years now, elections campaigns in Australia have been very presidential, and I knew that from that moment on, most of the responsibility for the Coalition's fortunes would rest with me'.[36] Howard later confessed that he was 'a great believer in the permanent campaign', indicating that this responsibility was not simply episodic but would continuously stay with him. Professional campaign management had progressively developed from the 1970s on, but the elaboration of the permanent campaign is strongly associated with Howard's leadership.[37] In turn, it transferred attention from parliament and the party to the leader, facilitating his command of communication.

Relations with the party organisation were important in the strategic articulation of Howard's pitch. It was there that expertise had been developed—by successive federal directors Andrew Robb and Lynton Crosby, working with pollster and analyst Mark Textor—in combining quantitative surveys with focus group insights to mobilise underlying attitudes or shift opinions. Howard was quick to appreciate the value of this advice. It enabled a focus on the voters needed for victory in campaigns, and thereafter to dominate the agenda.[38] Crosby and Textor would leave to set up a commercial consultancy in 2001. However, their firm was retained by the next federal Liberal director, Brian Loughnane, to maintain the provision of such services.

Howard's preferences determined characteristic features of his public communication. He was hands-on in shaping the message of the day, and PMO advisers then coordinated advisers in other ministerial offices to ensure consistency.[39] Howard set the public agenda by means of radio interviews. He believed that 'a fairly clear majority of working journalists do tend to be of a centre-left disposition'. The choice of talkback radio was a means of bypassing them.

> The reason I chose to use radio a lot was that it is the one medium where you are guaranteed that if you've got something to say, somebody will hear it in its entirety if they want to sit and listen. You do a news conference … and you are beholden to the gatekeeper as to what is then reported to the public … When it comes to radio … you did have the opportunity of actually getting a message across.[40]

It was to have a significant impact upon the conventions of prime-ministerial communication. Press conferences became rare and access was diminished. The Hawke government's amendments to media regulation had enabled aggregation of radio networks. Two were dominant: the

Macquarie Network and Southern Cross. By concentrating on engaging with the hosts of their leading morning programs—Alan Jones at 2UE (Macquarie) and Neil Mitchell at 3AW (Southern Cross)—Howard could reach millions across the country, unedited, in just two sessions, with moderated calls from the public. Furthermore, his sessions were recorded and televised, with transcripts and vision offered to journalists, obviating the need for 'all-in' press conferences. The transcripts became the source for quotes, information and television grabs. Follow-up queries to the PMO hit a dead end: journalists were referred back to the transcripts.[41]

Press secretaries had figured in the PMO since Billy Hughes' appointment of Lloyd Dumas in 1917. With the expansion of ministerial staff under Whitlam, they became a feature of all ministers' offices. Fraser cut back their numbers and ensured coordination by establishing both the Ministerial Committee on Government Communication (MCGC) and the Government Information Unit (GIU) to 'make sure that information relevant to Government decisions is disseminated in the widest possible way so that there can be the widest possible understanding of the nature of Government decisions and their impact for the well being of the broad Australian community'.[42] Hawke and Keating capitalised on the latter by transforming it into the National Media Liaison Service (NMLS, nicknamed aNiMaLS), ostensibly intended to perform much the same functions as Fraser's GIU, but well known as a 'dirt unit' monitoring the media to gather ammunition to be used against the opposition.

Outraged, Howard undertook to abolish the NMLS, and did so immediately he gained office. He then replaced it with the Government Members Secretariat, intended to assist Coalition MPs in dealing with the media, which soon was known as 'baby aNiMaLS' because its monitoring was also devoted to capturing whatever could be used against the opposition. In addition, in 1998, the more orthodox Government Communication Unit, responsible for strategic advice on government communication and for ensuring the efficient delivery of government information (including anything produced by the public affairs units of government departments), was established within PM&C. Howard also maintained the MCGC. Overall, then, Howard gathered up and enhanced the resources introduced by his predecessors, to ensure comprehensive oversight and control of all aspects of publicity. And public servants were told to report all calls from journalists to the PMO.[43]

Not everything can be contained despite the existence of means for comprehensive oversight if some of those within the system choose to communicate informally with those outside it. All governments suffer from leaks by those with privileged information. The Howard government took an unusually vigorous line in attempting to identify and punish leakers. Following a series of high-profile raids and investigations, public servants ceased to respond to journalists even on matters that might once have been regarded as routine. An audit by a conglomerate of media organisations—both public and private—noted that:

> Overwhelmingly journalists complain they are denied access to information, particularly background information on government decisions. They say the flow of information is controlled, largely because of the centralisation of the source of government information. In what now appears to be the majority of cases, public servants are prohibited from giving journalists information directly. Journalists are either referred to the department's media section or the minister's office.[44]

The result, said Tony Walker, a journalist with the *Australian Financial Review*, was 'that there is practically no information outside the government line'. Howard's Coalition, he said, was 'the most controlling government' he had 'ever come across'.[45]

Howard skilfully articulated his project for government, persuasively linking it with national needs, shared history and common values. He adopted rhetorical strategies attuned to those who were to be mobilised, and targeted those he could never win over as the 'elite' enemies of common aspirations. He selected a means of dissemination that circumvented media gatekeepers. He refined available institutional resources to ensure a control of communication that promoted a singular message and limited debate. It was a masterful demonstration of how to manage the contemporary expectation that a leader must serve as the government's chief communicator. It may have been the principal element in his electoral success.

Establishing Authority

Leadership, as Howard insisted, was the gift of the party: 'The key there is to listen and understand you are a creature of the party room ... That's where you get your authority from ... you should never take that for granted'.[46] Governing was the remit of the executive in collaboration with the parliamentary party. Advice and implementation depended upon the relationship between the executive and the public service: in reality, the fulcrum was now the interaction between bureaucratic agencies and the PMO. Developments since 1950 had accentuated the centrality of prime-ministerial performance in managing each of these domains, and Howard was acutely conscious that his authority hinged on their orchestration.

Howard had devoted twelve years to party activism and networking before being elected to parliament. Given his subsequent ministerial experience and leadership travails in opposition, he knew that philosophical direction was a necessary but not sufficient condition to hold the party together. He must ensure that the party machine—which he now knew intimately—worked for him: 'From the moment I returned to the leadership, I had established a good relationship between my office and the federal secretariat of the Liberal Party'.[47] The close ties between Tony Eggleton, as federal director, and Malcolm Fraser might have been a model, and now Eggleton worked with Howard, who would ensure similar closeness with Eggleton's successors: Robb, Crosby and Loughnane. He involved them in strategy and listened to their advice. Indeed, Robb and Crosby were integral to the communication and refinement of his message, in teaching him how to capture public opinion. He was assiduous in his commitment to state and federal conferences, and when federal party presidents caused problems—as John Elliott and Shane Stone did[48]—or state branches needed attention, Howard could rely on the federal secretariat to swing behind him.

In the parliamentary party, he remained visible and accessible, joining backbenchers for a meal in the members' dining room, inviting colleagues to drinks at the Lodge, staying back at the end of parliamentary party meetings to allow anyone who wanted to catch him informally to approach him. He reminded his ministers of the importance of visiting electorates, even marginal seats, as he never ceased to do. It was a way to refresh information. As political journalist Paul Kelly observed, 'He is the most domestically travelled Prime Minister in the nation's history, in the regions and in the cities, and is proud of his local knowledge'.[49] This won the loyalty of MPs, demonstrated good faith to the party base, and connected with constituents. Management of party sentiment, ability in working with the party organisation and the generation of loyalty were essential to the party discipline Howard was able to instil and to his hold on power.

Relations with ministers were carefully managed. There was a core group: Downer (foreign affairs), Peter Reith (industrial relations, and later defence) and Costello (treasurer). Downer and Costello served until 2007; Reith retired in 2001. Downer and Reith were reliable friends. That Costello aspired to Howard's job made for a fraught association. Howard, however, ensured that proper relations were maintained with his treasurer and they agreed on core policy so the government's direction was secure. Howard, scarred by divisions within the Coalition in 1987, preserved harmony by cultivating successive leaders of the National Party: Tim Fischer and John Anderson. An inner circle of about six senior ministers met with Howard each day to discuss issues, strategy and coordination. After losing seven ministers in his first term because of failure to meet stringent guidelines on ministerial conduct, Howard decided instead to defend his ministers to the hilt—usually with the effect of transferring responsibility for setbacks to the public service. It was an added incentive for loyalty. Departing or disaffected ministers were not left on the backbench but eased out into extra-parliamentary appointments. The leader's prerogative of ministerial choice was manifest in patronage: loyalists were rewarded; Costello's supporters were kept out until late in Howard's administration.

Action of course depended upon cabinet. Howard was both committed to and respectful of cabinet government. 'I was determined that the system would function properly and productively', he said. 'The key was to restore a fully functioning and orderly system of cabinet government, with all the major decisions … being made by cabinet or its properly functioning committees.'[50] The three core committees were the ERC, the Parliamentary Business Committee (PBC) and the National Security Committee (NSC). They were means of keeping large amounts of business under ministerial control but away from the main cabinet.[51] And because the ERC determined budget allocations and the NSC became an instrument central to Howard's mission, they were where core ministers and key officials held sway.

Soon after his election, Howard established a cabinet policy unit (CPU) whose head was to be cabinet secretary. Adjacent to his office, and run initially by his adviser Michael L'Estrange, it was a transfer of the management of cabinet business from PM&C to Howard's own strategists. It facilitated two streams of advice—departmental and political—enabling Howard to determine the balance, but ensuring political control of policy. L'Estrange's successor, Paul McClintock, said that:

> Howard described at it as the 'link point between the office and the bureaucracy'. Neither totally inside one or the other … We certainly didn't see ourselves as part of the PMO … But we weren't part of the bureaucracy either. We were the go-to people from both ends.[52]

Yet decisions went back through cabinet, where Howard's behaviour ensured a calm, deliberative process.

> I sat through Cabinet for two-and-a-half years. I don't remember anybody raising their voices or using language that you wouldn't be comfortable [with] on TV … it was a very controlled, gentle and respectful environment. Now that's not always the case and that reflects John Howard's personal style.[53]

Howard tried 'to give everybody a go' to ensure that 'cabinet ministers were involved', after which he insisted, whether ministers won or lost, that they defend the decision.[54]

Broad changes in party structures in the late twentieth century—weaker voter attachments encouraging greater focus on leaders as the 'selling point', as Howard had recognised—not only made the leader responsible for the party's fortunes but also gave him more leverage. Ministers were aware that the prime minister's power over political careers had been much enhanced. Furthermore, Howard embraced a narrow version of ministerial responsibility, for which the working rule, according to Paul Kelly, was 'that ministers, in effect, are responsible not to the Parliament or to the party but to the Prime Minister. The test Howard applies or rationalises is that of ministerial responsibility to the people with the Prime Minister interpreting the public will'.[55] David Kemp, a minister under Howard, commented that 'he used cabinet as an instrument to keep the government united'. There were no reports of him not getting his way. Indeed, one observer noted, 'On one occasion, every single minister at the table was opposed but he agreed with it and that is what they did'.[56]

The result: in Kelly's view, Howard became one of the most effective postwar practitioners of cabinet government, running ideas though the party room and into cabinet, insisting on debate, focusing presentations, listening to views but then locking his colleagues into determinations, and achieving a dominance that deterred dissidents and leaks.[57] His cabinet was the most unified since that of Menzies. It was a tight, secretive and collective group whose processes were rarely penetrated. None of the discrete elements of Howard's cabinet control was especially novel—he built upon trends already evident in the practices of his predecessors—but he carried them to a new level. And after 2001, the introduction of one new dimension—the prime minister as national security chief—significantly enhanced his authority: 'In the hands of an astute leader such as Howard it represents a fusion of greater political authority and electoral popularity'.[58]

Howard's assertion of executive control over the public service was both overt and controversial. He had inherited his family's suspicion of the public sector, argued that private sector actors with proper incentives would perform more effectively than bureaucrats, habitually mapped the likely political inclinations of those with whom he must deal, and believed that Canberra was 'a Labor town' and that most of those who would advise him would vote against him.[59] Menzies and Fraser had both believed that public duty, expertise and a professional ethic outweighed political inclinations and disavowed interest in the political preferences of their closest public service advisers. Howard in contrast was sceptical about public service neutrality and responsiveness. Ministerial resources were strengthened, and the PMO grew from seventeen under Hawke and thirty under Keating to over forty under Howard.[60] On taking office, his government, in an unprecedented move, sacked six departmental secretaries—a third of the total. It set about slashing public sector staff (by 1998 there were roughly 60 000 fewer APS staff than there had been in 1986, though numbers would begin to recover after 2001).[61] He made non-routine appointments to central roles—Max Moore-Wilton, a former public servant but then at the Australian Stock Exchange, as secretary of PM&C; his adviser, L'Estrange, to the new CPU (and as cabinet secretary). Whatever their personal virtues, these were seen as Howard's men. It was no surprise that a former departmental secretary remarked to one writer, 'This government asks, "Are you one of us?"',[62] though the situation was hardly so simple.

Howard's actions were no more than the realisation of the logic of what his predecessors had initiated. That the careers of senior APS officers had become dependent on the goodwill of government was implicit in Labor's *Public Service Reform Act 1984* and later explicit with Keating's introduction of contract appointments and limited tenure. Howard took this further: his government's *Public Service Act 1999* gave the prime minister the power to appoint and terminate secretaries. It was a power soon tested when Paul Barratt, secretary of the Department of Defence, was dismissed on the grounds that he had lost the confidence of his minister: Barratt appealed to the Federal Court, which found that the prime minister did not require a cause to dismiss a secretary.[63] Some of Howard's predecessors had disrupted expectations in exercising decidedly individual choice rather than observing APS orthodoxy in determining key appointments—Gorton in appointing Lenox Hewitt and Whitlam in appointing John Menadue to head PM&C.

The increasing significance of ministerial staff, and prime-ministerial staff in particular, as political actors had been registered since the mid-1970s. That there would be more competition and devolution to non-public-sector agents in sourcing policy had already been manifest in the recourse to contract appointments and consultancy advice by previous governments. Yet the manner in which Howard's reservations about the relations between executive government and the public sector were expressed, the way in which he approached this relationship and the scale on which he acted initially caused estrangement between these arms of government. The test in the longer term would be how Howard's approach worked once relations had settled down.

Change in the institutional culture of the APS was driven from the top, by the prime minister's agenda: to take control of the public service. Moore-Wilton, whose reputation for decisive, no-nonsense, aggressive action was captured in the sobriquet 'Max the Axe', was regarded by departmental staff as the prime minister's man in their domain. Smart, able to see problems from new angles, quick in apprehending detail, swift to move, he dominated through force of personality.[64] Many were intimidated, but some colleagues noted that his confrontational propensity was matched by fearlessness in dealing with his masters: one insider remarked, 'Max, for his eccentricities, was very straight-forward and courageous' in telling the prime minister when he disagreed with him.[65]

Nonetheless, Moore-Wilton warned colleagues of what they should expect, that 'it is now presidential style government'.[66] Like Hewitt, he was said to spend more time in the prime-ministerial precinct than in the department. Like Alan Carmody, his stress was on responsiveness to the government, and perhaps more than anyone other than Carmody, on service to the prime minister.[67] His blunt insistence on this, and on the authority of cabinet as determining issues for action, was seen by some as abandonment of the convention of considered advice.

He intimated that being perceived as on-side with the government was a prerequisite for serious engagement. For example, Moore-Wilton told a well-regarded deputy secretary in his department, Dr Meredith Edwards, that she 'wouldn't get anywhere under this government because of my genes, meaning my father'.[68] It was an apparent reference to events nearly fifty years earlier. Edwards' father, John Burton, appointed secretary of the Department of External Affairs in 1947 by Evatt and known for his left-liberal views, had been targeted by conservative politicians in the 'nest of traitors' debates of the period as a suspected communist sympathiser. What arose from Howard's intentions, and what from overzealous interpretation, remains a moot point however: 'I don't know', added Edwards, 'whether [Moore-Wilton] was the messenger for Howard or whether he was anticipating where Howard might have come from'. It was an unsettling climate for experienced professionals.

The baton passed to Dr Peter Shergold in 2003 after Moore-Wilton returned to the private sector. Shergold's style was decidedly different: smooth, forensic and disciplined, he was a policy enthusiast, an accomplished expositor rather than a heavy.[69] His strength was in spelling out the logic for the Howard-era reforms of the public sector, and the case for policy objectives. Despite very different styles, the project of both Moore-Wilton and Shergold was integrated governance, with attention to government priorities, strategic central agency coordination and monitoring of implementation and delivery, under the purview of PM&C.

Shergold's appointment also suggests qualification to the argument that Howard was only interested in those who might be counted as 'one of us'. He notes,

> … having been almost personally appointed by Bob Hawke … in the Office of Multicultural Affairs, [then] the Aboriginal and Torres Strait Islander Commission … I have little doubt that, when the Howard Government came into power in '96, I would have been seen as a Labor sympathiser, if not apparatchik.[70]

Yet Shergold had demonstrated high competence in working with Reith on public service matters and, as secretary of Employment, Workplace Relations and Small Business, in managing the controversial waterfront disputes in 1998. Howard may have given more attention to likely partisan affiliation than did Menzies or Fraser: he was too shrewd to discount effectiveness in its favour.

Howard was good to work with. He was invariably on top of submissions and papers, administratively efficient, calm, courteous and measured. Public servants said he was easy to brief:

> Keating thinks in pictures. So when you brief Keating and … you're a left-brain, linear person … it's really hard to know where he's at. With Howard it was very easy. He did the … linear brain stuff … You'd give him all the facts and he absorbed them and then he'd be asking for more information and he'd take it all in. So it was very different in style … He was very clear in what he wanted.[71]

Clarity, civility and effective working relations facilitated by Moore-Wilton and Shergold ensured productive interaction with the APS for the most part. Yet there was an undeniable edge: Howard's tenacity translated into tackling apparent divergence from the government line, not to mention public service leaks and whistleblowers, with uncommon punitive vigour, which some have argued was intentionally intimidatory.[72]

Moore-Wilton inculcated the stress on service to the executive and prime minister. Shergold insisted on the need to infuse policy advising with attention to evidence *and* to the political climate. That entailed knowing how far the evidence would take you, once conscious of the prime minister's preferences: 'how far do you keep pushing when you can see the prime minister is saying no? How many times can you say, "Well Prime Minister, let me just give you more evidence on this"?'[73] There was increased emphasis on performance management across the service, and on the vetting of key appointments. Task forces, in which members were expected to forget departmental allegiances and apply their expertise to particular problems, were formed to facilitate government objectives. It was a means of 'allowing the prime minister to take the lead without imposing too heavily on the minister … [and] a way of keeping PM&C involved in this "whole of government" sense'.[74] It fostered horizontal collaboration and coordination, but with a hierarchical dimension, underpinned by political authority.[75] Policy and program control and integration was, as always, achieved through cabinet, central agencies and departments, but the system after 1996 reinforced the potential of the prime minister as the locus of power. Inevitably, that engaged the staff closest to him in the PMO.

After the Liberal Party defeat in the 1993 election, there had been discussion of the need for a more professional approach to staffing of and recruitment to support roles. An even earlier review, chaired by then Liberal Party president John Valder following the Coalition defeat in 1983, established the principles on which Howard's PMO would be developed. The Valder Report had argued that support for cabinet (the catalyst for the CPU), and more support and more political focus in ministerial offices and the PMO, were imperative.[76] Thirteen years later, Howard adopted its principles. There were teething problems at first in establishing this political focus in the PMO. Howard's first chief of staff, Nicole Feely, had efficiently restructured his office in opposition but lacked public service networks and experience, and had some difficulty in engaging with the Canberra policy bureaucracy.[77] She was replaced after fourteen months by long-term Howard confidant Grahame Morris, but his tenure too was brief. He departed after four months when, in the course of a controversial inquiry into improper claiming of travel allowances (which claimed three ministerial scalps), there were discrepancies in accounts of when the PMO had been advised of the problem, for which Morris took the fall.[78] Initially, the performance of Howard's office was unimpressive.[79]

The tide turned following the appointment of Arthur Sinodinos, certainly a partisan loyalist but also an experienced public servant, to head the PMO in 1997. He brought to bear political understanding, appreciation of the prime minister's objectives, and bureaucratic experience in achieving order in the PMO and facilitating the networks necessary for policy development. An office insider remarked on his ability to maintain 'a very good balance of policy and administration and political nous'.[80] The establishment of the CPU relieved the PMO of responsibility for long-term planning and freed it to concentrate on day-to-day and tactical imperatives, yet policy objectives remained primary. Complementing the CPU's responsibility for dealing with departments, the stable relationships fostered by Sinodinos were crucial. Peter Shergold said:

> There would probably have been no day when I was not in touch with one of the policy advisers in the prime minister's office about something. And I would have regular contact in person or by telephone with the

> prime minister … A lot of the relationship was about policy and Arthur … well, I think he was quite exceptional … because he liked policy.[81]

In 1998 Sinodinos reorganised the office. The principal private secretary, Tony Nutt, headed the personal staff, provided political advice and was Howard's 'fixer' and 'enforcer'. An advisory group numbered between ten and twelve, with senior advisers specialising in substantive policy areas and in some cases mirroring divisions in PM&C. In accordance with Howard's preoccupation with controlling communication, the media unit, with eight staff, was the largest of any Australian prime minister. It not only advised the prime minister but also coordinated the thirty-four media advisers working in other ministerial offices and became progressively more engaged with the public affairs and media sections of departments.[82]

The PMO structure, once settled by Sinodinos, remained stable. There was relatively little staff turnover: Howard's equable treatment of his staff encouraged loyalty. In 2003, Sinodinos commented, 'We've all been around a long time. It's a team rather than individuals fighting for access to the emperor's ear'.[83] Moreover, Howard ensured that his office remained aware of the different roles to be played by public servants and private office staff. According to Shergold,

> John Howard … had a very traditional view of Westminster and public servants … he was very clear in understanding the difference between Arthur's role and my role. He would conscientiously remind others in his office, more junior policy advisers or particularly the media advisers, of that role.[84]

Ideally, policy development and implementation would be collaborative. But the intention behind the development of the PMO was clear: it was to be an office with the capacity not only to engage with but to direct the public service, and an unrivalled ability to dictate the government's story.

John Howard, through his relations with his party secretariat, attention to the parliamentary backbench and the party base, and feeling for party sentiment, gained the unqualified admiration of Liberals: by 2001 even critics remarked 'he can hang on as long as he wants ... he owns the party'.[85] By then, too, instances of ministerial failure to observe codes of conduct that had led to a number being dropped during his first term were forgotten: his exercise of exemplary cabinet discipline was manifest. He had ensured responsiveness in the APS by key appointments, and by the capacity of his strategists in the CPU and the PMO to ensure that the government's objectives determined policy direction and implementation. He had identified the best means of managing the media to disseminate his message and contain critics. He was a controlling prime minister, but no more so than Fraser. However, such was his authority that he did not have to contend with a disruptive group in the party room, as had Fraser. He did not lose battles in cabinet or Caucus, as had Whitlam. And, by extending the logic of public sector reform and private staffing infrastructure inherited from his predecessors, he had fully realised the means for prime-ministerial government.

Prime-ministerial Government Redux

Before Howard, Fraser had consolidated leadership resources and fine-tuned leader centrality in a manner reflecting what British Labour leader Richard Crossman, writing in 1972, had described as prime-ministerial government—the transition from collective executive responsibility to prime-ministerial dominance.[86] Hawke, however, adopted a different approach: the core elements of his mode of governing were his partnership with Keating complemented by a more general exercise of distributed leadership. Keating as prime minister swung the leadership pendulum back. But, as Paul Kelly has argued, it was Howard who most comprehensively revived and perfected prime-ministerial government in the Australian context.[87] It was not that Howard abandoned cabinet government. On the contrary, he insisted that he was a cabinet traditionalist, and was one of its most accomplished practitioners. Nor did it mean that he consistently intervened or overrode his ministers, or that he laid claim to every initiative. But it did mean that when necessary he could prevail: he reportedly always got his way. Since his authority rested with the party, he was not dependent on cabinet: big decisions could be taken outside it and legitimised within.[88] And the big decisions always related to the objectives Howard identified, initially in the economic sphere and later in the security domain.

Howard was courageous in the cause of what he believed to be right. Although always attentive to what he called the broad church of his party and the Coalition, he had the capacity to carry them with him in contentious decisions—such as on gun control and the GST—despite trenchant opposition from some within his ranks. He was not captive to dissidents. On the other hand, nor was he sufficiently responsive to distractions (such as the emergence of Pauline Hanson and her One Nation Party) or to what he regarded as self-interested minorities. His distaste for climate activists, welfare advocates and the 'Aboriginal industry' hindered open-minded engagement with their claims for most of his term.[89] In Howard's mind these matters were incidental to economic imperatives. It was there that clarity about what he wanted and adept recourse to prime-ministerial government, when necessary, enabled Howard to put his stamp on the reform agenda.

Howard continued with the unfinished business of the Hawke–Keating era. In Kelly's view, there were three planks: 'fiscal consolidation and government debt reduction based on a commitment to surplus budgets; a formal agreement on central bank independence to entrench a low inflation culture; and a deregulated labour market in the cause of individual freedom, more jobs and higher productivity'.[90] It was the agenda he had developed ever since the Coalition loss in 1983. Despite tensions as Costello grew increasingly impatient about leadership succession, common policy objectives enabled Howard to continue working closely with his treasurer. Their aims were pursued incrementally and were largely achieved. They involved spending cuts, the sale of public assets, commercialisation of social service delivery, taxation reform, tariff revision, labour law reform and more efficient targeting (rather than abolition) of regulation.

The reliable delivery of surplus budgets was 'prudent economics and brilliant politics': it was the buffer against economic crises; the burden fell on those interest groups and Labor voting blocs Howard judged he would never win; and it provided the means for canny redistribution to those he must persuade.[91] Howard also profited from a period of unparalleled economic growth, triggered by the Hawke–Keating reforms, but with the added advantage that the mid-1990s to the mid-2000s were boom years for the world economy, the best decade for global growth since the 1970s. Between 1990 and 2005, Australian housing values doubled, share prices trebled, stock exchange values of Australian companies increased sixfold, and unemployment dropped to levels not matched since the 1970s.[92] It was not simply luck. Economic liberalism, promoted by the policies of Hawke, Keating and Howard, generated prosperity even if equitable redistribution remained a matter of contention. Targeted regulation, such as the Australian Prudential Regulation Authority, introduced by Costello, ensured economic resilience and saved Australia from the excesses that would create the global financial crisis (GFC) in 2008–09. And the prime minister, despite Costello's success in innovative regulation, managing budgets and winning parliamentary battles,[93] remained the chief spruiker, putting the Liberal stamp on all that was achieved and reinforcing his own centrality. After winning three elections, Howard was described as the leader who '"brought home the bacon"—a glowing 83 per cent of voters who rated the economy as the main issue believe he has managed the economy well or quite well'.[94] It was argued that economic management was *the* key reason why 'Australians … re-elected the Howard Government three times to give it 10 years in office'.[95]

Even so, there was disquiet. By the late 1990s, 74 per cent of survey respondents had little confidence in federal government; 84 per cent distrusted both major parties; and there had been a 30 per cent drop in confidence in government over the preceding thirteen years.[96] A few years later, a survey showed that there was more consistent public support for old economic institutions than for the new market-based and deregulated institutional arrangements advocated by governments of both persuasions: reformers had not won consensus for 'the new consensus'.[97] Social researcher Peter Saunders, following another survey, concluded that there was 'a sense of alienation and powerlessness in which a gulf has opened up between the values and priorities of ordinary Australians and those in positions of political power and influence'.[98]

Paul Kelly signalled the danger of Coalition hubris following the 2001 election, and places the death of the reform project—and a subsequent series of botched policies—around 2003.[99] By then, bipartisan commitment had failed: Labor, capitalising on public disquiet to challenge the Coalition, had retreated from the Hawke–Keating economic legacy. Perhaps to counter the emerging fragility of the reform project, or the exhaustion of its big ideas, Howard sought other means to reinforce his position. Kelly noted the manner in which, after the 9/11 attacks on America and the inauguration of the 'war on terror', Howard took on a role analogous to 'commander in chief' and used the upgraded NSC and the security agenda to enhance his executive authority.[100] Border control and sovereignty became his watchwords, and he deployed them both in mobilising a critical response to asylum seekers and in marshalling the case for Australian participation in the war on terror. In parallel, with repeated electoral ascendancy, colleagues were inclined to cede to Howard ever greater authority and autonomy.

Howard had long shown a proclivity for unilateral decision-making when he deemed it warranted by the circumstances, as had most of his predecessors. Indeed, his much-lauded introduction of gun control legislation following the 1996 Port Arthur massacre was one such instance. The bold decision to introduce a GST, in consultation with Costello alone, was another. And previous prime ministers had certainly made decisions about security and conflict engagement without recourse to cabinet. In Howard's case, however, especially from 2001 on, a number of instances provoked widespread critical discussion. They indicate the potential for overreach inherent in the exercise of prime-ministerial government. Two cases can serve as examples: the 'children overboard' affair, and the closeted decision-making leading to Australia's commitment to the 'coalition of the willing' and the Iraq war.

In August 2001, following the *Tampa* incident, the government hastily established a new border protection regime. The *Tampa*, a Norwegian ship, rescued asylum seekers from a boat that was foundering and sought to land them on Christmas Island. It was refused. When it entered Australian maritime waters, Australian troops boarded and took control of the ship. Eventually the Australian navy transported the asylum seekers to Nauru. In parallel, the government developed the 'Pacific' solution: provision for the navy to intercept sea-faring asylum seekers and to transport them to offshore centres (initially Nauru) where they would be held until their claims were processed. Two months later, shortly before the 2001 election, ministers Philip Ruddock, Reith and Howard himself, acting on incomplete information and images, announced that asylum seekers whose boat was intercepted by the navy had thrown their children into the sea in the hope that rescue would secure passage to Australia. What actually happened was that as the boat was sinking, navy personnel had leapt into the sea to rescue children and others. Yet persistent debate about the nature of the evidence between ministers and their advisers ensured that a more accurate picture did not emerge until after the election. Some believed this to be deliberate obfuscation.

Even more contentious was Howard's solo post-9/11 pledge to stand with America against its enemies, and the government's subsequent commitment to the Iraq war, despite adverse public opinion and insufficient intelligence as to the alleged trigger for invasion: Saddam Hussein's possession of weapons of mass destruction (WMDs). Decisions were restricted to an inner circle, though later strongly supported by cabinet. It was apparent that countervailing advice was not welcome, and that neither DFAT nor Defence conveyed reservations about the available intelligence or the Iraq strategy to government. 'In my view', said Ashton Calvert, secretary of Defence, 'they didn't need advice on what they should do because they had, in effect, made up their minds'.[101]

It is acknowledged that previous prime ministers typically made decisions about military engagement and security in camera. But the extensive discussion provoked by each of these examples seemed to reveal a common pattern.[102] There were serial failures of senior public servants to tell Howard and his ministers when they were wrong. Their efforts to find evidence to support the government's story in relation to 'children overboard' and Iraq's alleged WMD capacities, for example, were striking. This persistence convinced both veteran commentators—such as Paul Kelly—and public sector insiders who had engaged in reform—such as Andrew Podger and Mike Keating—that public service 'responsiveness' had gone so far as to inhibit officials from telling government other than what it wanted to hear.[103]

Peter Shergold argued strongly against this position, saying that in most instances ministers will not decide upon the detail of policy until they have received advice, but also suggesting a secretary can never be 'too responsive in the most fundamental of respects—that is, in accepting that it is the minister who has the responsibility to decide a policy'.[104] Yet in each of these cases, as Calvert in particular indicates, ministers had made up their minds, and public servants (true to Shergold's principal that it is the minister's responsibility to decide policy) were disinclined to point out what at least some knew to be wrong.

Furthermore, when such events achieved high political salience, ministerial staff became significant intermediaries, not simply cooperating with officials but improperly attempting to direct them. Patrick Weller's study of 'children overboard' showed staffers to have intervened in departmental processes and mediated between the political and administrative domains. They drove, sieved and skewed departmental advice to ministers, insisting upon what ministers wanted as opposed to the public interest or the integrity of the policy process. Weller's conclusion was that ministerial staff had become 'the "junk-yard attack dogs" of the political system: the hard men and the hit men. They are politically dispensable, convenient scapegoats who will take the bullet for their ministers and protect them from political fallout'.[105] Thus it was that when inconvenient details emerged, the prime minister and his ministers consistently defended themselves from criticism by maintaining that advisers (both public servants and personal staffers) did not pass on crucial information. Then (on the grounds that they had not been properly informed) they denied responsibility for 'mistakes', while refusing to allow their staffers to be questioned by parliament. In cases where private office staffers had played key roles, they could not be called to account—leaving public servants to take most of the heat.[106]

One might accept that the government wholeheartedly believed in what it was doing. It can also be argued that these were exceptional cases: Howard's decade-long success relied on a pragmatism in which such extremes were rare. But where such instances arose they could not easily be explained as 'mistakes, from which we have to learn',[107] given the pattern underlying such 'mistakes'.[108] They were manifestations not of contestability and adjudication between alternative options, but of funnelling everything in terms of what the leader was alleged to need, or had already decided.

By late in Howard's final term, what was once the exception, when Howard bypassed cabinet to work with a small inner circle, became more common. One precursor was that the Coalition gained control of the Senate at the 2004 election, removing one of the constraints on prime-ministerial government. Howard then felt free to push through measures that had always been intended but had previously been diluted by Senate 'obstruction'. The most controversial was his radical WorkChoices legislation that deregulated workplaces, truncating the power of unions and shifting the balance in negotiating wages and conditions decisively in favour of employers. Tellingly, Howard resisted the concerns of some of his ministers and misjudged the community unease this Bill provoked. It would provide an opening for unions to run an expensive and effective scare campaign against the government.

Howard sensed in 2006 that the tide had begun to run out, but he was far from alone.[109] His colleagues were increasingly uneasy as polls showed the Labor opposition leading by a widening margin. Yet Howard had come from behind in successive elections and had always prevailed. He remained convinced that he was the person most likely to lead the Coalition to another victory in 2007. But the rankling issue of leadership succession was always a factor at such times. The expectation that Costello was the logical successor, recurrent media speculation about the appropriate timing of any transition, and Costello's thinly veiled frustration had been persistent since 2001. A story broke in July 2006 that an understanding had been reached between Howard and Costello in 1994, during negotiations over Downer standing aside to allow Howard's accession to the party leadership unopposed. Costello would retain the deputy leadership, and in the event that the Coalition won in 1996, Howard would govern for a term or so, expecting to hand over to Costello during a second term in about 2000.

It never happened. Howard and Costello have each published accounts of this, but as Costello concedes, 'Howard was an expert at manoeuvring over the leadership', and despite recurrent approaches from Costello and others, he would never go voluntarily.[110] Howard argued that the leadership was not his to give; it was the gift of the party room. Anyone had a right to challenge, but he would remain as long as the party wanted him. Costello's view was that an orderly transition, rather than a divisive battle such as that between Keating and Hawke, was in the party's best interests, especially in 2006–07 as prospects looked increasingly adverse. That the history of this argument was now in the public domain meant that it was an issue that could no longer be ignored, despite Costello 'loyally' declining to challenge and Howard turning his efforts to campaigning.

In 2007, in what amounted to a year-long election campaign, the focus on prosperity and reform that had served Howard so well was diffused, on the one hand by what appeared to be a step too far—the Work Choices initiative—and on the other by a subsidiary but interventionist prime-ministerial agenda. Suddenly, problems of lengthy duration were elevated as policy concerns and now said to be so urgent, and so challenging, that only experienced government could manage them. In relation to the social breakdown in Indigenous communities, the states' administration of hospitals and management of the Murray-Darling river system, for instance, it was argued that only central government intervention and strong leadership could serve as the circuit-breaker. At the core were real and serious problems, and action arguably arose from good intentions, but it begged the question of why they had been ignored for so long, and why they now should be addressed in a matter of months, using startling measures (such as mobilising the army to facilitate intervention in the Northern Territory's Indigenous communities). In these cases, a handful of cabinet colleagues, senior civil servants and personal staff became Howard's reference group. Initiatives were driven from the top; consultation was rare; urgency of action was the watchword.

The consistency of purpose and calm control that had been admired aspects of Howard's government were diluted by a sense of confected crisis management. The success of the Labor and union campaign against WorkChoices confirmed the reservations some of Howard's ministers had expressed. The loss of focus allowed Labor leader Kevin Rudd to step in, claiming to speak for economic orthodoxy and the consistent management that had been Howard's strengths. From a position that had long seemed unassailable (between 2001 and early 2006), public support was eroded to such an extent that the fall of Howard's government at the federal election of 2007 came to be widely predicted. When, at Howard's invitation, and only weeks from the election, a majority of his cabinet colleagues indicated that Howard should relinquish the leadership in favour of Peter Costello, he refused to accede. After consulting his family and invoking the authority stemming from his support in the extra-parliamentary party, he challenged them to remove him. They caved in: the prime minister's predilections trumped the concerns of his colleagues. Howard remained in power until the voters removed him.

A Prime-ministerial Machine

Some of those long experienced in the practices and evolution of federal government see the process of professionalising the public service (beginning with Curtin, Chifley and Menzies) and the accretion of executive resources devised by Wilenski and Whitlam, refined by Fraser and Kemp, and built upon by every successor, as having created a political and policy machine of considerable power and sophistication. This occurred in conjunction with a weakening of parties and party loyalty, and a transition in media practices that directed increasing attention to leaders and influenced public expectations. The combination of a responsive public sector, integrated by a 'can do' PM&C, and a finely attuned, politically loyalist private office was suited both to the complex challenges of managing dynamic policy problems and the political imperatives stemming from party, media and electoral expectations. This was the intention behind their development. Arguably such a prime-ministerial machine reached its height during the administrations of Hawke, Keating and Howard.

It demanded balance and a sure touch, however. Said Alan Rose, after lengthy service in senior APS roles:

> If a prime minister comes in and doesn't understand the history of the machine … they're inheriting, they're at a grave disadvantage and are likely to be chewed up by it … Outside of the government, outside of the prime minister's office—the media, the lobbies—all have grown to have a particular understanding of what the prime minister is capable of. I don't mean personally but what … his or her machine is capable of, what they're responsible for and what they should be doing. It's not so much the character of the individual but the office and what the office has become that dictates the way it works … Now John Howard commanded it superbly. He knew what he was getting … he commanded it … He took it on in a particular way and ran it in his way.[111]

Howard's cabinet secretary, Paul McClintock, accentuated the positive and negative propensities:

> The office reflects the minister: it's not the other way around. A bad minister will normally have a bad office and a good minister will normally have a good one … The office amplifies the prime minister. So, if the prime minister is in strife, he amplifies that, makes it worse. If the prime minister is on top of the job, it amplifies it … the leader is assessed and re-assessed all the time … the fortunes of the government rise and fall on that one individual. And the power of the office, to some extent, also reflects the fact that they all know that.[112]

Yet the inherent flaws in the ministerial staffing system, with the PMO at its apex, introduced under Whitlam and refined under Fraser, had been there from the first. An enhanced capacity for direction and control was not matched by systematic constraints or, above all, by transparent scrutiny and accountability. Terry Moran, a young public servant when the Whitlam reforms were introduced, recalled:

> I was in the Public Service Board in early 1973 when the request came in from the Prime Minister's Office … to have a look at the ministerial staff. And I was the one who … as a young graduate recruit, suggested … that what they really needed was a career structure … But

> I wasn't experienced enough to realise that you've got to define what the different roles do ... It didn't happen when it should have happened ... Nobody bothered much about getting the definition of the roles right much less the accountabilities right ... it wasn't a great problem because there were always a very large number of seconded public servants in ministerial offices.[113]

Hence, adverse potential had been held in check because there had been a balance between the partisan element and bureaucratic realism: namely, the practice by prime ministers of retaining experienced public servants in key roles within the private office. Bureaucratic networks were known, the inherent APS concern for a professional ethic was understood, cooperative endeavour and mutual trust could develop. This was evident during the Hawke and Keating administrations and for the most part under Howard.

For much of the twentieth century, those prime ministers with a marked propensity for control, such as Stanley Bruce and Malcolm Fraser, were constrained by needing to maintain mass party structures and lacked the resources to exercise prime-ministerial government, even though the germ of such an approach emerged under Fraser. The advent of electoral-professional parties, with much more reliance on the leader, accentuated by ever greater media focus on leadership performance rather than party or policy, and the development of the machine described above provided the opportunity for Howard to bring prime-ministerial government to fruition. But the potential for executive overreach and disruptive asymmetry in the relations between a leader, his private office staff and the public service was always present.

In general, Howard's long experience, controlling instinct, political nous and pragmatism ensured that he maintained the balance within this machine. His self-mastery was as remarkable as his mastery of the political levers now available to him. Furthermore, with the experienced bureaucrat Arthur Sinodinos as his chief of staff, his office resisted the lure of unwanted intervention. Given Howard's longevity, the achievement of much that he sought and indeed the transition he engineered towards a more individualist, choice-oriented and entrepreneurial political culture, his was a largely successful exercise of prime-ministerial government.

Yet the incidence of adverse cases indicates that there were lapses—moments when prime-ministerial government went too far—when seemingly propitious circumstances, perceived threat, political temptation or urgency intervened. And their proliferation as Howard's authority became more unquestioned (coincident with Sinodinos leaving the stage in 2006, before the final curtain) suggests that with increasing hubris born of long dominance, the machine went into overdrive. The electorate at last was unimpressed. Concocted crises, the refusal to backtrack on the unpopular decision to join the disastrous Iraq intervention, and overreach with WorkChoices legislation, instead of confirming strong leadership, mobilised opinion against the Coalition, and Howard lost office.

Howard's administration was the bridge in developing the executive government and public sector resources that his predecessors had built up into the means of prime-ministerial government. He succeeded in controlling communication in a manner that limited debate and accentuated the government's message; in seizing control of the public service; and in developing a machine of unparalleled influence, but with the potential that it would encourage overreach and amplify poor decisions as well as good leadership. His lengthy political and electoral dominance confirms that, at his best, on top of the job, it was indeed a machine that facilitated successful leadership. But later, accustomed to control, he would succumb to a degree of hubris and then, as he himself felt the tide beginning to turn, to desperation. Then, choices were made that illuminated the flaws in the machine. In the longer view, such instances might be accounted as marginal in relation to what Howard had otherwise achieved, but they would contribute to his eventual defeat. The question for his successors was clear: could they manage the machine they had inherited, or would they be chewed up by it?

6

HARBINGERS OF DECLINE? KEVIN RUDD, JULIA GILLARD AND TONY ABBOTT

'I FIRMLY BELIEVE that our party is better than this, that our government is better than this and, by God, that our country is so much better than this', prime minister Tony Abbott implored the nation, and more particularly his Liberal parliamentary colleagues, in September 2015 as he announced a party room ballot to resolve a challenge to his leadership by Malcolm Turnbull.[1] Abbott's effort to give patriotic gloss to the preservation of his prime ministership was in vain. He lost the contest to Turnbull, becoming the third prime minister to be removed from office by party colleagues in five years. On this occasion there was little of the public astonishment that had greeted the first of these political regicides: Labor prime minister Kevin Rudd's deposition by Julia Gillard in June 2010. In part this was because Abbott's hold on power had been tenuous since early 2015 when he had staved off a leadership spill motion, but the almost nonchalant nature of the response also suggested that voters had become inured to the spectacle of prime-ministerial assassination. Internationally, however, the latest leadership upheaval in Canberra piqued curiosity and more than a little bemusement. The BBC reported Abbott's downfall under the headline, 'Australia: Coup capital of the democratic world', and its correspondent mischievously compared the serial political bloodletting to a Quentin Tarantino movie.[2]

Australian prime ministers have historically been vulnerable to palace revolt because of the relative ease of the means of overthrowing them. Until a traumatised Labor Party changed its system for electing and deselecting leaders in 2013 by granting rank-and-file members a role in the process, prime ministers on either side of the political fence survived between elections exclusively on the sufferance of their parliamentary colleagues. Moreover, they could conceivably face a party room challenge at any time.[3] Equally, there have been previous periods when prime-ministerial office in Australia has resembled a revolving door. The immature party system of the infant Commonwealth saw eight separate ministries and five prime ministers in a decade; the knife-edge parliament of early World War II occasioned turbulence with three prime ministers in the second half of 1941; and the retirement in 1966 of the bulwark of the postwar political order, Robert Menzies, ushered in another spell of unsettled national leadership.

Instability at the top has thus been a recurrent feature of the Australian political system. Nevertheless, the deposition of three prime ministers and five incumbencies in eight years following John Howard's reign (Rudd, December 2007 – June 2010; Gillard, June 2010 – June 2013; Rudd, June–September 2013; Abbott, September 2013 – September 2015; and Turnbull, September 2015–) invited the impression that holding the office has rarely been so confounding. To some observers the leadership churn signalled a profound malaise in the political system. The most insistent exponent of this view, Paul Kelly, wrote that the role of prime minister had become 'a more arduous task' in a situation in which 'volatility and fragmentation' were the defining features of a political culture blighted by intensified partisanship and collapsing public trust. This imperilled the kind of transformative leadership that Australia enjoyed in the 1980s: 'it is by no means certain that Bob Hawke or Paul Keating would have succeeded in the contemporary environment'.[4] Other seasoned political commentators, however, were sceptical of the idea of systemic decline. Instead, by some accounts, rather than be panicked by the recent prime-ministerial merry-go-round, we could take comfort that 'the system' was functioning as it ought to by having 'weeded out' a run of poor leaders.[5]

Rudd, Gillard and Abbott endured travails as each struggled to manage the prime-ministerial government machine developed under their predecessors. Their collective story is one of individual fallibility but also of the hazards inherent in that machine and of the larger destabilising forces increasing the difficulties and onerousness of office.

Kevin Rudd: a Micromanager in the Lodge

Because of its originating collectivist principles, the Labor Party has found it especially challenging to accommodate domineering leaders. Historically, they have had a combustible effect on the party, none more so than Billy Hughes. Yet in modern times, beginning with Whitlam and continuing through the Hawke–Keating era, the party has progressively adapted itself, albeit grudgingly, to greater prime-ministerial assertiveness. If these incumbencies were stepping stones to Kevin Rudd's, he would take leadership centralism to a higher plane and push the party towards another tipping point. In many ways, his leadership record represents a textbook case study of personalisation, throwing into sharp relief the opportunities but also the perils of the autonomous leader. His prime ministership would also shape the circumstances of his successors, Julia Gillard and Tony Abbott. The trio became intertwined in a mutually destructive cycle.

When Kevin Rudd won the Labor Party leadership in December 2006, it was the fifth time the party had changed leader during a decade in opposition. By way of contrast, the party's previous five leadership transitions had stretched out over nearly thirty years.[6] This alone said much about the compressed time cycle of contemporary politics and the growing flakiness of parties, both of which fed a culture of leadership disposability. Rudd was in many ways the very model of a modern leader. Having entered the House of Representatives at the October 1998 federal election, when he became prime minister at the end of 2007 he had been in parliament for nine years. With the exception of Hawke, who had his own extraordinary trajectory to office and who, while formally outside the political sphere, had been deeply enmeshed within it and the Labor Party, this meant that Rudd had much less parliamentary experience upon obtaining the prime ministership than any predecessor since World War II. Nor, unlike most of those forerunners, had Rudd been a minister.

The youngest of four children, Rudd was brought up in country south-east Queensland in a politically conservative and religious family.[7] Straitlaced and fastidious, he was also precociously curious about the wider world. Despite the trauma of the sudden death of his father and the ensuing family upheaval, Rudd flourished at secondary school. As a teenager he first evinced interest in the Labor Party 'not by virtue of tribalism but because of intellectual commitment to Whitlam's China policy'.[8] Leaving Queensland, he enrolled in Asian Studies at the ANU. Rudd eschewed campus politics to concentrate on his studies, and devoted his extracurricular involvement to the student Christian evangelical network. Upon graduation he entered the Department of Foreign Affairs and Trade, where his talents marked him out for a bright future. Following a second overseas posting, however, Rudd took leave to join the staff of Queensland Labor opposition leader and soon to be premier Wayne Goss. Appointed principal private secretary to Goss, he was subsequently elevated to director-general of the office of cabinet—a position that, according to some, he exploited to become de facto second-in-command within the government. Winning mixed reviews in the role, Rudd exhibited traits that would define his prime-ministerial leadership: prodigious drive matched by a ferocious work ethic and a voracious appetite for information. But he was also highly controlling, prone to bullying those around him, intellectually vain, had a cavalier disregard for keeping to schedule, and a fetish for the minutiae of policy detail.[9] Under his direction, one staffer noted, the government's administrative structure 'was built around a single choke point: Rudd'.[10]

Once in the federal parliament, Rudd was relentlessly oriented towards personal advancement. At the end of 2003, Simon Crean followed Kim Beazley to become the second of Labor's old guard to be discarded as opposition leader, and the party looked to its up-and-coming MPs for a successor. Rudd had designs on the job. Largely aloof from the party's factions and without a support base within its industrial wing, however, he could not yet muster anything like the Caucus numbers to be a credible candidate. Rudd was at the same time turning that distance to his advantage. An assiduous courter of the media, in 2001 he had debuted on the morning breakfast television program *Sunrise*. Those regular appearances were refined into a popular segment, 'Big guns of politics', in which he was eventually paired with the genial Liberal minister Joe Hockey. By that time *Sunrise*'s ratings were soaring.[11] With its relaxed informality the segment became a crucial platform for Rudd to reach beyond his party to a mainstream audience and to craft a 'non-political persona'.[12] Prolific activity in other outlets further burnished Rudd's media profile as he demonstrated a rare adeptness at modulating presentations for different audiences. Rudd would construct, as the journalist and political commentator George Megalogenis later observed,

> a persona for every demographic. There was Kevin the erudite for the ABC set. Kevin the dag for FM radio and the Twitterverse. Kevin the genial dad for the Seven network's *Sunrise* program. Kevin the bloke for *Today Tonight* and *A Current Affair*.[13]

Though Rudd's media performances provided a means to circumvent the party, he could not afford to ignore it outright. His stillborn leadership candidacy of 2003 spurred him to embark on a campaign of networking with parliamentary colleagues and Labor's organisational powerbrokers. In the words of one admirer, former NSW premier Bob Carr, 'He couldn't be overlooked. He was always in your diary or at your door'.[14] Neither could the party disregard Rudd's remarkable tenacity in pursuing the Coalition government in his role as Labor's foreign affairs spokesperson, nor his burgeoning public profile. It was the backing of the NSW right faction and that state branch's secretary, Mark Arbib, which was ultimately decisive in elevating Rudd as a legitimate contender as leadership instability continued to plague Labor into the fourth term of the Howard government. In a recurring scenario, internally commissioned polling was wielded as a weapon to precipitate a leadership contest in late 2006. That research showed that the public was familiar with and interested in Rudd—a recognition factor Arbib attributed to *Sunrise*.[15] The final hurdle to Rudd's ascension was cleared through an accommodation with another of the rising stars of Caucus, Julia Gillard, who agreed to put her ambition on hold in favour of him. Her explanation for deferring to Rudd had ominous implications for her own prime ministership: 'Kevin had to be leader in our alliance because I understood that I was not what Labor needed at that point: a woman, not married, an atheist. I would not be perceived as the embodiment of safe change'.[16]

Rudd was 'the embodiment of safe change' throughout the 2007 election year.[17] Policy differences to the Coalition were staked out, particularly in industrial relations and climate change, but otherwise a disciplined Rudd declined to allow the government to bait him. He presented as a younger and more energetic version of Howard, brandishing his economic conservatism and distancing himself from labour movement militancy. The party's campaign pitch revolved around him both exploiting and reinforcing his celebrity politician status. The election year began with a television advertisement, scripted by and featuring Rudd, introducing viewers to his life narrative. By August the leader-centred campaign fully bloomed into 'Kevin 07', complete with website, 'KMAIL', branded T-shirts and other presidential-like paraphernalia, while closer to polling day there was personalised text-messaging and skywriting.

Rudd and a small team of advisers were in the driving seat of Labor's campaign (though ironically, the iconic 'Kevin 07' slogan was created without his consent). He had given public expression to his determination to dictate to the party on the evening he was elected opposition leader by announcing that if he became prime minister he would overturn the century-old rule that Caucus chose the ministry: 'I'll be leading this show and when it comes to the outcomes that I want, I intend to get them'.[18] The party meekly submitted—as it did to a highly orchestrated 2007 national conference that was a showcase for Rudd and paved the way for increased leadership influence over candidate preselections.[19]

Within Rudd's camp there were few doubts that he was the party's chief asset and key to its success. One campaign insider noted that 'self-evidently it was Rudd, not Labor, that was going to win the election'.[20]

According to another, the party's focus groups were telling them: 'people were voting for KR (Kevin Rudd) despite him being Labor ... There was no love for Labor as a party, brand, movement ... It was all KR'.[21] The Australian Election Study, a national survey conducted after every federal election since 1987, confirmed Rudd's personal popularity with voters. He was the most highly rated leader to that time, narrowly surpassing the response to Bob Hawke in 1987. On the other hand, the swing to Labor had been due to broader factors: the Coalition's unpopular industrial relations policy, its laggard conversion to tackling climate change, and general fatigue with the more-than-a-decade-old government and its prime minister.[22] Even so, when one combined Rudd's undeniable appeal to voters, his dominance of Labor's campaign and the fact he would steer the party to power less than a year after becoming leader, it was perhaps inevitable the view that, as one senior party figure expressed it, this had been 'entirely Kevin's victory' would assume irresistible force.[23]

Kevin 24/7

Rudd's election night victory speech of November 2007 was a peculiarly deflating affair that left the Labor faithful cold. He referred to a shopping list of broad policy ambitions for the incoming government, arguably enough for several terms, before warning that there was no time for celebrations because, 'Tomorrow, and I say this to the team, we roll up our sleeves, we're ready for hard work'.[24] Rudd meant it. From the outset, he operated in office at an almost superhuman pace. Within weeks of the election, 'Kevin 07' was reported to have morphed into 'Kevin 24/7' as stories circulated of the new prime minister's sleepless schedule and the extraordinary demands he was placing upon staffers and bureaucrats alike.[25] Nor was this simply an initial burst of energy: the whirlwind showed no signs of abating, and after several months Rudd was dubbed the nation's 'Workaholic-in-Chief'.[26]

The breakneck work rate was a symptom of Rudd's highly personalised approach to governing. It revealed an inherent lack of faith in the capacity of other people—with the exception of a small inner circle—as well as an inability to delegate. In his own mind everything depended on him. This was reflected too in his 'Sisyphean quest to be on top of every issue … always demanding a briefing paper to be written for him'.[27] A sympathetic biographer attributed this absorption in detail to Rudd's 'appreciation' of 'complexity' and an intensely analytical rather than intuitive mind.[28] Yet the breadth of matters in which he became involved and the volume of information he required was inimical to structured and timely government decision-making. Delays and policy paralysis ensued: the system waited for the leader to decide, and the leader was otherwise occupied or demanded yet more briefings. This problem was compounded by hyperactivity that saw him flit between issues while simultaneously dressing up the government's objectives in grand terms that inflated expectations. There was to be nothing less than an 'education revolution', for instance. At the same time, short-term tactics often trumped long-term strategy. Hoarding his leadership capital—built mainly on personal popularity in the electorate—was a prime consideration from the start, translating into an obsession with commanding the daily media cycle.

To be fair, important steps were taken towards instituting effective executive practices that might have countervailed Rudd's leadership quirks.[29] As foreshadowed in opposition, he broke with the Labor tradition of Caucus electing the ministry, which was substantially different in composition from the opposition frontbench. But Rudd had not exercised unfettered choice. He consulted Gillard and two of the party's factional 'wise old owls' to assemble a factionally balanced ministry that also took account of state and Senate representation.[30] Though not boasting the same experience, compelling personalities or depth of talent as Hawke's 1983 government, cabinet had powerful players other than the prime minister, particularly deputy prime minister Gillard (who held the 'mega-portfolio' of education, employment and workplace relations, social inclusion) and the treasurer, Wayne Swan.

In the executive machinery, there was a change from the Howard government with the abolition of the CPU. Its secretariat functions were returned to the PM&C, while Labor veteran John Faulkner was appointed cabinet secretary. The choice of Faulkner was shrewd. One of the few in the government who had previously been a cabinet member, he had the experience and acumen to fulfil a role that positioned him as 'Cabinet gatekeeper, troubleshooter and guardian of government strategy'.[31] The cabinet committee system was also refreshed with four main committees: the Climate Change Committee (CCC) that had charge of designing a policy response to what Rudd in opposition had labelled the 'greatest moral challenge of our generation'[32]; the ERC, now a longstanding feature of governments; the NSC; and the Strategic Priorities and Budget Committee (SPBC). Initially, these committees and the cabinet were regarded as functioning effectively, notwithstanding teething problems caused by, among other things, a lack of punctuality by an overloaded prime minister.[33]

As special minister of state, Faulkner was charged with another machinery of government innovation: a code of conduct for ministerial staffers. This initiative had grown out of concerns about the activities of advisers during the Howard years that had been crystallised by the 'children overboard' affair. One of the code's objectives was a sharper demarcation of authority and responsibilities between private offices and departments. It stipulated that staffers 'did not have the power to direct' public servants.[34] The bureaucracy was further encouraged by Labor fulfilling its promise not to replicate Howard's early purge of senior officials, and Rudd's statements that he wanted a renewal of the public service's capacity as a source of policy advice for government. As it turned out, there was considerable turnover of departmental secretaries during the Rudd government's term. This started with the almost immediate departure of Peter Shergold from PM&C, which complicated the transition process. Nevertheless, when the new secretary, Terry Moran, who was recruited from Victoria where he was the state's top bureaucrat, arrived in March 2008 he promptly embarked upon strengthening the strategic policy functions of PM&C.[35] Meanwhile, the recruitment of staffers, which Rudd insisted on being merit-based, resulted in a PMO that included seasoned hands, among them a veteran of the Hawke–Keating governments, David Epstein, as chief of staff.

These developments augured well for the government. But there were also troubling counter-indications. The PMO soon acted as an instrument of Rudd's controlling instincts and became heavily focused on the day-to-day media cycle. A highly centralised media management system was implemented: advisers dubbed it 'command and control'. The PMO daily supplied backbenchers and ministers alike with tightly scripted messages as well as strictly choreographing government media activities.[36] A staffer in one ministerial office received an early taste of the extent of micromanagement when a media conference was interrupted by a curt directive from the PMO: 'Okay, shut it down now, call "enough" on the questions and get out of there'.[37] The government's relationship with the bureaucracy was also being tested as officials struggled to adapt to Rudd's exhausting schedule and capricious demands and became frustrated by the lack of orderly processing of paperwork by the prime minister. When grumblings filtered into the media and there were allegations of leaks by overstretched departments, Rudd's response was unrepentant:

> I understand that there has been some criticism around the edges that some public servants are finding the hours a bit much. Well, I suppose I've simply got news for the public service—there'll be more. The work ethic of this government will not decrease. It will increase.[38]

The prime minister's early activities invited a mixture of optimism and unease in other ways. Few doubted his good intentions or could fault the aplomb with which he delivered on symbolic yet significant Labor pledges. Most notable was the ratification of the Kyoto agreement on climate change and a moving apology to the Indigenous stolen generations delivered before a packed House of Representatives public gallery in February 2008.[39] There were also gestures towards encouraging greater public engagement with government.[40] One expression of this was the inauguration of community cabinet meetings—a practice pioneered by the Queensland state Labor government a decade earlier and subsequently copied by its counterparts in other states—that were billed by the prime minister as a means to better connect the federal government to the public.

The same spirit informed Rudd's convening of a '2020 summit' in April 2008 to bring together 'the best and brightest brains' to hothouse ideas for the nation's long-term future.[41] It generated images of the prime minister humbly seated on the floor listening to the deliberations. However, like much of his activity, there was suspicion of a lack of substance. While the summit spawned a report bulging with 900 recommendations, there were few tangible outcomes. Where it did appear to yield an early result—a sweeping review of the tax system—that was driven by the need for a so-called 'announceable' from the event. Treasurer Swan was only informed of the review, which ultimately became a millstone for the government, hours before the prime minister announced it on national television.[42]

Still, Rudd's honeymoon with voters was unquestioned. He was a breath of fresh air following a decade of Howard, and the public was impressed by his élan and the apparent surety with which he had taken to the role—an ease displayed during frequent international travels that saw him overshadow foreign affairs minister Stephen Smith. His popularity soared. Yet perceptive commentators began to sound warnings that the stratospheric poll ratings were being purchased at the cost of evading tough decisions, and that underneath the veneer of a confident beginning lay dysfunction at the heart of government. By mid-2008, Rudd was christened with a label that would come to stick: 'Captain Chaos'.[43] A measured but sobering assessment of Labor's transition to office delivered around the same time concluded that the prime minister was struggling 'to develop a sustainable operational tempo'.[44]

The GFC: Boon and Burden

Crises can make and unmake a leader. According to Gillard, the global financial crisis was for Rudd 'a great boon' but equally 'a great burden'.[45] The collapse of American financial conglomerates and an ensuing crash of stock markets in the spring of 2008 triggered the most serious breakdown of the international financial system since the Great Depression. Though Australia was partially insulated by a robust domestic banking system and other cushioning factors such as its buoyant trade relationship with China, it was not immune to the dire economic scenarios. For a prime minister and government still struggling for definition nearing their first anniversary in office, responding to the GFC instilled urgency and purpose. Rudd's decision-making was distinguished by a resolve that belied much of his prime-ministerial leadership. Explaining the contrast, Swan later wrote that the severity and immediacy of the crisis 'forced upon Kevin tight frames for disciplined decision-making'.[46]

In other ways, however, the GFC was a challenge tailor-made for Rudd.[47] Grasping early the gravity of the situation, he personally set out about mastering the intricacies of the international financial system, while also convening daily with Swan and senior public servants to monitor the ominous developments overseas and war-game responses. Having to manage an international crisis appealed to Rudd's sense of self-importance. An indefatigable networker, as global credit markets went into paralysis Rudd was in regular contact with fellow world leaders and was prominent among those who successfully lobbied for the G20 (the grouping of the world's twenty major economies) to become a key forum for coordinated multilateral action to stabilise the international economy and reform global financial governance arrangements. His dexterity with ideas was also to the fore. Laying aside his earlier incarnation as an 'economic conservative', Rudd apprehended early that the crisis would weaken the hegemony of tiring neoliberal assumptions and potentially herald a shift in policy thinking. He published a lengthy essay indicting 'free-market fundamentalism' for the GFC and described it as a watershed for the rejuvenation of social democracy.[48] Above all, the emergency environment suited and justified his preference for decision-making in a powerful inner circle centred on him. The government's policy response to the GFC was dictated by the SPBC, comprising Rudd, Gillard, Swan and finance minister Lindsay Tanner, with advice supplied by leading officials headed by Moran and the secretary of treasury, Ken Henry. Cabinet was bypassed in the formulation of Labor's initial $10 billion stimulus spending announced in October 2008, left only 'to ratify the package when all the key decisions had been made and the press releases printed'.[49]

Within the SPBC, the prime minister was chiefly responsible for the big calls on the size and content of the two major economic stimuluses delivered by the government—the second, $42 billion package, focused mainly on fast-tracking capital works, was unveiled in February 2009. 'I took charge of it and drove it', was how Rudd subsequently explained the government's management of the GFC.[50] Rudd's insight and boldness in this period impressed officials such as the experienced Henry. Henry's own advice that government 'go early, go hard, go households' to stimulate economic demand had been influenced by Treasury's dilatory response to the recession of the early 1990s. With the first stimulus package, Rudd was prepared to go further than the Treasury secretary recommended: a prime-ministerial judgement that on Henry's reckoning was vindicated by events.[51]

Yet Labor's handling of the GFC became a matter of sustained dispute.[52] To some extent, the government was a victim of its success. By ameliorating the domestic effects of the international economic disturbance, the dire scenarios did not materialise: Australia became one of only three OECD countries to avoid recession in this period. This, however, emboldened opponents to argue that the dangers had been overblown and the policy response disproportionate. There were also criticisms that parts of the second stimulus package, especially a home insulation scheme that was ultimately connected to several deaths, had been rushed in design and poorly implemented. Beguiled by the notion of a 'double dividend' on policy—an idea borrowed from American president Barack Obama—Rudd had disregarded bureaucratic caution to push for 'policies that would not only stimulate the economy but also achieve environmental outcomes'.[53] PM&C secretary Moran also witnessed a deterioration of process associated with the second stimulus. SPBC members and officials chased Rudd around, including grabbing time with him on a VIP flight to Papua New Guinea where he was attending the South Pacific Forum, to finalise its details, and there was inadequate testing of measures with relevant departments.[54] In addition to costing Labor political capital when flaws in the second stimulatory package began to emerge, the GFC had a damaging legacy by routinising the predominance of the SPBC, or 'gang of four' as it became widely known. Whereas cabinet and Caucus had been willing to tolerate the concentration of authority during the peak of the GFC crisis, its persistence inevitably fuelled internal resentments as well as affording little constraint on the increasingly erratic decision-making practices of the prime minister.

The GFC had other adverse consequences. Because of the inadequate management of processes and flaws in implementation, not only were the merits of the innovation Rudd had attempted obscured, but momentum was lost for the larger policy reorientation he had gestured towards. Prime-ministerial talk of reinvigorating social democracy fizzled out. Instead, the government was left with question marks over its competence, with recurrent deficits to address, a weakened defence against opposition accusations of Labor profligacy, and a leader who seemed neither a committed economic conservative nor social democrat revivalist. Furthermore, the crisis so consumed Rudd and other leading ministers that it overshadowed other government activity. This was painfully true of climate change policy.[55] The GFC collided with a major milestone on Labor's climate change policy timetable with the release of a white paper in December 2008. Problems had already been built into that process with Rudd having effectively disbanded the CCC earlier that year due to concern about leaks and a characteristic determination to monopolise the information flow. This left responsibility for policy development chiefly with the prime minister, a similarly heavily taxed Swan, and the minister for climate change, Penny Wong. Key departments were also sidelined, while the newly set up Department of Climate Change was left to fend for itself practically without resources and support. But the distraction and draining effects of coping with the GFC also contributed to a damaging lack of engagement with voters over the issue. Despite Rudd portentously declaring at the white paper's launch that 'our generation stands at the crossroads of history',[56] he was publicly missing from the climate change field during the following months. The result was poor community understanding of Labor's policy and a corresponding falling away of support for climate action.

Finally, coming less than twelve months after his ascent to office, the GFC derailed the prime minister's adaptation to government—it 'interrupted any learning process'.[57] From the beginning, Rudd's natural predisposition was to govern in overdrive, but senior cabinet members considered that the GFC diminished the prospect of him finding equilibrium. Foreign minister Stephen Smith later remarked: 'Kevin thrived on the sense of crisis, the 24-hour news cycle, requests for immediate advice, urgent phone calls and briefings. The GFC decision-making format came to define the government permanently'.[58]

Failed Relationships

What would undo Rudd's leadership above all was a string of dysfunctional relationships—within the PMO, and between the office and the wider government and bureaucracy; and between the prime minister and the Labor Party, cabinet and, fatally, Caucus as a whole. A common source of these failed relationships was Rudd's refusal to devolve power.

Some of the problems of Rudd's PMO reflected the evolution of ministerial staffing systems. Under Rudd, however, the control-oriented short-termism that characterised its performance manifested early and aggressively. This was despite Labor's intentions to introduce greater accountability for ministerial staff, to better delineate the relationship between private offices and the bureaucracy, and Rudd's desire for merit-based advisory appointments. Interviewed not long after Labor came to office, Howard's former chief of staff, Arthur Sinodinos, identified two conditions for an effective PMO. First was 'the right mix of people in the right jobs, people who understand the bureaucracy, people who get the politics, people to manage the paper flow'. Second was 'to guard against the urgent crowding out the important'.[59] Neither was achieved under Rudd.

Experience in the PMO rapidly leached away. Epstein resigned as chief of staff in October 2008. He had been powerless to overcome the prime minister's erratic administrative habits: 'His office was chaotic. Briefs would just pile up and be arranged across the floor. He would commission multiple briefs and then not read them because other issues became more pressing'.[60] Another who departed quickly was former senior Victorian bureaucrat Rod Glover, who had vainly tried to assist the prime minister prioritise objectives, but was left frustrated by Rudd positioning himself 'smack bang in the middle of the debate on everything, on micro issues that should have been a million miles away from him'.[61] The exodus continued into 2009. In the colourful description of another seasoned adviser, Rudd 'burned through a generation of staff'.[62]

The attrition rate was such that within two years of Labor's election, twenty-three of thirty-nine staff had gone from the PMO.[63]

These losses were not only at the top end. Junior staff tended to bear the brunt of Rudd's volatile temper: being frozen out was a common punishment. However, most damaging was the haemorrhaging of experience. Epstein's replacement was his 29-year-old deputy, Alister Jordan—only Jim Spigelman had been younger when he became Whitlam's chief of staff in 1974 at a time when the PMO was in its infancy. Moreover, Jordan, unlike most of his other predecessors, did not have a public service background.[64] The other two central figures in the PMO hierarchy—Rudd's chief economics adviser, Andrew Charlton, and director of communications, Lachlan Harris—were also shy of thirty when appointed. Though undoubtedly talented and extraordinarily hardworking, the youthfulness of this triumvirate compounded a risk inherent in partisan private offices dominated by personal loyalists. Their extreme intensity of operation and associated high turnover in membership makes them liable to be deficient in organisational memory and deep knowledge of government processes, and so, susceptible to poor judgement and practices.[65] Moreover, given the age profile of the key staff, no-one had the stature or authority to protect Rudd against himself—to tell him what he didn't want to hear. As one journalist shrewdly observed, there was no equivalent of Sinodinos to Howard, Don Russell to Keating, or Peter Barron, Graham Evans, Dennis Richardson or Geoff Walsh to Hawke.[66] Inexperience might also explain the insecurity that permeated the office: staff jealously guarded their own influence with Rudd rather than encouraging a plurality of voices to be heard on major decisions.[67]

An instrument of its boss's intimidating quest for dominance, the PMO's operation undercut good process and healthy relationships across the government. The office's peremptory demands for work that frequently went nowhere were a major bugbear for the public service, while another was the clogging up of paperwork in the PMO. One senior official later remarked that under Rudd the private office 'became a giant black hole, nothing ever seemed to emerge from it'.[68] Over time the bureaucracy was also sidelined by the PMO from some key decision-making forums. Moran was frozen out from meeting with the prime minister for several months in the first half of 2010. Remarkably, the prime minister seemed oblivious to the exclusion of his senior public servant, and when Moran finally broke through the impasse Rudd 'enthusiastically welcomed' his secretary in from the cold.[69] Moran's concerns about the PMO's behaviour had included its subversion of an orderly cabinet agenda.[70] By early 2010 journalists were reporting a breakdown of cabinet procedure, with ministers receiving some submissions only a day before meetings, without adequate vetting by departments.[71] Meanwhile, the PMO continued its practice of highly centralised media management. Ministerial offices were expected to deliver regular 'announceables', tying up their energies and, as one adviser subsequently observed, fostering 'a terrible culture' across the government.[72]

According to Simon Crean—a veteran minister of the Hawke–Keating era—Rudd 'never used the collective cabinet properly'. Instead, he 'operated a "hub and spokes" system: he dealt separately with ministers', with the PMO a conduit to those dealings.[73] Rudd's capacities as a chair of cabinet received mixed reviews from ministers. But it seems clear that processes suffered from the prime minister stretching himself thinly across so many areas of government activity. Gillard recalled that meetings 'would turn into rolling seminars because it was obvious that Kevin had not read any of the papers'.[74] Rudd also frayed relations with ministers by cutting across their authority. A dramatic illustration was the *Oceanic Viking* episode of October–November 2009 that was triggered by the prime minister striking a deal with Indonesian president Susilo Bambang Yudhoyono to prevent a boatload of Sri Lankan asylum seekers from coming to Australia. Neither the responsible minister nor the relevant department had been consulted. The intervention itself was an ill-conceived attempt by Rudd to prove his mettle on border control amid a growing influx of asylum-seeker vessels into Australian waters that the Coalition blamed on Labor's unpicking of the Howard government's border protection regime. But it had the opposite effect when the asylum seekers refused to disembark from the Australian Customs vessel and the Indonesian authorities declined to cooperate.

The extended stand-off dented Rudd's reputation in the public eye and fuelled discontent among his colleagues.[75]

A more fundamental problem with the prime minister's relationship with his cabinet stemmed from its habitual supplanting by the SPBC as the government's supreme decision-making body. Members grumbled at cabinet being reduced to a 'tick-and-flick exercise' for resolutions of the SPBC.[76] Beyond the 'gang of four', other ministers, where appropriate, were invited into the SPBC, but the dominance of that committee regularly left ministers 'bit players'.[77] Nor did it help that the practices of the SPBC were chaotic. By 2010 its members and other ministers routinely chased Rudd hither and thither to obtain an audience with him. Its agenda had grown unwieldy.[78] Greg Combet, a rising star of the ministry, later wrote that by 2010 'everyone seemed to think the SPBC process was nuts'.[79] Moran had earlier suggested reforming the SPBC, only to be bluntly told by the PMO that the committee was Rudd's 'playground'.[80]

As prime minister, Rudd was also insufficiently solicitous of his Labor colleagues both inside and outside his government. In Crean's view, Rudd 'fell for the classic deception, that you can do it all without the party'.[81] Symbolic of a lack of sensitivity towards the wider party was Labor's 2009 national conference, when Rudd's PMO not only heavily vetted the program but appointed a 'four-man troubleshooting team' to keep delegates from straying off course.[82] Within his government, Rudd was rarely accessible to backbenchers (many grumbled that once he had won their vote in the 2006 leadership contest he cut them off) outside of appearances at Caucus meetings. His phone was permanently diverted to a staff member.[83] The difficulties of the prime minister's relationship with party colleagues, however, went beyond remoteness. One of his harshest critics among those colleagues observed that the leadership insurrection against Rudd of mid-2010 could only 'be understood with an appreciation of the insufferable atmosphere of fear and intimidation that prevailed amongst [Labor] MPs and senators'.[84] In a portent of this, in late 2009 a senior member of the Canberra press gallery spoke of Rudd having 'cowed his party, his caucus, his cabinet'. Presciently, he warned of growing internal resentment: 'they say when he falls … it will be with blinding speed as his own party rushes in to tear down the statue'.[85]

Demise

'Rudd's view was that his power was derived not from his caucus or from his government but from his ascendancy in the opinion polls', later observed Gary Gray, a parliamentary secretary in Rudd's administration and a former Labor Party national secretary.[86] For Rudd, those opinion polls remained consistently high throughout 2008 and 2009, but ebbed by the beginning of 2010.[87] Heavily invested in communication performance to maintain polling supremacy, he was unquestionably a skilful media entrepreneur, tailoring performances to different platforms. Yet over time this 'celebritisation' wore thin. The 'excess of accessibility' through an endless cycle of stage-managed stunts and 'announceables' progressively diminished respect for Rudd and his office.[88] Furthermore, presenting such a prominent target, journalists relished opportunities to expose the confections of Rudd's media image and the dissonance between the amiable face he presented to the public and the backstage realities of his relationships with subordinates.[89] When reports surfaced in the first half of 2009 about Rudd having shouted at a flight attendant, press gallery doyen Laurie Oakes shrewdly noted that the story was 'dangerous' for the prime minister because it was 'the first public confirmation of claims that there are two Rudds—the cheerful Kevin that viewers of Seven Network's *Sunrise* program came to know and a darker figure'.[90]

Questions over Rudd's authenticity intensified, and by late 2009 Labor's internal polling detected that, while the prime minister was still rating comparatively well, focus groups were 'struggling to describe him'. The perception was taking hold in the electorate that 'he was not being genuine, it was just an act'.[91] Journalists shared this view of a prime-ministerial chameleon: 'There are so many Kevins, depending on who you are … He tries to reflect back at you'.[92] The gnawing public doubts about Rudd's sincerity dramatically escalated in late April 2010 with a meek prime-ministerial confirmation of a newspaper leak that the government had shelved its carbon emissions reduction scheme.[93] This debacle had been months in the making and its ingredients exemplified many of the shortcomings of his government's administrative style: excessively centralised decision-making, flawed internal coordination of policy and poor knowledge exchange, inadequate external consultation, indecision, and short-run political tactics taking precedence over policy outcomes. The scheme's abandonment followed a period of drift in the wake of the major setback of the December 2009 Copenhagen international summit on climate change. Rudd's labours in Copenhagen were herculean, but when hopes for a binding agreement on carbon emission reduction targets were dashed by differences between major polluting nations, he emerged debilitated. There was undoubtedly something manic about Rudd's conduct in the first half of 2010 as, paralysed by indecision about whether to pursue a double-dissolution election on climate change, he embarked on a frenzied round of consultations on hospital reform. Even the circumspect Ken Henry would later reluctantly agree that the government had begun to resemble a 'train wreck' by that time.[94]

The abandonment of Labor's climate change scheme was eventually settled within the SPBC, but months of prevarication meant the decision had come about more by default than firm resolution. The impact on community sentiment towards the prime minister when the public learned of the decision, however, was stark. In the space of a fortnight polling cycle, his leadership rating plummeted deep into negative territory.[95] For Rudd, the effects undoubtedly had been magnified because Labor's climate change policy had been so closely identified with him. This was another hazard of leadership centralisation—while a predominant prime minister may receive most of the plaudits for government success, they reap a correspondingly large share of the opprobrium for failure. With his chief asset of public popularity melting away, Rudd was deeply exposed. Exacerbating his plight were other policy difficulties swamping the Labor government, including botched plans for a super profits tax on mining—an episode that replicated aspects of the climate change fiasco.[96]

Rudd was removed as prime minister by a party room revolt in June 2010. The circumstances of his deposition became the subject of bitter recriminations that plagued Labor for the following three years.[97] What is plain, however, is that while the decline in polling left Rudd vulnerable, he would have been better placed to weather that downturn had his governing practices not degenerated to such an extent and had his alienation of colleagues not been so complete. Similarly, if factional heavyweights instigated the move against Rudd, once the rebellion was underway it gathered irresistible force. As Combet observed, 'Yes, there would have been scheming and plotting. But when it got to it, Kevin Rudd's support in the Caucus just appeared to vanish'.[98] A disempowered cabinet, rather than forming a defensive perimeter around the prime minister, was impotent, with many ministers bystanders to the insurrection. Though the figures cannot be verified because Rudd declined to contest a ballot to try to save his leadership (itself tacit admission of the magnitude of his loss of support), rivals estimate that he could have counted on the votes of less than one-fifth of Caucus.[99] Ironically, the demise of this most imperious of leaders had served as a remedial lesson that the prime ministership remained the gift of the party room.

The Broken 'Dream Team'

When Kevin Rudd and Julia Gillard formed a joint ticket to challenge Kim Beazley for the Labor leadership in late 2006, the media anointed them a 'dream team'.[100] That stylisation had a sharp edge. Theirs was recognised as a marriage of convenience between two ambitious up-and-comers. Yet it was also an allusion to the pair representing a generational shift to a post-Hawke/Keating era, with both having entered the House of Representatives in 1998. They were also seen as balancing each other's claims: gender wise, factionally (Rudd deriving his principal support from the right while Gillard was aligned with the left) and stylistically.

Gillard's background was very different from Rudd's.[101] The eldest child of Welsh working-class immigrants who settled in the Adelaide suburbs when she was four years old, Gillard was a naturally shy child but fortified by a plentiful supply of self-belief endowed by her close-knit family. Bright and hardworking, she made the most of educational opportunities that had been unthinkable for her parents. Labor tribalism was another component of her inheritance: 'Dad was pro-Labor, Mum was pro-Labor, that's just who we were. That was our team'.[102]

If Rudd's journey had been one of largely going around the labour movement, Gillard became intimately enmeshed within it virtually from the time she joined the party as an arts/law student at the University of Adelaide. It was a path from which she did not deviate: as an officer with the Australian Union of Students, as a lawyer with the Labor-aligned firm Slater and Gordon, as chief of staff to Victorian Labor opposition leader John Brumby, and as an aspiring parliamentarian. Gillard had to struggle, though, to fulfil the latter goal. She required a combination of talent, perseverance and a streak of pragmatism to finally best the men who thrice checked her ambitions for a political career. A foundation member of the Labor women's network, Emily's List, and beneficiary of its support, she was typically candid about how she finally overcame the resistance to her preselection: 'I'm not Doris Day who's just somehow parachuted into Canberra. I had to fight hard to get preselected, I had to play a factional game to do that. I had to count numbers, I had to make deals'.[103]

In opposition, Gillard made her mark mastering thorny portfolio areas. She supported Crean and his successor as leader, Mark Latham. The latter became notorious for astringent commentary on his colleagues, yet he admired Gillard: 'she has a go ... feisty, irreverent, good sense of humour ... Not afraid of policy innovation but also steady and sensible'.[104] Her status as an unmarried, childless woman singled her out for attention and prejudice—perhaps the tawdriest example being a crusty Liberal senator questioning her fitness for leadership because of her choice to 'remain deliberately barren'.[105] Gillard's decision to throw in her lot with Rudd was another demonstration of her pragmatism and recognition that her profile within the electorate was not yet sufficiently developed. Lachlan Harris, Rudd's communications director, observed a potent alchemy between the novice leadership pairing during Labor's election-winning year of 2007:

> Rudd was all energy and emotion and Gillard was all discipline and delivery ... He was incredibly good in the media; he was likeable, he had the kind of big picture stuff. Gillard was much more straight down the line, much more disciplined, in the weeds of the hard draft of policy.[106]

As deputy prime minister in the Rudd government, Gillard was a perfect foil to the eccentricities of its leader: focused, able to sustain an enormous workload in her multiple portfolios, dependable and calm. Where Rudd exhibited a 'smartest man in the room' complex, Wayne Swan, who had viewed Gillard warily in opposition and had been against the challenge to Beazley, discovered working alongside her in government that she had a knack 'to consistently sound as though she is the most sensible person in the room'.[107] Where Rudd was a haphazard and often dilatory administrator, Gillard was orderly and time efficient. Her frequent stints as acting prime minister—by the beginning of 2009 she had been in that position for almost a quarter of Labor's period in office—were a salve for frustrated colleagues and public servants alike, as political journalist Annabel Crabb observed: '"Bring out your dead!" she would holler on entering the PMO, seeking out long-stalled ambassadorial appointments, out-of-favour briefs and slumbering cabinet submissions'.[108] Where Rudd was temperamentally volatile, oscillating between charm and prickliness, Gillard was known for her equanimity, good humour and self-effacement. Where Rudd hoarded authority and was seemingly incapable of extending trust beyond a small circle of disciples, Gillard was an enabler of others. She was expert at mediating differences and negotiating outcomes and won abiding affection from those she worked with. Yet Gillard could not match some of Rudd's strengths. Highly task-oriented, she lacked his imagination or creativity with big ideas. While a forceful advocate and feisty parliamentary performer, and with a rare gift for working one-on-one or in small groups, Gillard did not have Rudd's flair for connecting with or inspiring the public. As opposed to his (often hollow) grandiosities, her forte was the unglamorous yet tangible business of navigating a path to policy delivery.

On the surface, they were a formidable complementary team, evoking echoes of the best years of the Hawke–Keating partnership. Yet there was an inherent tension in its hierarchy since Gillard had a strong power base in the party while Rudd did not. Furthermore, as Paul Kelly noted, the relationship had an 'unhealthy' aspect: 'Gillard did the cleaning up after Rudd, a fact that became notorious across the government'.[109] In her description, she became 'the fix-it person': soothing and jollying colleagues, advisers and bureaucrats, while doing what she could to keep the wheels of government turning.[110] It is impossible to ignore the gender stereotypes in these respective roles. An episode at the 2008 Victorian Labor Party state conference illustrated the dynamic between leader and deputy. Rudd was to deliver a centrepiece address but failed to surface at the appointed time, instead bunkering down while he furiously rewrote his speech. With the cameras rolling, desperate organisers hurriedly conscripted Gillard to the stage to humour delegates. When the prime minister finally emerged to speak: 'it wasn't worth the wait. It was long and tedious'.[111]

The balance of evidence is that Gillard stood by Rudd's leadership virtually until the moment she resolved to challenge him.[112] The chance of ambition, a sense of obligation to right a listing government and simply being swept up in the stampede of rebellion against Rudd are likely to have influenced that fateful choice. Gillard has spoken poignantly about the 'loneliness of that moment. It comes down to you … I've never tried to suggest I was inveigled or persuaded … by others'.[113] It is clear, however, that in striking against Rudd she not only irrevocably sundered their relationship but misread the character of the slain prime minister by not foreseeing that this would create a vengeful and remorseless enemy.[114]

Could the 'dream team' have been sustained? A prerequisite for a successful leadership tandem is that the partners have complementary qualities, which Rudd and Gillard self-evidently had, but it relies ultimately upon a prime minister to make the tandem work. Andrew Fisher and Billy Hughes worked productively together because the modest Fisher allowed latitude for the other's dynamism. On the other hand, once he replaced Fisher, the authoritarian Hughes could never treat any of his colleagues as anything remotely like an equal. Egalitarian by nature, John Curtin and Ben Chifley formed an alliance rooted in a deeply held sense of common purpose and mutual affection. A key ingredient in the durability of the Hawke–Keating tandem was that Hawke's sense of self was sufficiently unassailable for him to tolerate his treasurer sharing the limelight and not be threatened by Keating's extraordinary capacities. Rudd's egotism, however, was of a defensive and brittle kind, lessening the chances of a lasting unity. Yet, in supplanting Rudd, Gillard perhaps never quite appreciated their interdependence or took enough account of her own limitations. Nor once the decision was taken was she prepared to entertain that, despite the provocations and manifest difficulties, continued forbearance to prop up the partnership might have been the wiser course: 'I don't see what alternate reality was possible: other than the ones we lived through … people are really wistfully hoping for something that was never going to be'.[115]

Julia Gillard: A Perfect Storm

> It was a perfect storm for her [Gillard]. Perhaps she could have survived minority government, perhaps she could have survived Kevin Rudd undermining her, perhaps she could have survived the carbon tax, perhaps she could have survived Tony Abbott, but throw them all into the mix and there's not a chance.[116]

This catalogue of adversities Gillard encountered during her tumultuous three years in office, as recited by Sean Kelly, senior media adviser in the Labor governments of Rudd and Gillard, is daunting enough. The list of ruinous circumstances could also easily be expanded, however, to include the liability of the means by which she became prime minister, budget difficulties as ambitious reform collided with straitened post-GFC government finances, a disrupted media industry that encouraged a febrile reporting environment and the bedevilling influence of gender prejudice. Though the nature of the problems that conspired against them cannot be compared, Gillard's incumbency has a claim as the most beleaguered since James Scullin's in the Depression era.

The forces arrayed against Gillard began with the way she obtained office. The precipitous coup against a first-term prime minister and squeamishness about publicly revealing the dysfunctionality of Rudd's leadership—apart from Gillard's unsatisfactory euphemism that 'a good government was losing its way'[117]—were millstones for her from the start. Regardless of whether they had been supporters or opponents of Rudd's deposition, her Labor colleagues were in hindsight united in their belief that it sullied Gillard's legitimacy.[118] The highly personalised basis of Rudd's leadership had a compounding effect. Encouraged to believe they were anointing a leader rather than voting for a party at the 2007 election, the electorate, despite their flagging opinion of him, felt disenfranchised by the abrupt overthrow of 'Kevin 07'.[119] Rudd protested a dishonouring of his personal mandate on the evening the challenge was announced—'I was elected by the people of Australia ... [not] by the factional leaders of the Labor Party'[120]—a mantra he would repeat in his efforts to subvert Gillard's prime ministership.

Polling immediately following the leadership change belied this problem for Gillard. Support for Labor surged and there was a favourable reaction to her leadership.[121] The party's market researcher detected, however, that voters retained an 'emotional connection' to Rudd and that his overthrow had elicited a wave of 'sympathy' for him. Indeed, it soon became obvious that his status in the public eye as a wronged leader allowed him to be disloyal to Gillard with relative impunity. Conversely, when the focus groups were asked to provide one-word responses to Gillard, the positive descriptions of her as 'strong' and 'determined' were offset by negatives such as 'backstabber' and 'traitor'.[122] Trust, in short, would be an abiding issue for Gillard's leadership—a factor also shot through by gender bias.

That Gillard headed a minority government for all but a few weeks of her prime ministership was another major handicap. Quickly calling a poll for August 2010 to capitalise on the goodwill that apparently surrounded her ascension and to gain legitimacy for her leadership, the election campaign was an unhappy experience for Gillard.[123] The challenges she faced were manifold: a need to defuse the policy dilemmas left over from Rudd's prime ministership, her own campaigning inexperience that caused significant missteps on the hustings, and a lack of preparation by the party. In addition, Labor's re-election bid was plagued by leaks thought to originate from Rudd. The most devastating suggested that as deputy prime minister Gillard had raised concerns in cabinet about Labor's paid parental leave scheme and a rise in the pension. As Gillard later wrote, the leak 'played to questions voters were already thinking about in relation to me—if I was unmarried, childless, could I really understand the pressures and concerns of families?'[124] It also reinforced the image of her as cold-hearted.

Despite a disappointing August 2010 election result that produced a hung parliament, Gillard successfully outmanoeuvred the Coalition leader, Tony Abbott, by securing the support of crossbench members in the House of Representatives to form a Labor minority government.[125] The attributes that Gillard displayed in achieving that arrangement—emotional intelligence, discipline, adaptability and a scrupulous attention to detail and the arguments of others—also placed her in good stead in wrangling a minority parliament. But her talent for brokering compromises was also readily construed as evidence of her opportunism, further encouraging perceptions of duplicity and expedience within a sceptical electorate.

Equally, the alien nature of minority administration at the federal level—it was the first since World War II—was ripe for exploitation by the gladiatorial opposition leader Abbott, who continued to protest the government's illegitimacy. The government's reputation was also tarnished by relying on tainted votes to shore up its precarious parliamentary position, as exampled by a damaging delay in cutting loose a Labor backbencher who was under investigation and later convicted of defrauding his trade union. And because of those finely balanced numbers, Gillard was constrained from bringing to heel disloyal elements on her own side.[126] The cumulative effect was that the government frequently resembled a soap opera, notwithstanding a record of legislative productivity.

The most destructive element, however, was Rudd's campaign of 'political terrorism' to regain the prime ministership.[127] Swan compared the deposed prime minister to 'a grand chess master' in orchestrating the destabilisation of Gillard's leadership.[128] Showing off his superior skills in that domain, the media was a primary focus of Rudd's insurgency. This involved backgrounding and strategic leaks combined with highly choreographed and opportunistically timed media interventions. Rudd's relationship with selected journalists, newspaper editors and media powerbrokers abetted these activities whereas Gillard had never cultivated anything like the same connections. 'I was not a graduate of the boys' drinking circles involving male editors, male reporters and male politicians', she subsequently complained.[129] The media's trigger-finger reporting of leadership speculation also stemmed from the prosaic reality that, late to the scene of Rudd's political assassination, journalists were determined to not be caught off guard again. They overcompensated by forecasting with almost comic regularity Gillard's impending demise.[130] The incessant cycle of opinion polls—mostly delivering dire numbers for the government—consistently provoked this speculation. Metaphorically speaking, the polls became a rack for Gillard.

Compounding the toxic environment in which Gillard governed was the fact that the media was in the midst of profound upheaval. Though the collapse of the traditional business model of the press had been in train for a number of years, Gillard's prime ministership coincided with major waves of redundancies of journalists. The intrusion of social media had also reached a critical level, disrupting conventional reporting practices and further accelerating the news cycle. As a result, 'fewer journalists covering more stories in less time, contributed to a shallower, more frenetic, tweet first, check later, news reporting culture'.[131] In a more familiar story, the Labor government was the target of hostile coverage by Australia's dominant Rupert Murdoch–owned News Limited press stable as well as from conservative elements within the broadcast media. Meanwhile, the largely uncensored world of social media was having a coarsening influence on public discourse, with Gillard's gender a lightning rod for incivility.

Like Rudd before her, Gillard found it hard to achieve a suitable operating rhythm within the 24-hour news cycle. From the beginning, however, she was determined to distinguish herself from her media-obsessed predecessor. She signalled this in a lighthearted speech that nevertheless had a serious intent:

> The task of government is [not] to deliver reforms exclusively in line with the contemporary media cycle … 'What do we want? Long-term reform.'—Yes, agreed. 'When do we want it? Before we tape our *Insiders* segment.'—Sorry, ain't gunna happen.[132]

Moreover, there was some relaxation under her leadership of the command-and-control media practices of the Rudd government, with her PMO delegating greater autonomy to ministerial offices.[133]

The results, though, were mixed. Gillard later lamented that, despite her objective to avoid distraction by short-term demands transmitted by contemporary communication technologies ('It beeps and buzzes and pings at you 24 hours a day'), she did not manage to isolate sufficient 'thinking time, the quiet time, the unplugged time, to work out what is important, rather than just attending to the urgent'.[134] At the same time, she and her senior staff concluded that their initial attempt to step back from the whirlwind of the media cycle had been largely counterproductive—the void was being filled by the voices of government critics.[135] Her (second) chief of staff, Ben Hubbard, also observed the limited scope for decentralising communications because of the imperative to coordinate announcements to 'feed the [media] beast'. Astounded by evidence of the increasing scale of political news traffic on social media, Hubbard later mused whether the government should have diverted more resources into that field rather than channelling its message predominantly through the press gallery.[136] In the hurly-burly of events, however, the opportunity for innovation mostly passed by.

The Stoic Administrator

The productivity metrics of the Gillard prime ministership are impressive. Her minority government enacted 561 Bills. This was more than were passed during the final Howard government, which enjoyed majorities in both Houses of parliament, and considerably more than the 409 pieces of legislation passed by the Rudd government.[137] Indeed, the rate of legislative productivity as measured by Bills passed per sitting day under Gillard was the greatest for any contemporary prime minister—the next highest was Bob Hawke.[138] This output was achieved in the teeth of fierce obstruction by the Abbott-led Coalition, with the proportion of government Bills contested by the opposition more than double the level in parliaments over the preceding two decades.[139]

The legislation enacted during Gillard's prime ministership included major reforms.[140] Among these were the Clean Energy Future (CEF) package that priced carbon and contained complementary measures to encourage renewable energy and energy efficiency; the National Disability Insurance Scheme, which has been characterised as the most significant social reform since the advent of universal health care; a needs-based funding system for schools; the National Broadband Network; a plan for managing the water resources of the Murray-Darling Basin; government-subsidised dental care for children and low-income adults; a national agreement on hospital funding with the states; an internationally pioneering measure to enforce plain packaging of tobacco products; and the establishment of a landmark royal commission into institutional responses to child sexual abuse.

Some of these measures involved closing on initiatives commenced by Rudd (for example, the hospital funding agreement) and some would not survive the fall of Gillard's government (the carbon price was repealed by the Abbott Coalition government in 2014). Others were marred by flaws and the policy successes offset by fiascos. An instance of the latter was a hasty and poorly devised deal to revise the Rudd government's proposed tax on mining super profits. By returning only a fraction of the revenue it had been forecast to reap (a problem in part resulting from a collapse in commodity prices), the tax became a symbol of Labor's budget woes.[141] Caught between the political imperative to restore budget equilibrium following the GFC stimulus expenditure (despite arguably having the opportunity for a more enterprising fiscal policy), its big-ticket reform ambitions and an unanticipated steep fall in government revenue, Labor undermined its economic credentials by repeated unfulfilled promises to deliver a surplus. Yet another policy dilemma inherited from Rudd's period in office was the inflow of unauthorised vessels that further increased during Gillard's prime ministership, with hundreds of asylum seekers drowning at sea. In August 2011 the High Court unexpectedly struck down a creative attempt by Labor to mitigate the problem through a 'people swap' arrangement with Malaysia, and its plan to salvage the scheme by enabling legislation was then thwarted in the parliament by the Greens and the Coalition—an obstruction that Abbott later regretted as a missed opportunity to 'step back from … hyper partisanship'.[142]

Even allowing for these deficiencies and misfortunes, Gillard's government boasted a substantial record of policy achievement eked out in inhospitable circumstances. The conundrum was her inability to parlay that record into electoral favour. By autumn 2011, Labor's polling figures had sharply declined. With the exception of a short-lived rally in late 2012, they were ruinous for Gillard's prime ministership. Her leadership ratings were equally bleak: a small consolation being that her opponent, Abbott, was also unpopular with voters.[143] As suggested above, Gillard's political capital was low from the start because of public disapproval of the means by which she entered the office, and it was difficult to replenish due to the minority parliament and the corrosive effects of persistent leadership destabilisation that fed off the poor polling. In addition, public aversion to the government's carbon pricing scheme was a lead weight on the prime minister's standing from early 2011. However, Gillard's inability to win over voters was also due to a leadership style that was grudging in the domain of public performance. Gillard had, as one writer observed, 'the prefect's belief that by her deeds she will be known'.[144] Yet those deeds alone were insufficient to impress the electorate.

Both instinctively and because Gillard expressly set about correcting the excesses of Rudd, her approach to governing was in most respects the antithesis of her predecessor. Here we find an echo of earlier instances of prime-ministerial chaos giving rise to a successor intent on instilling order, such as the methodical Stanley Bruce following the erratic Billy Hughes, and Fraser succeeding Whitlam. Upon toppling Rudd, Gillard vowed to 'run a cabinet system of government ... all substantial decisions will go to the full cabinet', as well as promising to empower Caucus to create a collective governing enterprise.[145] She also extolled Bob Hawke as 'the gold standard for any Australian head of government'. The traits she admired in his prime-ministerial practice—and, by implication, she wished to emulate—were a capacity to take advice, an orderly sense of administration, confidence in delegating to ministers, and effectiveness as a cabinet chair.[146]

Against these benchmarks Gillard mostly succeeded. The SPBC, at the heart of the erosion of cabinet process under Rudd, was abolished.[147] Three other changes were made to ensure the centrality of cabinet to government decision-making and to improve its functioning.[148] First was a reliable meeting schedule laid down well in advance. Second was an insistence on timely cabinet submissions and an accompanying curtailing of so-called 'under-the-line' items. Meant to be reserved for urgent matters of procedural rather than policy nature, or matters sufficiently uncomplicated not to require a formal submission, or appointments, these had it was reported ballooned to nearly 60 per cent of items coming before cabinet in the final year of Rudd's prime ministership. In contrast, in the first year of Gillard's tenure they declined to around 15 per cent.[149] Third, while during Rudd's leadership cabinet committees had tended to operate as independent silos, under Gillard there was a renewed emphasis on committees 'articulating up into the cabinet'.[150] This difference was illustrated by the operation of the committees charged with designing climate change policy during the respective Labor administrations. The Rudd committee was stripped down to a troika of ministers and its deliberations largely occurred in isolation from cabinet. By comparison, the minister heading the multi-party committee set up by Gillard to deal with climate change, Greg Combet, exhaustively referred to cabinet for approval of negotiating positions.[151]

Gillard was generally regarded as a skilled chair of cabinet. According to Moran, who stayed on as secretary of PM&C following the change of prime minister, she was 'a great reader ... incredibly well informed'.[152] Gillard was also deft at structuring debates, patient and attentive to colleagues' views and measured in her own contributions. She allowed ministers leeway to pursue policy outcomes, generally intervening only when an impasse was reached. The development of the CEF package was a case in point: Combet was charged with the frontline negotiations while Gillard and the Greens leader, Bob Brown, resolved sticking points.[153]

Yet the decision-making processes of her government were not impeccable. Gillard's transactional leadership style was occasionally manifest in policy deals that were far from optimal, such as the bungled revision of the mining tax, and the dilution of the needs-based principle in the reformed school-funding system due to varied arrangements struck with the different states and territories and school sectors. Politically besieged for much of her tenure, it was perhaps inevitable that she should also have succumbed at times to small-circle decision-making. Gillard subsequently regretted that she did not 'reach out much more often to seek other perspectives'.[154] The treachery of Rudd and his supporters also compromised cabinet's operation. This was especially a problem in early 2013 when, according to Gillard, cabinet discussions 'were very likely to be distorted or leaked [so] there were times where I felt we couldn't chew through it as much as I would have liked'.[155] A concern about leaks led to contentious proposals on media reform being 'walked into' cabinet in March 2013.[156] The haste and lack of consultation surrounding the proposals diminished what slender chance there was for them receiving a considered public reception amid a predictable firestorm of vested hostility from the media industry. Equally, because of the internal pressure on her position, Gillard was guilty of unwise assertions of authority. Most notable was her insistence in November 2012 that cabinet fall in behind a position that Australia should vote against a resolution granting Palestine observer status in the United Nations, despite the opposition of a majority of her ministers. Her brinkmanship threatened to provoke a Caucus revolt that was only averted by a last-minute prime-ministerial backdown.[157]

Still, there is little question that Gillard was far more solicitous of her relationship with party colleagues than had been Rudd. Her PMO had a practice of conscientious response to Caucus member concerns and the prime minister was readily accessible to them.[158] In return, she enjoyed a rapport with, and the respect of, most colleagues. The most compelling demonstration of the regard in which Gillard was held—and the depth of antipathy towards Rudd—was that her leadership survived for so long despite persistently disastrous opinion polls. Along the way she comprehensively defeated a challenge from Rudd in February 2012, while another was stillborn in March 2013. Three months later, against a background of party polling painting apocalyptic scenarios of Labor being reduced to a rump at the impending September election, ongoing agitation by the Rudd forces and the media baying for her head, Gillard's support finally broke. In a dramatic showdown, she called a leadership ballot and, effectively terminating her political career, insisted on the condition that the loser quit parliament. Even then the margin was relatively tight (Rudd won by fifty-seven votes to forty-five) and the decision enveloped in sadness rather than enthusiasm for her conqueror.

Trade union–based factional voting blocs had shored up Gillard's leadership, as her detractors claimed,[159] but she earned a genuine loyalty from her party room never sought or matched by Rudd.

Other relationships were righted under Gillard. Exasperated bureaucrats must have emitted sighs of relief when she replaced Rudd. Moran seized upon the opportunity of the leadership change to reboot relations between the PMO and PM&C and the public service more widely. He invited to Canberra Gillard's former chief of staff (between 2006 and 2008), Ben Hubbard, who devised 'a clear structure for putting the relationship back together'.[160] Moran remained as secretary of PM&C until the second half of 2011, departing an admirer of Gillard's administrative capabilities.[161] His successor was the secretary of defence, Ian Watt, who was appointed by the 'conventional route' of advice by the APS Commissioner.[162] According to Hubbard, who had returned permanently to Canberra as Gillard's chief of staff, replacing Amanda Lampe in early 2011, the lines of communication between the PMO and PM&C remained strong throughout the life of the government. Watt regularly met with Gillard and there was close dialogue between the office and department.[163]

The PMO took time to settle. Hubbard's history with Gillard dated back to the 1990s when they had worked together in the office of state Labor opposition leader John Brumby. He also had been a principal adviser to Victorian Labor premier Steve Bracks. A seasoned political operator, therefore, when he teamed up with Gillard again in February 2011, Hubbard overhauled the PMO to enhance its strategic planning capacity and sharpen its functioning. Meeting and reporting procedures were revised, and a clearer demarcation of responsibilities established between the office's communications, strategy, policy and government business units.[164] Meanwhile, Labor's promise in opposition to cut back on ministerial staffing had been shelved: Gillard's PMO was in excess of fifty strong—some ten more than Howard's office at the end of his prime ministership and three times the size of Hawke's.[165]

Gillard's PMO attracted considerably less attention and opprobrium than Rudd's. Nevertheless, grumbles about the prime minister operating 'in a shrinking circle of advisers' surfaced towards the end of the government—although arguably these criticisms were proxy for the leadership assault on Gillard.[166] Hubbard had difficulty in attracting experienced media and political staffers because of the perception the government was living on borrowed time. His decision to recruit the high-profile John McTernan, a former adviser to British Labour prime minister Tony Blair, as director of communications was motivated by a desire to instil 'toughness' into the office.[167] Upon joining Gillard's staff in November 2011, McTernan diagnosed an urgent need to give greater priority to 'retail politics'.[168] Among those who worked in Gillard's PMO, two features stood out about the office. The first was its calmness.[169] Taking their cue from Gillard, the staff mantra was to soldier on irrespective of the maelstrom swirling around them. The other was the strength of affection for their boss.[170] Inseparable from that sentiment, however, was the frustration they felt, as one former senior adviser wrote, at 'the chasm that existed between the public perception' of Gillard and the prime minister they knew 'as warm, good-humoured, dignified, hardworking and courageous'.[171] It was a dilemma that even the wily McTernan later admitted he was powerless to fix.[172]

Climate change policy encapsulated the strengths and weaknesses of Gillard's governance.[173] The Rudd government's attempt to legislate a price on carbon had been characterised by overblown rhetoric, closeted decision-making, the prioritising of short-term political advantage over policy delivery, leadership prevarication and, ultimately, capitulation. With the public's patience already strained, when Gillard became prime minister she struggled unconvincingly to manage the issue through the 2010 election campaign. Though signalling that Labor remained in favour of a market-based mechanism to curb emissions, she ended the campaign fatefully vowing not to introduce a carbon tax. Once her minority government was in place, Gillard established an innovative multi-party committee, chaired by Combet and including four independent experts, to examine options for pricing carbon. By February 2011, the committee had agreed on the framework of a scheme. This was followed by several months of arduous policy development that involved intense negotiations within the committee, dialogue with a diverse range of stakeholders, close collaboration between the prime minister and Combet, and the settlement of impasses by Gillard and Brown. This activity culminated in legislation of the CEF package in the second half of 2011 for start-up by July 2012.

Ambitious and brave, the package constituted 'a huge achievement in rapid public policy-making'.[174] However, it was poisoned by politics. The announcement of the framework months before the policy details were settled left it prey to an inflammatory scare campaign by the Coalition, sections of the business community and elements of the media. Moreover, the symbolism of Gillard making that announcement at a joint press conference with the Greens and independents further undermined her authority. The most devastating miscalculation, though, was Gillard's admission that the carbon price was a tax. This exposed her to the accusation that she had reneged on her 2010 election campaign pledge. Cabinet had agreed to the use of the term 'tax' to describe the carbon price, but ministers retrospectively claimed the deliberation was inadequate. Nor, Gillard later rued, were its consequences sufficiently war-gamed with her staff.[175] Combet emphatically believed it mischaracterised the policy, which was an emissions trading scheme with a three-year transitional fixed price.[176]

Labor's and Gillard's polling nose-dived in the wake of the statement. The anti-carbon tax campaign monstered the prime minister. The nadir was a rally outside Parliament House where Abbott infamously spoke against a background of placards bearing the slogans 'Juliar', 'Bob Brown's Bitch' and 'Ditch the Witch'. Amid the calumnies and hysteria, Gillard valiantly maintained that the lived experience of the policy would reveal the hollowness of opponents' claims—as it did: once the scheme commenced in 2012, community anxiety about its effects dissipated.[177] But the carbon tax had irrevocably damaged her reputation. According to the national secretary of the Labor Party, George Wright, the 'broken bond of trust' between Gillard and the public could not be mended.[178]

Lapses of political judgement and deficient communication were the Achilles heel of Gillard's prime ministership. As purposeful as her leadership project was, she struggled to convey that the sum of its parts formed a cohesive whole. In the absence of a unifying message and rhetorically anodyne, she relied on her government's policy objectives to amount to a self-evident vision. Gillard struggled too to develop an emotional affinity with the electorate. She had a thinly concealed disdain for the media vanities of Rudd—at various stages she pointedly remarked that the Labor leadership was not 'an episode of celebrity *Big Brother*' and warned her party against seduction by 'the number of positive media profiles, or the amount of time spent schmoozing media owners and editors, or the frippery of selfies'.[179]

Yet if Rudd confused the line between celebrity and national leadership and along the way sacrificed the gravitas of the prime-ministerial office, Gillard frequently presented as scripted, wooden and stubbornly undemonstrative on the public stage. She made tentative but never quite satisfactory attempts to account for her constrained persona. Styling herself as 'the shy girl who studied and worked hard', she told the National Press Club in mid-2011, 'I'm a decision maker by nature and I have tended to let the decisions speak for themselves … I've brought a sense of personal reserve to this, the most public of professions'.[180] At other times, she betrayed frustration at the expectation that she unbend before the media. Questioned by a veteran journalist about whether she intended to modify her 'innate style of holding back a fair bit', she retorted: 'I'm not a talk show host. I'm not on breakfast TV, I'm not appearing in a drama on Australian television, I'm the Prime Minister'.[181]

Gillard's insistence on being judged on administrative competence and a functioning, productive parliament rather than as communicator-in-chief put her out of step in an age of personalised politics in which there is an intensified onus on leaders to develop a 'virtual relationship' with voters—to become an 'intimate stranger' to the electorate.[182] Gillard recognised but bemoaned the expectation for leaders 'to emote' and the trend towards 'the politician as celebrity'.[183] By not meeting those demands, Gillard was also disadvantaged against Rudd, who was an artful communicator and whose incumbency had heightened the bar of prime-ministerial media entrepreneurship. Gillard appeared publicly parsimonious by contrast. Her speechwriter, Michael Cooney, observed the cost this exacted within the electorate:

> Gillard's reserve was a heavy barrier to the wider task of communicating with Australians who could never know her privately and relied on her

> media performances to understand her leadership. It made it hard for her to humble herself before the people; to tell them they were right and she wanted their support to deliver for them. Without being silly about it, if you keep telling people popularity doesn't matter to you, they can be inclined to reward you by agreeing that you don't need to be popular.[184]

'It Explains Some Things'

In an insightful essay published towards the end of Gillard's tenure, the writer Anna Goldsworthy directly linked the prime minister's stoical leadership style and battle to establish an affinity with the public to gender. Noting that Gillard's habit was 'to deflect any speculation about who she is', Goldsworthy continued:

> Despite having more to explain than the average prime minister—besides her gender, there is her professed atheism; her childlessness; her de facto living arrangements—she has not provided any reassuring narrative of self … Instead, she just keeps on *doing* stuff, resilient as a Duracell bunny: forging alliances, making deals, retracting promises, passing legislation. *Getting on with it* speaks to a recognisable truth of female pragmatism.[185]

Gillard spent much of her time in office trying to neutralise the issue of her pioneering gender role. She set the tone on the day she was sworn in. 'I didn't set out to crash my head against any glass ceilings', Gillard declared, and joked about being the nation's first red-haired leader.[186] 'It was so obvious that I was the first woman to do this job', she later said of this reticence, 'that I didn't need to hark on about it'.[187] She also calculated that the novelty would 'peter out'.[188] From the outset, however, gender coloured the reception of her prime ministership. The impact in the electorate showed up at the 2010 election with Gillard's leadership 'galvanising women' to support Labor to an extent that may have been decisive in the party clinging to government.[189] The flipside, however, was a cool response from male voters: a coolness that turned to frigidity by the later stages of her prime ministership.

Much of the gendered reaction to Gillard mimicked patterns encountered by women leaders internationally. For example, the negativity emanating from the way she obtained the office was consistent with evidence that overt displays of ambition and assertiveness by women, by transgressing stereotypes of gender behaviour, impair their 'likeability' and 'popularity'.[190] Equally predictable from overseas experience was the magnified focus on personal issues and her appearance in media reporting of Gillard's prime ministership. Her choice of clothes, the size of her earlobes, the way she walked and, piqued by a shameless intervention by one-time feminist icon Germaine Greer, her 'big arse' became media talking points.[191] In the face of this scrutiny, Gillard reluctantly began taking advice on styling. She keenly felt the double standard, though, of the 'complexity' of her grooming routine while male counterparts had the luxury of a standard uniform of suit and tie.[192]

There was a darker side still to the gender reaction to Gillard that revealed an ugly strain of sexism and a coarsening of the political culture. She became the brunt of offensive name calling such as 'bitch', 'witch' and 'cow', perverse questions about her partner's sexuality, crude references to her menstrual cycle and lewd jokes about her genitalia. Social media became a hothouse of misogynistic abuse of Gillard.[193] Focus group research showed the gender hostility percolated into the electorate:

> As soon as she [Gillard] would come up, the [focus] group would kind of come to life and people would come out with this stuff about her and it was always nasty. It quite often ended in the word 'bitch'.[194]

As part of downplaying her gender, Gillard turned her cheek to the sexist stereotyping and vitriol. By 2012, however, her office concluded this was counterproductive: 'she was now getting the worst of both worlds—all the backlash and none of the benefit'. Moreover, continued 'silence' risked looking 'like weakness and even consent'.[195] The silence ended with Gillard's now famous 'misogyny speech' to the House of Representatives on 9 October. It was, as a female journalist described, 'a blow up of pure frustration: volcanic and howling in intensity because the prelude to the explosion is a long period of not saying'.[196]

The reaction to the speech was polarised. The press gallery initially missed its significance. Gillard was also accused of hypocrisy, of a politically contrived playing of the 'gender card' and of provoking a 'gender war', so confirming another of the 'double binds' that bedevil female leaders.[197] On the other hand, the prime minister's expression of pent-up rage elicited empathy and even rejoicing among women of all ages, and well beyond Australia's borders. As the same journalist wrote: 'What woman can't relate to that? We've all been there, not saying, broiling about the injustice of not saying'.[198]

Yet when Gillard continued to beat the drum of gender into 2013, the politics were calamitous. By then her standing among male voters was in collapse and it was one of the factors that made her downfall take on an air of inevitability.[199] In her parting speech that June, she made up for the omission at the beginning of her incumbency by directly addressing 'the reaction to being the first female prime minister'. Her summary of the effect of gender on her prime ministership was that 'It doesn't explain everything, it doesn't explain nothing, it explains some things'.[200] In a further reflection shortly after leaving office, she ruefully observed that 'smashing through a glass ceiling is a dangerous pursuit. It is hard not to get lacerated on the way through'.[201]

Tony Abbott: An Unequal Protégé

Rudd's second coming as prime minister was short-lived.[202] It lasted from June 2013 to the September election when Labor was comprehensively defeated by the Tony Abbott–led Liberal–National Party Coalition. Rudd's return did deliver an initial dramatic poll bounce that saw Labor draw level with the Coalition on two-party-preferred terms and Rudd surge ahead of Abbott as preferred prime minister. Abbott, however, was not unnerved by what he derisively labelled as the 'electoral alchemy' of Rudd.[203]

Abbott's scepticism proved right once the August–September election campaign was underway. Abbott stuck resolutely to the script he had recited ad nauseam over the past three years to compelling effect. He promised a Coalition government would stop asylum-seeker boats, abolish the carbon and mining taxes and end Labor's alleged economic mismanagement. Equally uncomplicated and yet devastating were his references to Labor's leadership civil war. 'Do you want another three years like the last six?' Abbott asked voters and pledged to revive 'grown-up government'. On the other hand, unable or unwilling to pitch his re-election bid on Gillard's reform record, Rudd's campaign, as a senior journalist observed, was predicated 'on the Rudd persona … almost independent of the Labor Party'.[204] The effect on the polls of the leadership change was already fading, however, by the time the election was called. On the hustings, Rudd micromanaged schedules and strategies and issued grandiose, unplanned and unrelated ideas that were derided as 'thought bubbles'. Come polling day, Rudd did have the consolation of being credited with sparing Labor from the electoral annihilation predicted under Gillard. Yet for a prime minster who had elevated leadership personalisation to new heights, his second term ended surreally with a concession speech exuberantly invoking Labor tradition.

The scale of Abbott's achievement of bringing the Coalition back into government in September 2013 could not be denied. When he had become Liberal leader in December 2009, it was regarded as something of a rogue outcome. Like Labor during the second half of Howard's prime ministership, in opposition from late 2007 the Liberal Party indulged in leadership musical chairs. Following Brendan Nelson and Malcolm Turnbull, Abbott was its third leader in two years. His elevation was described as an 'accident' and Abbott was viewed as an unlikely future prime minister. He had won the leadership as the candidate of conservative elements of the party rebelling against Turnbull's determination to negotiate an emissions trading scheme with the Labor government. In an initial three-way contest against Turnbull and Joe Hockey, Abbott prevailed in the second ballot by a single vote.[205] Two years before, Abbott had nominated to succeed Howard but withdrew from the contest humbled when it became apparent he could muster only a handful of supporters.

Growing up in comfortable circumstances on Sydney's north shore, Abbott was marked early for great things by doting parents and sisters: his mother spoke of him as either a future prime minister or leader of the Catholic Church.[206] Educated by the Jesuits at the elite

Saint Ignatius' College, Riverview, he then studied law and economics at the University of Sydney. He catapulted into student politics. Joining the Democratic Club, a satellite of BA Santamaria's National Civic Council, the youthful Abbott extolled a blend of Anglophilia and Catholic social conservatism. Campaigning for the university Student Representative Council (SRC) presidency, he promised to replace SRC posters of Che Guevara with portraits of the Queen and the pope. However unfashionable his outlook, Abbott was a formidable scourge of the 'permissive' left. He confronted opponents with a flood of written words and strongarm tactics. These were enduring features of Abbott's political persona: part aspiring philosopher king, part bare-knuckled pugilist, a traditionalist but militant in practice. Temperamentally, he was also a volatile mix of swaggering blokey charm and the quixotic: the windmill tilting perhaps a means of atoning for a weakness for earthly pleasures. Gillard, who developed a rapport with Abbott while she was an opposition frontbencher and he a minister, came to regard him as a 'likeable, knockabout Australian character. But he's a deeply eccentric human being'.[207]

Abbott's journey into politics suggested restlessness of mind and spirit. There were stints as a Rhodes scholar at Oxford University, a seminarian for three years, a journalist with the *Bulletin* and the *Australian*, a staffer with Liberal opposition leader John Hewson, and executive director of the Australians for Constitutional Monarchy organisation. He won preselection for the blue-ribbon Sydney electorate of Warringah in 1994 with the encouragement of John Howard, who was Abbott's next significant political mentor after Santamaria. His timing in entering the House of Representatives could not have been much better and, while initially frustrated at being confined to the role of a parliamentary secretary when the Coalition formed government two years later, he gained a junior portfolio in 1998 and entered Howard's cabinet by early 2001.

Abbott earned a record as a capable if unimaginative administrator. But he was also given to distraction, a maverick who courted controversy. He was not a philosophical fellow traveller of the government's economic liberals—he showed little heart for expenditure cutting and was a sceptic of the deregulatory Work Choices industrial relations regime that finally undid Howard. In cabinet he championed unconventional spending schemes that fellow ministers ribbed as a throwback to Santamariaism. While Howard treated him with the forbearance of a favoured political son, Abbott's freewheeling tendencies tested the patience of colleagues. An erratic performance during the Coalition's losing 2007 election campaign and a view that he was branded within the electorate as a Catholic-inspired conservative accounted for the absence of enthusiasm for him succeeding Howard as leader. Out of favour, he temporarily went into a funk. One way he found solace during that period was by authoring a manifesto, *Battlelines*, in which he paid glowing tribute to Howard as an exemplar of how to manage a government:

> Political leadership is not like running a company or being captain of a ship. Prime ministers can direct public servants, but, for all their prominence and influence, they can rarely give orders to their colleagues. Howard understood that respect had to be earned, affection had to be won, and authority had to be used sparingly if it was to be effective.[208]

Because of his reputation for having an idiosyncratic world view and temperament (his nickname was the 'Mad Monk'), Abbott's elevation to leader was initially interpreted as a gift to the Labor government.[209] The suspicion was he would self-destruct. Abbott, however, was once again fortunate in his timing. He gained the leadership when Rudd was becoming increasingly brittle and then was pitted against a Labor successor whose prime ministership was compromised from the start. Still, Abbott made his own luck. In an afterword to *Battlelines* written after he became leader, Abbott referenced Winston Churchill, and there was an element of Churchillian war-like zeal to Abbott's crusade to defeat his Labor opponents unconditionally.[210] Supported by a small, disciplined team, headed by his chief of staff, Peta Credlin, Abbott set a new benchmark for trenchant aggression in opposition. First, his ferocious campaign against Labor's emissions trading scheme at the beginning of 2010 (unleashing the deadly 'great big tax on everything' slogan) helped spook Rudd into abandoning the scheme.[211] Second, having been outflanked by Gillard in winning the support of the independent members following that year's election, he then relentlessly portrayed her as an illegitimate leader. His formula was simple but sustained assaults on Labor's record on asylum seekers and carbon pricing and its management of government finances.

Having felled two prime ministers in less than four years, by the time he won office in 2013 Abbott was being counted among Australia's most effective opposition leaders.[212] There was a question, however, about whether he qualified for that rank since he had succeeded through implacable negativity and resort to incivility rather than the kind of philosophical and policy creativity that had enabled Menzies in the 1940s and Whitlam in the 1960s to mobilise new constituencies of support. Indeed, Abbott had arguably failed his own benchmark for achievement in opposition as articulated in *Battlelines*: 'Constructing a clear alternative ... is almost as important as attacking the government'.[213] Furthermore, his hyper-aggression had come at the price of the public not warming to him. He was the first opposition leader in modern times to win office despite being negatively rated by the electorate.[214]

An Unloved Prime Minister

In office, Abbott would combine and magnify the flaws of his Labor predecessors. Like Rudd, he demonstrated little capacity for administration and failed to manage crucial relationships effectively. Like Gillard, he often displayed a tin ear politically and was incapable of developing an emotional connection with voters.

Any public goodwill towards Abbott and his government evaporated alarmingly quickly.[215] He recorded a modest positive leadership rating in the first weeks of his prime ministership. That honeymoon—if it could be called that—was over by early December 2013, with his rating falling back into negative territory and the Coalition behind Labor on two-party-preferred terms. Things never recovered. Following the government's first budget of May 2014, Abbott's dissatisfaction rating hit 60 per cent and he trailed opposition leader Bill Shorten as preferred prime minister—an unusual plight, especially for a first-term incumbent. The polling nadir for Abbott came in February 2015 when more than two-thirds of voters disapproved of his performance. Among recent prime ministers, only Keating and Gillard had plumbed such depths and neither had suffered a decline quite so precipitous. In making his case for a change of prime minister that September, Turnbull pointed out that under Abbott's leadership the Coalition government had been behind in thirty consecutive Newspolls.[216]

Abbott's lack of appeal was connected to his inability to make the transition in the public's consciousness from opposition gladiator to a leader governing for all Australians. His prime-ministerial persona became a caricature of the 'strong leader' type once delineated by the Australian political psychologist Graham Little. The defining traits of the strong leader are 'a malignly dichotomous world [view], a world of win or lose, lead or be led, control or be controlled' and a corresponding mercilessness towards opponents. The objective, according to Little, 'is not to contribute to debate; the intention is to overcome and then marginalise contrary views out of existence'.[217] These are leaders that stoke fears and thrive best in a crisis setting.

There were abundant 'crises' for Abbott to exploit during his prime ministership: a 'budget emergency', border control, and the spectre of home-grown and external militant Islamic terrorism. Abbott could claim his government 'stopped the boats', even if the policy's implementation on the high seas was cloaked in operational secrecy. He also won kudos in mid-2014 for his resolute action when Malaysian Airlines flight 17 (MH17) was shot down over Ukraine, claiming two dozen Australian lives. But for the most part his security threat responses were bereft of rhetorical or tactical 'nuance'.[218] Polarising language was his stock in trade. He employed the apocalyptic term 'death cult' to describe the jihadist militant group Islamic State, which he warned was 'coming after us', while new arrivals to Australia were lectured that they must join 'team Australia'. He raised diplomatic eyebrows by threatening to 'shirt-front' Vladimir Putin when the Russian president visited Australia for the 2014 G20 conference, over that country's suspected complicity in the downing of MH17. There were stories too of Abbott entertaining rash Dr Strangelove–like schemes for sending troops to secure the crash site of MH17 and despatching soldiers to battle Islamic State in Iraq.[219] These reports were likely exaggerated, but they contributed to the image of a leader who looked at the world through a glass darkly and whose instinct was always to fight: a prime minister who had no other métier than aggression.

The mishandling of the 'budget emergency' was perhaps most disastrous for Abbott's relationship with voters.[220] To some degree, the stringency of his government's first budget followed the playbook used by Howard when he entered office. Once again, however, Abbott paid a price for a lack of proportion in opposition. Having fanatically pursued Gillard for reneging on her 2010 election campaign pledge not to introduce a carbon tax, his government's 2014 budget contained large expenditure reductions in areas—including health and education—that Abbott had assured voters on the eve of the 2013 election would be spared from cuts. Predictably, he too now was condemned for betraying the public's trust and seen as making a mockery of his pre-election vow that his would be a government of 'no surprises'. Moreover, the harshness of the budget medicine relied on economic nostrums of declining currency: the public reacted with scepticism and anger at the perceived unfairness of its measures. Unlike Howard, Abbott also lacked an effective economic spokesperson to smooth the budget's way. Treasurer Joe Hockey's ham-fisted presentation of the cuts reinforced a picture of hardheartedness. The budget folly was then compounded by Abbott's stubborn denial that it had broken promises, an inability to negotiate a number of the measures through the Senate, and confusing policy twists and surrenders (the latter exercise styled by Abbott as 'barnacle clearing'). The Coalition delivered a more benign and better-received 2015 budget, but by walking away from the 'fiscal crisis' mantra obsessively used by Abbott and his colleagues in opposition and in their first year in office, he was left looking like another in a line of economically muddled prime ministers.

Nor could Abbott's idiosyncrasies be contained. The most spectacular manifestation of him being out of step with community sentiment was the announcement on Australia Day 2015 of the conferral of a knighthood on Prince Philip.[221] Abbott had reinstated the titles of knights and dames the previous year to the astonishment of his cabinet and party room, and despite his mentor, John Howard, counselling him against it.

That decision was met with bemusement, but the prime-ministerial 'captain's call' of knighting Prince Philip aroused worse: nationwide incredulity and ridicule. It was a catalyst for a sharp deterioration in Abbott's already poor standing in the opinion polls and spurred the first attempt by his disaffected colleagues to depose him. While unsuccessful, that move left his grip on the prime ministership tenuous after less than a year and a half in office.

Abbott's struggle to cultivate broad appeal in the electorate was not helped by his tribal attitude to the media.[222] Similar to Gillard before him, Abbott initially sought to manage the news cycle by stepping back from it. On coming to office he complained that 'too much empty talk' had emanated from governments over recent years and signalled his administration would only be heard from when it had something substantive to say.[223] True to that strategy, Abbott made himself only sparingly available to journalists early in his term. But as the government settled in, the most striking feature of the prime minister's media relationships was that they were skewed towards sympathisers: conservative columnists in News Limited newspapers and prominent right-wing radio talkback hosts. It was a pattern replicated by his PMO that conspicuously favoured the Murdoch-owned *Daily Telegraph* and *Australian* (the latter's editor-in-chief was a prime-ministerial confidant) with exclusives and leaks. Conversely, Abbott entered into a 'low-level culture war' against what he clearly regarded as antagonistic media organisations, especially the ABC.[224] 'Whose side are you on?' he demanded of the national broadcaster and expressed his wrath at aspects of its performance by banning ministers from appearing on one of its flagship current affairs programs.[225]

There was an echo here of Howard's preference for targeting his communications through ideologically reliable channels and his prosecution of the 'culture wars'. Abbott's approach, though, was neither as discriminating nor adept. Where Howard was a highly agile interlocutor and acutely aware of the audience he was trying to persuade (and calculating about who he could afford to alienate), Abbott was rhetorically inflexible and over time appeared to speak to a diminishing conservative circle. An interview in the dying days of his prime ministership in which he robotically parroted the phrases 'the boats have stopped' and the 'carbon tax has gone' in answering questions about his government's economic record emphasised the aridity of his communication technique.[226] Abbott's narrow-minded approach to the media was also reflected in an unimaginative engagement with non-traditional media in which he showed little interest or understanding. Responding to the deluge on social media pillorying the knighting of Prince Philip, he dismissed it as 'electronic graffiti', and added: 'You wouldn't report what's sprayed up on the walls of buildings'.[227]

Abbott's Rasputin

Perversely, the same kind of paranoid them-against-us mentality permeated the management of Abbott's government. The PMO, or more precisely, the chief of staff, Peta Credlin, was the principal enforcer of this culture. In the two years of Abbott's prime ministership, Credlin gained a level of notoriety unprecedented for a ministerial staffer: her power and the nature of her relationship with Abbott became a source of media fascination.[228] After a year of internal rumblings about Credlin, Abbott issued a public defence of her: 'do you really think my chief of staff would be under this kind of criticism if her name was P-E-T-E-R as opposed to P-E-T-A?'[229] This sensitivity to gender prejudice must have left Julia Gillard spinning in her political grave. Abbott nevertheless had a point. Credlin's stereotyping as a 'dominatrix' was consistent with the pattern of treatment of women in positions of authority in Australian politics.[230] She subsequently protested at having been judged differently to male counterparts: 'If I was a guy I wouldn't be bossy, I'd be strong. If I was a guy I wouldn't be a micromanager. I'd be across my brief, or across the detail'.[231]

Even so, there is little question that under Credlin's direction, the 'command-and-control style' of operation to which modern PMOs have been prone 'was taken to an extreme'.[232] Whereas Hawke and Howard had seen the wisdom of a chief of staff with bureaucratic experience, Credlin's appointment continued the recent trend of a political functionary filling the position. She had not spent time in the public service but rather was a Liberal Party partisan par excellence. Her career path before becoming Abbott's chief of staff when he was elected opposition leader comprised a series of appointments in the offices of senior party members.[233] Credlin was, in Abbott's words, 'the smartest and fiercest political warrior I've ever worked with'.[234] That by itself might have given pause as to whether she was a suitable choice for supervising management of the government and whether she had the necessary complementary skills to Abbott. Rather than moderating it, Credlin would reinforce his combative partisanship.

The symbiosis between prime minister and his chief of staff was all the more problematic because of how much Abbott depended on Credlin. This reliance included her doing his make-up and hair, choosing his ties, controlling his diary, and sitting in and speaking for him in key forums.[235] So indivisible were they that, according to one account of the government, Credlin 'became a proxy for the prime minister himself'.[236] The dependence had developed in opposition when Credlin was virtually Abbott's shadow, vigilantly preventing him going off the rails. By the time he assumed office, her support was indispensable to him. It invited speculation that she was a psychological crutch for a gnawing self-doubt that he was not up to the job.[237] Abbott was certainly unwilling to countenance prime-ministerial life without Credlin. Despite a chorus of complaints from colleagues about her role, the prime minister rebuffed their advice—including from Howard—that he let her go. 'You wouldn't be here if it wasn't for Peta', he told her detractors.[238]

Though originating more from the chief of staff than the prime minister, Abbott's PMO had distorting effects on the Coalition's administration that were reminiscent of problems that had occurred under Rudd.[239] First, because Credlin sought to control so much—from vetting draft cabinet briefing submissions and overseeing the prime minister's schedule, to micromanaging the minutiae of designing staff business cards, drawing up wine lists for major functions and organising VIP flight seating arrangements—administrative bottlenecks emerged. In the description of one adviser, the PMO became 'constipated'.[240] Second, because the office respected few boundaries it choked the autonomy of ministers, inhibiting initiative and breeding resentment. Credlin's reach extended to attending cabinet and ERC and NSC meetings, where she was known to intervene to grill ministers and officials. Her ubiquity and influence led one observer to conclude that she 'had more power than most ministers'.[241] The PMO's vetting of ministerial staffing arrangements was a particular source of internal grievance and brought Credlin into sharp conflict with senior government members, among them Liberal deputy leader and foreign minister Julie Bishop. Credlin was seen to be manipulating staffing appointments to consolidate her control by inserting loyalists throughout the administration. The atmosphere of intimidation and mistrust within the government was further aggravated by the PMO's practice of leaking against its own. Arthur Sinodinos, Howard's former chief of staff and a newly elected Liberal senator and assistant treasurer in the government, was the victim of a leak in late 2014, alienating him from Abbott.[242] Third, the PMO constricted advice to the prime minister to an unhealthy degree. Credlin was accused of jealously guarding access to Abbott and freezing out parliamentary colleagues and key Liberal Party officials. 'The problem is', complained one government senator, 'there is a funnel into the PM's office … The funnel is Peta Credlin, and no ideas can get to Abbott unless people get them through Credlin'.[243]

Distrust also coloured Abbott's and his chief of staff's approach to the public service. Upon entering government, the Coalition instigated a scaled-down version of Howard's 'night of the long knives' by dismissing three departmental secretaries, while another, the head of treasury, Martin Parkinson, was informed he would be required to leave within twelve months.[244] Astonishingly, the treasurer, Joe Hockey, learned of his departmental secretary's fate only after Parkinson had been put on notice. He was unable to reverse the decision despite preferring Parkinson to stay.[245] The sins of these officials were that they were implicated in the previous Labor governments' policies on climate change and asylum seekers and one was a former chief of staff to Paul Keating. In other words, the bureaucratic cleansing was another example of the obsessive political and philosophical tribalism of Abbott and Credlin. This was also reflected in the close control exercised over statutory authority and senior advisory appointments and a pattern of installing conservative fellow travellers in those positions.[246] The cowing of the bureaucracy was in turn compounded by the Coalition's plans for substantial cuts to staffing numbers and Abbott's war of words with public institutions like the ABC and the Human Rights Commission.

Estranging Cabinet and Party Room

Despite being a student and avowed admirer of Howard's canny management of his cabinet and party room, Abbott fell short of those standards. It surely did not help Abbott's relationship with his ministers that Credlin became resented for wielding greater authority than some of them. Abbott's predilection for what became known as 'captain's calls' was another cause of strain. The most notorious of these exercises of unilateral leadership was the knighting of Prince Philip, but there were others such as Abbott's foisting on his colleagues a costly paid parental leave scheme that dated back to opposition days and that he only abandoned under sufferance in 2015.[247]

During 2015 Abbott also incensed ministers by trying to 'ambush' them with a highly controversial proposal for stripping citizenship from suspected terrorists. He had it brought before them as an 'under-the-line' item. Both the proposal and the process generated heated dissension in cabinet, and a leak to the press of what had occurred, in embarrassingly elaborate detail. According to that leak, Abbott's soon to be conqueror, Malcolm Turnbull, rebuked the prime minister over the disregard of process: 'Here we go again. Talking about something as momentous as this and there is nothing in front of us. There's a discussion paper that only a few of us have seen. This is a shambles'.[248] When Turnbull successfully challenged for the leadership a few months later, he returned to the theme of Abbott's mishandling of cabinet and pointedly referenced Howard:

> We need to restore traditional Cabinet government. There must be an end to policy on the run and captain's calls. We need to be truly consultative with colleagues … we have to remember that we have a great example of good Cabinet government. John Howard's government most of us served in, and yet few would say that the Cabinet government of Mr Abbott bears any similarity to the style of Mr Howard.[249]

The most conclusive measure of Abbott's failure to manage relationships in his government was that he haemorrhaged support so swiftly in his party room as to be deposed within two years of his triumph in returning the Coalition to office. Indeed, it might have been earlier had not Abbott locked his cabinet in behind him in February 2015 when his leadership was first threatened. An unorganised and largely spontaneous uprising by government backbenchers, it was born out of anxiety at the Coalition's unfavourable polling and frustration at the prime minister's political missteps. But the backbench disaffection also sprang from feelings they were being neglected by a remote prime minister.[250] Crossbench senators would similarly complain about the prime minister's aloofness, despite their importance to the progress of the Coalition's legislative program.[251] Following the February 2015 leadership scare, Abbott took steps to improve his accessibility to parliamentary colleagues and relax the PMO's control of them. Moreover, while the prime minister ignored calls to remove Credlin as chief of staff, for a time at least she became less conspicuous.[252]

The poor polls and blunders kept coming, though. Abbott's convening of a joint Liberal and National Party room meeting in August, in a transparent stratagem to thwart the wishes of elements within his party for a parliamentary conscience vote on same-sex marriage, angered moderates and raised more questions about his judgement and openness to colleagues' views. And it signalled a prime minister fighting a rearguard action against community sentiment that was largely in favour of marriage equality.[253] When his tenure ended ignominiously the following month—the shortest and least consequential prime ministership since McMahon's—Credlin reputedly issued an edict to staffers that 'No one is to work for the other side'.[254] It epitomised a rabid partisanship.

Extreme Personality and Extreme Contingency

Writing after the 'madness' of 2007–10, a former senior adviser in the Rudd government reflected:

> Is it the case that systems of government are so large, complex and robust and involve so many actors that even the most wilful political

> leader cannot control them; or can a leader's extreme personality and style make good government practically impossible? I used to be a believer in systems, conventions, and good government sailing serenely on over the chaos of even the most extreme personality. I'm no longer sure any more.[255]

'Extreme personality' is part of the explanation for the prime-ministerial upheavals of the period here.[256] Kevin Rudd was a creative fashioner of ideas, a gifted political communicator and had an enviable ability to inspire optimism in the electorate. Yet he was a poor driver of the prime-ministerial government machine: manic and chaotic, incapable of recognising his own limitations and cavalier of key relationships. Suffering from the conceit that he enjoyed a personal mandate and could govern around rather than through his party, his fortunes exemplified the autonomous leader in the contemporary media age: 'simultaneously both stronger and weaker. As long as they can ride the tiger of an increasingly fickle public opinion, they can "go it alone": once public support begins to dwindle, however, they are left with few allies'.[257] Tony Abbott too fits the 'extreme personality' category. A formidable warrior in opposition, he singularly failed to adapt to governing. This inability to make the transition was said to have dismayed and mystified his role model, Howard.[258] Instead, Abbott seemed compulsively locked into a militant, paranoid and ultimately self-destructive tribalism.

Gillard's is a different story. She was a superior driver of the prime-ministerial government machine than either Rudd or Abbott. Possessing a strong sense of purpose, she was orderly, collegial and tenacious. Having endured and learned from the excesses of Rudd, Gillard later insisted she was 'as ready as you can be' for office. Yet her incumbency was continuously beset by crisis, beginning with the original sin of overthrowing a first-term prime minister.[259] Her chief dilemma was not 'extreme personality' but rather

> 'extreme contingency' ... As Malcolm Tucker would say in *The Thick of It* [a BBC satire about British government], it was an 'omnishambles'; it was shambolic, no matter how you looked at it. Of course, all prime

> ministers have to deal with one damn thing after another. It is a matter of degree. For Gillard, personally and politically it was extreme.[260]

At the same time, Gillard's aptitude for administration was not matched by her public communication performance—a major deficit in an era when media entrepreneurship is a crucial element of the prime-ministerial repertoire.

Neither extreme personality nor extreme contingency is sufficient, though, to explain the prime-ministerial vicissitudes of this period. For one, there are the philosophical uncertainties and skittishness of contemporary political parties. In their weakened state, both the major parties began to demonstrate serial poor judgement in making leadership choices, resorting to candidates 'outside the leadership mainstream' or those not adequately road-tested for office.[261] They also displayed little ability to constrain leaders—save through the destructive sanction of deposition. The power and long tentacles of prime-ministerial offices exacerbated this problem by facilitating rather than checking leadership idiosyncrasies: they amplified the effects of 'extreme personalities'. Overbearing and intimidating, both Rudd's and Abbott's offices clogged up and narrowed decision-making processes. The asymmetry in influence between partisan private offices and the bureaucracy is another factor that seems to have diminished the restraints on prime ministers.

Though personal failings and institutional weaknesses played key parts, the political instability of the last few years cannot be divorced from other, larger forces. The decline of voter loyalty to the major parties accelerated, creating a volatile governing environment. The public was unforgiving in its judgement of incumbents, with rolling public opinion polls an instrument of expression of the mood of popular discontent. It is no coincidence that adverse polling helped seal the fate of each of these prime ministers. Rudd, Gillard and Abbott were also condemned to be in office during a period of major disruption in the media. The round-the-clock news cycle and insatiable hunger for content placed extra demands on each of them as communicator-in-chief, while the fragmentation of the media landscape simultaneously complicated the task of crafting and maintaining an authentic public persona. These prime ministers sought to cope in different ways. Rudd became 'Australia's first 24/7 PM, both by temperament and necessity'.[262] On the other hand, Gillard and Abbott experimented with taming the media cycle by withdrawing from it. None of these approaches worked. Finally, the GFC left all prime ministers of the era to govern in a climate of policy flux. The core economic liberalising ideas championed by Hawke, Keating and Howard in the vaunted era of reform were losing traction, but a clear alternative had not yet materialised.

There is little to suggest that these trying circumstances will ease any time soon. If anything, they are being exacerbated by geopolitical instability and a deepening backlash against the socioeconomic insecurities wrought by 'globalisation'. No matter how individually skilled they are, the prime ministers who follow Rudd, Gillard and Abbott are likely to be severely tested by governing in such a climate of endemic turbulence and popular resentment. A fundamental lesson of this study has indeed been that it is naïve to expect too much of leaders alone: successful government has mostly been the product of a confluence of propitious historical conditions, robust institutions and shared rather than solo leadership. And so it is likely to be in the future.

7

FROM PRE-EMINENCE TO PARADOX: THE AUSTRALIAN PRIME MINISTERSHIP, 1949–2016

'THERE HAS NEVER been a more exciting time to be alive than today and there has never been a more exciting time to be an Australian', Malcolm Turnbull enthusiastically proclaimed upon becoming prime minister in September 2015.[1] His optimism appeared to be contagious. The electorate responded buoyantly to the removal of Tony Abbott and his replacement by Turnbull. Having cited the Coalition government's dire unpopularity under his predecessor's leadership as a core motive for challenging Abbott, Turnbull was able to bask in the latter months of 2015 in the glow of opinion polls showing that the government had surged ahead of the Labor opposition, and in dizzying ratings for his own performance. It did not last. By early 2016, the gloss was rapidly falling off Turnbull as the (excessive) expectations of him went unfulfilled and the constraints he was operating under grew manifest. Long regarded as a philosophical outlier in the Liberal Party because of his progressive inclinations, Turnbull was unable or unprepared to rock the boat on conservative policy positions established under Abbott, most emblematically in the areas of climate change and same-sex marriage. With his standing in the polls faltering, Turnbull called an early double-dissolution election with the aim of clearing out a hostile Senate, but also to gain legitimacy for his leadership and, anticipated many commentators, to attain the necessary authority to assert his true colours within his government and party. Yet at the July 2016 election the Coalition lost substantial ground, only scraping back into government with a one-seat majority in the House and its position in the Senate worse. Turnbull's authority, rather than being enhanced, had been diminished and his internal Liberal Party critics were emboldened. In the wake of the election, the polls turned stubbornly against the government.

We must be cautious in jumping to conclusions about the fate of Turnbull's prime ministership. Nevertheless, the topsy-turvy nature of his first year in office suggested at least two things. The first was that, despite the discomfiture of the prime ministership since 2007, the public clung to a residual faith in the office's redemptive capacities given the right person to fill it: hence the initially heady response to Turnbull's ascension. But, equally, the swift onset of disillusionment with him—a fall in standing similar to that suffered by his three immediate predecessors—lent credence to the argument of those who believe that the recent malaise affecting the office goes beyond a run of poor leaders to something deeper and structural. Three benighted prime ministers in succession might perhaps be rationalised away, but four appeared beyond a coincidence.

The fickle voter response to Turnbull is symptomatic of a broader trend in public attitudes to political leadership in Australia. Surveys from the beginning of this century that coincided with the later stages of what has generally been recognised as one of Australia's most significant and successful eras of reform under the successive stewardship of Bob Hawke, Paul Keating and John Howard revealed significant ambivalence towards that reform project. They suggested most Australians accepted the benefits of free trade and valued economic growth, but many rejected privatisation. Protectionist policy (and a mixed economy) still appealed. Big business was thought to have too much power and income inequality to be too great, and an active role for government was preferred.[2] Moreover, the disquiet about economic reform was accompanied by increasing disillusionment with politicians and disengagement from conventional political processes. Those in the most disadvantaged economic groups were the least trusting of others.[3] And even when those same reforms were seen to have fortified the nation with a resilience that few other countries enjoyed, when the GFC struck in 2008, the level of disenchantment only grew more pronounced.

By 2016, the Australian Election Survey revealed that trust in government had reached an all-time low of 26 per cent; 74 per cent of respondents believed that people in government looked after themselves; and only 12 per cent thought government was run for 'all the people', while 56 per cent thought it served 'a few big interests'.[4] Perhaps most intriguingly, a subsequent survey seemed to confirm a latent messiah complex within the electorate. It reported that 70 per cent of Australians believed 'the nation needs a strong leader to take the country back from the rich and powerful', and that Australians emerged as more likely than most to support closing the door on globalisation.[5] These trends were worldwide, but it was striking that Australians, who suffered less than most, were more disenchanted than the global average, indicating that something more than shared problems was in play.[6]

How do we most convincingly account for the malaise that the prime ministership—an institution established as apparently unassailable by the time Robert Menzies left office in the mid-1960s and then reinforced in pre-eminence when Gough Whitlam, Hawke, Keating and Howard demonstrated what it was capable of setting in motion—has fallen into over the past decade? How much of the institutional developments responsible for elevating the authority and prominence of the office, and which were capitalised upon by those leaders, carried within them the seeds of the present fragilities? Or is it changes over recent decades in the contextual landscape in which politics is played—particularly in the political parties, the media and the policy cycle—to which we must chiefly look for an explanation? And how do we make sense of public yearning for strong, transformative leadership and the pattern of precipitous giving up on leaders? In answering these questions, it is worthwhile to first recap prime-ministerial leadership and institutional evolutions since the middle of last century.

Leader Performance: the Prime-ministerial Government Machine

Prime ministers in the first half of the twentieth century all worked to achieve the means of executive authority to exercise genuine national leadership. They discovered that their remit was limited and that proposing constitutional reform—referendums—to address constraints on what they thought necessary for such purposes was mostly fruitless. They learned that progress instead depended almost solely on mobilising institutional and popular support for their measures. The authority for this could not be assumed as an entitlement of office. It had to be won through access to and control of information supporting policy objectives, command of a broad-based party organisation, the exercise of discipline in cabinet and the parliamentary party room, and effective communication with the people. Access to expert advice—a professional public service—was essential. And financial power to implement genuinely national programs and induce states to cooperate was key. It was finally achieved as a result of the wartime exercise of emergency powers, then confirmed by taxation legislation. These things, seeming so self-evident now, were only gradually gained. But by the 1940s they had come to fruition. The governments of John Curtin and Ben Chifley appeared, finally, to have the 'big levers' to govern Australia. The prime minister's role had been firmly established and its authority secured.[7]

Yet the country continued to develop, with enormous socioeconomic and demographic change. In Australia, population growth (from 8.3 million in 1950 to 19.2 million by 2000), targeted to support development and industrialisation, and with a diversification of migrant source countries, saw a transition from Anglo-Celtic assumptions to multiculturalism. Rapid urban expansion and planning problems in the cities, as well as a decline in the proportion of rural population, were engendered. Education was promoted both as the means of personal development and an economic necessity, though access favoured urban populations while opportunities for young country people disappeared. Developmentalism, cushioned by protection and smoothed by Keynesian economics, gave way to demands to open up markets and integrate with the global economy: manufacturing was supplanted, the knowledge economy and service industries grew. Many benefited, but others saw their lives and communities disrupted. Policy solutions intended to address the challenges of such transitions were devised, but as integration into the global economy advanced, their purchase would become limited. Yet issues both of appropriate policy responses for generating and capturing benefits, and of means to address the loss of opportunities some experienced, demanded national leadership. So, in interaction with geopolitical developments, inevitably the prime-ministerial office too changed.

This book has concentrated upon the way in which groups of post-war prime ministers, in addressing the issues specific to their periods of incumbency, responded to those challenges. The institutions with which, and in which, they operated had to adapt—sometimes in reaction to historical contingency, sometimes as a result of an incumbent's action and performance, sometimes a combination of both—and so the office continued to evolve. Several patterns underlaid that evolution: enhanced public expectations of what leaders should or could do; an increase in the resources thought necessary for leadership; changes in parties that have accentuated leader-centralism; and transitions in media and technology that have profoundly influenced the practice of political communication.

Effective prime ministers had always managed to gain public attention, but it was Curtin's and Chifley's successful crisis management in a national emergency—World War II—and the ambition of their post-war programs that gave impetus to the expectation that leaders were central to public wellbeing. Menzies, however, added new dimensions to such expectations. He was the colossus of postwar politics, and his performance set new benchmarks. He had, in effect, created his own party and with it a version of liberalism that mobilised a constituency—the 'moral middle class'[8]—which would be its source of strength for decades. Speaking for a cause was always important, but Menzies came to personify what liberalism meant. He assumed effortlessly the role of communicator-in-chief for his party and government, setting a standard that others would struggle to match. His command of parliament, control of party and cabinet, ruthless despatch of rivals, international statesmanship (and renown) and his performance on the public stage established a template that successors would strive to emulate. It was a significant reinforcement of leader-centric party practice and of public expectations.

War and postwar reconstruction had provided the impetus for the expanded and intellectually high-calibre public service that Menzies inherited from Curtin and Chifley. But here, too, Menzies' contribution was substantial. His encouragement of, trust in and reliance upon the ambitious mandarins emerging from postwar reconstruction facilitated the professionalisation of the Australian public service. Paul Hasluck described it as perhaps Menzies' greatest achievement. It would not stop there. John Gorton, in service to his own concept of strong leadership and vision for the country, breached what had become convention by appointing his own man, Lenox Hewitt, as secretary of PM&C, and with the intention of making it the lead agency of government. Whitlam, having experimented with using his private office to drive an ambitious agenda, soon saw its limits and he too turned to a personal appointment—John Menadue—to recalibrate PM&C for his purposes. Malcolm Fraser, building on the trend, counted on his PM&C secretary, Alan Carmody, as would Hawke on Mike Codd, and Paul Keating on Mike Keating, to focus whole-of-government attention on the political executive's aims. Howard, famously, brought in a semi-outsider, Max ('the Axe') Moore-Wilton, to shake up the service, and then Peter Shergold to transmit the logic of reform and the case for government objectives. Every step was an amplification of PM&C as a 'can do' department and as the lead agency in whole-of-government coordination and responsiveness to prime-ministerial direction.

The PMO, a small, primarily secretarial operation, was dramatically transformed in the transition from Menzies and his successors to Whitlam. It was thought a policy-smart, politically oriented office would be the catalyst for reforms not welcomed by a public service habituated to conservative rule. It was an underestimation of the public service capacity and willingness to respond, and an indirect incentive for the readiness of the service to adapt when the private office proved no match for Whitlam's ambitions. And yet the concept of a division between politically attuned staff at the prime minister's side and their capacity to debate and challenge public service tradition, or to unsettle constraining orthodoxy, would not be abandoned. No subsequent prime minister would revert to a small secretarial office.

Numbers in the PMO grew inexorably, as did a reliance on political loyalists alongside policy experts and consultants. The intention was to ensure debate and contest from which robust decisions would emerge. It was also intended to give prime ministers a stronger hand in dealing with lead agencies such as Treasury. Fraser, for instance, came to rely on a combination of PM&C officers (such as Ian Castles and Ed Visbord) alongside private office staffers (such as John Rose) to provide the firepower with which to control Treasury's dominance of economic decision-making. The practice would spread to other policy domains, and prove a significant resource in ensuring informational control over other ministers and hence the initiation of prime-ministerial, rather than cabinet, government. Staffers such as David Kemp with Fraser, Graham Evans and Sandy Hollway with Hawke, Don Russell with Keating, and Arthur Sinodinos with Howard became key players in managing the balance between their prime ministers' political and policy agendas. Yet even as the PMO expanded, and gained capacity, cooperation rather than conflict was sustained, largely because prime ministers retained experienced public servants, with their knowledge of Canberra networks and systems, in key roles, usually as chief of staff.

The vaunted reforms of the late twentieth century owed much to the combinations and flexibility afforded by the pairing of a 'can do' PM&C and a politically savvy PMO. Indeed, the pairing, when all was going well, made for a sophisticated political machine of considerable policy capacity and political nuance. It reached its height under Hawke, Keating and Howard. In the right circumstances, it amplified good leadership. Yet there was an inherent asymmetry, with public servants bound to systems of accountability and transparency from which private office staff were free. In challenging situations, where staffers had the last word, or could act as gatekeepers to the inner circle, they could have disproportionate influence with little fear of consequences. When hubris or conviction on the part of a leader overcame prudence, then the loyalty of staffers to the boss rather than to the public good could reinforce poor decisions. Even a leader of great self-control, experience and shrewdness could succumb. Such was the case in the few, but damaging, policy fiascos that marked the closing years of the Howard administration. Those who lacked Howard's self-knowledge, experience and political nous would find the going much tougher.

Parties changed in the closing years of the twentieth century in ways that reinforced leader centrality and further augmented public expectations. The mass parties of the mid-twentieth century depended on patterns of socioeconomic identification—the embattled worker, the middle-class 'backbone' of the country—and associated ideologies that lost traction as prosperity and aspirations increased. As 'rusted-on' party identifiers dwindled, the major parties transformed into 'electoral professional' parties, more reliant on expert advice and market-based campaigning than on tribal loyalties, and on leader communication than shared ideology as the means of electoral mobilisation.

Menzies had a gift for such communication, but later it became an imperative for all. And here, the importance of media organisations, and the ability of prime ministers and their staff to utilise what they offered, was crucial. One element was the professional campaign based on an iconic leader ('It's Time' 1972 as the inception) transitioning by the Howard era into the permanent campaign (incessant, advertorial leader promotion). But more important was leader performance and media management. The capacity to achieve the latter became a core responsibility of the PMO. The leaders deemed most effective—from Menzies to Howard—all relied upon broadcast models to disseminate messages. It was a practice dependent upon media conglomerates, predictable news cycles and reaching wide audiences, with broadsheet press and opinion-leading 'god' journalists and media presenters setting the agenda, facilitating trickle-down influence on television and radio news. The pattern was bookended at the one end by Curtin (expert in understanding journalists and cultivating the press gallery) and Menzies (using radio broadcasting to disseminate a philosophy and create a constituency), and at the other by Keating (at his best, like Curtin, persuading the press gallery that his was the only argument in town) and Howard (using talkback radio not only to reach supporters but also to lay out an argument uninterrupted and as virtually the only avenue though which journalists could access prime-ministerial copy).

These were systems that complemented the reliance of the parties on leaders as their communicators-in-chief, since monopolies and their influential journalists and broadcasters served to aggregate opinion and hence to channel the prime minister's message. But in the twenty-first century, this too became much tougher. The business model of the media conglomerates began to fail; the desperate attempt to retain audiences through 'infotainment' made 'god' journalists extinct; and internet access and customer choice led to an extreme of 'narrowcasting', where individuals could access (or be channelled towards) only those opinions with which they already agreed and social media threatened to become the news aggregator of choice. This disruption, both institutional and contextual, would hobble the aspirations of more recent prime ministers to match their predecessors.

From Pivot of Power to 'Impossible Job'?

Despite the institutional transformations described, no linear pattern in the accrual of prime-ministerial power can be assumed. As with any role, much depends on the capacity of incumbents. Hence, the deference extended to individuals and the efficacy with which they sought and used their licence to exercise leadership has varied markedly between prime ministers—McMahon and Abbott being at the low end of the continuum and Menzies, Hawke (with Keating) and Howard at the high end. Sometimes there were notable variations within one incumbent's period in office. Even Menzies, the seemingly unassailable and 'eternal' prime minister, experienced fluctuations in his personal popularity, the political strength of his party and electoral performance. Critics turned against him in his final years in office. Likewise, Hawke and Howard, each now remembered by their parties as exemplary role models, varied markedly in their ability to 'get things done' at different junctures during their long tenures. This might be expected: Australian prime ministers are not exempt from the normal process of accumulating, spending and exhausting the 'leadership capital' a head of government is accorded during their time in office.[9]

However, during the most recent decade, a more disturbing trend has set in. Post-Howard, the credit lines necessary to exercise effective leadership—keeping the nation's ear even when delivering unpopular messages, articulating a policy agenda, having institutional reforms passed and delivered, and leading from the front (staring down one's own colleagues and constituencies when necessary)—have eluded successive incumbents. Prime ministers have at their command a formidable political machine, comprising better resources for advice and policy development than ever before. And still, since 2007, prime ministers have struggled to resolve major policy problems, and all experienced serious erosion of their personal popularity and political authority remarkably quickly after achieving office. The trend is so distinctive and has proved so debilitating that it cannot be ignored.

Both sides of politics share in the malaise. The fact that, despite their marked personal, political and stylistic differences, Rudd, Gillard, Abbott and, most recently, Turnbull all swiftly found themselves in deep and disabling political trouble makes it implausible to argue that Australia has suffered a series of substandard politicians. Certainly, each has had personal idiosyncrasies. And each has made sometimes grave errors of judgement. But so have many predecessors. Yet the sense that there is a crisis of leadership at the centre of the Australian political system is widespread.[10] How can we account for the apparent decline of prime-ministerial efficacy, authority and longevity when neither lack of institutional resources nor general incompetence of office-holders (albeit, with some exceptions) plausibly applies? And how might this play out into the future?

This analysis of prime-ministerial leadership relies on three pillars: personalities, institutions and context. And it is in this third pillar that there have been epochal changes over the last decades, changes that have conspired to make the job of prime minister progressively more challenging. For a start, post-2007 leaders are, like Whitlam and Fraser in the 1970s and 1980s, struggling with policy regime exhaustion: in their case, the endpoint of the neoliberal experiment. It is common to all the advanced economies. The financial crisis starting in 2008 was seen at the time as a turning point, as the moment when—in Kevin Rudd's view, for instance—social democracy must save capitalism from itself. Rudd failed to effect that salvation. Much was said about the necessity of a new social contract, regulation that would manage market failure, measures that would address inequality in resource distribution, and the need to stem the pervasive and increasing conviction among many that reform was not working for them. It demands new ideas and a refreshed policy regime. Yet leaders seem unable to move on from the market liberalisation model and are instead, in George Megalogenis' deft phrase, struggling to 'release themselves from the spell cast by the leader they wish to be, Paul Keating'.[11]

Party change and party fragmentation has them ensnared. The two-party system that emerged at the end of the first decade of the twentieth century reached its peak in the mass parties of the post–World War II period, but the transition to electoral professional parties hollowed out support, and ultimately has led to excessive leader centralism. As these parties turned increasingly to 'the leader' as the point of brand differentiation and the spokesperson for all that the party represented and intended, leaders were given greater responsibility and authority, but also threatened with blame and retribution if party fortunes suffered.

And in the new century, as party membership continued to dwindle and 'professionals' dictated policy and strategy, there was increasing fragmentation and factionalisation within parties. Splinter parties on the left and right emerged, and there was a growing divergence in the opinions of the residual party membership and majority public opinion.[12] 'Broad church' arguments, such as those with which Howard persisted, became difficult to sustain. By 2015, polls of opinion divergence between Liberal Party members and the public illustrated the conundrum faced by Coalition prime ministers: their position depended on party favour, yet their task was to mobilise majority opinion to ensure electoral success. To hew closely to party views—and especially to the vocal advocacy of ideological purists—rapidly extinguished public popularity. But to do what the public wanted was to court factional challenge and loss of leadership in a party-room vote.

Just as the main parties became sundered between professionals and members, and between the party base and the public, the mass media 'broadcast' model of public communication that had served parties well in the twentieth century broke down. The old model had conferred on prime ministers the ability to build relations with media proprietors and the press gallery, to use radio and television to speak directly to a broad audience, to lay out arguments, and to calculate the timing of releases. Twentieth-century leaders knew this game and structured their communication to achieve a match between their own skills and the options then available.

In the twenty-first century, however, the business models that sustained such practices were susceptible to changing perceptions of what would trigger audience 'choice', with 'infotainment' and celebrity undermining investigative journalism. Above all, they were eclipsed by the new technology of dissemination, the internet, which frayed the monopolies on which the model had depended. The anarchic, real-time, 'post-fact' logic of social media eroded the press gallery's quasi-monopoly on meaning-making about politics for the public. New social media platforms became significant in opinion formation. In effect, 'mass' media was eviscerated by a new form of narrowcasting. How were leaders to reach voters at large? How could genuine debate on alternatives be sustained? Above all, how could coalitions of interests be mustered when attention was paid only to preordained fragments of information?

While prime ministers were busy augmenting executive power within Canberra, the Australia they were governing altered substantially as a result of the demographic, sociocultural, technological, economic and geopolitical changes we have noted. Some of these contextual changes were the result of purposeful Australian government policy; many were not and were neither foreseeable nor controllable by political office-holders, who nevertheless have to live with their consequences. Yet with neither parties nor the media now serving as effective means for explaining and justifying policy responses and promoting opinion aggregation, the incumbency advantage in national debate so strongly enjoyed by prime ministers from Curtin on has dissipated. From Menzies through to Keating and Howard, prime ministers could dominate countrywide conversations through a combination of well-timed speeches, press gallery control, parliamentary prowess and selective radio and television appearances. Those days are gone, probably forever.

It has made governing far more complicated, not just in Australia but worldwide. Executive resources have increased, but in terms of public policy realities, traction may well have decreased considerably from Curtin to Turnbull. Yet, crucially, there has not been a corresponding decrease in public expectations of the government's capacity to protect, create and deliver the things the public demands. Politicians have continued trading in hope, practising the politics of promises while stretching the art of the possible. But in a globalising world, national governments are no longer the powerhouses they once were, not even in 'domestic' policy. They struggle to create jobs and seem virtually powerless to preserve them when technological imperatives and transnational corporate decision-making conspire to eliminate or move them. Still, in an almost tragic self-undermining fashion, they continue to claim that they do.

The sense of control slipping is not limited to the domain of prime-ministerial communication. In the early postwar decades, prime-ministerial leadership was underpinned by the institutional authority of the office. Incumbents benefited from the ever-expanding remit and resources of the federal government. Relatively high levels of public trust gave them the benefit of the doubt. They could take time to devise smart and politically palatable solutions to the problems of the day. Now, institutional authority has eroded, replaced by what has been called performative authority.[13]

It has two strands. First, prime ministers and governments are now expected to 'perform' in terms of *delivery*: they need to legitimise their existence by getting results, right now, day in, day out. Hence the preoccupation with translating campaign promises into 'announceables' and into 'KPIs' (key performance indicators) for the bureaucracy; and the concern to micromanage ministers and agencies to make sure the desired outcomes are being achieved.[14] Twenty-first-century citizens ask: 'What have they done for us lately?' And, electronic devices in hand, they do not hesitate to make their voices heard when they don't like what they see.

Second, prime ministers have also to become 'performers' in the sense of *public meaning-making*. They have to *feel* authoritative: looking and sounding competent, human and credible. And they have to do so in the midst of a Zeitgeist of rampant resentment against 'elites' who promised a 'fair go' as prosperity increased but created rising social inequality and growing uncertainty for 'Australian families'. The twenty-first-century 'netizen' asks: 'Who do I choose to listen to, who do I choose to believe and who am I prepared to forgive?' And, within the ideological echo chambers they have constructed via the web, they are quicker than ever to reach the conclusion that whoever happens to be in the Lodge falls short of the mark.

As the 'delivery' aspect of governing has proven ever more elusive, the emphasis in the prime-ministerial entourage has skewed towards message control and the spruiking of imagery in increasingly desperate attempts at managing the inevitable disappointments. All prime ministers since Howard have been caught in this self-negating bind. Rudd, Abbott and until now Turnbull have overpromised and underdelivered. Gillard's problem was different but no less damaging: she delivered legislation and reform but failed in the communicative performance required to get the public to understand the choices and the compromises involved in dragging these outcomes across the line.

Every prime minister since Howard has wrestled, largely unsuccessfully, with the conjunction of problems here presented. At the time of writing, Coalition prime minister Malcolm Turnbull perfectly represents the quandary this presents. He gained office because the Liberal party room feared that Tony Abbott's insistence on a strong leader's prerogatives, dependence on an insular warrior cast in the PMO, and deep unpopularity would lead them to oblivion. But what people at large saw in Turnbull was performative authority: a sense of both promise and of delivery on issues that concerned them. Turnbull recognised, as had Howard, that excessive tribalism was self-defeating and that Abbott had been overreliant on a narrow constituency (the party base that, as noted earlier, has diverged from majority opinion). He must appeal to a broader audience. He came to office promising to listen, to consult and to heed that audience. He would pursue innovation and ideas, and promote sensible, informed debate. His popularity soared.

As soon as Turnbull intimated initiatives that could be seen as more attuned to the broader audience on which his popularity depended, however, he was beset by radio shock-jocks, the twitterverse and, most significantly, those claiming to speak for the party base in the party room (Abbott's remaining supporters prominent among them). He countered and compromised, but it was never enough completely to satisfy internal critics. The promise of a positive agenda receded—he could not deliver. Both elements of performative authority were compromised and his popularity slumped. It was an impossible situation. He might be voted out in the party room because of an uprising from the party base (which was constantly implied). He might equally be voted out on the grounds that the improvement in the polls his advent had promised had collapsed. The Coalition won the 2016 election so narrowly, and with an unwieldy Senate in which fringe-party cross-bench senators would need to be managed, that it did nothing to reinforce his much-diminished authority. So the critics continued to circle and policy stasis threatened.

Has the prime minister's job, then, become impossible? Arguably, three things give cause for hope of a way out of the disenchantment that now seems so widely felt. First, policy cycles come and go. If the limitations of the big ideas of the 1980s and 1990s and their unintended consequences have become apparent to many people, provoking disillusion, we have been there before. The innovative Deakinite 'Australian settlement' was in large part a reaction to the Australian experience of the 1890s depression: it took the first commonwealth decade and more to achieve. The disasters of the 1930s were followed by years of frustration for then prime ministers James Scullin, Joseph Lyons and Menzies (mark 1) before the catalyst of war and postwar reconstruction fostered the Keynesian breakthrough, led by Curtin, Chifley and Menzies (mark 2). This met the problems of that time but, inevitably, circumstances changed again and the assumptions of the 1940s no longer served in the 1970s and 1980s. Though Treasury began to question those assumptions and to revisit classical economics as early as 1971, it was not until 1983 that Hawke, Keating and later Howard drove the reforms that have since been memorably described as 'the Australian moment'. That reform has produced problems of its own.[15] The lags and transitions as policy regimes wane and reinventions occur are never short-term—they may take ten or fifteen years. But history suggests that they are usually achieved. A new dawn will arrive.

Second, Australian institutional responses to changing circumstances have been robust, in part because of imaginative leadership. To remark only on the institutions supporting executive government, there is a good story to tell here about the professionalisation of the public service—its considered answer to the need for responsiveness to government, and its retention of ethical clarity as it has contended with trying circumstances. The development of an activist PMO was intended to assist in contested policy debate. It would always threaten to become too partisan, too intensely political, if not carefully managed. For the most part, from the mid-1970s to the mid-2000s, it was—largely because prime ministers ensured that not only loyal but also bureaucratically experienced chiefs of staff ran it. At its best, working together with the public service, it contributed to good policy. At its worst, it amplified bad leadership—but the inherent problems of accountability and transparency have long been recognised, and are clearly capable of resolution.[16] The prime-ministerial machine can be recalibrated.

Third, and finally, let us talk more specifically of leadership. At times of crisis or deep disillusion, there is typically a call for strong leadership—and Australians have registered just such a plaint in polls published at the time of writing. There has been no dearth of strong leaders (Menzies, Fraser, Howard) and aspirant strong leaders (Abbott), and we have acknowledged their achievements. But their limitations are also apparent: a conviction that they must take everything on themselves (Fraser); a tendency towards cognitive closure in the face of complex problems that require flexibility (Abbott); encouragement of inner circles that may encourage groupthink (Howard); and a possible leaning towards role-induced hubris (Menzies and Howard, for all their acquired self-control and political astuteness, overreaching in policy fiascos such as the Suez intervention, the Iraq War and WorkChoices).

There is now a considerable critique of 'the myth of the strong leader' along with equally rich research that demonstrates the value of ensemble approaches to multifaceted social problems.[17] Our study has shown that the complex challenges of social change have been best addressed by prime ministers who have fostered just such talented ensembles, capable of applying diverse skills to the task. The standout instances have been Alfred Deakin (with a rare capacity for attracting disciples and crafting alliances), Curtin and Chifley (united in cooperative endeavour by robust common sense allied with personal humility), and Hawke (who improbably matched overweening egotism with an inherent gift for orchestrating distributed leadership). In each case, they operated at the turning point of a political cycle: Deakin inaugurating 'the Australian settlement', Curtin and Chifley initiating 'Australia's boldest experiment',[18] and Hawke (with Keating) instigating the reform cycle that assured prosperity and resilience as globalisation disrupted Australian expectations. It perhaps seems a vain hope to trust in the wisdom or capacity of the right individuals simply to emerge again, but in the past, difficult circumstances have conspired to produce them. And the prime ministership has been a hardy and adaptable institution. It might yet prove so again.

Notes

Introduction

1 Paul Kelly, *Triumph and Demise: The Broken Promise of a Labor Generation*, Melbourne University Press, Melbourne, 2014, p. 335.

2 Peter Hennessy, *The Prime Minister: The Office and Its Holders Since 1945*, Penguin Books, London, 2000, p. 36.

3 The speaker was Sir William McMillan, a New South Wales delegate to the 1891 Federation Convention. See *National Australasian Convention 1891*, Sydney, 12 March 1891, pp. 272–3.

4 Since our first volume was published, further insight into Curtin's media management practices has been provided in Caryn Coatney, *John Curtin: How He Won over the Media*, Australian Scholarly Publishing, Melbourne, 2016.

5 This phrase is borrowed from Hennessy, *The Prime Minister*, p. 549.

Chapter 1 The Politics of Consolidation

1 'Australia: Out of the Dreaming', *Time Magazine*, vol. LXXV, no. 14, 4 April 1960.

2 Clyde Cameron, Labor MP (1949–80), quoted on the dust jacket of AW Martin, *Robert Menzies: A Life, Volume 2 1944–1978*, Melbourne University Press, Melbourne, 1999.

3 John Howard, *The Menzies Era: The Years that Shaped Modern Australia*, HarperCollins, Sydney, 2014.

4 AW Martin, *Robert Menzies: A Life, Volume 1 1894–1943*, Melbourne University Press, Melbourne, 1993, pp. 383, 386.

5 David Day, *Menzies and Churchill at War*, Angus & Robertson, Sydney, 1986, ch. 15; Martin, *Robert Menzies: A Life Volume 1*, ch. 17.

6 RG Menzies, *Afternoon Light: Some Memories of Men and Events*, Cassell Australia, Melbourne, 1967, ch. 12.
7 RG Menzies, 'The Forgotten People' (1942), in Graeme Starr (ed.), *The Liberal Party of Australia: A Documentary History*, Drummond/Heinemann, Melbourne, 1980, pp. 57–63.
8 Graeme Starr's assessment, ibid., p. 57.
9 Judith Brett, *Robert Menzies' Forgotten People*, Pan Macmillan, Sydney, 1992, pp. 31–73.
10 Ibid., pp. 41, 42.
11 See David Kemp, 'The Political Philosophy of Robert Menzies', in JR Nethercote (ed.), *Menzies: The Shaping of Modern Australia*, Connor Court Publishing, Brisbane, 2016, pp. 1–26.
12 Institute of Public Affairs, *Looking Forward: A Post War Policy for Australian Industry*, IPA, Melbourne, 1944.
13 LF Fitzharding, *The Little Digger 1914–1952: William Morris Hughes, a Political Biography, Vol. 2*, Angus & Robertson, Sydney,1979, p. 661.
14 Martin, *Robert Menzies: A Life, Volume 1,* p. 406.
15 This paragraph paraphrases Martin, ibid., pp. 406–7.
16 Ibid., p. 422.
17 Menzies, *Afternoon Light*, p. 284.
18 Ian Hancock, *National and Permanent? The Federal Organisation of the Liberal Party of Australia 1944–1965*, Melbourne University Press, Melbourne, 2000, p. 35.
19 Ian Hancock, 'The Liberal Party Organisation: 1944–1966', in Scott Prasser, JR Nethercote and John Warhurst (eds), *The Menzies Era: A Reappraisal of Government, Politics and Policy,* Hale & Iremonger, Sydney, 1995, p. 81.
20 Ibid., p. 81.
21 Ian McAllister and Rhonda Moore (eds), *Party Strategy and Change: Australian Electoral Speeches Since 1946*, Longman Cheshire, Melbourne, 1991, pp. 163–4.
22 Quoted in Martin, *Robert Menzies: A Life, Volume 2 1944–1978*, p. 57.
23 Ibid., pp. 58–61.
24 *Sydney Morning Herald*, 8 December 1949, quoted in Martin, *Robert Menzies: A Life, Volume 2*, p. 122.
25 Ian Ward, 'The Early Use of Radio for Political Communication in Australia and Canada: John Henry Austral, Mr Sage and the Man from Mars', *Australian Journal of Politics and History*, vol. 45, no. 3, 1999, pp. 311–29.
26 McAllister and Moore, *Party Strategy and Change*, pp. 169, 172; Martin, *Robert Menzies: A Life, Volume 2*, p. 116.
27 Martin, *Robert Menzies: A Life, Volume 2*, p. 126.
28 Graeme Starr, 'Menzies and Postwar Prosperity', in JR Nethercote (ed.), *Liberalism and the Australian Federation*, Federation Press, Sydney, 2001, pp. 177–95.
29 Michael Keating, 'The Evolution of Australian Macroeconomic Strategy Since World War 2', in Simon Ville and Glenn Withers (eds), *The Cambridge Economic History of Australia*, Cambridge University Press, Melbourne, 2015, pp. 439–45; Ian W McLean, *Why Australia Prospered: The Shifting Sources of Economic Growth,*

Princeton University Press, Princeton, 2013, pp. 176–209 (the sentence quoted is on p. 209).

30 This paragraph draws heavily on McLean, *Why Australia Prospered*, pp. 176–209.

31 RG Menzies, 'Address to the Liberal Party Federal Council', 6 April 1964, in Starr, *The Liberal Party of Australia*, p. 217.

32 Ibid.

33 Cf. Graeme Starr, 'Menzies and Postwar Prosperity', p. 179.

34 Judith Brett, *Australian Liberals and the Moral Middle Class: From Alfred Deakin to John Howard*, Cambridge University Press, Melbourne, 2003, pp. 120–5.

35 Graeme Davison and Barbara Davison, 'Suburban Pioneers', in Graeme Davison, Tony Dingle and Seamus O'Hanlon (eds), *The Cream Brick Frontier: Histories of Australian Suburbia*, Monash Publications in History, no. 19, Monash University, Melbourne, 1995, pp. 41–50; Brett, *Australian Liberals and the Moral Middle Class*, p. 125.

36 Gwen Gray, 'Social Policy', in Prasser, Nethercote and Warhust, *The Menzies Era*, p. 222.

37 RG Menzies, *Central Power in the Australian Commonwealth*, Cassell Australia, Melbourne, 1967.

38 Brett, *Australian Liberals and the Moral Middle Class*, p. 125; Hugh Stretton, *Ideas for Australian Cities*, Georgian House, Melbourne, 1971.

39 For a fine account, see Nicholas Brown, *Governing Prosperity: Social Change and Social Analysis in Australia in the 1950s*, Cambridge University Press, Melbourne, 1995.

40 The leading figures are well captured in Samuel Furphy (ed.), *The Seven Dwarfs and the Age of the Mandarins: Australian Government Administration in the Postwar Reconstruction Era*, ANU Press, Canberra, 2015.

41 This paraphrases political scientist AF Davies, quoted in James Walter, 'Bureaucracy and Democracy in the American Century: AF Davies on Administration and the "Knowledgeable Society"', *Australian Journal of Public Administration*, vol. 58, no. 1, 1999, p. 28.

42 Martin, *Robert Menzies: A Life, Volume 2*, p. 431.

43 Menzies, 'Address to the Liberal Party Federal Council', p. 217; Brown, *Governing Prosperity*, p. 106.

44 See Greg Whitwell, *The Treasury Line*, Allen & Unwin, Sydney, 1986.

45 See, for example, Heather Henderson (ed.), *Letters to My Daughter: Robert Menzies, Letters, 1955–1975*, Murdoch Books, Sydney, 2011, p. 5.

46 See David Lee, 'Sir Roland Wilson', in Furphy, *The Seven Dwarfs*, pp. 136–8.

47 Keating, 'The evolution of Australian Macroeconomic Strategy Since World War 2', p. 441.

48 McAllister and Moore, *Party Strategy and Change*, p. 172.

49 For instance, Ken Buckley, Barbara Dale and Wayne Reynolds, *Doc Evatt: Patriot, Internationalist, Fighter and Scholar*, Longman Cheshire, Melbourne, 1994, pp. 369–81; Humphrey McQueen, 'Menzies', in his *Gallipoli to Petrov: Arguing with Australian History*, Allen & Unwin, Sydney, 1984, pp. 167–75. Quotation from

RG Menzies, 'The Defence Call to the Nation', 2nd broadcast, 22 September 1950, cited in David Lowe, *Menzies and the 'Great World Struggle': Australia's Cold War 1948–1954*, UNSW Press, Sydney, 1999, p. 2. Lowe's fine study influences much of the discussion here.

50 Martin, *Robert Menzies: A Life, Volume 2*, ch. 7.

51 This paragraph draws primarily on Lowe, *Menzies and the 'Great World Struggle'*, pp. 135, 149–51; and LJ Louis, *Menzies' Cold War: A Reinterpretation*, Red Rag Publications, Melbourne, 2001, especially chs 1 and 3—Louis describes Menzies' economic model as 'the Keynesian warfare state'.

52 Ann Genovese, '*Australian Communist Party of Australia v The Commonwealth*: Histories of Australian Legalism', *Australian Historical Studies*, vol. 44, no. 1, 2013, p. 12.

53 McAllister and Moore, *Party Strategy and Change*, p. 173.

54 John Roskam, 'The Liberal Party's Response to the Split', in Brian Costar, Peter Love and Paul Strangio (eds), *The Great Labor Schism: A Retrospective*, Scribe, Melbourne, 2005, p. 262.

55 These points are stressed by Murray Goot and Sean Scalmer in 'Party Leaders, the Media and Political Persuasion: The Campaigns of Evatt and Menzies on the Referendum to Protect Australia from Communism', *Australian Historical Studies*, vol. 44, no. 1, 2013, pp. 71, 77.

56 Peter Crockett, *Evatt: A Life*, Oxford University Press, Melbourne, 1993, pp. 296–7.

57 Robert Manne, *The Petrov Affair: Politics and Espionage*, Pergamon Press, Sydney, 1987; RG Menzies, 'The Petrov Spy Case', in his *The Measure of the Years*, Cassell, London, 1970, pp. 154–97; Buckley, Dale and Reynolds, *Doc Evatt*, pp. 369–81; Crockett, *Evatt*, pp. 236–49.

58 Crockett, *Evatt*, pp. 297–300.

59 Makin is quoted in Christopher Waters, 'The Great Debates: HV Evatt and the Department of External Affairs, 1941–1949', in Joan Beaumont, Christopher Waters, David Lowe and Garry Woodard (eds), *Ministers, Mandarins and Diplomats: Australian Foreign Policy Making, 1941–1969*, Melbourne University Press, Melbourne, 2003, p. 47.

60 See Henderson (ed.), *Letters to My Daughter*, passim.

61 Ibid., pp. 12, 20, for example.

62 See Menzies, *The Measure of the Years*, p. 155 (footnote).

63 Ibid., p. 156.

64 *Commonwealth Parliamentary Debates* (*CPD*), vol. 217, 27 May 1952, pp. 808–9, 870–5.

65 Martin, *Robert Menzies: A Life, Volume 2*, p. 254.

66 National Archives of Australia (NAA), A6122/47, 1886-1888–Security–personnel security risks in the Commonwealth Public Service, NSW returns, vols 1–3; NAA, A11099, 1/6, 5 September 1952, p. 5.

67 Phillip Deery, 'Decoding the Cold War: Verona, Espionage and "the Communist Threat"', in Peter Love and Paul Strangio (eds), *Arguing the Cold War*, Red Rag Publications, Melbourne, 2001, pp. 107–115.

68 These comments are quoted by Menzies, *The Measure of the Years*, pp. 172–3.

69 Evatt's statement is reproduced in Robert Murray, *The Split: Australian Labor in the Fifties*, Cheshire, Melbourne, 1970, pp. 179–81. Press coverage was extensive; see, for example, 'Dr Evatt Accuses Labor Party Group of Disloyalty', *Canberra Times*, 6 October 1954.

70 Geoffrey Bolton, *The Middle Way: The Oxford History of Australia Volume 5, 1942–1988*, Oxford University Press, Melbourne, 1990, p. 142.

71 Crockett, *Evatt*, pp. 282–4; Peter Love, 'The Great Labor Split of 1955: An Overview', in Costar, Love and Strangio, *The Great Labor Schism*, pp. 12–16.

72 Love, 'The Great Labor Split of 1955', pp. 1–20.

73 *CPD*, vol. 8 (new series), 19 October 1955, pp. 1694–718.

74 *CPD*, vol. 8 (new series), 25 October 1955, pp. 1858–74; Manne, *The Petrov Affair*, pp. 258–64; Martin, *Robert Menzies: A Life, Volume 2*, pp. 310–11.

75 Menzies, *The Measure of the Years*, p. 191.

76 Martin, *Menzies: A Life, Volume 2*, p. 311.

77 Ibid., p. 313; 'Election to Clear the Air', *Canberra Times*, 26 October 1955.

78 Menzies, *The Measure of the Years*, pp. 196–7.

79 Ibid., p. 44.

80 Ibid., pp. 44–65.

81 Menzies, quoted in Garry Woodard, '"A Radical Tory": Sir Garfield Barwick', in Beaumont, Waters, Lowe and Woodard, *Ministers, Mandarins and Diplomats*, p. 110.

82 Amos J Peasley, quoted in Martin, *Robert Menzies: A Life, Volume 2*, p. 296.

83 *Sydney Morning Herald*, 24 June 1959.

84 WJ Hudson, *Blind Loyalty: Australia and the Suez Crisis, 1956*, Melbourne University Press, Melbourne, 1989.

85 RG Menzies, 'My Suez Story', in his *Afternoon Light*, pp. 149–85.

86 See, for instance, Graham Freudenberg's account of his 'road to Damascus' in his *A Figure of Speech: A Political Memoir*, John Wiley, Brisbane, 2005, pp. 13–21, and especially the letter to his parents about Suez, pp. 19–20.

87 Menzies, 'My Suez Story', passim.

88 Beale, quoted in Woodard, 'A Radical Tory', p. 111.

89 This paragraph draws on Martin, *Robert Menzies: A Life, Volume 2*, pp. 400–29 (Menzies' letters to his wife and to Harrison are quoted, pp. 428–9); Woodard's summary in 'A Radical Tory', pp. 110–11; and John Darwin, 'Britain's Withdrawal from East of Suez', in Carl Bridge (ed.), *Munich to Vietnam: Australia's Relations with Britain and the United States*, Melbourne University Press, Melbourne, 1991, pp. 140–58.

90 Menzies Papers, MS 4936, 13, National Library of Australia (NLA).

91 Menzies (to Dame Pattie Menzies), quoted in Martin, *Robert Menzies: A Life, Volume 2*, p. 422.

92 Ibid., pp. 336 and 569, for instance.

93 See Furphy (ed.), *The Seven Dwarfs and the Age of the Mandarins*.

94 Paul Hasluck, *Sir Robert Menzies: Daniel Mannix Memorial Lecture*, Melbourne University Press, Melbourne, 1980, p. 9.

95 John Bunting, *R.G. Menzies: A Portrait*, Allen & Unwin, Sydney, 1988, p. 104.

96 Menzies, *The Measure of the Years*, pp. 149–50.

97 HC Coombs, *Trial Balance: Issues of My Working Life*, Sun Books, Melbourne, 1983, p. 268; Sir Peter Lawler, interview with James Walter, 6 February 2012.

98 Tony Eggleton, interview with James Walter, 6 July 2012. Menzies' reference was almost certainly to Lawler, who had in fact, at Bunting's urging and in response to Menzies' good grace, resigned from the Labor Party years before Eggleton joined the PMO.

99 Sir William Heseltine, *'I Did but See Him Passing by': The Second Menzies Lecture*, The Sir Robert Menzies Centre for Australian Studies, London, 1989, p. 4.

100 Martin, *Robert Menzies: A Life, Volume 2*, p. 217.

101 Ibid.

102 Heseltine, *'I Did but See Him Passing by'*, p. 4.

103 Bunting, *R.G. Menzies*, pp. 96–127. The subtitle 'Menzies' Boys' is adapted from Sir John Bunting's affectionate account of Menzies' relations with senior public servants, 'The Boys'.

104 Ibid., pp. 96–7.

105 Ibid., p. 119.

106 See Paul Strangio, Paul 't Hart and James Walter, *Settling the Office: the Australian Prime Ministership from Federation to Reconstruction*, The Miegunyah Press, Melbourne, 2016, pp. 228–30.

107 Davies, quoted in Walter, 'Bureaucracy and Democracy in the American Century', p. 28.

108 Hasluck, *Sir Robert Menzies*, p. 12.

109 Bunting, *R.G. Menzies*, p. 107.

110 The prime minister's office was generally referred to as the private office until the 1970s, when it first became a significant institution. The designation 'prime minister's office' (and the acronym PMO) emerged then, but we use it throughout as a term journalists have made familiar to contemporary readers.

111 Heseltine, *'I Did but See Him Passing by'*, p. 2.

112 Bunting, *R.G. Menzies*, p. 102.

113 Eggleton, interview.

114 Henderson, *Letters to My Daughter*, passim.

115 On the credit squeeze and the 1961 election, see Martin, *Robert Menzies: A Life, Volume 2*, pp. 430–6; on the competition between the seven dwarfs, see Furphy, *The Seven Dwarfs*, passim; on Brown's aspiration and the conversations between Brown and Menzies that led to Menzies' 1955 memorandum altering the functions of PMD, see Patrick Weller, Joanne Scott and Bronwyn Stevens, *From Postbox to Powerhouse: A Centenary History of the Department of the Prime Minister and Cabinet 1911–2010*, Allen & Unwin, Sydney, 2011, pp. 50–4.

116 Weller, Scott and Stevens, *From Postbox to Powerhouse*, pp. 47–60.

117 RG Menzies, 'Developments in Higher Education', in his *The Measure of the Years*, pp. 81–97.

118 Martin, *Robert Menzies: A Life, Volume 2*, pp. 398–9.

119 Grant Harman, 'Development of Higher Education', in Prasser, Nethercote and Warhurst, *The Menzies Era*, pp. 239–57.
120 David Headon, 'Convert to the Faith: Menzies and Canberra', in Nethercote, *Menzies*, pp. 361–84.
121 See RG Menzies, 'Canberra: The Making of a City', in his *The Measure of the Years*, pp. 142–8; Martin, *Robert Menzies: A Life, Volume 2*, pp. 382–8.
122 Keating, 'The Evolution of Australian Macroeconomic Strategy Since World War 2', p. 440.
123 Menzies, *The Measure of the Years*, pp. 49–50, 62–4.
124 Ibid., pp. 60–5
125 Jenny Stewart, 'Trade and Industry Policies', in Prasser, Nethercote and Warhurst, *The Menzies Era*, pp. 185–201.
126 RG Menzies, 'Politics: "Fine Art and Inexact Science"', *New York Times*, 28 November 1948; 'A Retrospective Survey of the Art and Science of Politics', in his *The Measure of the Years*, pp. 3–12.
127 Menzies, 'Politics: "Fine Art and Inexact Science"', n.p.
128 Menzies, 'A Retrospective Survey of the Art and Science of Politics', excerpts pp. 7–9.
129 On 'Sundays at The Lodge', see Bunting, *R.G. Menzies*, pp. 121–5; on the other instances in this sentence, see Martin, *Robert Menzies: A Life, Volume 2*, passim.
130 Coombs, *Trial Balance*, p. 223.
131 Ibid.
132 Gavin Souter, *Acts of Parliament: A Narrative History of the Senate and House of Representatives, Commonwealth of Australia*, Melbourne University Press, Melbourne, 1988, p. 435.
133 Hasluck, *Sir Robert Menzies*, p. 9.
134 This paragraph draws on David Lee, 'Cabinet', in Prasser, Nethercote and Warhurst, *The Menzies Era*, pp. 123–36; and Patrick Weller, *Cabinet Government in Australia 1901–2006*, UNSW Press, Sydney, 2007, pp. 95–118.
135 Weller, *Cabinet Government in Australia 1901–2006*, pp. 6, 8–9.
136 Ibid., p. 15.
137 Brian Costar, 'The Politics of Coalition', in Prasser, Nethercote and Warhurst, *The Menzies Era*, pp. 93–110.
138 Weller, Scott and Stevens, *From Postbox to Powerhouse*, p. 47.
139 See, for example, the discussion of one such, Athol Townley, in Martin, *Robert Menzies: A Life, Volume 2*, pp. 270–1.
140 *Sydney Morning Herald*, 3 July 1952.
141 Quoted in Martin, *Robert Menzies: A Life, Volume 2*, p. 360.
142 Brett, *Robert Menzies' Forgotten People*, pp. 20–1.
143 Carrington again, quoted in Martin, *Robert Menzies: A Life, Volume 2*, p. 360.
144 For an early, exemplary instance, see Goot and Scalmer, 'Party Leaders, the Media and Political Persuasion', pp. 74–5.
145 *Age*, 13 November 1963.
146 Colin Hughes and John Western, *The Prime Minister's Policy Speech: A Case Study in Televised Politics*, ANU Press, Canberra, 1966, p. 30.

147 Martin, *Robert Menzies: A Life, Volume 2*, p. 2.
148 Stewart Cockburn, once Menzies' press secretary, gives detailed examples; see CJ Lloyd, *Parliament and the Press: The Federal Parliamentary Press Gallery, 1901–88*, Melbourne University Press, Melbourne, 1988, p. 175.
149 Menzies, 'My Suez Story', p. 159.
150 Lloyd, *Parliament and the Press*, pp. 128–9.
151 Ibid., pp. 174–211; Bridget Griffin-Foley, *Party Games: Australian Politicians and the Media from War to Dismissal*, Text Publishing, Melbourne, 2003, pp. 8–34, 85–116.
152 Lloyd, *Parliament and the Press*, p. 174.
153 Martin, *Robert Menzies: A Life, Volume 2*, p. 381.
154 Hasluck, *Sir Robert Menzies*, p. 12.
155 Judith Brett, 'Prime Ministers and Their Parties in Australia', in Paul Strangio, Paul 't Hart and James Walter (eds), *Understanding Prime Ministerial Performance: Comparative Perspectives*, Oxford University Press, Oxford, 2013, p. 184.

Chapter 2 The Burden of Succession

1 Brown to Menzies, 1 June 1965, quoted in Martin, *Robert Menzies: A Life, Volume 2*, p. 505.
2 Donald Horne, *The Lucky Country: Australia in the Sixties*, revised edition, Penguin Books, Melbourne, 1964, p. 239.
3 Ibid., p. 201.
4 JD Pringle, *Australian Accent*, Chatto and Windus, London, 1958, pp. 48–9.
5 Horne, *The Lucky Country*, both passages quoted, p. 205, but see pp. 201–13 for elaboration.
6 Heather Henderson (ed.), *Letters to My Daughter: Robert Menzies, Letters, 1955–1975*, Murdoch Books, Sydney, 2011, p. 206.
7 See David Kemp, 'The Political Philosophy of Robert Menzies', in JR Nethercote (ed.), *Menzies: The Shaping of Modern Australia*, Connor Court Publishing, Brisbane, 2016.
8 See, for instance, John Bunting, *R.G. Menzies: A Portrait*, Allen & Unwin, Sydney, 1988; Paul Hasluck, *Sir Robert Menzies: Daniel Mannix Memorial Lecture*, Melbourne University Press, Melbourne, 1980; John Howard, *The Menzies Era: The Years that Shaped Modern Australia*, HarperCollins, Sydney, 2014; AW Martin, *Robert Menzies: A Life, Volume 2 1944–1978*, Melbourne University Press, Melbourne, 1999, pp. 430–43; Patrick Weller, *Cabinet Government in Australia 1901–2006*, UNSW Press, Sydney, 2007, pp. 95–122.
9 Horne, *The Lucky Country*, pp. 212–13, emphasis in original.
10 See Carrington's foreword to Bunting, *RG Menzies*, pp. v–vi.
11 Ibid., p. vii.
12 Martin, *Robert Menzies: A Life, Volume 2*, p. 360.
13 Carrington, foreword to Bunting, *RG Menzies*, p. vii.
14 Henderson, *Letters to My Daughter*, p. 206.
15 WJ Hudson, *Casey*, Oxford University Press, Melbourne, 1986, pp. 213–17, 274–7, 284–8.
16 Martin, *Robert Menzies: A Life, Volume 2*, pp. 528–9.

17 David Lowe, *Australian between Empires: The Life of Percy Spender*, Pickering & Chatto, London, 2010, pp. 120–41.
18 David Marr, *Barwick*, Allen & Unwin, Sydney, 1980, pp. 132–209.
19 Quoted, ibid., p. 209.
20 Henderson, *Letters to My Daughter*, p. 206; Gavin Souter, *Acts of Parliament: A Narrative History of the Senate and House of Representatives, Commonwealth of Australia*, Melbourne University Press, Melbourne, 1988, p. 455.
21 Geoffrey Bolton, *Paul Hasluck: A Life*, UWA Publishing, Perth, 2014, passim.
22 Ibid., p. 421.
23 Horne, *The Lucky Country*, p. 202.
24 Henderson, *Letters to My Daughter*, pp. 88–9.
25 Cf. David Owen and Jonathan Davidson, 'Hubris Syndrome: An Acquired Personality Disorder? A Study of US Presidents and UK Prime Ministers over the last 100 years', *Brain*, vol. 132, 2009, pp. 1396–1406.
26 Bunting, *RG Menzies*, p. 112.
27 Weller, *Cabinet Government in Australia 1901–2006*, pp. 117–18.
28 Ibid., pp. 95–121.
29 Arthur Calwell, *Be Just and Fear Not*, Lloyd O'Neil, Melbourne, 1972, p. 206.
30 This and the next paragraph draw on Martin, *Robert Menzies: A Life, Volume 2*, ch. 16; Tom Frame, *The Life and Death of Harold Holt*, Allen & Unwin/National Archives of Australia, Sydney, 2005, pp. 106–14; Gavin Souter, *Company of Heralds*, Melbourne University Press, Melbourne, 1981, pp. 378–85; and Souter, *Acts of Parliament*, pp. 447–50.
31 Henderson, *Letters to My Daughter*, pp. 61–62.
32 CB Schedvin, *In Reserve: Central Banking in Australia, 1945–75*, Allen & Unwin, Sydney, 1992, p. 320.
33 *Australian Financial Review*, 21 January 1966.
34 Quoted in Frame, *The Life and Death of Harold Holt*, p. 110.
35 Ian McAllister and Rhonda Moore (eds), *Party Strategy and Change: Australian Electoral Speeches Since 1946*, Longman Cheshire, Melbourne, 1991, pp. 69–75, 188–91.
36 Quoted in Souter, *Acts of Parliament*, p. 449.
37 Quoted in Souter, *Company of Heralds*, p. 383.
38 AF Davies, 'Politics in the New Suburb', *Australian Journal of Politics and History*, vol. 8, no. 2, 1962, pp. 214–23.
39 Jennifer Clark, *Aborigines and Activism: Race, Aborigines and the Coming of the 1960s to Australia*, UWA Publishing, Perth, 2008, ch. 6.
40 Ralph V. Summy, 'Militancy and the Australian Peace Movement, 1960–67', *Politics*, vol. 5, no. 2, 1970, pp. 148–62.
41 Judith Brett, *Australian Liberals and the Moral Middle Class: From Alfred Deakin to John Howard*, Cambridge University Press, Melbourne, 2003, ch. 6.
42 See Davies, 'Politics in the New Suburb'.
43 James Walter, *What Were They Thinking? The Politics of Ideas in Australia*, UNSW Press, Sydney, 2010, ch. 8.
44 Weller, *Cabinet Government in Australia 1901–2006*, p. 118.

45 Thomas Ford (1580–1648), 'There Is a Lady Sweet and Kind'.

46 Peter Edwards, 'The Liberals as Managers of the Australian–American Alliance', *Australian Journal of Politics and History*, vol. 51, no. 3, 2005, p. 454.

47 Ibid., pp. 454–5.

48 Ibid., pp. 455–6.

49 John Elliott, quoted in Edwards, 'The Liberals as Managers of the Australian–American Alliance', p. 456.

50 This paragraph draws on James Walter and Carolyn Holbrook, 'Housing in a Federation: From Wicked Problem to Complexity Cascade?', *Australian Journal of Public Administration*, vol. 74, no. 4, 2015, p. 452.

51 Quoted in Martin, *Robert Menzies: A Life, Volume 2*, p. 478.

52 *Sydney Morning Herald*, 2 December 1963.

53 Martin, *Robert Menzies: A Life, Volume 2*, pp. 515–42.

54 Menzies' rueful comment after Harold Holt's death, reported by Malcolm Fraser in *Malcolm Fraser: The Political Memoirs* (with Margaret Simons), The Miegunyah Press, Melbourne, 2010, p. 138.

55 Kevin Perkins, *Menzies: Last of the Queen's Men*, Rigby, Adelaide, 1958, p. 185.

56 Sources for this and the previous paragraph, IR Hancock, 'Holt, Harold Edward (1908–1967)', *Australian Dictionary of Biography, Vol 14 1940–1980*, Melbourne University Press, Melbourne, 1996, pp. 474–80; Frame, *The Life and Death of Harold Holt*, passim.

57 Hancock, 'Holt, Harold Edward', p. 477.

58 John Hawkins, 'Harold Holt: An Urbane Treasurer', *Economic Roundup*, no. 1, 2012, pp. 59–71.

59 Frame, *The Life and Death of Harold Holt*, p. 137.

60 Quoted in Edgar Holt, *Politics Is People: The Men of the Menzies Era*, Angus & Robertson, Sydney, 1969, p. 137.

61 Bolton, *Paul Hasluck*, p. 393.

62 Frame, *The Life and Death of Harold Holt*, pp. 150–1.

63 Tony Griffiths, *Contemporary Australia*, Croom Helm, London, 1977, p. 98.

64 Frame, *The Life and Death of Harold Holt*, p. 151.

65 Clem Lloyd, 'Prime Ministers and the Media', in Patrick Weller (ed.), *Menzies to Keating: The Development of the Australian Prime Ministership*, Melbourne University Press, Melbourne, 1992, p. 119.

66 CJ Lloyd, *Parliament and the Press: The Federal Parliamentary Press Gallery, 1901–88*, Melbourne University Press, Melbourne, 1988, pp. 244–5.

67 Frame, *The Life and Death of Harold Holt*, p. 148.

68 Quoted, ibid., p. 161.

69 Paul Rodan, 'Harold Holt's Foreign Policy', *Australian Journal of Politics and History*, vol. 25, no. 3, 1979, pp. 310–12.

70 WR Crocker, *Australian Ambassador*, Melbourne University Press, Melbourne, 1971, p. 204; see also Rodan, 'Harold Holt's Foreign Policy', p. 316.

71 Paul Ham, 'Allies in Name Alone', *Griffith Review*, no. 48, 2015, https://griffithreview.com/articles/allies-name-alone/ (accessed 7 October 2016).

72 Zara Holt, *My Life and Harry: An Autobiography*, The Herald, Melbourne, 1968, p. 150.
73 The relevant section of Holt's speech is reproduced in Sally Warhaft (ed.), *Well May We Say … The Speeches that Made Australia*, Black Inc., Melbourne, 2004, pp. 123–4.
74 Frame, *The Life and Death of Harold Holt*, p. 183.
75 G Barclay and J Siracusa (eds), *Australian–American Relations since 1945*, Holt, Rinehart and Winston, Sydney, 1976, p. 82.
76 Frame, *The Life and Death of Harold Holt*, pp. 166–70, 188–9.
77 Don Chipp and John Larkin, *The Third Man*, Rigby, Melbourne, 1968, p. 58.
78 Patrick Weller, Joanne Scott and Bronwyn Stevens, *From Postbox to Powerhouse: A Centenary History of the Department of the Prime Minister and Cabinet 1911–2010*, Allen & Unwin, Sydney, 2011, pp. 60–3.
79 Frame, *The Life and Death of Harold Holt*, pp. 226–34; Hancock, 'Holt, Harold Edward', p. 478; Ian Hancock, *The VIP Affair, 1966–67: The Causes, Course and Consequences of a Ministerial and Public Service Cover-up*, Australian Study of Parliament Group, Canberra, 2004, pp. 19–25; Weller, Scott and Stevens, *From Postbox to Powerhouse*, p. 63.
80 Gerard Henderson, quoted in Frame, *The Life and Death of Harold Holt*, p. 199.
81 Frame, *The Life and Death of Harold Holt*, passim; Ian Hancock, 'Liberal Governments, 1966–1972', in JR Nethercote (ed.), *Liberalism and the Australian Federation*, Federation Press, Sydney, 2001, pp. 200–1; Rodan, 'Harold Holt's Foreign Policy', pp. 313–17; TB Millar, 'Vietnam', in Carl Bridge (ed.), *Munich to Vietnam: Australia's Relations with Britain and the United States since the 1930s*, Melbourne University Press, Melbourne, 1991, pp. 174–93.
82 Frame, *The Life and Death of Harold Holt*, pp. 235–41.
83 Quoted, ibid., p. 241.
84 Quoted, ibid., p. 224.
85 Alan Reid, *The Power Struggle*, Shakespeare Head Press, Sydney, 1969, pp. 7–18.
86 Ibid., pp. 19–28; Ian Hancock, *John Gorton: He Did It His Way*, Hodder, Sydney, 2002, pp. 137–40; Hudson, *Casey*, pp. 309–11.
87 Hancock, *John Gorton*, pp. 141–59; Bolton, *Paul Hasluck*, pp. 406–11; Barry Jones, *A Thinking Reed*, Allen & Unwin, Sydney, 2006, pp. 185–90.
88 Sir Leslie Martin, chair of the AUC, delivered a report in 1964 that in due course led to the establishment of colleges of advanced education from 1967. Gorton was active throughout the planning and implementation.
89 This and the previous paragraph rely on Hancock, *John Gorton*, passim.
90 John Gorton, interviewed on ABC TV's *Monday Conference*, 22 January 1968; quoted in Hancock, *John Gorton*, p. 154, emphasis added.
91 Cf. Weller, *Cabinet Government in Australia 1901–2006*, p. 118.
92 Malcolm Fraser, interview with James Walter, 12 December 2012.
93 Jones, *A Thinking Reed*, pp. 191–2; Ian Ward, '"Culture up to Our Arseholes": Projecting Post-Imperial Australia', *Australian Journal of Politics and History*, vol. 51, no. 1, 2005, pp. 53–66.

94 Robert Menzies, *Central Power in the Australian Commonwealth: An Examination of the Growth of Commonwealth Power in the Australian Federation*, Cassell Australia, Melbourne, 1967.
95 Weller, Scott and Stevens, *From Postbox to Powerhouse*, p. 68.
96 Hancock, *John Gorton*, p. 399; see also Weller et al., *From Postbox to Powerhouse*, pp. 65–9.
97 Hancock, *John Gorton*, pp. 162–4, 362.
98 Ibid., pp. 399–400.
99 Weller, Scott and Stevens, *From Postbox to Powerhouse*, p. 69.
100 Weller, *Cabinet Government in Australia 1901–2006*, pp. 119–20.
101 This and the preceding paragraph draw on Fraser, interview; Hancock, *John Gorton*, pp. 168–72; Colin Hughes, *Mr Prime Minister: Australian Prime Ministers 1901–1972*, Oxford University Press, Melbourne, 1976, p. 184; Reid, *The Gorton Experiment*, pp. 194–9; Weller, *Cabinet Government in Australia 1901–2006*, pp. 119–20.
102 Ward, '"Culture up to Our Arseholes"', pp. 56, 57.
103 Ibid., pp. 57, 58.
104 Hancock, *John Gorton*, pp. 181–5.
105 Ibid., pp. 186–9.
106 Ibid., pp. 272–81; Hughes, *Mr Prime Minister*, p. 187–8; Weller, *Cabinet Government in Australia 1901–2006*, p. 120.
107 Peter Edwards, *A Nation at War: Australian Politics, Society and Diplomacy during the Vietnam War 1965–1975*, Allen & Unwin, Sydney, 1997, pp. 192–3.
108 David Lowe, *Menzies and the 'Great World Struggle': Australia's Cold War 1948–1954*, UNSW Press, Sydney, 1999, pp. 140–3; Wayne Reynolds, *Australia's Bid for the Atomic Bomb*, Melbourne University Press, Melbourne, 2000.
109 Lachlan Clohesy and Phillip Deery, 'The Prime Minister and the Bomb: John Gorton, W.C. Wentworth and the Quest for an Atomic Australia', *Australian Journal of Politics and History*, vol. 61, no. 2, 2015, pp. 217–32; Christopher Hubbard, 'From Ambivalence to Influence: Australia and the Negotiation of the 1968 Nuclear Non-Proliferation Treaty', *Australian Journal of Politics and History*, vol. 50, no. 4, 2004, pp. 526–43; Fraser, *Malcolm Fraser*, pp. 195–6.
110 Edwards, 'The Liberals as Managers of the Australian–American Alliance', p. 456.
111 Fraser, *Malcolm Fraser* , p. 185.
112 Susan Read, 'How Electors Confound the Pundits: The Vietnam War, 1969', *Politics*, vol. 10, no. 2, 1975, p. 201.
113 Ibid., pp. 204–5.
114 Hancock, 'Liberal Governments, 1966–72', p. 197; Hughes, *Mr Prime Minister*, p. 187.
115 Reid, *The Gorton Experiment*, pp. 368–72.
116 Bridget Griffen-Foley, 'Sir Frank Packer and the Leadership of the Liberal Party, 1967–71', *Australian Journal of Political Science*, vol. 36, no. 3, 2001, pp. 499–513.
117 Bolton, *Paul Hasluck*, p. 438; Fraser, *Malcolm Fraser*, pp. 195–6, 205–7; Hancock, *John Gorton*, pp. 292–4.

118 Fraser, *Malcolm Fraser*, pp. 208–23; Hancock, *John Gorton,* pp. 314–28; Reid, *The Gorton Experiment*, pp. 416–44.
119 *Commonwealth Parliamentary Debates* (*CPD*), House of Representatives (H of R), vol. 71, 9 March 1971, pp. 679–84.
120 Julian Leeser, 'McMahon, Sir William (Billy) (1908–1988)', *Australian Dictionary of Biography*, http://adb.anu.edu.au/biography/mcmahon-sir-william-billy-15043/text26240 (accessed 13 June 2016).
121 John Hawkins, 'William McMahon: The First Treasurer with an Economics Degree', *Economic Round-up*, no. 2, 2012, http://www.treasury.gov.au/PublicationsAndMedia/Publications/2012/Economic-Roundup-Issue-2/Report/William-McMahon (accessed 13 June 2016).
122 Paul Strangio, 'Evaluating Prime Ministerial Performance: The Australian Experience', in Paul Strangio, Paul 't Hart and James Walter (eds), *Understanding Prime Ministerial Performance: Comparative Perspectives*, Oxford University Press, Oxford, 2013, pp. 272, 274, 284.
123 Frank Stillwell, *Political Economy: The Contest of Economic Ideas*, Oxford University Press, Melbourne, 2002, pp. 148–52; Greg Whitwell, *The Treasury Line*, Allen & Unwin, Sydney, 1986, pp. 178–81.
124 Whitwell, *The Treasury Line*, pp. 176–204.
125 Weller, Scott and Stevens, *From Postbox to Powerhouse*, p. 70.
126 See Hawkins, 'William McMahon'; Weller, Scott and Stevens, *From Postbox to Powerhouse*, p. 70.
127 Griffen-Foley, 'Sir Frank Packer and the Leadership of the Liberal Party, 1967–71', pp. 502–3.
128 Quotations from Menzies and Bury are cited in Hawkins, 'William McMahon', notes 23 and 24; the long list of those willing to criticise also appears there. The source for the comment about Wilson is at note 54.
129 Paul Hasluck, *The Chance of Politics*, Text Publishing, Melbourne, 1997, p. 185.
130 See Hancock, *John Gorton,* p. 154.
131 John Gorton, 'I Did It My Way', *The Australian*, 8 August 1971.
132 Souter, *Acts of Parliament*, p. 496.
133 Quoted in Laurie Oakes and David Solomon, *The Making of an Australian Prime Minister*, Cheshire, Melbourne, 1973, p. 269.
134 Hughes, *Mr Prime Minister*, p. 196.
135 Souter, *Acts of Parliament*, pp. 497–8.
136 Cited in Oakes and Solomon, *The Making of an Australian Prime Minister*, p. 64.
137 Edwards, *A Nation at War*, pp. 302–5; Hancock, 'Liberal Governments, 1966–72', pp. 211–12; Hughes, *Mr Prime Minister*, pp. 195–8; Leeser, 'McMahon, Sir William'; Souter, *Acts of Parliament*, pp. 498–505; Whitwell, *The Treasury Line*, pp. 187–204.
138 Souter, *Acts of Parliament*, p. 501.
139 Hancock, 'Liberal Governments, 1966–72', p. 211.
140 Donald Horne, *Time of Hope: Australia 1966–1972*, Angus & Robertson, Sydney, 1980.
141 Quoted in Souter, *Acts of Parliament*, p. 498.

Chapter 3 Harnessed by History

1 Sally Warhaft (ed.), *Well May We Say … The Speeches that Made Australia*, Black Inc., Melbourne, 2004, p. 399.

2 See https://www.youtube.com/watch?v=RjqtuUXnm2g&index=5&list=PLhunE3Hi143lm95cJ0Jb2gtq9QeZjgMAP (accessed 24 June 2016).

3 Quoted in Tony Wright, 'The Line's Broken: Malcolm Fraser Mourns his Friend Gough Whitlam', *Sydney Morning Herald*, 21 October, 2014, http://www.smh.com.au/federal-politics/political-news/the-lines-broken-malcolm-fraser-mourns-his-friend-gough-whitlam-20141021-119a5d.html (accessed 24 June 2016).

4 Ibid.

5 See, for instance, Malcolm Fraser's own listing of such continuities in his '2012 Gough Whitlam Oration', *The Conversation*, 6 June 2012, https://theconversation.com/malcolm-fraser-2012-gough-whitlam-oration-7524 (accessed 15 September 2016).

6 See Jenny Hocking, *Gough Whitlam: A Moment in History*, The Miegunyah Press, Melbourne, 2008, pp. 15–57; see also James Walter, *The Leader: A Political Biography of Gough Whitlam*, University of Queensland Press, Brisbane, 1980, pp. 199–229.

7 Quoted in Hocking, *Gough Whitlam: A Moment in History*, p. 32.

8 Fred Daly, interview with James Walter, 25 July 1977.

9 Ibid.

10 *Australian Financial Review*, 30 May 1972.

11 See Hocking, *Gough Whitlam: A Moment in History*, pp. 149–53.

12 Quoted in Graham Freudenberg, 'The Program', in Fabian Papers, *The Whitlam Phenomenon*, McPhee Gribble/Penguin, Melbourne, 1986, p. 134.

13 EG Whitlam, 'The Relevance of the Whitlam Government Today', in Jenny Hocking and Colleen Lewis (eds), *It's Time Again: Whitlam and Modern Labor*, Circa, Melbourne, 1973, pp. 21–2.

14 *Australian Financial Review*, 30 May 1972.

15 Walter, *The Leader*, p. 24.

16 Jim Cairns, interview with James Walter, quoted in *The Leader*, p. 24.

17 *Australian Financial Review*, 30 May 1972.

18 Hocking, *Gough Whitlam*: A Moment in History, pp. 192–4; Walter, *The Leader*, p. 24.

19 John Menadue, quoted in Hocking, *Gough Whitlam: A Moment in History*, p. 234.

20 Laurie Oakes and David Solomon, *The Making of an Australian Prime Minister*, Cheshire, Melbourne, 1973, p. 13.

21 Graham Freudenberg, *A Certain Grandeur: Gough Whitlam in Politics*, Penguin Books, Melbourne, 1987, pp. 85–106, 129–37, 151–78; Hocking, *Gough Whitlam: A Moment in History*, pp. 234–71; John Menadue, *Things You Learn along the Way*, David Lovell Publishing, Melbourne, 1999, pp. 39–74.

22 Freudenberg, *A Certain Grandeur*, p. 100.

23 Gough Whitlam, 'Gough Whitlam's Caucus', in John Faulkner and Stuart Macintyre (eds), *True Believers: The Story of the Federal Parliamentary Labor Party*, Allen & Unwin, Sydney, 2001, pp. 108–9.

24 Paul Strangio, 'Whitlam vs. Cairns: Colliding Visions of Labor', in Hocking and Lewis, *It's Time Again*, pp. 354–5; and see Freudenberg, *A Certain Grandeur*, pp. 129–37.

25 Hocking, *Gough Whitlam: A Moment in History*, pp. 293–4; Walter, *The Leader*, p. 30.

26 Peter Wilenski, interview with James Walter, 20 July 1977.

27 Menadue, *Things You Learn along the Way*, pp. 63–6; Alan Hutchings, interview with Patrick Troy, Don Dunstan Foundation Oral History Project, pp. 2–4, http://dspace2.flinders.edu.au/xmlui/bitstream/handle/2328/15063/Troy_Pat_Cleared.pdf?sequence=4 (accessed 1 July 2016); Patrick Troy, interview with James Walter, 22 March 2016; James Walter, *The Ministers' Minders: Personal Advisers in National Government*, Oxford University Press, Melbourne, 1986, pp. 69–74.

28 Gough Whitlam, interview with David Frost, August 1972, in *Whitlam and Frost*, Sundial Books, London, 1974, p. 44.

29 *Australian Financial Review*, 30 May 1972.

30 Billy Griffiths, *The China Breakthrough: Whitlam in the Middle Kingdom, 1971*, Monash University Publishing, Melbourne, 2012.

31 Walter, *The Ministers' Minders*, pp. 50–8.

32 See Jenny Hocking, *Gough Whitlam: His Time,* The Miegunyah Press, Melbourne, 2012, pp. 34–7.

33 EG Whitlam, 'Foreword', in Irwin Young, *Theodore: His Life and Times*, Alpha Books, Sydney, 1971, p. ix.

34 Ibid., p. viii.

35 Murray Goot, '"It's Time": Spectrum's Market Research, Modern Campaigning, and Whitlam's Mandate', in Jenny Hocking (ed.), *Making Modern Australia: The Whitlam Government's 21st Century Agenda*, Monash University Publishing, Melbourne [in press].

36 Ibid.; see also Mick Young, 'The Build-up to 1972', in Fabian Papers, *The Whitlam Phenomenon,* p. 105.

37 All details here from Goot, '"It's Time"'.

38 Murray Goot and RW Connell, 'Presidential Politics in Australia?', *Australian Quarterly*, vol. 44, no. 2, 1972, p. 33.

39 Sally Young, *The Persuaders: Inside the Hidden Machine of Political Advertising*, Pluto Press, Melbourne, 2004, pp. 8–28.

40 Stephen Mills, *The Professionals: Strategy, Money and the Rise of the Political Campaigner in Australia*, Black Inc., Melbourne, 2014, pp. 72, 74–86.

41 Stephen Mills, *The New Machine Men: Polls and Persuasion in Australian Politics*, Penguin, Melbourne, 1986, p. 97.

42 Vicky Braund, 'Timely Vibrations: Labor's Marketing Campaign', in Henry Mayer (ed.), *Labor to Power: Australia's 1972 Election*, Angus & Robertson/APSA, Sydney, 1973, p. 28.

43 Young, 'The Build-up to 1972', pp. 107–8.

44 Gough Whitlam, *The Whitlam Government 1972–1975*, Penguin, Melbourne, 1985, p. 26. See also Hocking, *Gough Whitlam: His Time*, pp. 60–2.

45 Whitlam, *The Whitlam Government 1972–1975*, p. 1; and see ch. 1, 'A Mandate for Change', pp. 1–24 for elaboration.
46 Clyde Cameron, *The Cameron Diaries, 1976–1977*, Allen & Unwin, Sydney, 1990, p. 155.
47 Goot, '"It's Time"'.
48 It is significant that his memoir is boldly titled *The Whitlam Government.*
49 Whitlam, 'The Relevance of the Whitlam Government Today', p. 11.
50 Whitlam, *The Whitlam Government 1972–1975*, pp. 15–22.
51 Ibid., pp. 19–22; see also Freudenberg, *A Certain Grandeur*, pp. 239–42; Hocking, *Gough Whitlam: His Time*, pp. 16–27; Troy Bramston, 'The Whitlam Government through the Cabinet Papers', in Troy Bramston (ed.), *The Whitlam Legacy*, Federation Press, Sydney, 2013, pp. 97–9.
52 Graham Freudenberg, *A Figure of Speech: A Political Memoir*, John Wiley, Brisbane, 2005, p. 137.
53 Ibid.
54 Whitlam, *The Whitlam Government 1972–1975*, pp. 25–182.
55 Gordon Bilney, 'Foreign and Defence Policy', in Bramston, *The Whitlam Legacy*, p. 271.
56 Peter Wilenski, 'Ministers, Public Servants and Public Policy', *Australian Quarterly*, vol. 51, no. 2, 1979, pp. 37–8.
57 RFI Smith, 'Ministerial Advisers: The Experience of the Whitlam Government', *Australian Journal of Public Administration*, vol. 36, no. 2, 1977, pp. 157–8. He is quoting a study commissioned by the Royal Commission on Australian Government Administration, which reported in 1976.
58 John Edwards, quoted in Walter, *The Ministers' Minders*, p. 54.
59 Robert Haupt, 'Treasury Opts Out', *Australian Financial Review*, 27 August 1974.
60 Correspondence with the author, quoted in Walter, *The Ministers' Minders*, p. 57.
61 For details, see *Parliamentary Handbook of the Commonwealth of Australia, Twentieth Edition: 1978*, AGPS, Canberra, 1978, p. 318 [note]; see also JR Nethercote, 'The Public Service', in Bramston, *The Whitlam Legacy,* pp. 129–45.
62 Freudenberg, *A Certain Grandeur*, p. 256; Patrick Weller, Joanne Scott and Bronwyn Stevens, *From Postbox to Powerhouse: A Centenary History of the Department of the Prime Minister and Cabinet 1911–2010*, Allen & Unwin, Sydney, 2011, pp. 72–8; Wilenski, interview.
63 Freudenberg, *A Certain Grandeur*, p. 256.
64 Bill Hayden, *Hayden: An Autobiography*, Angus & Robertson, Sydney, 1996, p. 166.
65 Weller, Scott and Stevens, *From Postbox to Powerhouse,* pp. 75–7.
66 Menadue, *Things You Learn along the Way*, pp. 118–38.
67 Weller, Scott and Stevens, *From Postbox to Powerhouse*, pp. 80–1,
68 Ibid., pp. 79–2.
69 Bernard Schaffer and Geoffrey Hawker, 'The Rise and Fall of RCAG', in RFI Smith and P Weller (eds), *Public Service Inquiries in Australia*, University of Queensland Press, Brisbane, 1978, p. 35.
70 Whitlam, *The Whitlam Government 1972–1975*, p. 382.

71 Hayden, *Hayden*, p. 178; see also Hocking, *Gough Whitlam: His Time*, pp. 164–9; Greg Whitwell, *The Treasury Line*, Allen & Unwin, Sydney, 1986, pp. 214–15.
72 Menadue, *Things You Learn along the Way*, p. 123.
73 Allan Barnes, 'Whitlam's First Twelve Months', *Age*, 1 December 1973.
74 Patrick Weller, 'Caucus Control of Cabinet: Myth or Reality?', *Public Administration* (Sydney), vol. 33, no. 4, 1974, p. 306.
75 See Hocking, *Whitlam: His Time*, pp. 163–8; Walter, *The Leader*, pp. 45–8.
76 Patrick Weller, *Cabinet Government in Australia 1901–2006*, UNSW Press, Sydney, 2007, pp. 124–30.
77 Ibid., pp. 131–2.
78 Hayden, *Hayden*, p. 216.
79 Quoted in Walter, *The Leader*, p. 53.
80 Reported in *Canberra Times*, 14 July 1975.
81 Weller, *Cabinet Government*, p. 133.
82 Hocking, *Whitlam: His Time*, pp. 196–236; Menadue, *Things You Learn along the Way*, pp. 139–48.
83 Paul Strangio, *Keeper of the Faith: A Biography of Jim Cairns*, Melbourne University Press, Melbourne, 2002, pp. 325–8.
84 Quotation from Walter, *The Leader*, p. 51.
85 Whitlam, quoted in Strangio, 'Whitlam vs Cairns', p. 348.
86 John Howard, *The Menzies Era: The Years that Shaped Modern Australia*, HarperCollins, Sydney, 2014, pp. 576–606.
87 Michael Keating, 'The Evolution of Australian Macroeconomic Strategy Since World War 2', in Simon Ville and Glenn Withers (eds), *The Cambridge Economic History of Australia*, Cambridge University Press, Melbourne, 2015, pp. 445–46; Ian W McLean, *Why Australia Prospered: The Shifting Sources of Economic Growth*, Princeton University Press, Princeton, 2013, pp. 212–15; John O'Mahony, 'Economic Policy', in Bramston, *The Whitlam Legacy*, pp. 166–74.
88 O'Mahony, 'Economic Policy', p. 175.
89 Ibid., pp. 169–76; Whitwell, *The Treasury Line*, pp. 207–17.
90 O'Mahony, 'Economic Policy', p. 174.
91 Troy Bramston and Paul Kelly, 'The Untold Story of the Dismissal', in Bramston, *The Whitlam Legacy*, pp. 311–32; Jenny Hocking, *The Dismissal Dossier: Everything You Were Never Meant to Know about November 1975* (updated edn), Melbourne University Press, Melbourne, 2016.
92 Alan Reid, *The Whitlam Venture*, Hill of Content, Melbourne, 1976, p. 408.
93 Hayden, *Hayden*, p. 278.
94 The great exposition of this psychological and political disposition is Thomas Hobbes, *Leviathan* (1651).
95 John Edwards, *Life Wasn't Meant to Be Easy: A Political Profile of Malcolm Fraser*, Mayhem, Sydney, 1977, pp. 75–6; Fraser, *Malcolm Fraser: The Political Memoirs* (with Margaret Simons), The Miegunyah Press, Melbourne, 2010, pp. 236–237; Little, *Strong Leadership*, pp. 182–183.
96 See Fraser, *Malcolm Fraser*, pp. 255, 272–3, 294–5, 299–300, 314.

97 Edwards, *Life Wasn't Meant to Be Easy*, p. 97; Hayden, *Hayden*, p. 236.
98 See his account of these events in Fraser, *Malcolm Fraser*.
99 Russell Paltridge, quoted in Paul Kelly, 'John Malcolm Fraser', in Michelle Grattan (ed.), *Australian Prime Ministers*, New Holland, Sydney, 2000, p. 363.
100 See Paul 't Hart, 'Symbols, Rituals and Power: The Lost Dimensions of Crisis Management', *Journal of Contingencies and Crisis Management*, vol. 1, no. 1, 1993, pp. 36–50; Arjen Boin and Paul 't Hart, 'Public Leadership in Times of Crisis: Mission Impossible?', *Public Administration Review*, vol. 63, no. 5, 2003, pp. 544–53.
101 Fraser, *Malcolm Fraser*, p. 95.
102 Philip Ayres, *Malcolm Fraser: A Biography*, William Heinemann Australia, Melbourne, 1987, pp. 1–12; Edwards, *Life Wasn't Meant to Be Easy*, pp. 13–18; Fraser, *Malcolm Fraser*, pp. 15–40.
103 Fraser, *Malcolm Fraser*, p. 33.
104 Ibid., ch. 3.
105 See ibid., chs 14 and 15, and on international free trade, pp. 467–9.
106 See, for example, Fraser, '2012 Gough Whitlam Oration'.
107 For example, Robert Manne, 'Fraser's Great Conservative Achievement: Cementing Whitlam's Progress on Race', *The Guardian*, 20 March 2015, https://www.theguardian.com/commentisfree/2015/mar/20/frasers-great-conservative-achievement-cementing-whitlams-progress-on-race (accessed 15 September 2016).
108 See Andrew Campbell, 'Malcolm Fraser: Political Decadent', *National Observer*, no. 52, 2002, p. 62.
109 Fraser, interview.
110 Ibid.
111 Fraser, *Malcolm Fraser*, ch. 11; Patrick Weller, *Malcolm Fraser PM: A Study in Prime Ministerial Power in Australia*, Penguin Books, Melbourne, 1989, pp. 214–73.
112 Fraser, *Malcolm Fraser*, pp. 364–6; see also Ayres, *Malcolm Fraser*, pp. 214–15, 358–60, 413–18.
113 Weller, *Malcolm Fraser PM*, p. 271.
114 Fraser, *Malcolm Fraser*, p. 355.
115 Ibid., p. 369.
116 Ibid., p. 372.
117 Paul Kelly, *The Hawke Ascendancy*, Angus & Robertson, Sydney, 1984, p. 407
118 Fraser, *Malcolm Fraser*, p. 606.
119 Howard, *The Menzies Era*, p. 599.
120 See Paul Kelly, *The End of Certainty: Power, Politics and Business in Australia*, Allen & Unwin, Sydney, 1994, ch. 2.
121 Jim Carlton, interview with James Walter, 7 December 2005.
122 Howard, quoted in Gerard Henderson, *Menzies' Child: The Liberal Party of Australia 1944–1994*, Allen & Unwin, Sydney, 1994, p. 260; the following phrases paraphrase Henderson.
123 For example, Richard Allsop, 'The Fading Legacy of Malcolm Fraser', *IPA Review*, June 2010, pp. 11–14; Campbell, 'Malcolm Fraser', pp. 50–63; Charles Richardson,

'The Fraser Years', in JR Nethercote (ed.), *Liberalism and the Australian Federation*, Federation Press, Sydney, 2001, pp. 214–29.

124 Kelly, 'John Malcolm Fraser': the quoted line is at p. 378; on Fraser and prime ministerial government, see p. 363.

125 Jan Pakulski and András Körösényi, *Toward Leader Democracy*, Anthem Press, London, 2012, ch. 3.

126 Richard Crossman, *Inside View: Three Lectures on Prime Ministerial Government*, Cape, London, 1972.

127 See James Walter and Paul Strangio, *No, Prime Minister: Reclaiming Politics from Leaders*, UNSW Press, Sydney, 2007.

128 Both quotes from Weller, *Cabinet Government in Australia 1901–2006*, p. 156; this passage and the preceding paragraph draw on that book, pp. 135–58; and on Weller, *Malcolm Fraser PM*, pp. 395–409.

129 For details, see Kelly, 'John Malcolm Fraser', p. 367.

130 Tony Eggleton, interview with James Walter, 6 July 2012.

131 See Mills, *The Professionals*, pp. 105–6.

132 See Weller, *Malcolm Fraser PM*.

133 See Walter, *The Ministers' Minders*, pp. 83–4.

134 Ed Visbord, interview with James Walter, 26 March 2013.

135 John Rose, interview with Zareh Ghazarian, 7 May 2013.

136 Mike Keating, interview with James Walter, 3 February 2012.

137 Quotes from Menadue, *Things You Learn along the Way*, pp. 171 and 170, respectively.

138 Alan Rose, interview with James Walter, 3 February 2012.

139 For details, see Ayres, *Malcolm Fraser*, p. 316.

140 For details, see Weller, Scott and Stevens, *From Postbox to Powerhouse*, pp. 101–2.

141 Quoted ibid., p. 90.

142 Ibid., p. 91.

143 Alan Rose, interview.

144 Menadue, *Things You Learn along the Way*, p. 126.

145 Weller, Scott and Stevens, *From Postbox to Powerhouse*, p. 94. This paragraph draws on ibid., pp. 92–5.

146 Young, *The Persuaders*, p. 15.

147 Ayres, *Malcolm Fraser*, pp. 209–10, 213–14, 239–40; Fraser, *Malcolm Fraser*, pp. 251–3.

148 Mills, *The Professionals*, pp. 102–7; Young, *The Persuaders*, pp. 95–6.

149 Walter and Strangio, *No, Prime Minister*, p. 60.

150 On policy cycles and the politics of disjunction, see Stephen Skowronek, *Presidential Leadership in Political Time: Reprise and Reappraisal*, University Press of Kansas, Lawrence, 2011; on Fraser and the politics of disjunction, see Matthew Laing and Brendan McCaffrie, 'The Politics Prime Ministers Make: Political Time and Executive Leadership in Westminster Systems', in Paul Strangio, Paul 't Hart and James Walter (eds), *Understanding Prime Ministerial Performance: Comparative Perspectives*, Oxford University Press, Oxford, 2013, pp. 79–101.

151 Kelly, 'John Malcolm Fraser', p. 357.
152 Fraser, *Malcolm Fraser*, pp. 349, 544.
153 Charles Moore, *Margaret Thatcher: The Authorised Biography, Vol. 1*, Allen Lane, London, 2013, ch. 22.
154 See Anthony Giddens, *Runaway World: How Globalization Is Reshaping Our Lives* (2nd edn), Profile Books, London, 2002, pp. 7–9.
155 Fraser, quoted in Allsop, 'The Fading Legacy of Malcolm Fraser', p. 13.
156 Whitlam, quoted by John Faulkner, in Wendy Guest and Gary Gray (eds), *Not Just for This Life: Gough Whitlam Remembered*, NewSouth, Sydney, 2016, p. 274.
157 See, for instance, Hocking and Lewis, *It's Time Again*; Bramston, *The Whitlam Legacy*.
158 Menadue, *Things You Learn along the Way*, pp. 168, 175.
159 See, for example, Richardson, 'The Fraser Years', pp. 216, 227, 228–9.
160 Fraser, *Malcolm Fraser*, p. 439.

Chapter 4 Agents of Change

1 Bill Kelty, 'The Accord, Industrial Relations and the Trade Union Movement', in Susan Ryan and Troy Bramston (eds), *The Hawke Government: A Critical Retrospective*, Pluto Press, Melbourne, 2003, p. 339.
2 Gerry Bloustien, 'Legitimacy, Governance and Consensus: A Candid Conversation with Graham Freudenberg', in Gerry Bloustien, Barbara Comber and Alison Mackinnon (eds), *The Hawke Legacy*, Wakefield Press, Kent Town, SA, 2009, p. 35.
3 The distinction between 'eventful' (shaped by 'events') and 'event-making' (agenda-setting, highly consequential, epoch-creating) leadership comes from Sidney Hook, *The Hero in History: A Study in Limitation and Possibility*, Beacon Press, Boston, 1955 (originally published 1943).
4 See Troy Bramston, *Paul Keating: The Big-Picture Leader*, Scribe Publications, Melbourne, 2016, pp. 2–3.
5 Hugh V Emy and Owen E Hughes, *Australian Politics: Realities in Conflict*, Macmillan, Melbourne, 1991, p. 9.
6 Carol Johnson, *The Labor Legacy: Curtin, Chifley, Whitlam, Hawke*, Allen and Unwin, Sydney, 1989.
7 Dean Jaensch, *The Hawke–Keating Hijack*, Allen and Unwin, Sydney, 1989, uses the term 'hijack' to denote Hawke and Keating's impact on their party's ethos, structure and practice, but in a non-judgemental fashion. In contrast, David Day, 'Hawke and the Labor Tradition', in Ryan and Bramston, *The Hawke Government*, pp. 399–407, gives voice to the claims that Hawke and Keating flouted 'Labor tradition'. See also Barry Jones, 'The Hawke Government: An Assessment from the Inside', in Ryan and Bramston, *The Hawke Government*, pp. 421–5.
8 Paul Kelly, *The End of Certainty: Power, Politics and Business in Australia*, Allen & Unwin, Sydney, 1994, p. 685.
9 Peter Walsh, *Confessions of a Failed Finance Minister*, Random House, Sydney, 1995, p. 150; Chris Bowen, *The Money Men: Australia's 12 Most Notable Treasurers*, Melbourne University Press, Melbourne, 2015, pp. 312–15.

10 George Megalogenis, *The Australian Moment: How We Were Made for These Times*, Penguin, Melbourne, 2012.
11 James Walter and Carolyn Holbrook, 'Political Memory and Policy Achievement: Leaders in Retrospect', Political Studies Association conference paper, Sheffield, UK, 2015, https://www.psa.ac.uk/sites/default/files/conference/papers/2015/Political%20memory%20and%20policy%20achievement%20_final.pdf (accessed January 2016).
12 Julian Fitzgerald, *On Message: Political Communications of Australian Prime Ministers 1901–2014*, Clareville Press, Mawson, ACT, 2014, pp. 146–7.
13 John Hurst, *Hawke PM*, Angus & Robertson, Sydney, 1983; Robert Haupt with Michelle Grattan, *31 Days to Power: Hawke's Victory*, George Allen & Unwin, Sydney 1983; Anne Summers, *Gamble for Power: How Bob Hawke Beat Malcolm Fraser—The 1983 Election*, Thomas Nelson, Melbourne, 1983; Paul Kelly, *The Hawke Ascendancy*, Angus & Robertson, Sydney, 1984.
14 Pal Ahluwalia and Greg McCarthy, 'The Politics of Intimacy: A Conversation with Bob Hawke', in Bloustien, Comber and Mackinnon, *The Hawke Legacy*, pp. 15–29.
15 Graham Richardson, *Whatever It Takes*, Bantam Books, Sydney, 1994, p.124.
16 Walsh, *Confessions of a Failed Finance Minister*, p. 280.
17 Amanda Buckley, 'Hawke and the Australian People', in Ryan and Bramston, *The Hawke Government*, p. 31.
18 Troy Bramston, 'The Hawke Leadership Model', in Ryan and Bramston, *The Hawke Government*, p. 63.
19 Blanche d'Alpuget, *Robert J Hawke*, Schwartz Penguin, Melbourne, 1982, p. 307; Tom Uren, *Straight Left*, Random House, Sydney, 1994, p. 400.
20 Stephen Mills, *The Hawke Years: The Story from the Inside*, Viking, Sydney, 1993, p. 55.
21 Ibid., p. 28; see also Uren, *Straight Left*, p. 401.
22 Mills, *The Hawke Years*, pp. 141–50. See Bill Hayden, *Hayden: An Autobiography*, Angus & Robertson, Sydney, 1996, p. 464, for a less-than-kind assessment of this particular propensity: 'Perhaps it was just another instance of Hawke's egocentric presumption [that] he could transfer his indisputable local industrial relations skills to the "big canvas of international relations"'.
23 Gareth Evans, *Inside the Hawke Keating Government: A Cabinet Diary*, Melbourne University Press, Melbourne, 2014, p. 155.
24 George Megalogenis, *The Longest Decade*, Scribe, Melbourne, 2008, p. 25.
25 Sol Encel first characterised the larrikin PM, referring to George Reid, Billy Hughes, Arthur Fadden and Gorton; see his *Cabinet Government in Australia*, Melbourne University Press, Melbourne, 1974 (2nd edn), pp. 170–1.
26 Graham Freudenberg, 'The Passionate Persuader', in Ryan and Bramston, *The Hawke Government*, p. 90.
27 Michael Pusey, *The Experience of Middle Australia: The Dark Side of Economic Reform*, Cambridge University Press, Melbourne, 2003.
28 Quoted in Frank Bongiorno, *The Eighties: The Decade that Transformed Australia*, Black Inc, Melbourne, 2015, p. 113.

29 Paul Strangio, 'Evaluating Prime-ministerial Performance: The Australian Experience', in Paul Strangio, Paul 't Hart and James Walter (eds), *Understanding Prime Ministerial Performance: Comparative Perspectives*, Oxford University Press, Oxford, 2013, pp. 264–90.
30 Emy and Hughes, *Australian Politics*, pp. 51–61.
31 Mills, *The Hawke Years*, p. 39.
32 Carol Johnson, 'The Hawke Government and Consensus', in Bloustien, Comber and Mackinnon, *The Hawke Legacy*, p. 5.
33 Don Russell, interview with James Walter, 7 March 2013.
34 Emy and Hughes, *Australian Politics*, p. 560.
35 Shaun Goldfinch, *Remaking New Zealand and Australian Economic Policy*, Georgetown University Press, Washington DC, 2000, pp. 152–7, 178–82; and Peter Ewer, Ian Hampson, Chris Lloyd, John Rainford, Stephen Rix and Meg Smith, *Politics and the Accord*, Pluto Press, Sydney, 1992.
36 There are various accounts of the events surrounding the float, including Bramston, *Paul Keating*, pp. 208–21; Bongiorno, *The Eighties*, pp. 42–50; Edna Carew, *Paul Keating: Prime Minister*, Allen & Unwin, Sydney, 1992, pp. 104–15; John Edwards, *Keating: The Inside Story*, Penguin, Melbourne, 1996, pp. 205–35; and Gregory McCarthy and David Taylor, 'The Politics of the Float: Paul Keating and the Deregulation of the Australian Exchange Rate', *Australian Journal of Politics and History*, vol. 41, no. 2, 1995, pp. 219–38.
37 Bob Hawke, *The Hawke Memoirs*, William Heinemann, Melbourne, 1994, p. 169.
38 Bramston, *Paul Keating*, p. 219.
39 Bongiorno, *The Eighties*, p. 49.
40 Keating, quoted in Kerry O'Brien, *Keating*, Allen & Unwin, Sydney, 2015, p. 134, and see pp. 134–7; Bramston, *Paul Keating*, pp. 192–4.
41 Kelly, *The End of Certainty*, p. 79.
42 Peter Cook quoted in Bramston, *Paul Keating*, p. 225.
43 Quoted ibid.
44 Particularly vivid participants' accounts of the tax discussions can be found in Uren, *Straight Left*, p. 374ff and Evans, *Inside the Hawke Keating Government*, pp. 120–45.
45 Goldfinch, *Remaking New Zealand and Australian Economic Policy*, p. 180; Ross McMullin, *The Light on the Hill: The Australian Labor Party 1891–1991*, Oxford University Press, Melbourne, 1991, pp. 442–4.
46 John Button, *As It Happened*, Text Publishing, Melbourne, 1998, p. 320.
47 Tom Conley, *The Vulnerable Country: Australia and the Global Economy*, UNSW Press, Sydney, 2010, pp. 2–3.
48 Marian Wilkinson, *The Fixer: The Untold Story of Graham Richardson*, Heinemann, Melbourne, 1996, p. 202.
49 Informative accounts of the 'greening' of the Hawke government and the tensions it generated include: Kelly, *The End of Certainty*, pp. 524–43; Wilkinson, *The Fixer*, pp. 298–300, 317–21; Phillip Toyne and Simon Balderstone, 'The Environment', in Ryan and Bramston, *The Hawke Government*, pp. 170–83.
50 Mills, *The Hawke Years*, pp. 59, 79–87.

51 Neal Blewett, 'Robert James Lee Hawke', in Michelle Grattan (ed.), *Australian Prime Ministers*, New Holland, Sydney, 2000, p. 409.
52 David Bradbury, 'The Institutions of Governance', in Ryan and Bramston, *The Hawke Government*, p. 392; Patrick Weller, *Cabinet Government in Australia 1901–2006*, UNSW Press, Sydney, 2007, p. 244.
53 Blanche d'Alpuget, *Hawke: The Prime Minister*, Melbourne University Press, Melbourne, 2010, pp. 67–75.
54 Bloustien, 'Legitimacy, Governance and Consensus', pp. 35–7.
55 Mills, *The Hawke Years*, p. 161.
56 James Walter, *The Ministers' Minders: Personal Advisers in National Government*, Oxford University Press, Melbourne, 1986, pp. 89–93.
57 Anne Tiernan, *Power without Responsibility: Ministerial Staffers in Australian Governments from Whitlam to Howard*, UNSW Press, Sydney, 2007, p. 61.
58 RAW Rhodes and Anne Tiernan, *Lessons in Governing: A Profile of Prime Ministers' Chiefs of Staff*, Melbourne University Press, Melbourne, 2014, p. 69.
59 Sandy Hollway, interviewed by James Walter, 14 February 2013.
60 Freudenberg, 'The Passionate Persuader', p. 93.
61 Mills, *The Hawke Years*, p. 92.
62 John Halligan and John Power, *Political Management in the 1990s*, Oxford University Press, Melbourne, 1992, p. 77.
63 Goldfinch, *Remaking New Zealand and Australian Economic Policy*, pp. 130–1.
64 Quote abridged from Rhodes and Tiernan, *Lessons in Governing*, p. 150.
65 Kelty, 'The Accord', p. 330.
66 Mike Steketee, 'Labor in Power: 1983–96', in John Faulkner and Stuart Macintyre (eds), *True Believers: The Story of the Federal Parliamentary Labor Party*, Allen & Unwin, Sydney, 2001, p. 140.
67 Quoted ibid., p. 143.
68 Neal Blewett, 'The Hawke Cabinets', in Ryan and Bramston, *The Hawke Government*, pp. 77–82; see also McMullin, *The Light on the Hill*, p. 416.
69 Hawke, *The Hawke Memoirs*, p. 169.
70 Blewett, 'The Hawke Cabinets', p. 75.
71 On the latter, see Richard Lucy, *The Australian Form of Government: Models in Dispute*, Macmillan, Melbourne, 1993, pp. 125–7.
72 Weller, *Cabinet Government in Australia 1901–2006*, p. 160; Lucy, *The Australian Form of Government*, pp. 151–2.
73 Lucy, *The Australian Form of Government*, p. 122.
74 Quoted in d'Alpuget, *Hawke: The Prime Minister*, p. 78.
75 Weller, *Cabinet Government in Australia 1901–2006*, p. 171.
76 Useful accounts of some of these reform episodes include Button, *As It Happened*, pp. 245–78; Emy and Hughes, *Australian Politics*, pp. 419–30; Wilkinson, *The Fixer*, pp. 280, 287–9, 298–300, 317–22, is vivid about the environmental decisions, but see Walsh, *Confessions of a Failed Finance Minister*, pp. 205ff for a cynical portrayal.
77 Hayden, *Hayden*, p. 477, who also credits Hawke, his erstwhile rival, with having 'a great reservoir of something I was short of—patience', p. 480.

78 An illustrative account of one such instance can be found in Evans, *Inside the Hawke Keating Government*, pp. 26–30.
79 Ibid., p. 51.
80 Lucy, *The Australian Form of Government*, pp. 250–60.
81 Arthur Hoyle and Cecil Carr, 'Administrative Chronicle', *Australian Journal of Public Administration*, vol. 44, no. 2, 1985, p. 113.
82 Michael Keating, 'The Public Service and Management of the Public Sector', in Ryan and Bramston, *The Hawke Government*, p. 371.
83 Weller, *Cabinet Government in Australia 1901–2006*, pp. 101–2.
84 Mills, *The Hawke Years*, pp. 67–78, quotes are from p. 73 and p. 77 respectively.
85 McMullin, *The Light on the Hill*, pp. 412–13.
86 Steketee, 'Labor in Power', p. 147.
87 This paragraph is largely based on ibid., pp. 145–53.
88 Quoted in McMullin, *The Light on the Hill*, p. 413.
89 Margaret Simons, *Fit to Print: Inside the Canberra Press Gallery*, UNSW Press, Sydney, 1999; Clem Lloyd, 'Prime Ministers and the Media', in Patrick Weller (ed.), *Menzies to Keating: The Development of the Australian Prime Ministership*, Melbourne University Press, Melbourne, 1992, p. 127; Ian Ward, 'An Australian PR State?', *Australian Journal of Communication*, vol. 30. no. 1, 2003, p. 31.
90 A point observed by Bowen, *The Money Men*, p. 302.
91 Blewett, 'The Hawke Cabinets', p. 85.
92 Michael Gordon, *A True Believer: Paul Keating*, University of Queensland Press, St Lucia, Qld, 1996, p. 74.
93 Quoted in O'Brien, *Keating*, p. 140.
94 Edwards, *Keating*, p. 167.
95 Kelly, *The End of Certainty*, p. 55.
96 Russell, interview.
97 James Walter, *What Were They Thinking? The Politics of Ideas in Australia*, UNSW Press, Sydney, 2010, pp. 258–9.
98 For example, Graham Maddox, *The Hawke Government and Labor Tradition*, Penguin, Melbourne, 1989.
99 Don Watson, *Recollections of a Bleeding Heart: A Portrait of Paul Keating PM*, Knopf, Sydney, 2002, p. 24.
100 Evans, *Inside the Hawke Keating Government*, p. 145.
101 David Love, *Unfinished Business: Paul Keating's Interrupted Revolution*, Scribe, Melbourne, 2008, p. 77.
102 Troy Bramston, 'Peter Walsh: Labor's Fiscal Powerhouse', *Australian*, 14 April 2015.
103 Graham Little, 'The Two Narcissisms: Comparing Hawke and Keating', in Judith Brett (ed.), *Political Lives*, Allen & Unwin, Sydney, 1997, pp. 16–27.
104 Megalogenis, *The Longest Decade*, p. 31.
105 For Keating's insistence that he was effectively the true driving force of the Hawke government from late 1984 onwards, see Bramston, *Paul Keating*, p. 301; and O'Brien, *Keating*, p. 305.
106 Quoted in Bramston, *Paul Keating*, p. 309.

107 Keating's public life has been documented by a series of biographers (journalists, former staffers and an historian): Bramston, *Paul Keating*; Carew, *Paul Keating*; David Day, *Paul Keating: The Biography*, Fourth Estate, Sydney, 2015; Edwards, *Keating*; Gordon, *A True Believer*; and Watson, *Recollections of a Bleeding Heart*. O'Brien's *Keating* is the closest we are likely to come to a Keating autobiography.

108 Quoted in O'Brien, *Keating*, p. 28.

109 Quoted ibid., p. 27; see also Phillip Adams, 'Former PM Paul Keating and Historian Frank Cain Discuss Jack Lang's Life', *Late Night Live*, 17 November 2005, ABC Radio National streaming audio.

110 Archie Brown, *The Myth of the Strong Leader: Political Leadership in the Modern Age*, Basic Books, New York, 2014.

111 Hence the 'Brawler Statesman' epithet, taken from Jim Chalmers, 'Brawler Statesman: Paul Keating and Prime Ministerial Leadership in Australia', PhD thesis, School of Social Sciences, Australian National University, Canberra, 2004, the most thorough academic analysis of Keating's modus operandi as prime minister.

112 Quoted in Margaret Bowman and Michelle Grattan, *Reformers: Shaping Australian Society from the 60s to the 80s*, Collins Dove, Melbourne, 1989, p. 155.

113 Adding that 'you were scrambling to catch up with his head': Mary Ann O'Loughlin, interview with James Walter, 21 September 2012.

114 Gordon, *A True Believer*, p. 68.

115 Tom Uren, quoted in Bowman and Grattan, *Reformers*, p. 156.

116 Some of the characteristic Keating-speak is covered in Russell Marks (ed.), *The Book of Paul: The Wit and Wisdom of Paul Keating*, Black Inc., Sydney, 2014. Systematic analyses of his rhetoric can be found in James Curran, *The Power of Speech: Australian Prime Ministers Defining the National Image*, Melbourne University Press, Melbourne, 2004, pp. 255–315; John Uhr, 'Political Leadership and Rhetoric', in Geoffrey Brennan and Francis G Castles (eds), *Australia Reshaped: 200 Years of Institutional Transformation*, Cambridge University Press, Melbourne, 2002, pp. 261–94.

117 Gordon, *A True Believer*, p. 194.

118 Quoted in Carew, *Paul Keating*, p. 103.

119 This is a central theme of Watson's memoir, *Confessions of a Bleeding Heart*.

120 Bowman and Grattan, *Reformers*, p. 157.

121 Quote taken from Gordon, *A True Believer*, pp. 3–13, who also provides a vivid account of the context and consequences of the speech.

122 Watson, *Confessions of a Bleeding Heart*, pp. 655–61.

123 Paul Kelly, *The March of Patriots: The Struggle for Modern Australia*, Melbourne University Press, Melbourne, 2009, p. 117.

124 Paul Strangio, Paul 't Hart and James Walter, *Settling the Office: The Australian Prime Ministership from Federation to Reconstruction*, The Miegunyah Press, Melbourne, 2016, p. 216.

125 Chalmers, 'Brawler Statesman', pp. 100–6; see also Pamela Williams' tell-all story of the machinations within both parties in the 1996 campaign: *The Victory: The Inside Story of the Takeover of Australia*, Allen & Unwin, Sydney, 1997.

126 Quoted in Day, *Paul Keating*, p. 444.
127 Watson, *Confessions of a Bleeding Heart*, p. 616.
128 Ibid., p. 470.
129 Kelly, *The March of Patriots*, p. 35; see also: http://www.news.com.au/national/tony-abbott-escapes-being-our-most-unpopular-prime-minister-that-title-goes-to-paul-keating/story-fncynjr2-1226923638349 (accessed February 2016).
130 Kelly, *The March of Patriots*, pp. 38–9.
131 For example, his continued support for Carmen Lawrence, his hand-picked West Australian recruit whose past as premier of that state was catching up with her in a politically inspired inquiry; see Gordon, *A True Believer*, pp. 310ff.
132 As quoted in Chalmers, 'Brawler Statesman', p. 116, and re-quoted in Weller, *Cabinet Government in Australia 1901–2006*, p. 173.
133 Chalmers, 'Brawler Statesman', p. 154.
134 Edwards, *Keating*, p. 460.
135 Cited in Bramston, *Paul Keating*, p. 480.
136 Quoted in Chalmers, 'Brawler Statesman', p. 139.
137 Gordon quotes various Labor figures expressing the view that the 1993 acceptance speech already hinted at what would become apparent throughout the second term: that Keating failed to understand that the electorate had first and foremost repudiated Hewson, rather than endorsed him. Gordon, *A True Believer*, pp. 262–3.
138 Bramston, *Paul Keating*, p. 478.
139 Ibid.
140 Geoff Kitney, 'Small Fuse, Big Row', *Sydney Morning Herald*, 4 June 1993.
141 Chalmers, 'Brawler Statesman', p. 145.
142 Button, *As It Happened*, p. 243.
143 Kelly, *The March of Patriots*, p. 34.
144 Ibid. p. 35.
145 Chalmers, 'Brawler Statesman', p. 144.
146 Ibid., p. 119.
147 For more such examples of Keating pre-empting cabinet, see Weller, *Cabinet Government in Australia 1901–2006*, p. 174.
148 Watson, *Confessions of a Bleeding Heart* powerfully describes Keating's ambivalence (so powerfully that Keating resented it, and regarded the book as a breach of trust); Kelly, *The March of Patriots*, p. 36.
149 Kelly, *The March of Patriots*, p. 56.
150 Bramston, *Paul Keating*, pp. 482–3.
151 Watson, *Confessions of a Bleeding Heart*, p. 43.
152 Ibid., pp. 44–5.
153 Gordon, *A True Believer*, p. 190.
154 Watson, *Confessions of a Bleeding Heart*, p. 210.
155 O'Loughlin, interview.
156 Day, *Paul Keating*, p. 451 (largely based on Watson, whose account Keating resented).
157 Keating quoted in O'Brien, *Keating*, p. 455.

158 O'Loughlin, interview.

159 John Halligan, 'Labor, the Keating Term and the Senior Public Service', in Gwynn Singleton (ed.), *The Second Keating Government: Australian Commonwealth Administration 1993–1996,* Centre for Research in Public Sector Management/ Institute of Public Administration Australia, Canberra, 1997, p. 54.

160 Hollway, interview.

161 For instance, in late 1995 when Don Russell, meeting ministers individually in the lead-up to the 1996 election, belatedly 'discovered there were something like 19 ministerial statements all planning to be made before the end of 95'. Quoted in Chalmers, 'Brawler Statesman', p. 174.

162 Bramston, *Paul Keating*, p. 404.

163 Walsh, *Confessions of a Failed Finance Minister*, p. 251; Button, *As It Happened*, p. 242.

164 O'Brien, *Keating*, p. 436.

165 Kelly, *The March of Patriots*, p. 93.

166 Megalogenis, *The Longest Decade*, pp. 67, 70–8.

167 On *One Nation*'s genesis and impact, see: Megalogenis, *The Longest Decade*, pp. 68–70, 145, and Goldfinch, *Remaking New Zealand and Australian Economic Policy*, pp. 183–8. On *Working Nation*, see Jim Jose and John Burgess, 'Working Nation: Context and Consequences', *Journal of Economic and Social Policy*, vol. 9, no. 2, 2005, pp. 1–17.

168 Kelly, *The March of Patriots*, p. 142.

169 Ibid., pp. 109–17.

170 Goldfinch, *Remaking New Zealand and Australian Economic Policy*, pp. 188–92.

171 Kelly, *The March of Patriots*, pp. 134–47.

172 A term borrowed from Curran's interpretation of Keating's identity leadership: Curran, *The Power of Speech*, pp. 190–234.

173 It was a position from which he would not budge: the quotes in this sentence are not from the 1992 speech but from a 2013 interview with the *Guardian* on the same subject: https://www.theguardian.com/world/2013/nov/11/paul-keating-describes-first-world-war-as-a-war-devoid-of-any-virtue (accessed February 2016).

174 http://www.keating.org.au/shop/item/anzac-day---25-april-1992 (accessed February 2016).

175 Quoted in Bramston, *Paul Keating*, p. 500.

176 Elaborate detail about the complexity and gruelling nature of the Mabo processes can be found in Peter Butt, Robert Eagleson and Patricia Lane, *Mabo, Wik and Native Title,* Federation Press, Sydney, 2001; and Murray Goot and Tim Rowse (eds), *Make a Better Offer: The Politics of Mabo*, Pluto Press, Sydney, 1994.

177 http://www.keating.org.au/shop/item/redfern-speech-year-for-the-worlds-indigenous-people---10-december-1992 (accessed February 2016).

178 On that diplomacy, see Bramston, *Paul Keating*, pp. 414–28.

179 Kelly, *The March of Patriots*, p. 148.

180 See also Gordon, *A True Believer*, pp. 195–6.

181 Kelly, *The March of Patriots*, p. 127.

182 The details of that process can be found ibid., pp. 124–31.
183 Shaun Carney and Innes Willox, 'A Week Is a Long Time in Politics', *Age*, 23 October 1993.
184 Kelly, *The March of Patriots*, p. 79.
185 Quoted in Gordon, *A True Believer*, p. 277.
186 Day, *Paul Keating*, p. 480.
187 On this point, see Bramston, *Paul Keating*, pp. 586–9.
188 Bongiorno, *The Eighties*, p. xi.
189 Ibid., p. 58.

Chapter 5 Speaking for the Mainstream

1 Nick Cater (ed.), *The Howard Factor: A Decade that Changed a Nation,* Melbourne University Publishing, Melbourne, 2006.
2 John Howard, *Lazarus Rising: A Personal and Political Autobiography*, HarperCollins, Sydney, 2010, p. 180.
3 See Rod Tiffen, 'The Geoffrey Boycott of Australian Politics', *Australian Review of Public Affairs*, 23 February 2006, http://www.australianreview.net/digest/2006/02/tiffen.html (accessed 30 October 2016).
4 This is the period that Paul Kelly and George Megalogenis—who have been most influential in celebrating Howard's contribution, along with those of Hawke and Keating, to economic reform—identify as fundamental to Australia's success in the late twentieth century; see Paul Kelly, *The March of Patriots: The Struggle for Modern Australia*, Melbourne University Press, Melbourne, 2009, and George Megalogenis, *The Australian Moment: How We Were Made for These Times*, Penguin, Melbourne, 2012.
5 Howard, *Lazarus Rising*, p. 18. The paragraph above draws on Howard's account, ibid., pp. 3–25.
6 See Wayne Errington and Peter van Onselen, *John Winston Howard: The Biography*, Melbourne University Press, Melbourne, 2007, pp. 86–90; Paul Kelly, *The End of Certainty: The Story of the 1980s*, Allen & Unwin, Sydney, 1992, pp. 50–2.
7 Christine Wallace, *Hewson: A Portrait*, Sun Australia, Sydney, 1993, p. 122.
8 Malcolm Fraser, *Malcolm Fraser: The Political Memoirs* (with Margaret Simons), The Miegunyah Press, Melbourne, 2010, pp. 523–54.
9 Howard, *Lazarus Rising*, p. 136.
10 Kelly, *The End of Certainty*, p. 95, and see ch. 5, passim.
11 Howard, *Lazarus Rising*, p. 141.
12 Tony Eggleton, interview with James Walter, 6 July 2012.
13 Howard, *Lazarus Rising*, pp. 149–51.
14 See Errington and van Onselen, *John Winston Howard*, pp. 174–205.
15 Howard, *Lazarus Rising*, p. 233.
16 Ibid., p. 232.
17 Ibid., p. 141; and see Kelly, *The End of Certainty*, ch. 5.
18 See ML Murray, 'John Howard: A Study in Policy Consistency', PhD thesis, Discipline of Politics, University of Adelaide, 2010.

19 See Kelly, *The End of Certainty*, pp. 183, 236, 397–8; Geoff Kitney, 'The Hawke Government: An Assessment from the Outside', in Susan Ryan and Troy Bramston (eds), *The Hawke Government: A Critical Retrospective*, Pluto Press, Melbourne, 2003, p. 437.

20 For instance, John Howard, 'The Liberal Tradition: The Beliefs and Values which Guide the Federal Government', The 1996 Sir Robert Menzies Memorial Lecture, http://pmtranscripts.pmc.gov.au/release/transcript-10171 (accessed 1 March 2017); and for its precursors, see Murray, 'John Howard', pp. 110–41.

21 See Paul Kelly, 'Re-thinking Australian Governance: The Howard Legacy', Cunningham Lecture 2005, Academy of the Social Sciences in Australia, Canberra, 2005.

22 Judith Brett, *Australian Liberals and the Moral Middle Class: From Alfred Deakin to John Howard*, Cambridge University Press, Melbourne, 2003, pp. 183–212.

23 Ibid.

24 Howard, 'The Liberal Tradition', p. 12. Emphasis added.

25 John Howard, 'A Century of Nationhood', Melbourne Press Club Address, 22 November 2000, p. 5, http://pmtranscripts.pmc.gov.au/release/transcript-11678 (accessed 8 March 2017).

26 Ibid.

27 David Marr and Marion Wilkinson, *Dark Victory*, Allen & Unwin, Sydney, 2004; Stuart Macintyre and Anna Clark, *The History Wars*, Melbourne University Press, Melbourne, 2003.

28 Brett, *Australian Liberals and the Moral Middle Class*, pp. 194–6, 206–12; George Megalogenis, *The Longest Decade*, Scribe, Melbourne, 2006, pp. 274–7; Murray, 'John Howard', pp. 181–227.

29 See Russel Ward, *The Australian Legend*, Oxford University Press, Melbourne, 1958.

30 Brett, *Australian Liberals and the Moral Middle Class*, pp. 202–6.

31 Howard, 'The Liberal Tradition', p. 2.

32 Macintyre and Clark, *The History Wars*, p. 3.

33 Quotes, ibid., pp. 9–10; Howard, 'A Century of Nationhood', pp. 1–2.

34 See this exemplified in 'Transcript of the Prime Minister, The Hon John Howard MP, Address to the National Press Club, Great Hall, Parliament House, Canberra, 7 October, 2004', http://www.pm.gov.au (accessed 9 October 2004).

35 Harold Lasswell, *World Politics and Personal Insecurity*, Free Press, New York, 1935; Harold Lasswell, 'The Garrison State', *American Journal of Sociology*, vol. 46, 1941, pp. 455–68.

36 Howard, *Lazarus Rising*, p. 222.

37 Peter van Onselen and Wayne Errington, 'The Democratic State as a Marketing Tool: the Permanent Campaign in Australia', *Commonwealth & Comparative Politics*, vol. 45, no. 1, 2007, pp. 78–94; the phrase quoted from Howard appears on p. 78.

38 Stephen Mills, *The Professionals: Strategy, Money and the Rise of the Political Campaigner in Australia*, Black Inc., Melbourne, 2014, pp. 174–94.

39 David McKnight, 'Shaping the News: Media Advisers under the Howard and Rudd Governments', *Australian Journalism Review*, vol. 37, no. 1, 2015, pp. 21–31.

40 John Howard, 'Politics and the Media: The Good, the Bad and the Ugly', public lecture at the Centre for Advanced Journalism, University of Melbourne, 10 August 2009, http://newsroom.melbourne.edu/news/n-103 (accessed 22 November 2016).

41 Helen Ester, 'The Media', in Clive Hamilton and Sarah Maddison (eds), *Silencing Dissent*, Allen & Unwin, Sydney, 2007, pp. 118–22.

42 Malcolm Fraser, *Commonwealth Parliamentary Debates* (*CPD*), House of Representatives (H of R), vol. 122, 7 April 1981, p. 1350.

43 This and the previous paragraph draw on Greg Barns, *Selling the Australian Government: Politics and Propaganda from Whitlam to Howard*, UNSW Press, Sydney, 2005; Ester, 'The Media'; Ian Ward, 'An Australian PR State?', *Australian Journal of Communication*, vol. 30, no.1, 2003, pp. 25–42; van Onselen and Errington, 'The Democratic State as a Marketing Tool'.

44 Irene Moss, *Report of the Independent Audit into the State of Free Speech in Australia*, commissioned by Australia's Right to Know Coalition, Sydney, 31 October 2007, p. ii; and see ch. 4, pp. 13–48.

45 Walker is quoted in Ester, 'The Media', p. 114.

46 Howard, quoted in Michael Gordon, 'Howard Reveals Secrets of his Political Success', *Age*, 29 February 2016.

47 Howard, *Lazarus Rising*, p. 220.

48 Ibid., pp. 172–3, 368–9.

49 Kelly, 'Re-thinking Australian Governance', p. 10.

50 Howard, *Lazarus Rising*, p. 237.

51 Patrick Weller, *Cabinet Government in Australia 1901–2006*, UNSW Press, Sydney, 2007, p. 183; and see pp. 182–4.

52 Paul McClintock, interview with James Walter, 2 February 2012.

53 McClintock, interview.

54 Howard, *Lazarus Rising*, p. 236; Kelly, *The March of Patriots*, p. 256.

55 Kelly, 'Re-thinking Australian Governance', p. 11.

56 Kemp is quoted in Kelly, *The March of Patriots*, p. 256, where the claim that there were no instances where Howard did not get his way also appears; the following quotation is from Anne Tiernan and Patrick Weller, *Learning to Be a Minister: Heroic Expectations, Practical Realities*, Melbourne University Press, Melbourne, 2010, p. 194.

57 Kelly, 'Re-thinking Australian Governance', pp. 3–4; Weller, *Cabinet Government in Australia 1901–2006*, ch. 10.

58 Kelly, 'Re-thinking Australian Governance', p. 16.

59 On the family view of the public sector, and on Canberra as a Labor town, see Howard, *Lazarus Rising*, pp. 24, 647; on a properly incentivised private sector vs. the public sector, see Howard, 'A Century of Nationhood', p. 5; on Howard's mapping, see, for example, his listing of the political disposition of individuals in the press gallery, in John Howard, 'The Press Gallery's Part in Our Downfall', *Independent Monthly*, July 1989, p. 19.

60 RAW Rhodes and Anne Tiernan, *Lessons in Governing: A Profile of Prime Ministers' Chiefs of Staff*, Melbourne University Press, Melbourne, 2014, p. 69.

61 John Halligan, 'Public Service Reform under Howard', in Gwynneth Singleton (ed.), *The Howard Government*, UNSW Press, Sydney, 2000, p. 54.
62 Quoted in Geoffrey Barker, 'The Public Service', in Hamilton and Maddison, *Silencing Dissent*, p. 125.
63 Anne Tiernan, *Power without Responsibility: Ministerial Staffers in Australian Governments from Whitlam to Howard*, UNSW Press, Sydney, 2007, pp. 112–13.
64 Patrick Weller, Joanne Scott and Bronwyn Stevens, *From Postbox to Powerhouse: A Centenary History of the Department of the Prime Minister and Cabinet 1911–2010*, Allen & Unwin, Sydney, 2011, pp. 126–30.
65 Roger Beale, interview with James Walter, 9 February 2012.
66 Meredith Edwards, quoted in Weller, Scott and Stevens, *From Postbox to Powerhouse*, p. 136.
67 Weller, Scott and Stevens, *From Postbox to Powerhouse*, p. 128.
68 Meredith Edwards, interview with James Walter, 8 February 2012.
69 Weller, Scott and Stevens, *From Postbox to Powerhouse*, pp. 139–43.
70 Peter Shergold, interview with James Walter, 22 February 2012.
71 Edwards, interview.
72 Barker, 'The Public Service', pp. 129–33.
73 Shergold, interview.
74 Weller, Scott and Stevens, *From Postbox to Powerhouse*, p. 136: Jenny Goddard, deputy secretary, quoted p. 142.
75 John Halligan, 'The Search for Balance and Effectiveness in the Australian Public Service', in Chris Aulich and Roger Wettenhall (eds), *Howard's Fourth Government: Australian Commonwealth Administration 2004–2007*, UNSW Press, Sydney, 2008, pp. 13–30.
76 Tiernan, *Power without Responsibility*, pp. 85–6.
77 Rhodes and Tiernan, *Lessons in Governing*, pp. 59–60.
78 Tiernan, *Power Without Responsibility*, pp. 160–163.
79 Anne Tiernan, 'Advising Howard: Interpreting Changes in Advisory and Support Structures for the Prime Minister of Australia', *Australian Journal of Political Science*, vol. 41, no. 3, 2006, pp. 309–24.
80 Quoted, ibid., p. 316.
81 Shergold, interview.
82 This paragraph draws on Tiernan, 'Advising Howard', pp. 314–15, 317–18.
83 Quoted in the *Age*, 20 September 2003.
84 Shergold, interview.
85 Guy Rundle, *The Opportunist: John Howard and the Triumph of Reaction*, Quarterly Essay No. 3, Black Inc., Melbourne, 2001.
86 Richard Crossman, *Inside View: Three Lectures on Prime Ministerial Government*, Cape, London, 1972.
87 Kelly, 'Re-thinking Australian Governance', passim.
88 Cf Kelly, *The March of Patriots*, p. 258.
89 'Aboriginal industry' was a term used increasingly in the 1990s, on one hand by commentators intent on categorising one set of what they saw as welfare

scroungers, and on the other, as early as 1996, by critics of Howard's Indigenous policies—see, for example, Geoff Pryor's *Sydney Morning Herald* cartoon of 15 July 1996 at http://nla.gov.au/nla.obj-156991103/view (accessed 8 March 2017).

90 Kelly, *The March of Patriots*, pp. 265–6.

91 Ibid., pp. 281, 284.

92 Murray Goot, 'The New Millennium', in Alison Bashford and Stuart Macintyre (eds), *The Cambridge History of Australia, Vol. 2: The Commonwealth of Australia*, Cambridge University Press, Melbourne, 2013, p. 188.

93 See Peter Costello, with Peter Coleman, *The Costello Memoirs*, Melbourne University Press, Melbourne, 2008.

94 Karen Kissane, 'A Lasting Impression', *Age*, 20 February 2005. The term 'bringing home the bacon' was likely an ironical reference to a phrase minted earlier by Keating when claiming his own economic success.

95 Tim Colebatch, 'The Money Man', *Age*, 22 February 2006.

96 Elim Papadikis, 'Constituents of Confidence and Mistrust in Australian institutions', *Australian Journal of Political Science*, vol. 34, no. 1, 1999, pp. 75–94; Ian Marsh and David Yencken, *Into the Future: The Neglect of the Long Term in Australian Politics*, Australian Collaboration/Black Inc., Melbourne, 2004.

97 Michael Pusey, *The Experience of Middle Australia: The Dark Side of Economic Reform*, Cambridge University Press, Melbourne, 2003.

98 Peter Saunders, *The Ends and Means of Welfare: Coping with Economic and Social Change in Australia*, Cambridge University Press, New York, 2002.

99 Kelly, *The March of Patriots*, pp. 613–27; Paul Kelly, 'How to Design and Deliver Reform that Makes a Real Difference: What Recent History Has Taught Us as a Nation', in EA Lindquist, S Vincent and J Wanna (eds), *Delivering Policy Reform: Anchoring Significant Reforms in Turbulent Times*, ANU E Press, Canberra, 2011, pp. 43–51.

100 Kelly, 'Re-thinking Australian Governance', pp. 14–16.

101 See Kelly, *The March of Patriots*, pp. 260–2; Calvert is quoted, p. 261.

102 Patrick Weller, *Don't Tell the Prime Minister*, Scribe Books, Melbourne, 2002; Marr and Wilkinson, *Dark Victory*; Robert Garran, *True Believer: John Howard, George Bush & the American alliance*, Allen & Unwin, Sydney, 2004; Parliamentary Joint Committee on ASIO, ASIS and DSD, *Intelligence on Iraq's Weapons of Mass Destruction*, Parliament of the Commonwealth of Australia, Canberra, 2003; Philip Flood, *Report of the Inquiry into Australian Intelligence Agencies*, Australian Government, Canberra, 2004.

103 Kelly, 'Re-thinking Australian Governance', pp. 5–7; Andrew Podger, 'What Really Happens: Department Secretary Appointments, Contracts and Performance Pay in the Australian Public Service', *Australian Journal of Public Administration*, vol. 66, no. 2, 2007, pp. 143–6; Michael Keating, 'In the Wake of "A Certain Maritime Incident": Ministerial Advisers, Departments and Accountability', *Australian Journal of Public Administration*, vol. 62, no 3, 2003, pp. 92–7.

104 Peter Shergold, 'What Really Happens in the Australian Public Service: An Alternative View', *Australian Journal of Public Administration*, vol. 66, no. 3, 2007, p. 369.

105 Weller, *Don't Tell the Prime Minister*, p. 72.
106 Keating, 'In the Wake of "A Certain Maritime Incident"', pp. 92–3; Tiernan, *Power without Responsibility*, pp. 171–232; Weller, *Don't Tell the Prime Minister*.
107 See Peter Shergold, '"Lackies, Careerists, Political Stooges"? Personal Reflections on the Current State of Public Service Leadership', *Australian Journal of Public Administration,* vol. 63, no. 4, 2004, p. 11.
108 See Tiernan, *Power without Responsibility*; James Walter, 'Why Prime Ministers Go Too Far: The Case of John Howard', in Derek McDougall and Peter Shearman (eds), *Australian Security after 9/11: New and Old Agendas,* Ashgate, Aldershot, UK, 2006, pp. 189–206; Weller, *Don't Tell the Prime Minister*.
109 Howard, *Lazarus Rising*, pp. 626–7.
110 Costello, *The Costello Memoirs*, ch. 12 (and see p. 234 for the line quoted); Howard, *Lazarus Rising*, ch. 44.
111 Alan Rose, interview with James Walter, 3 February 2012.
112 McClintock, interview.
113 Terry Moran, interview with James Walter, 20 July 2012.

Chapter 6 Harbingers of Decline?

1 'Tony Abbott's Speech in Full: "Our Country Is So Much Better than This"', *The Guardian* (Australian edition), 14 September 2015, http://www.theguardian.com/australia-news/2015/sep/14/tony-abbotts-speech-in-full-our-country-is-so-much-better-than-this (accessed January 2016).
2 Nick Bryant, 'Australia: Coup Capital of the Democratic World', *BBC News*, 14 September 2015, http://www.bbc.com/news/world-australia-34249214 (accessed January 2016).
3 This contrasted with other Anglo democracies such as Canada. See Patrick Weller, 'The Vulnerability of Prime Ministers: A Comparative Perspective', *Parliamentary Affairs*, vol. 36, no. 1, 1983, pp. 96–117; and Jonathan Malloy, 'Prime Ministers and Their Parties in Canada', in Paul Strangio, Paul 't Hart and James Walter (eds), *Understanding Prime-Ministerial Performance: Comparative Perspectives*, Oxford University Press, Oxford, UK, 2013, pp. 151–71.
4 Paul Kelly, *Triumph and Demise: The Broken Promise of a Labor Generation*, Melbourne University Press, Melbourne, 2014, pp. 498–500.
5 Niki Savva, 'Yes, We're Not a Banana Republic, and No, the System Ain't Broke', *Weekend Australian*, 19 September 2015. For Kelly's retort to Savva, see, Paul Kelly, 'Negative Politics the Biggest Enemy of Reform', *Weekend Australian*, 23 September 2015. For a summary of these and other contributions to this debate, see Mary Walsh, 'Five Prime Ministers: A Crisis, a Political Aberration or the New Normal?', in Chris Aulich (ed.), *From Abbott to Turnbull: A New Direction? Australian Commonwealth Administration 2013–2016*, Echo Books, West Geelong, Vic., 2016, pp. 323–42.
6 This contrast has been noted in George Megalogenis, *The Australian Moment: How We Were Made for These Times*, Hamish Hamilton, Melbourne, 2012, p. 322.
7 There are a number of sources on Rudd's pre-prime-ministerial life, including Robert Macklin, *Kevin Rudd: The Biography*, Viking, Melbourne, 2007; David Marr, 'Power Trip: The Political Journey of Kevin Rudd', *Quarterly Essay*, no. 38,

2010; Nicholas Stuart, *Kevin Rudd: An Unauthorised Political Biography*, Scribe Publications, Melbourne, 2007; and Patrick Weller, *Kevin Rudd; Twice Prime Minister*, Melbourne University Publishing, Melbourne, 2014, part I.

8 Kelly, *Triumph and Demise*, p. 17.

9 Marr, 'Power Trip', pp. 29–31; Weller, *Kevin Rudd*, ch. 4.

10 Quoted in Marr, 'Power Trip', p. 31.

11 Christine Jackman, *Inside Kevin 07: The People. The Plan. The Prize*, Melbourne University Press, Melbourne, 2008, pp. 30–3.

12 Jason Wilson, 'Kevin Rudd, Celebrity and Audience Democracy in Australia', *Journalism*, vol. 15, no. 2, 2014, p. 208.

13 George Megalogenis, 'Trivial Pursuit: Leadership and the End of the Reform Era', *Quarterly Essay*, no. 40, 2010, p. 8.

14 Quoted in Marr, 'Power Trip', p. 40.

15 Stuart, *Kevin Rudd*, p. 221. Also see Weller, *Kevin Rudd*, pp. 112–16.

16 Julia Gillard, *My Story*, Random House, Sydney, 2014, p. 5.

17 This summary of the 2007 election campaign chiefly draws on Jackman, *Inside Kevin 07*; but also see David Adams, 'Leadership', *Australian Journal of Cultural History*, vol. 27, no. 2, 2009, pp. 10–13; and Peter van Onselen and Philip Senior, *Howard's End: The Unravelling of a Government*, Melbourne University Press, Melbourne, 2008.

18 Quoted in Jackman, *Inside Kevin 07*, p. 92.

19 Glenn Kefford, 'The Presidentialisation of Australian Politics? Kevin Rudd's Leadership of the Australian Labor Party', *Australian Journal of Political Science*, vol. 48, no. 2, 2013, p. 140.

20 Quoted in Jackman, *Inside Kevin 07*, p. 214.

21 Quoted in Troy Bramston, *Looking for the Light on the Hill: Modern Labor's Challenges*, Scribe Publications, Melbourne, 2011, p. 81.

22 Clive Bean and Ian McAllister, 'The Australian Election Survey: The Tale of the Rabbit-less Hat. Voting Behaviour in 2007', *Australian Cultural History*, vol. 27, no. 2, 2009, pp. 205–18. Also see Kefford, 'The Presidentialisation of Australian Politics?', pp. 141–2; and Ian McAllister, *The Australian Voter: 50 Years of Change*, UNSW Press, Sydney, 2011, p. 249.

23 Quoted in Jackman, *Inside Kevin 07*, p. 214.

24 'Time to Roll up Sleeves for the Future', *Australian*, 26 November 2007.

25 Jennifer Hewett, 'No Yawning Folks, It's Time for Work, Says Kevin 24/7', *Weekend Australian*, 15–16 December 2007.

26 Ross Gittens, 'PM: Stop Running and Start Leading', *Age*, 2 June 2008.

27 Megalogenis, *The Australian Moment*, p. 330.

28 Weller, *Kevin Rudd*, pp. 306–7.

29 The chief source for this and the following paragraph is Anne Tiernan, 'The Rudd Transition: Continuity and Change in the Structures of Advice and Support to Australian Prime Ministers', Senate Occasional Lecture Series, 30 May 2008, http://www.aph.gov.au/About_Parliament/Senate/Whats_On/Seminars_and_Lectures/~/~/~/link.aspx?_id=B9667AA3F2A343F496ED51D1465738B5&_z=z (accessed February 2016).

30 Patricia Karvelas, 'Leader Opts for Talent over Tradition', *Australian*, 30 November 2007; Weller, *Kevin Rudd*, pp. 151–3.
31 Tiernan, 'The Rudd Transition'.
32 Quoted in Andrew Macintosh, Deb Wilkinson and Richard Denniss, 'Climate Change', in Chris Aulich and Mark Evans (eds), *The Rudd Government: Australian Commonwealth Administration 2007–2010*, ANU EPress, Canberra, 2010, p. 200.
33 Figures for the number of meetings are cited in John Halligan, 'The Australian Public Service: New Agendas and Reform', in Aulich and Evans, *The Rudd Government*, p. 42.
34 Quoted ibid., p. 38.
35 Terry Moran, interview with James Walter, 20 July 2012; Michelle Grattan and Paul Austin, 'Three Amigos from the Sunshine State', *Age*, 9 February 2008; RAW Rhodes and Anne Tiernan, *Lessons in Governing: A Profile of Prime Ministers' Chiefs of Staff*, Melbourne University Press, Melbourne, 2014, pp. 191, 220.
36 David McKnight, 'The Rudd Labor Government and the Limitations of Spin', *Media International Australia*, no. 159, May 2016, pp. 3–4. See also Greg Callaghan and Drew Warne-Smith, 'Rise of Rudd's Sentinels of Spin', *Weekend Australian*, 6–7 June 2009.
37 Quoted in McKnight, 'The Rudd Labor Government and the Limitations of Spin', p. 4.
38 Quoted in Lenore Taylor, 'Public Sector Says Rivets about to Pop', *Australian*, 30 May 2008.
39 For a summary of the prime minister's early activities, see Weller, *Kevin Rudd*, ch. 11.
40 See David Marsh, Chris Lewis and Paul Fawcett, 'Citizen-centred Policy Making under Rudd: Network Governance in the Shadows of Hierarchy?'. in Aulich and Evans, *The Rudd Government*, pp. 145–53.
41 Mark Davis, '2020 Vision: Rudd Summit to Map Future', *Sydney Morning Herald*, 4 February 2008.
42 Wayne Swan, *The Good Fight: Six Years, Two Prime Ministers and Staring Down the Great Recession*, Allen & Unwin, Sydney, 2014, p. 31.
43 John Lyons, 'Inner Circle', *Weekend Australian*, 21–22 June 2008. See also George Megalogenis, 'A Show about Nothing', *Weekend Australian*, 19–20 April 2008.
44 Tiernan, 'The Rudd Transition'.
45 Quoted in Kelly, *Triumph and Demise*, p. 151.
46 Swan, *The Good Fight*, p. 178.
47 For an account of the Labor government's response to the GFC, see Lenore Taylor and David Uren, *Shitstorm: Inside Labor's Darkest Days*, Melbourne University Press, Melbourne, 2010. Other useful accounts include Kelly, *Triumph and Demise*, ch. 11; and Swan, *The Good Fight*, chs 5–8.
48 Kevin Rudd, 'The Global Financial Crisis', *The Monthly*, February 2009, pp. 20–9.
49 Taylor and Uren, *Shitstorm*, p. 83.
50 Quoted in Kelly, *Triumph and Demise*, p. 159.
51 Ibid., pp. 160–5. Also see Sarah Ferguson (with Patricia Drum), *The Killing Season Uncut*, Melbourne University Press, Melbourne, 2016, p. 58.

52 See Anne Garnett and Phil Lewis, 'The Economy', in Aulich and Evans, *The Rudd Government*, pp. 183–5.
53 Laura Tingle, 'Political Amnesia: How We Forgot How to Govern', *Quarterly Essay*, no. 60, 2015, p. 28.
54 Moran, interview. Also see Taylor and Uren, *Shitstorm*, pp. 139–53.
55 This is based on Philip Chubb, *Power Failure: The Inside Story of Climate Politics under Rudd and Gillard*, Black Inc. Agenda, Melbourne, 2014, chs. 1–2.
56 Marian Wilkinson, 'PM Baulks at Crossroads of History', *Sydney Morning Herald*, 16 December 2008.
57 Weller, *Kevin Rudd*, p. 335.
58 Quoted in Kelly, *Triumph and Demise*, p. 151.
59 Katharine Murphy, 'Rudd's Will to Power', *Age*, 29 March 2008.
60 Quoted in Kelly, *Triumph and Demise*, p. 145.
61 Quoted in Joel Deane, *Catch and Kill: The Politics of Power*, University of Queensland Press, Brisbane, 2015, p. 304.
62 Rhodes and Tiernan, *Lessons in Governing*, p. 189.
63 Ibid.; and Cameron Stewart, 'Commander in Chief', *Weekend Australian Magazine*, 7–8 November 2009.
64 Rhodes and Tiernan, *Lessons in Governing*, pp. 72–5.
65 Ibid., pp. 33–5.
66 Lyons, 'Inner Circle'.
67 Moran, interview.
68 Helen Trinca, Brett Clegg, Tom Dusevic, Geoff Elliott, Richard Gluyas, Annabel Hepworth, Christian Kerr, Glenda Korporaal, George Megalogenis and Michael McKenna, 'The Enemy Within', *Weekend Australian*, 3–4 July 2010.
69 Moran, interview.
70 Kelly, *Triumph and Demise*, pp. 139, 152.
71 Laura Tingle, 'Tensions Escalate over Rudd's Kitchen Cabinet', *Australian Financial Review*, 8 March 2010.
72 McKnight, 'The Rudd Labor Government and the Limitations of Spin', p. 6.
73 Quoted in Kelly, *Triumph and Demise*, p. 154.
74 Gillard, *My Story*, p. 9. Gillard's account is collaborated by a number of those who worked inside the government; for example, see Chris Barrett, Swan's chief of staff, quoted in Deane, *Catch and Kill*, p. 303.
75 Kelly, *Triumph and Demise*, pp. 175–6, 183–5; Swan, *The Good Fight*, p. 182.
76 Michelle Grattan, 'Who Is the Real Kevin Rudd?', *Age*, 6 March 2010.
77 Gillard, *My Story*, p. 12.
78 One of the 'gang of four', Lindsay Tanner, while less critical of the SPBC process, nonetheless concedes it had grown dysfunctional by 2010. See Kelly, *Triumph and Demise*, p. 143.
79 Greg Combet (with Mark Davis), *The Fights of My Life*, Melbourne University Press, Melbourne, 2014, p. 230.
80 Moran, interview.
81 Quoted in Kelly, *Triumph and Demise*, p. 148.

82 Kefford, 'The Presidentialisation of Australian Politics?', p. 140.
83 Gillard, *My Story*, pp. 13–14.
84 David Feeney, quoted in Kelly, *Triumph and Demise*, p. 6.
85 Chris Ulhmann, quoted in Stewart, 'Commander in Chief'.
86 Quoted in Kelly, *Triumph and Demise*, p. 146.
87 This is based on a survey of archived Newspolls from the period 2008–10 that are housed at http://www.theaustralian.com.au/national-affairs/newspoll (accessed June 2016).
88 Megalogenis, 'Trivial Pursuit', p. 8.
89 See Wilson, 'Kevin Rudd, Celebrity and Audience Democracy in Australia'.
90 Quoted in James Button, *Speechless: A Year in My Father's Business*, Melbourne University Publishing, Melbourne, 2012, p. 69.
91 Quoted in Megalogenis, 'Trivial Pursuit', p. 47.
92 Quoted in Stewart, 'Commander in Chief'.
93 The following is principally based on Chubb, *Power Failure*, ch. 4, but also see Macintosh, Wilkinson and Denniss, 'Climate Change', pp. 200–14.
94 Ferguson, *The Killing Season Uncut*, p. 113.
95 See the archive of Newspoll polling data at http://www.theaustralian.com.au/national-affairs/newspoll (accessed June 2016).
96 Kelly, *Triumph and Demise*, ch. 20.
97 Kelly gathers up the greatest diversity of voices on the events of Rudd's overthrow, ibid., ch. 21.
98 Quoted in Ferguson, *The Killing Season Uncut*, p. 214.
99 Gillard, *My Story*, p. 23; Bill Shorten, *For the Common Good: Reflections on Australia's Future*, Melbourne University Press, Melbourne, 2016, p. 146; Swan, *The Good Fight*, p. 237.
100 For example, Jason Koutsoukis, '"Dream Team" Touted as Beazley Slips', *Sunday Age*, 19 November 2006.
101 This and the following paragraph are largely based on Jacqueline Kent, *The Making of Julia Gillard*, Viking, Melbourne, 2009.
102 Quoted ibid., p. 23.
103 Quoted in Julia Baird, 'Julia Gillard', *The Monthly*, August 2010.
104 Mark Latham, *The Latham Diaries*, Melbourne University Press, Melbourne, 2005, p. 268 (entry for 13 February 2004).
105 Senator Bill Heffernan quoted in Kent, *The Making of Julia Gillard*, p. 243.
106 Quoted in Ferguson, *The Killing Season Uncut*, p. 11.
107 Swan, *The Good Fight*, p. 246.
108 Annabel Crabb, 'Prime Minister, Interrupted', *The Monthly*, August 2011.
109 Kelly, *Triumph and Demise*, p. 140.
110 Gillard, *My Story*, p. 14.
111 Deane, *Catch and Kill*, pp. 308–9.
112 Haunted by the events surrounding Rudd's deposition, as prime minister Gillard offered to release press gallery journalists from any 'obligations' of confidentiality in challenging them to disclose any instances of her having destabilised Rudd's

leadership. See Chloe Hooper, 'On the Road with Julia Gillard: Sketches of a Prime Minister in Her Final Months', *The Monthly*, August 2013. Having considered a range of accounts of Rudd's downfall, the journalists Sarah Ferguson and Paul Kelly both conclude that there is little evidence of Gillard having actively plotted against the prime minister's leadership. See Ferguson, *The Killing Season Uncut*, p. 138; Kelly, *Triumph and Demise*, pp. 330–1.

113 Quoted in Ferguson, *The Killing Season Uncut*, p. 196.

114 Gillard has said she thought that Rudd, once having recovered from the initial 'shock' and 'hurt', might have felt 'relief' at being freed from the burdens of office given how 'miserable' he had become in the role by 2010. See Ferguson, *The Killing Season Uncut*, p. 221. Wayne Swan, who counselled against removing Rudd, had a far more realistic assessment of the fallen prime minister's character. He recalled 'a sense of foreboding about what he would do in the future'—Swan, *The Good Fight*, pp. 233–4, 237.

115 Quoted in *The Killing Season: Episode Three, The Long Shadow*, ABC Television.

116 Quoted in Ferguson, *The Killing Season Uncut*, p. 296.

117 Quoted in Michelle Grattan, 'Throw of the Dice for a Fresh Start', *Age*, 25 June 2010.

118 Kelly, *Triumph and Demise*, pp. 8–11, 335.

119 Polls and voter surveys revealed widespread disquiet at the leadership coup. See Barrie Cassidy, *The Party Thieves: The Real Story of the 2010 Election*, Melbourne University Press, Melbourne, 2010, p. 147; and Ian McAllister, Clive Bean and Juliet Pietsch, 'Leadership Change, Policy Issues and Voter Defection in the 2010 Australian Election', *Australian Journal of Political Science*, vol. 47, no. 2, June 2012, p. 196.

120 'Gillard Moves on Rudd', ABC News, 24 June 2010, http://www.abc.net.au/news/2010-06-23/gillard-moves-on-rudd/878810 (accessed September 2016).

121 McAllister, Bean and Pietsch, 'Leadership Change', p. 192; Cassidy, *The Party Thieves*, p. 147.

122 Ferguson, *The Killing Season Uncut*, pp. 237–8.

123 For an account of the 2010 election campaign and its aftermath, see Cassidy, *The Party Thieves*, parts III and IV. Also see Marian Simms and John Wanna, 'The Caretaker Election of 2010: "Julia 10" versus "Tony 10" and the Onset of Minority Government', in Marian Simms and John Wanna (eds), *Julia 2010: The Caretaker Election*, ANU EPress, Canberra, 2012, pp. 1–7.

124 Gillard, *My Story*, p. 40.

125 For an account of the period between the election date and formation of the minority Labor government, see Brian Costar, 'Seventeen Days to Power: Making a Minority Government', in Simms and Wanna, *Julia 2010*, pp. 357–70. The two regional-based independents, Rob Oakeshott and Tony Windsor, whose decision to side with Labor was decisive in enabling Gillard to form minority government in September 2010, both remark on her superior negotiating ability compared with Abbott. See Robert Oakeshott, *The Independent Member for Lyne: A Memoir*, Allen & Unwin, Sydney, 2013, pp. 58, 72–3; and Ruth Rae, *Tony Windsor: The Biography*, Allen & Unwin, Sydney, 2014, pp. 207–11.

126 Gillard identifies these complications. See *My Story*, p. 77.

127 The term 'political terrorism' was used by Labor backbencher David Feeney. See Kelly, *Triumph and Demise*, p. 455. For an exhaustive, albeit partisan, account of that campaign of subversion, see Kerry Ann Walsh, *The Stalking of Julia Gillard*, Allen & Unwin, Sydney, 2013.

128 Swan, *The Good Fight*, p. 305.

129 Gillard, *My Story*, p. 101. Gillard made a similar point to Chloe Hooper. See Hooper, 'On the Road with Julia Gillard'.

130 Walsh lists many of those reports in an appendix to her account, *The Stalking of Julia Gillard*, pp. 297–304.

131 Sally Young and Matthew Ricketson, 'Gillard, Her Government and the Media', in Chris Aulich (ed.), *The Gillard Governments: Australian Commonwealth Administration 2010–2013*, Melbourne University Press, Melbourne, 2014, pp. 286–7.

132 Quoted in Michael Cooney, *The Gillard Project: My Thousand Days of Despair and Hope*, Viking, Melbourne, 2015, pp. 51–2.

133 Ben Hubbard, interview with Paul Strangio, 20 September 2016.

134 Samantha Lane, 'Gillard: "I Should Have Gone into Cone of Silence More"', *Age*, 14 May 2016.

135 Gillard, *My Story*, p. 80; Tom Bentley, interview with James Walter, 1 August 2012; Hubbard, interview.

136 Hubbard, interview.

137 Gwynneth Singleton, 'The Legislative Record of a "Hung" Parliament', in Aulich, *The Gillard Governments*, p. 45.

138 Nick Evershed, 'Revealed: How Tony Abbott's Government Was the Least Productive since 1971', *The Guardian* (Australian edition), 17 September 2015, https://www.theguardian.com/news/datablog/2015/sep/17/tony-abbotts-government-how-productive-was-it (accessed October 2016).

139 Michelle Grattan, 'Looking Back on the Hung Parliament', *The Conversation*, 17July 2013 (first delivered as the Earle Page Lecture), http://theconversation.com/looking-back-on-the-hung-parliament-16175 (accessed October 2016).

140 For a measured summary of that legislative record, see Singleton, 'The Legislative Record of a "Hung" Parliament', pp. 43–54.

141 Gillard, *My Story*, pp. 345–6; Kelly, *Triumph and Demise*, pp. 343–5.

142 Quoted in James Massola, 'Reflective Abbott Reopens Racial Hate-speech Debate', *Age*, 13 August 2016. Also see Kelly, *Triumph and Demise*, chs 26, 28.

143 For a consolidated summary of polling figures for the Gillard minority government, see Brenton Holmes, 'Hard Days and Nights: the Final 147 Days of the Gillard Government', Research Paper Series 2013–14, 8 November 2013, Parliamentary Library, Parliament of Australia, Appendices 3–5, http://www.aph.gov.au/About_Parliament/Parliamentary_Departments/Parliamentary_Library/pubs/rp/rp1314/GillardGovernment (accessed October 2016).

144 Hooper, 'On the Road with Julia Gillard'.

145 Patricia Karvelas, 'Decisions to Involve the Full Cabinet—Gillard in Power', *Australian*, 29 June 2010. See also Megalogenis, 'Trivial Pursuit', p. 74.

146 Michelle Grattan, 'Hawke Set the Gold Standard: Gillard', *Age*, 13 July 2010.
147 Malcolm Farr, 'On the Fifth Day, she Closed the Kitchen Cabinet', *Daily Telegraph*, 29 June 2010.
148 Much of what follows in this paragraph is based on the Hubbard interview.
149 Crabb, 'Prime Minister, Interrupted'.
150 Hubbard, interview.
151 Chubb, *Power Failure*, pp. 15–17; Kelly, *Triumph and Demise*, p. 367.
152 Moran, interview.
153 Gillard, *My Story*, p. 389; Kelly, *Triumph and Demise*, p. 368.
154 Gillard, *My Story*, p. 357.
155 'The Prime Ministership According to Julia Gillard', *Anne Summer Reports*, no. 3, July 2013, p. 22, http://www.annesummers.com.au/wp-content/uploads/2014/11/ASR_Issue_3.pdf (accessed October 2016).
156 Hubbard, interview.
157 There are varying accounts of these episodes, including Bob Carr, *Diary of a Foreign Minister*, NewSouth Publishing, Sydney, 2014, pp. 229–49; Gillard, *My Story*, pp. 209–11; and Kelly, *Triumph and Demise*, pp. 434–7.
158 Hubbard, interview.
159 Kelly, *Triumph and Demise*, p. 446.
160 Hubbard, interview. Also see Rhodes and Tiernan, *Lessons in Governing*, p. 201.
161 Moran, interview.
162 Michelle Grattan, 'Reshuffle as PM's Right-hand Man Decides to Retire', *Age*, 5 August 2011.
163 Hubbard, interview.
164 Ibid. Also see Rhodes and Tiernan, *Lessons in Governing*, pp. 201–2.
165 RAW Rhodes and Anne Tiernan, *The Gate Keepers: Lessons from Prime Ministers' Chiefs of Staff*, Melbourne University Press, Melbourne, 2014, pp. 6–9.
166 David Crowe, 'PM's Inner Circle of Trust', *Australian*, 8 February 2012.
167 Hubbard, interview.
168 Samantha Maiden, 'Return of the Spin King', *Sunday Telegraph*, 5 February 2012.
169 Hubbard, interview; Bentley, interview. See also Mary Delahunty, *Gravity: Inside PM's Office during Her Last Year and Final Days*, Hardie Grant Books, Melbourne, 2014.
170 The most effusive statement of that affection can be found in the memoir of the government by speechwriter Michael Cooney, *The Gillard Project*.
171 Nicholas Reece, 'Secret Softie: The Cold Truth is Gillard's Warmth Couldn't Be Conveyed to Voters', *Sydney Morning Herald*, 1 July 2013.
172 John McTernan, 'The Julia I Know and Love But You Never Really Met', *Sunday Telegraph*, 21 July 2013.
173 The following two paragraphs are mostly based on Chubb, *Power Failure*, chs 5–11.
174 Kelly, *Triumph and Demise*, p. 368.
175 Quoted in Chubb, *Power Failure*, p. 161.

176 Combet, *The Fights of My Life*, p. 252.
177 Gillard, *My Story*, p. 392.
178 Quoted in Kelly, *Triumph and Demise*, p. 367.
179 Quoted in Wilson, 'Kevin Rudd, celebrity and audience democracy in Australia', p. 213; Julia Gillard, 'Julia Gillard Writes on Power, Purpose and Labor's Future', *The Guardian* (Australian edition), 14 September 2013, https://www.theguardian.com/world/2013/sep/13/julia-gillard-labor-purpose-future (accessed October 2016).
180 Quoted in Walsh, *The Stalking of Julia Gillard*, p. 36.
181 Quoted in Carol Johnson, 'Playing the Gender Card: The Uses and Abuses of Gender in Australian Politics', *Politics & Gender*, vol. 11, no. 2, 2015, p. 302.
182 On this phenomenon, see Donatella Campus, 'Personalization of Politics in Italy and France: The Cases of Berlusconi and Sarkozy', *International Journal of Press/Politics*, vol. 15, no. 2, 2010, pp. 219–35; and Wilson, 'Kevin Rudd, celebrity and audience democracy in Australia'.
183 Quoted in Jacqueline Kent, *Take Your Best Shot: The Prime Ministership of Julia Gillard*, Penguin Books, Melbourne, 2013, p. 71.
184 Cooney, *The Gillard Project*, p. 230.
185 Anna Goldsworthy, 'Unfinished Business: Sex, Freedom and Misogyny', *Quarterly Essay*, no. 50, 2013, https://www.quarterlyessay.com.au/qe/50/unfinished-business/416 (accessed October 2016). Emphasis in the original.
186 Quoted in Johnson, 'Playing the Gender Card', p. 300.
187 'The Prime Ministership According to Julia Gillard'.
188 Gillard, *My Story*, p. 113.
189 David Denemark and Ian Ward, 'Gender and Leader Effects in the 2010 Australian Election', *Australian Journal of Political Science*, vol. 47, no. 4, December 2012, pp. 572–5.
190 Lauren J Hall and Ngaire Donaghue, '"Nice Girls Don't Carry Knives": Constructions of Ambition in Media Coverage of Australia's First Female Prime Minister', *British Journal of Social Psychology*, vol. 20, no. 3, 2012, pp. 631–47.
191 Gillard, *My Story*, pp. 97–104.
192 Ibid., pp. 281–2.
193 Examples of this abuse are documented in Anne Summers, *The Misogyny Factor*, NewSouth Publishing, Sydney, 2013, ch. 5.
194 Quoted in Ferguson, *The Killing Season Uncut*, p. 253.
195 Cooney, *The Gillard Project*, p. 196.
196 Quoted in Linda Trimble, 'Julia Gillard and the Gender Wars', *Politics & Gender*, vol. 12, no. 2, June 2016, p. 307.
197 For analysis of the reaction to Gillard's speech, including the media framing, see Ngaire Donaghue, 'Who Gets Played by "The Gender Card"?', *Australian Feminist Studies*, vol. 30, no. 84, 2015, pp. 161–78; Johnson, 'Playing the Gender Card', pp. 291–319; and Trimble, 'Julia Gillard and the Gender Wars', pp. 296–316.
198 Quoted in Trimble, 'Julia Gillard and the Gender Wars', p. 307.
199 Kelly, *Triumph and Demise*, pp. 466–8.

200 The text of that final statement is reprinted in Kent, *Take Your Best Shot*, pp. 118–21.
201 Quoted in Johnson, 'Playing the Gender Card', p. 312.
202 This and the following paragraph are largely based on Paul Strangio and James Walter, 'The Leadership Contest: An End to the "Messiah Complex"?', in Carol Johnson and John Wanna (with Hsu-Ann Lee) (eds), *Abbott's Gambit: The 2013 Australian Federal Election*, ANU Press, Canberra, 2015, pp. 49–63.
203 Kelly, *Triumph and Demise*, p. 476.
204 Michael Gordon, 'The Beauty Contest Is Over, Now It's a Character Test', *Age*, 24 August 2013.
205 Kelly, *Triumph and Demise*, ch. 17.
206 The following paragraphs are largely based on Tony Abbott, *Battlelines*, Melbourne University Press, Melbourne, 2009 (2013), ch. 1; and David Marr, 'Political Animal: The Making of Tony Abbott', *Quarterly Essay*, no. 47, 2012.
207 Gillard, quoted in Hooper, 'On the Road with Julia Gillard'.
208 Abbott, *Battlelines*, p. 42.
209 Kelly, *Triumph and Demise*, p. 270.
210 Abbott, *Battlelines*, p. 187.
211 Chubb, *Power Failure*, p. 97.
212 On this point, see Wayne Errington and Peter van Onselen, *Battleground: Why the Liberal Party Shirtfronted Tony Abbott*, Melbourne University Press, Melbourne, 2015, p. 10.
213 Abbott, *Battlelines*, p. 60.
214 Peter Hartcher, 'Not the Popular Choice: Emphatic Win but Approval Rating Could Be a Lot Better', *Sydney Morning Herald*, 9 September 2013. Abbott's unpopularity was also corroborated by a comparison of the leadership ratings data in the 2013 Australian Electoral Study with that of previous AES surveys dating back to 1987. This showed he was the second-worst-rated opposition leader over the past quarter of a century behind Andrew Peacock in 1990, and that he was easily the least popular opposition leader to have won office during that period (the others being Howard in 1996 and Rudd in 2007). See Clive Bean and Ian McAllister, 'Documenting the Inevitable: Voting Behaviour at the 2013 Australian Election', in Johnson and Wanna, *Abbott's Gambit*, pp. 411–24; and McAllister, *The Australian Voter*, pp. 249–56.
215 The following data is based on archived Newspolls housed at http://www.newspoll.com.au/opinion-polls-2/opinion-polls-2/ (accessed November 2016).
216 Errington and van Onselen, *Battleground*, p. 198.
217 Graham Little, *Strong Leadership: Thatcher, Reagan and an Eminent Person*, Oxford University Press, Melbourne, 1988, pp. 28, 42.
218 Michelle Grattan, 'There's Never Been a Better Time to Change Prime Minister', in Aulich, *From Abbott to Turnbull*, p. 10.
219 Ibid.; John Lyons, 'In Command and out of Control', *Weekend Australian*, 21–22 February 2015; Aaron Patrick, *Credlin & Co.: How the Abbott Government Destroyed Itself*, Black Inc., Melbourne, 2016, pp. 166–8; and Niki Savva, *The Road to Ruin: How Tony Abbott and Peta Credlin Destroyed Their Own Government*, Scribe Publications, Melbourne, 2016, pp. 175–80.

220 See here, in particular, Errington and van Onselen, *Battleground*, ch. 1, pp. 119–21; and Savva, *The Road to Ruin*, pp. 115–16, 140–1.

221 On this episode, see Errington and van Onselen, *Battleground*, pp. 92, 125–30; and Savva, *The Road to Ruin*, pp. 143–6.

222 This paragraph is mostly based on Matthew Ricketson and Katharine Murphy, 'The Media', in Aulich, *From Abbott to Turnbull*, pp. 95–116.

223 Quoted, ibid., p. 99.

224 Ibid., p. 105.

225 Daniel Hurst, 'Tony Abbott Bans Ministers from Q & A Program', *The Guardian* (Australian edition), 6 July 2015, https://www.theguardian.com/australia-news/2015/jul/06/tony-abbott-bans-cabinet-ministers-from-q-a-program (accessed November 2016).

226 'Last Thing We Want to Do Is Reward People Smugglers, Says PM on Accepting Syrian Refugees', *7.30*, Australian Broadcasting Corporation, 9 September 2015, http://www.abc.net.au/7.30/content/2015/s4309488.htm (accessed November 2016).

227 Quoted in Patrick, *Credlin & Co.*, p. 111. See also Errington and van Onselen, *Battleground*, p. 169.

228 John Lyons, 'Inside the Bunker with Credlin', *Australian*, 23 February 2015.

229 Quoted in Savva, *The Road to Ruin*, p. 69.

230 Rhodes and Tiernan, *Lessons in Governing*, p. 100.

231 Quoted, ibid., p. 37.

232 Grattan, 'There's Never Been a Better Time to Change Prime Minister', p. 4.

233 Lyons, 'Inside the Bunker with Credlin'; Savva, *The Road to Ruin*, pp. 15–16, 23–4.

234 Quoted in Errington and van Onselen, *Battleground*, p. 26.

235 Ibid., pp. 63–4; Lyons, 'In Command and Out of Control'; Savva, *The Road to Ruin*, pp. 24–31, 65–8.

236 Patrick, *Credlin & Co.*, p. 18.

237 Errington and van Onselen, *Battleground*, pp. 66–8; and Savva, *The Road to Ruin*, p. 24.

238 Lyons, 'In Command and Out of Control'. Also see Errington and van Onselen, *Battleground*, p. 133.

239 The following paragraphs on the operation of the PMO are chiefly drawn from Errington and van Onselen, *Battleground*, pp. 60–4; Patrick, *Credlin & Co.*, pp. 26, 51–3, 64–5; and Savva, *The Road to Ruin*, pp. 45–54, 50, 96, 117.

240 Quoted in Savva, *The Road to Ruin*, p. 47.

241 Patrick, *Credlin & Co.*, p. 34.

242 Errington and van Onselen, *Battleground*, pp. 112–14. Also see Pamela Williams, 'Eight Plotters, One Volvo: How to Stage a Coup', *Australian*, 20 October 2015.

243 Quoted in Lyons, 'In Command and Out of Control'.

244 Roger Wettenhall and Paddy Gourley, 'The Public Sector', in Aulich, *From Abbott to Turnbull*, p. 70.

245 Savva, *The Road to Ruin*, pp. 110–11.

246 Wettenhall and Gourley, 'The Public Sector', pp. 70–1.

247 Errington and van Onselen, *Battleground*, pp. 136–7.

248 Quoted in Peter Hartcher, 'Tony Abbott Rolled By His Own Ministers over Stripping Terrorists of Citizenship', *Sydney Morning Herald*, 1 June 2015, http://www.smh.com.au/comment/tony-abbott-rolled-by-his-own-ministers-over-stripping-terrorists-of-citizenship-20150529-ghcuxf.html (accessed December 2016). Also see Patrick, *Credlin & Co.*, pp. 230–7; and Amanda Vanstone, 'Lazy or Sneaky: What Were You Thinking, PM?', *Age*, 8 June 2015.

249 'Liberal Leadership: Malcolm Turnbull's Press Conference Announcing Challenge to Tony Abbott', *ABC News*, 15 September 2015, http://www.abc.net.au/news/2015-09-14/malcolm-turnbulls-full-press-conference/6774744 (accessed December 2016).

250 Errington and van Onselen, *Battleground*, p. 130.

251 Brenton Prosser, John Warhurst and Richard Denniss, 'New Wine, Old Wine Skins: Perspectives on the "Feral" Senate', in Aulich, *From Abbott to Turnbull*, pp. 45–67.

252 Errington and van Onselen, *Battleground*, pp. 130–4; Grattan, 'There's Never Been a Better Time to Change Prime Minister', p. 12; and Williams, 'Eight Plotters, One Volvo'.

253 Errington and van Onselen, *Battleground*, pp. 186–8.

254 Savva, *The Road to Ruin*, pp. 304–6.

255 Quoted in Walsh, *The Stalking of Julia Gillard*, p. 196.

256 The 'extreme personality and extreme contingency' schema that forms the title of this section has been borrowed from Rhodes and Tiernan, *Lessons in Governing*, pp. 204–5.

257 Thomas Poguntke and Paul Webb, 'The Presidentialization of Politics in Democratic Societies: A Framework for Analysis', in Thomas Poguntke and Paul Webb (eds), *The Presidentialization of Politics: A Comparative Study of Modern Democracies*, Oxford University Press, Oxford, UK, 2005, p. 22.

258 Williams, 'Eight Plotters, One Volvo'.

259 Quoted in Kelly, *Triumph and Demise*, p. 335.

260 Rhodes and Tiernan, *Lessons in Governing*, pp. 204–5.

261 Anne Tiernan, 'Beyond the Nadir of Political Leadership: Can Partisans Learn?', *Griffith Review: Fixing the System*, no. 51, 2015, p. 18.

262 Ricketson and Murphy, 'The Media', p. 98.

Chapter 7 From Pre-eminence to Paradox

1 'Transcript of the Hon Malcolm Turnbull MP and the Hon Julie Bishop MP Press Conference, Parliament House, 15 September 2015', http://www.malcolmturnbull.com.au/media/transcript-vote-on-the-liberal-party-leadership (accessed August 2016).

2 Michael Pusey and Nick Turnbull, 'Have Australians Embraced Economic Reform?', in Shaun Wilson (ed.), *Australian Social Attitudes: The First Report*, UNSW Press, Sydney, 2005, pp. 161–81.

3 Michael Pusey, *The Experience of Middle Australia: The Dark Side of Economic Reform*, Cambridge University Press, Cambridge, UK, 2003; Peter Saunders, *The*

Ends and Means of Welfare: Coping With Economic and Social Change in Australia, Cambridge University Press, Cambridge, UK, 2002; David Burchell and Andrew Leigh (eds), *The Prince's New Clothes: Why Do Australians Dislike their Politicians?*, UNSW Press, Sydney, 2002; Clive Bean, 'Is There a Crisis of Trust in Australia?' in Wilson, *Australian Social Attitudes*, pp. 122–140.

4 Sarah M Cameron and Ian McAllister, *Trends in Australian Political Opinion: Results from the Australian Election Study1987–2016*, Australian National University/ australianelectionstudy.org, Canberra, 2016, pp. 75–6. See also Mark Evans, Gerry Stoker and Max Haluptka, 'A Decade of Democratic Decline: How Australians Understand and Imagine their Democracy', in Chris Aulich (ed.), *From Abbott to Turnbull: A New Direction? Australian Commonwealth Administration 2013–2016*, Echo Books, West Geelong, Vic., 2016, pp. 23–41.

5 Inga Ting, 'Discontent Rising as Australia Echoes Trump's America, Survey Finds', *Age*, 18 January 2017.

6 See, for example, Edelman Trust Barometer 2017, http://www.edelman.com/trust2017/ (accessed January 2017).

7 See Paul Strangio, Paul 't Hart and James Walter, *Settling the Office: The Australian Prime Ministership from Federation to Reconstruction*, The Miegunyah Press, Melbourne, 2016.

8 Judith Brett, *Australian Liberals and the Moral Middle Class: From Alfred Deakin to John Howard*, Cambridge University Press, Cambridge, UK, 2003.

9 The capital analogy is borrowed from Mark Bennister, Paul 't Hart and Benjamin Worthy (eds), *The Leadership Capital Index: A New Perspective on Political Leadership*, Oxford University Press, Oxford, UK, 2017.

10 Influential long-term observers have encouraged this perception: see, for instance, Paul Kelly, 'The Australian Crisis', in his *Triumph and Demise: The Broken Promise of a Labor Generation*, Melbourne University Press, Melbourne, 2014, pp. 497–510; for devastating figures on public disillusion with politics and politicians, see Cameron and McAllister, *Trends in Australian Political Opinion*, passim.

11 George Megalogenis, 'Balancing Act: Australia between Recession and Renewal', *Quarterly Essay*, no. 61, Black Inc, Melbourne, 2016.

12 See, for instance, Kelly Fielding, Brian Head, Warren Laffan, Mark Western and Ove Hoegh-Guldberg, 'Australian Politicians' Beliefs about Climate Change: Political Partisanship and Political Ideology', *Environmental Politics*, vol. 21, no. 5, 2012, pp. 712–33; Zoe Leviston, Murni Greenhill and Iain Walker, *Australian Attitudes to Climate Change: 2010–2014,* CSIRO Canberra, 2015, pp. 44–7; Lowy Institute, *The Lowy Institute Poll 2015*, Lowy Institute, Sydney, 2015, pp. 3, 13–14; Jeff Sparrow, 'Don't Fear the People: A Plebiscite Will Confirm the Australian Public's Support for Marriage Equality and Marginalize Bigots', *The Monthly*, 26 July 2016, https://www.themonthly.com.au/blog/jeff-sparrow/2016/26/2016/1469500968/don-t-fear-people (accessed August 2016).

13 See, for instance, John Uhr, 'Rhetorical and Performative Analysis', in RAW Rhodes and Paul 't Hart (eds), *The Oxford Handbook of Political Leadership*, Oxford University Press, Oxford, UK, 2014, pp. 253–66.

14 This trend is epitomised in the unreservedly technocratic but nevertheless in government circles (within and beyond Australia) much-regarded account of Tony Blair's erstwhile micromanager in chief, Sir Michael Barber, *How to Run a Government*, Penguin, London, 2015.

15 See George Megalogenis, *The Australian Moment: How We Were Made for These Times*, Hamish Hamilton, Melbourne, 2012; and on how to address its unforeseen consequences, Megalogenis, 'Balancing Act'.

16 Ian Holland, *Accountability of Ministerial Staff?*, Research Paper no. 19, 2001–02, Department of the Parliamentary Library, Canberra, 2002; Anne Tiernan and Patrick Weller, *Ministerial Staff: A Need for Transparency and Accountability?*, Submission to the Senate Finance and Public Administration References Committee Inquiry into *Staff Employed under the Members of Parliament (Staff) Act*; *Report of the Senate Select Committee on a Certain Maritime Incident,* October 2002.

17 Archie Brown, *The Myth of the Strong Leader: Political Leadership in the Modern Age,* Bodley Head, London, 2014; and for a review of varieties of leadership research (including strong leader and distributed leadership debates), see Matthew Laing and James Walter, 'Great Expectations and Great Limitations: Walking the Tightrope of Leadership in the 21st Century', in John Storey, Jean Hartley, Jean-Louis Denis, Paul 't Hart and David Ulrich (eds), *The Routledge Companion to Leadership*, Routledge, Oxford, UK, 2017, pp. 209–24.

18 See Stuart Macintyre, *Australia's Boldest Experiment: War and Reconstruction in the 1940s,* NewSouth Publishing, Sydney, 2015.

Acknowledgements

The research on which this book, and the previous volume of our history of the Australian prime ministership, has been based would not have been possible without the generous support of an Australian Research Council Discovery Program Grant (DP1095243).

We are very grateful to all of those who agreed to be interviewed in the course of our research. The knowledge of those who worked with and for prime ministers is invaluable. While much has been used as background, all of it was enormously helpful in developing our interpretation of the way prime ministers operated and the development of the role. Direct attributions are cited (with permission) when individuals are quoted, but as some spoke off the record and others wished not to be identified, we do not provide a list of all who participated here.

This study has drawn upon the research of numerous scholars. In turn, many of our colleagues and friends have assisted directly and indirectly. The material gathered by Zareh Ghazarian, at the start of the project as a research assistant, remained a valuable resource for this volume. We wish particularly to thank those who read and commented upon successive drafts of chapters: Frank Bongiorno, Nicholas Brown,

John Nethercote and Anne Tiernan. Their expert feedback saved us from misapprehension: they are not responsible for arguments with which we have persisted. Others whose comments, conversation and communication have provided support and encouragement include Judith Brett, Nick Economou, Zareh Ghazarian, Murray Goot, Carolyn Holbrook, Matthew Laing, David Lowe and Stuart Macintyre.

Sally Heath, executive publisher at Melbourne University Publishing, has been an unflagging supporter of our project; Louise Stirling has once again judiciously overseen the editing process; and Paul Smitz has been an exceptionally patient and skilful copy-editor—for which we are profoundly grateful.

As always, we are indebted to the support and forbearance of our respective families, without whom we would never have reached the end of what proved to be a challenging and unexpectedly long enterprise. We love you all, and promise never to mention a prime minister again.

Paul Strangio, Paul 't Hart and James Walter.

Index

THE MIEGUNYAH PRESS

This book was designed and typeset by Patrick Cannon
The text was set in 11 point Minion with 15 points of leading
The text is printed on 80 gsm Woodfree

This book was edited by Paul Smitz

THE
MIEGUNYAH
PRESS

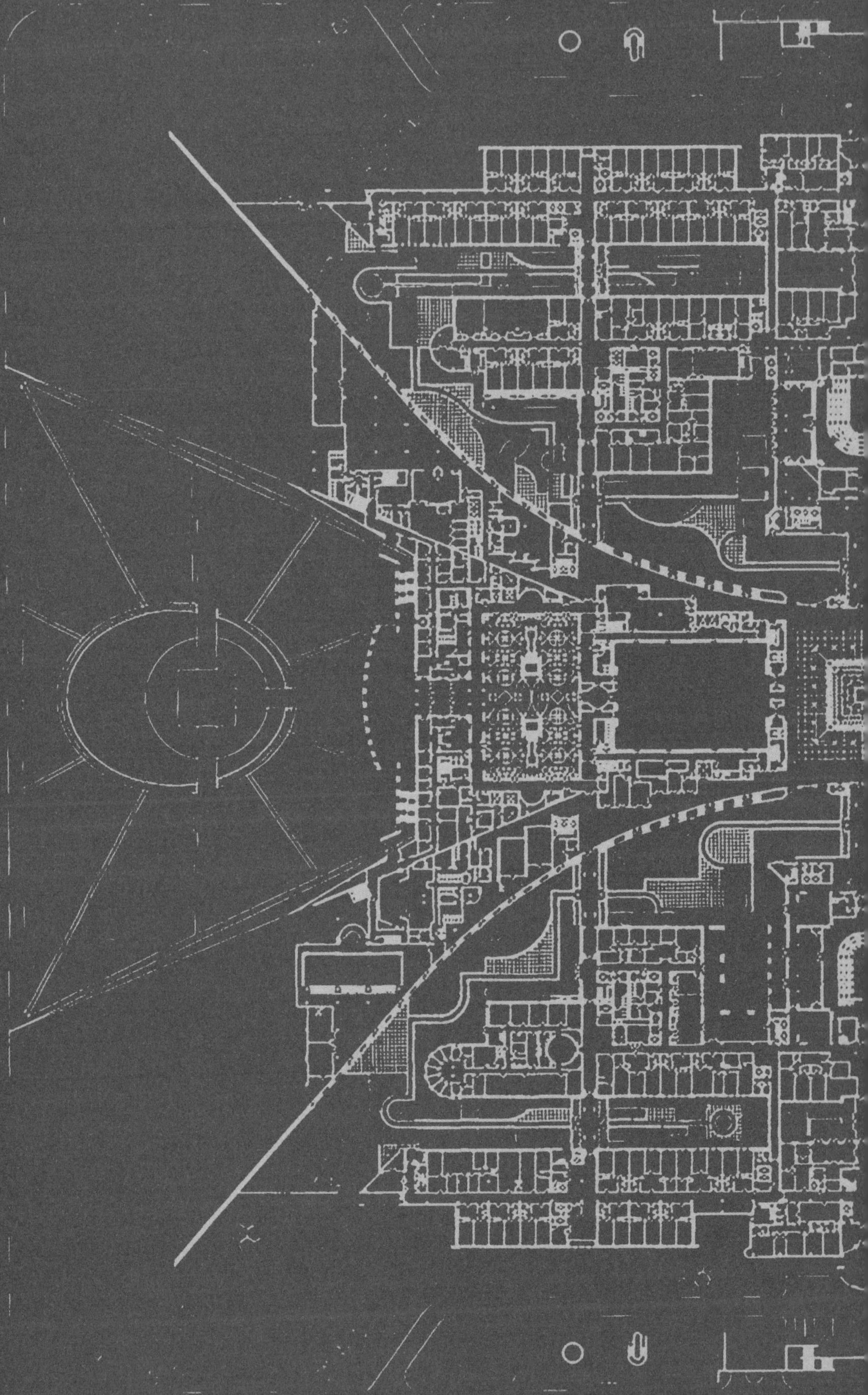